CZECH REFUGEES IN COLD WAR CANADA

STUDIES IN IMMIGRATION AND CULTURE

ISSN 1914-1459

ROYDEN LOEWEN, SERIES EDITOR

15 *Czech Refugees in Cold War Canada: 1945–1989*, by Jan Raska

14 *Holocaust Survivors in Canada: Exclusion, Inclusion, Transformation, 1947–1955*, by Adara Goldberg

13 *Transnational Radicals: Italian Anarchists in Canada and the U.S., 1915–1940*, by Travis Tomchuk

12 *Invisible Immigrants: The English in Canada since 1945*, by Marilyn Barber and Murray Watson

11 *The Showman and the Ukrainian Cause: Folk Dance, Film, and the Life of Vasile Avramenko*, by Orest T. Martynowych

10 *Young, Well-Educated, and Adaptable: Chilean Exiles in Ontario and Quebec, 1973–2010*, by Francis Peddie

9 *The Search for a Socialist El Dorado: Finnish Immigration to Soviet Karelia from the United States and Canada in the 1930s*, by Alexey Golubev and Irina Takala

8 *Rewriting the Break Event: Mennonites and Migration in Canadian Literature*, by Robert Zacharias

7 *Ethnic Elites and Canadian Identity: Japanese, Ukrainians, and Scots, 1919–1971*, by Aya Fujiwara

6 *Community and Frontier: A Ukrainian Settlement in the Canadian Parkland*, by John C. Lehr

5 *Storied Landscapes: Ethno-Religious Identity and the Canadian Prairies*, by Frances Swyripa

4 *Families, Lovers, and Their Letters: Italian Postwar Migration to Canada*, by Sonia Cancian

3 *Sounds of Ethnicity: Listening to German North America, 1850–1914*, by Barbara Lorenzkowski

2 *Mennonite Women in Canada: A History*, by Marlene Epp

1 *Imagined Homes: Soviet German Immigrants in Two Cities*, by Hans Werner

CZECH REFUGEES IN COLD WAR CANADA

JAN RASKA

UNIVERSITY OF MANITOBA PRESS

Czech Refugees in Cold War Canada, 1945–1989

22 21 20 19 18 1 2 3 4 5

University of Manitoba Press
Winnipeg, Manitoba, Canada
Treaty 1 Territory
uofmpress.ca

Cataloguing data available from Library and Archives Canada
Studies in Immigration and Culture, ISSN 1914-1459; 15
ISBN 978-0-88755-827-6 (PAPER)
ISBN 978-0-88755-572-5 (PDF)
ISBN 978-0-88755-570-1 (EPUB)

Cover design by Frank Reimer
Interior design by Karen Armstrong
Cover image: Czech demonstrators protest against the Soviet crackdown of the Prague Spring reform movement and communist aggression in Vietnam, Toronto, 22 August 1968. York University Libraries, Clara Thomas Archives and Special Collections, Toronto Telegram fonds, ASC41068.

Printed in Canada

The University of Manitoba Press acknowledges the financial support for its publication program provided by the Government of Canada through the Canada Book Fund, the Canada Council for the Arts, the Manitoba Department of Sport, Culture, and Heritage, the Manitoba Arts Council, and the Manitoba Book Publishing Tax Credit.

Funded by the Government of Canada | Canada

CONTENTS

A GUIDE TO CZECH PRONUNCIATION

á	*a* in "far"
c	*ts* in "cats"
č	*ch* in "church"
ch	*ch* in German "Bach"
ď	*d* in British "duke"
é	*e* in "bet"
ě	*ye* in "yell"
í	*i* in "machine"
j	*y* in "yet"
ň	*n* in "tenure"
ó	*o* in "home"
ou	*oa* in "goat"
ř	*r* followed by *z* and *h* (Czech composer Dvořák pronounced as Dvorzhak)
š	*sh* in "shoe"
ť	*t* in "venture"
ú, ů	*oo* in "moon"
y	*i* in "if"
ý	*ee* in "beef"
ž	*s* in "measure"

A NOTE ON SPELLING OF CZECH NAMES

In this book, male and female surname endings differ based on the Czech language's systems of gender adjectives. In Canada, it is common for many Czech female surnames to omit the suffixes "ová" and "á" in order to match a Czech male surname. Wherever possible, I have tried to respect the proper spelling of Czech names, while also acknowledging an individual's self-identification.

LIST OF ILLUSTRATIONS

Preface

Initially, my desire to learn about the shared past of Cold War refugees in Canada came from my own resettlement experience. In July 1985, just four years before the fall of the Berlin Wall, my family left Czechoslovakia in search of a better life and greater economic opportunities elsewhere. Like many Czech families, we applied for passports, in order to travel to communist Yugoslavia for "a vacation." It was the only way for most individuals and families to leave Czechoslovakia. After we drove through Hungary and arrived in Yugoslavia, my parents sent a letter informing their siblings of our departure, and we left our possessions to them before the communist authorities became aware of our emigration and confiscated them.

In Yugoslavia, we spent the first two weeks near the Adriatic Sea in Croatia. We eventually left for Belgrade and stayed there for several days in a motel where other refugees from Eastern Europe were awaiting permanent resettlement in the West. In the Yugoslav capital, my parents applied for refugee status, under the United Nations Refugee Convention, with the local office of the United Nations High Commissioner for Refugees (UNHCR). During their interview with a UNHCR official, my parents were asked why it had taken them two weeks to request refugee status. They informed the official that they had wanted to visit the Adriatic Coast before heading to Belgrade. The visibly annoyed official, who had handled hundreds of similar cases, subsequently denied our claim for refugee status. My parents were later informed by other refugees at the motel that they should have stretched the truth or fabricated a believable story in order to acquire refugee status. Without options, my father reached out to his sister, who had immigrated to Canada in the late 1960s.

In November 1985, we left Yugoslavia for Canada. Our journey involved a transatlantic flight from Belgrade to Montreal. After landing in Canada, immigration officials asked my parents how we pronounced our family name, Raška (pronounced Rash-ka), since no *háček* (a diacritical mark placed over certain letters in the Czech alphabet) existed above the letter *s* in the English language. The officials informed my parents that they could anglicize their surname to Rashka, or they could keep it the same, but the pronunciation would inevitably change. We eventually resettled in Ottawa and embraced our new Canadian home. Prior to receiving Canadian citizenship less than five years later, we officially chose to keep Raska as our family name.

Over the years, my parents have often told me stories about our journey to Canada. I soon began to consider the similarities and differences that our immigration experience had with other individuals and families from Eastern Europe, especially Czechs who came to Canada after the 1948 communist takeover of Czechoslovakia and the 1968 Warsaw Pact invasion. Although their motivations for leaving Czechoslovakia and resettling in Canada were diverse, they were often viewed by successive generations as individuals who had left their homes because of political persecution and everyday life under a totalitarian regime.

Yet this story was not drilled into me. As a youth, I attended summer camps in the Laurentian Mountains, where I spoke Czech, played sports, sang traditional songs, participated in the calisthenic exercises of the patriotic Sokol (Falcon) movement, and was taught about my ethnocultural heritage with other young Czechs. Apart from these early ethnocultural experiences, my family did not regularly participate in community events. I am well aware that my status as a community "insider-outsider"—a Canadian of Czech ancestry not active in community organizations—provides me with a unique lens through which to examine the history of Czech immigration to Canada during the Cold War.

In seeking insights into Czech refugee experiences in Canada, I began to collect stories, oral histories, archival documents, photographs, and published materials, no matter their political bent. I later learned that, during the Cold War, 36,531 individuals claimed Czechoslovakia as their country of citizenship upon entering Canada.[1]

But, more importantly, I discovered that a defining characteristic of this postwar migration of predominantly ethnic Czechs and Slovaks was the prevalence of anti-communist and pro-democratic values.

Diplomats, industrialists, workers, politicians, professionals, and students spoke about fleeing to the West in search of freedom, security, and economic opportunity. It was important to them that they might permanently resettle in Canada and become naturalized citizens. Yet it was never quite that simple. According to the 2016 Canadian census, 104,580 Canadians reported having full or partial Czech ethnicity. Closer analysis reveals that 81,330 Canadians claimed multiple ethnic origins, while 23,250 Canadians indicated having only Czech origins. Meanwhile, 40,715 Canadians reported having Czechoslovakian heritage.[2] The Czechs and the Slovaks formed separate ethnocultural groups. During Czechoslovakia's existence from 1918 to 1992, a majority of Slovaks opposed a common "Czechoslovak" nationhood often promoted by Czechs and a minority of Slovaks.

Existing scholarship on Slovak immigration to Canada has examined the postwar experiences of Slovak refugees in Canada. However, there remains a dearth of scholarship on Czech refugee experiences in Canada after the Second World War. As a result, a number of questions soon permeated my thinking about their immigration to Canada during the Cold War. Since many of these newcomers were political refugees, who were they? What made them choose Canada? When did they arrive in Canada? How did the Canadian government and local Czechoslovak community institutions influence their immigration and resettlement experiences? How did they create an identity that would make them welcome refugees in Canada?

Czech Refugees in Cold War Canada is the first full-length academic study of post–Second World War Czech immigration to Canada. It examines the admission, resettlement, and integration of Czech refugees during the Cold War. In using archival records and oral histories that illustrate diverse refugee experiences, I shed further light on the immigrant experience in Cold War Canada, ultimately demonstrating that refugees and their families were preoccupied with forging identities that would lead to their acceptance. They were intent on showing Canadians, the Canadian government, and their own compatriots that they were middle-class anti-communists beyond either Old World nationalism or subversive leftist agitation. By exposing the totalitarian nature of their homeland and the reasons for their forced migrations to the West, Czech refugees in Canada attempted to legitimize their experiences and navigate the Cold War norms found in their new country. For individuals and families who immigrated from Eastern Europe to Canada, the fear of being labelled communist sympathizers or Soviet spies and put under state surveillance became a significant factor in how they handled the moral panic in

Canadian society about the global spread of communism and Soviet influence. These individuals soon used pro-democratic and anti-communist rhetoric not only to appease Canadian officials and the greater public—suspicious of immigration from Southern and Eastern Europe because of preconceived notions about ethnoracial identity, work ethic, and ability to assimilate—but also to demonstrate their support for the cherished Canadian ideas of freedom, liberty, human rights, and democratic values.

Canadians remained apprehensive about the Cold War arrival of refugees from communist satellite states, fearing that they might become a drain on the economy. Federal officials, however, were concerned about the deprivations suffered by Czech refugees and how their experiences might lead to deviations from sociocultural and political norms in Cold War Canada. Nevertheless, bureaucratic pressure in support of liberalism and democracy and against communism to bring refugees fleeing Eastern Europe to Canada soon forced the Canadian government to help resettle displaced Czech refugees. In turn, federal officials promoted the resettlement of individuals and families from refugee-producing communist satellite states, labelling Czech refugees, for example, as the "cream of the crop," a "small gold mine of talent," and "good material" that would be socially and economically absorbed into the fabric of Canadian society.

In the years following their resettlement in Canada, some Czech newcomers continued to view themselves as "émigrés," believing that their relocation was temporary and that they would soon return to their old homeland after it was freed from the clutches of communism. I soon learned that many Czech refugees sensed that a democratic system of government would not easily return to Czechoslovakia and turned their attention to attaining social and cultural citizenship in Canada. In their attempts to legitimize their place in Canada, they cultivated a particular narrative. It focused on their displacement from their homeland and their subsequent resettlement in Canada in accounts told by articulate and politically minded Czech refugees who portrayed themselves as the true representatives of the Czechoslovak community to government officials and the Canadian public. To this end, they lobbied their fellow citizens for political support in returning a parliamentary democracy to Czechoslovakia while strengthening democratic values in Canada. It was all in an effort to integrate fully into their new country.

Introduction

During the Cold War, many thousands of Czech refugees left their homeland to come to Canada. Many emigrated because of a genuine fear of being persecuted for their middle-class beliefs on openness and free elections and their understanding of "democracy." Others left because of a lack of economic opportunity, a capitalist economy, and social mobility in their homeland. No doubt some even left because of a sense of adventure, but they were in the minority. The migration of Czech refugees during the Cold War was a class-based social movement.

They all came with stories about fighting the communists. Many of them carried out daring escapes to the West, only to languish later in European camps waiting for their opportunity to come to Canada. Initially, many of these individuals arrived in Canada with hopes of returning to their European homeland once it was freed from communism. Whether admitted into the country under the Displaced Person (DP) movement or later recognized as political refugees by Canadian and international law, many of the 36,531 immigrants who claimed Czechoslovakia as their country of citizenship (both Czechs and Slovaks) during the Cold War arrived with an evolving anti-communist narrative, affected by the culture of the Cold War, including how they thought Canadians perceived them.

The Cold War immigration of Czech refugees occurred in distinctive waves, and immigrants' narratives differed. Then, too, the immigration and resettlement experiences of these refugees were influenced both by changing Canadian government policies and by local Czechoslovak community institutions. At the same time, the very presence of these newcomers shaped Canada's Cold War anti-communist efforts, which in turn affected how Canadians viewed the newcomers. Existing scholarship on Canada and the Cold War has focused on the role of the Canadian state in regulating Cold War immigration, with a particular emphasis on the entry of individuals and families from Eastern Europe, as federal officials attempted to combat a "red scare" prevalent throughout Canadian society. Gerald Dirks, Reginald Whitaker, Gary Marcuse, and Steve Hewitt have demonstrated that refugee entry into Canada was heavily influenced by ideological and economic motives. In reality, a "double standard" existed whereby Canadian officials were passive to the admission of fascists and their sympathizers but screened more closely immigrants suspected of harbouring communist sympathies or affiliations.[1] Furthermore, individuals who fled communist states were permitted to settle as refugees in Canada, but officials treated them with caution. Meanwhile, leftists who fled conservative states were labelled as security risks.[2]

This book is also set in a historiography shaped by refugee histories that have illuminated the role of ethnocultural identity and political ideology in the process of refugee integration into Cold War Canada. Milda Danys has observed that, following their resettlement, Lithuanian refugees were far too conscious of their ethnocultural and political identity to be fully absorbed into Canadian society. As political exiles, they focused their efforts on influencing domestic and international opinions against the Soviet occupation of their homeland. Lubomyr Luciuk has argued that Ukrainian refugees believed that they would transmit their ethnocultural heritage to Canadians of Ukrainian heritage, thereby reinvigorating their community. The refugees' own notions of what it meant to be Ukrainian were shaped in a Soviet-occupied homeland and did not always conform to the Ukrainian identity formed in Canada. In reality, postwar Ukrainian refugees remained committed to the cause of liberating their homeland from Soviet oppression. Over time, two versions of Ukrainian identity took hold in Canada between the existing community (proponents of caution, pragmatism, and patriotism) and postwar arrivals (nationalistic, militant, and uncompromising). These community divisions ultimately led to further frustration and alienation. Franca Iacovetta has examined the role played by institutional gatekeepers—politicians, civil servants, and other professionals—in promoting a hegemonic and conservative Cold War consensus among recently arrived refugees. Her work has demonstrated that, during their resettlement and integration, newcomers' actions were circumscribed by public and private gatekeepers' views of Cold War societal and political norms. However, by using oral histories, personal stories, archival documents, and ethnocultural newspapers, I demonstrate that newcomers were often able to circumvent gatekeepers and establish their own paths toward social and cultural integration in Cold War Canada. Francis Peddie has suggested that, when Chilean refugees resettled in Canada, they had to rethink, to various degrees, how they self-identified and how they would live their lives in their new country. The connections formed by Chilean newcomers within their local community often determined how successful they were in their social integration in Canada. Meanwhile, the level of success shaped how newcomers defined themselves and were viewed by Canadian society.[3]

My work seeks to advance this historiography by focusing on the migration experiences of three successive waves of Czech refugees during the Cold War. An important question is how did refugees, who had secured admission as "desirable" immigrants, navigate existing social, cultural, and political norms in Canadian society during the Cold War? By answering this question, we can learn how many Czech refugees came to reinforce the existing conservative Cold War consensus. Following their resettlement in Canada, politically active, middle-class, and articulate Czech refugees established or joined existing Czechoslovak ethnocultural associations, in which they portrayed themselves as the true representatives of the Czechoslovak community in deliberations with government officials. To the federal government and their fellow Canadians, they presented themselves as "citizen allies," the very embodiment at the civilian level of the military alliance that most Canadians enthusiastically embraced.[4] Having experienced communist repression at home and a virulent anti-communist Canada, they soon became prominent members of Czechoslovak institutions in Canada, marshalling the rhetoric to help craft an identity that fit anti-communist sociocultural and political norms in Cold War Canada. This approach to achieving greater acceptance within Canadian society also entailed a public campaign to liberate their homeland from communism. This process ultimately paid dividends and helped these refugees to attain social and cultural citizenship in Canada.

In joining Canada's Cold War effort, these refugees also boosted their position within their ethnic community's elite. They joined community organizations out of self-interest to increase their socioeconomic standing and to promote their political views while denouncing political dissent from leftist sympathizers, whom they viewed as outside liberal democracy. Influenced by moral panic in Canadian society about the spread of communism, these "Czechoslovak" refugee elites used their anti-communist rhetoric through persuasive language, including words such as *fight, struggle,* and *liberate* in support of the cherished Canadian ideas of "freedom," "liberty," "democracy," and "human rights." They did so especially when lobbying other Canadians for their political support or encouraging them not to surrender to communist propaganda. However, this rhetoric often exceeded reality—in attempts to change Canadian public perceptions of Czechoslovakia and global communism. A considerable amount of anti-communist rhetoric was also anti-Soviet. Since Czechoslovak institutions and Canadian authorities were instrumental in the resettlement of Czech refugees, they also helped to determine what part of the newcomer's anti-communism was rhetoric—an attempt to embrace postwar Canadian norms or Czechoslovak community interests—and what was reality. Among Czech newcomers who initially considered themselves émigrés, longing for a return home to Czechoslovakia, their desire for repatriation eventually subsided.

The problem for Czech newcomers, of course, was that being an émigré was not possible. They met the definition of a "refugee": individuals and families without legal status seeking refuge, affecting international politics during the twentieth century. They were aware that, in the postwar period, nation-states had established mechanisms—including increasing administrative control over legislation, regulations, and border security—to prevent the "influx" of undesirable individuals because of political ideology, nationalism, xenophobia, and the suspicion of "others." Historian Jérôme Elie points out that the modern prevalence of forced migrations is largely the result of religious and political conflict in which refugee-producing states implement a "process of purification" to rid themselves of individuals who oppose their policies.[5] In the case of Czech refugees in Canada during the Cold War, they knew that the host society would suspect them of either harbouring Old World nationalisms or particular leftist ideologies. Their experiences relate to this broader trend. Individuals and families fled their homeland because of the communist regime's totalitarian nature and attempts to control all aspects of daily life. For many Czech refugees, this narrative would also guarantee their entry into Canada. After all, as refugees, they negotiated their own displacement, admission, and resettlement elsewhere. They attempted to legitimize their experiences and thus navigate the societal, cultural, and political norms found in Canada in an effort to integrate fully into the receiving society.

Czech Refugees in Cold War Canada focuses on ordinary refugees and thus incorporates personal accounts such as oral histories and stories—diverse refugee voices that contribute to, complement, and contest the refugee experience in Cold War Canada—to help us better understand how Czech refugees transplanted their ideological beliefs and influenced existing ethnocultural institutions and broader Canadian society during the Cold War.

Admissibility, Attitudes, and Waves of Czech Immigration

During the early years of the Cold War, Canadian immigration officials attempted to balance the economic need for skilled workers, who could also strengthen the conservative Cold War consensus, and the political necessity of recognizing the Canadian public's suspicions about immigration from communist satellite states. In turn, Czech refugees who wished to resettle in Canada were forced to confront evolving bureaucratic and societal notions of what constituted a "desirable" immigrant.

Admissibility was a fundamental premise underpinning Canada's shaping of immigration policy and its selection of immigrants. Previous Immigration Acts and legislation illustrated the development of a binary construction in which certain circumstances or qualities considered "desirable" ultimately led to the admission and inclusion of highly sought-after immigrants, whereas conditions labelled "undesirable" effectively led to inadmissibility and exclusion. Historically, desirability and admissibility were not only dependent on acts and regulations but often contingent on the local discretion and personal judgment of immigration officials who took into account various factors, including race, ethnicity, country of origin, ideology, gender, sexuality, finances, health, education, skills, and work experience. Immigrants who met Canada's prevailing sociocultural and political norms were considered admissible; for others, their undesirability excluded them from establishing new lives in Canada.[6]

For much of the twentieth century, Canada did not have an active refugee policy. Instead, federal officials relied on cabinet decisions, including individual orders-in-council and regulations, to either admit or refuse refugees. Although postwar Canadian governments remained committed to pursuing an international humanitarian agenda, they were also reluctant to resettle individuals and families in search of safe haven. Harold Troper notes that Canadian officials continued to deny that any moral or legal obligation to refugees existed within Canada's immigration policy. The introduction of a humanitarian class, which defined refugees as a separate group of immigrants, within the 1976 Immigration Act finally defined Canada's moral and legal responsibilities regarding refugees. The act also entrenched Canada's commitment to help find a permanent solution to the international refugee crisis. In the thirty years between the end of the Second World War and the introduction of the

1976 Immigration Act, Canada largely restricted the resettlement of refugees. In need of highly sought-after labour to appease an ever-growing postwar economy, the federal government established the DP movement that brought 186,154 persons to Canada between 1947 and 1952. At the time, immigration selection was heavily biased against non–Western European immigrants, partly because of societal prejudices; British immigrants were considered racially and culturally ideal applicants, whereas prospective immigrants from Southern and Eastern Europe were considered less desirable because of concerns about ethnoracial identity, work ethic, and ability to assimilate.[7] Although Canadian officials were heavily influenced by public opinion on immigration, Cold War politics soon overrode existing biases. Both federal officials and Canadian society were compelled to respond to the plight of thousands of individuals and families fleeing from the refugee-producing communist states of Eastern Europe.

The February 1948 communist takeover of Czechoslovakia provided the Canadian government with an important early propaganda victory. Thousands of Czechs fled their country, fearing persecution by the communists for their membership and participation in democratic political parties. After spending several months or even years in refugee camps in Allied-occupied Austria and Germany, and Italy, thousands of anti-communist academics, clergy, politicians, professionals, students, and tradespeople were admitted into and successfully resettled in Canada. Czechs in the West commonly referred to them as "1948ers" or "48ers." Refugee advocates promoted images of upheaval, displacement, and suffering to the Canadian public, while immigration officials declared that they had resettled the "cream of the crop" from the refugee camps in Europe. Canadian officials later publicized the democratic backgrounds of the refugees, labelling them as "Cold Warriors" and "freedom fighters."

All of this notwithstanding, the reactions of both the Canadian public and the Czech ethnocultural community to their arrival in Canada were mixed. Many of these refugees immediately joined or established organizations intent on promoting a democratic system of government in their old homeland, in the hope of returning home, while also instilling "Canadian" and middle-class values in successive generations of their community. In some cases, Czechs also attempted to unite with and represent Slovaks as "Czechoslovaks"—without regard for a separate Slovak ethnic identity—which increased mistrust and division between Czechs and nationalist Slovaks in Canada.[8]

Despite the Canadian government's attempts to portray these recently arrived refugees as democratic and anti-communist, the public remained apprehensive, fearing that the newcomers might become a drain on Canada's economy and society or that some of them might be communist spies. Public and private gatekeepers were also concerned about the psychological and physical tolls endured by the refugees during their flight from persecution, temporary housing in European camps, and eventual resettlement in Canada as contract manual labourers, family-sponsored immigrants, or students seeking to continue their interrupted studies. Canadian officials feared that the privations suffered by the refugees might lead to deviations from societal norms. As a result, federal authorities viewed ideological, moral, or sexual deviations from the established Cold War social standards of anti-communism, heteronormativity, and the nuclear family—with a male head of household and breadwinner and a female housewife and mother—as threats to the conservative Cold War consensus.

Two decades later and only twelve years after the Hungarian Revolution in 1956 had galvanized Canadian support for the resettlement of approximately 37,500 "freedom fighters," who fled the Soviet invasion of their homeland, the government was again compelled to consider resettling a significant wave of refugees. Warsaw Pact forces invaded Czechoslovakia in August 1968 to suppress the Prague Spring movement's attempts to reform and liberalize Communist Party rule in the country. In the early years after the invasion, over 150,000 individuals fled the state, seeking refuge in the West.[9] Many of those who left were young, well-educated, and trained professionals. In a special program, Canada accepted nearly 12,000 refugees from Czechoslovakia. Canadian officials claimed that Prague Spring refugees were a "small gold mine of talent" because of their educational background, multilingual ability, professional experience, and adherence to the anti-communist Cold War values of democracy, human rights, and justice.[10] Previous generations of Czech newcomers referred to these refugees as the "1968ers" or "68ers."

The 48ers who had arrived in Canada from refugee camps scattered across Europe included individuals who had fled the brutal repression of individual freedoms and civil rights through torture, imprisonment, and even death at the hands of the communist regime in the late 1940s and early 1950s. In contrast, the 68ers were fleeing a country in the midst of a sociopolitical upheaval in which the communist system was changing. Some 68ers had already left the country before the Warsaw Pact invasion occurred and therefore avoided the brutal Soviet-inspired "normalization" of their country. In the early hours, weeks, and months after the invasion, in the hope of getting rid of even more proponents of communist reform, Czechoslovakia had allowed its borders to remain open.

Canada's reaction to this wave of Czech immigrants stood in contrast to its previous response. The Canadian government was less enthusiastic about using resettlement of the 68ers as an anti-communist propaganda tool or example of its contribution to international humanitarianism. Instead, federal officials focused their attention on the economic and labour needs of the country, eventually labelling Prague Spring refugees as "good material."[11] The permanent resettlement of successive waves of Czech refugees demonstrates that Canadian immigration policy during the Cold War was ad hoc; although at times it was altruistic, it largely promoted national economic and political interests ultimately defined by anti-communist Cold War ideology.

Whereas the 48ers had experienced the effects of persecution during the communist takeover of Czechoslovakia and the initial period of Stalinization, the 68ers had lived through two decades of communism. Both Czech refugee movements consisted of educated and established professionals, students, and tradespeople. The 48ers initially struggled to integrate into Canadian society and to find suitable employment according to their academic training and professional experience. Like them, many of the individuals who arrived in 1968 and after were also underemployed, at least in their first few years in Canada. Compared with the 48ers, however, the 68ers integrated into Canadian society more rapidly and assumed positions in their respective fields.

During the 1970s and 1980s, a third wave of Czech refugees arrived to resettle permanently in the West. These Cold War immigrants were not fleeing their homeland in response to a sudden crisis but chose to leave it during the post-1968 period of "normalization." This group consisted of academics, professionals, students, and skilled tradespeople in construction, manufacturing, and service industries. These newcomers also reinvigorated the anti-communist and pro-democracy identity of the Canadian Czechoslovak community and its organizations.

"Czechoslovak" Institutions

Czech newcomers adapted ethnocultural values and political identities to their country of permanent resettlement. In Canada, Czech refugees sought to establish or join community organizations that mirrored their ideological beliefs in areas where their compatriots or neighbouring ethnic groups already existed. In order to understand better the emergence of Czechoslovak institutions in Canada, we must first understand the political events in Central Europe that led to the development of a Czechoslovak identity.

With the demise of Austria-Hungary in 1918, a newly established multinational state, Czecho-Slovakia, became home to over 13.4 million inhabitants: 6.8 million Czechs, 3.1 million Sudeten Germans, 1.9 million Slovaks, 745,000 Hungarians, 461,000 Subcarpathian Ruthenians, 180,000 Jews, and 238,000 persons listed as "others." In February 1920, a new constitution was published with a preamble declaring a "Czechoslovak" political ideology. The constitution aimed to establish a unitary nation-state for Czechs, who largely viewed the Slovaks as Slovak-speaking Czechs.[12] The hyphen, which symbolized a political federation between the Czech and Slovak nations, was removed. The new Czechoslovak constitution promoted a "Czechoslovak" language—an amalgam of the Czech and Slovak languages—and civic nationalism. From Prague, Czech political leaders co-opted Slovaks to form a sizable (65 percent) "Czechoslovak" majority in Czechoslovakia.

Scholars have asserted that Czechoslovak civic nationalism was constructed from two contested principles: first, that the newly conceived Czechoslovak nation-state was the historical culmination of earlier contact and collaboration between the Czech and Slovak nations, which maintained similar languages; second, that the smaller Slovak nation would accept being merged with a larger Czech population to form a Czechoslovak nation.[13] Therefore, proponents of Czechoslovak civic nationhood based their claims upon the erroneous assumption that the Czech and Slovak nations were not separate ethnic groups—with their own historical territory, language, and culture. This ideology continued to cause political and social tensions between Czechs and Slovaks.

Beginning in the 1920s, the politics of identity contested in Czechoslovakia were transplanted to Canada. State-sponsored Czechoslovakism was promoted by Prague's diplomatic representatives in Canada and opposed by nationalist Slovaks, who defended a distinct Slovak ethnic heritage and homeland in Slovakia.[14] During the Cold War, Czech refugee identity in Canada was not only shaped by political ideologies and personal backgrounds but also tied to a civic nationalism established in Europe.

Throughout the Cold War, Czechs and a minority of Slovaks who professed a belief in a common Czechoslovak identity organized community institutions to promote their ethnocultural heritage in Canada. Since the Czech and Slovak nations shared a common statehood in Czechoslovakia, it is important to recognize the similarities and differences between the Czech and Slovak ethnic groups in Canada. Beginning in the late nineteenth century, because of a familiarity with their cultures, both groups settled in areas where other Central and Eastern Europeans already resided. Within these communities, Czechs and Slovaks were numerically fewer compared with other European groups—which included Ukrainians, Russians, Poles, Germans, and Hungarians—and their patterns of assimilation differed.

Elena Jakešová and M. Mark Stolárik have argued that Slovaks in Canada tended to maintain strong ties within their ethnic community, upholding three pillars of Slovak life: the family, the fraternal benefit society, and the parish. Approximately 80 percent of Slovak immigrants were Catholic, about 15 percent were Lutheran, almost 5 percent were Greek Catholic, and a few individuals were of Reform (Calvinist) background. Prior to the First World War, Slovaks relied on the fraternal benefit society to build parishes where mass was delivered in the Slovak language. With an increase in Slovak immigration after 1918, many national parishes and congregations were created across Canada to serve local Slovak communities, both Catholic and Protestant. During the interwar period, many sojourners found their initial experiences in Canada difficult and chose to remain within their community. As a result, they did not learn English or French and never adapted to Canadian culture and customs. Subsequent generations of Slovaks often intermarried with other Slavic groups and with individuals of similar religious backgrounds. For example, Slovak Catholics often intermarried with individuals from French, Hungarian, Irish, Italian, or Polish backgrounds. After the Second World War, Slovak immigrants arrived in Canada with higher levels of education and experience and quickly improved their socioeconomic status. These newcomers established community schools for their children, where they were taught Slovak culture and history and could learn the Slovak language. Catholic Slovaks often enrolled their children in separate schools, whereas Protestant Slovaks largely placed their children in public schools. In recent decades, Slovak Canadians have continued to support local community institutions and their ethnic press.[15] To this day, a majority of Slovaks in Canada espouses a distinct Slovak ethnic identity and culture, and only a minority supports a common Czechoslovak identity with Canadian Czechs.

Compared with Slovaks, Czechs in Canada have achieved a higher level of institutional assimilation. Although they have often retained their ethnic identity, they are less likely to participate in Czech or Czechoslovak institutions, choosing instead to join non-ethnic Canadian organizations and groups. Approximately 75 percent of Czechs in Canada are Catholic, whereas a minority belongs to the Protestant churches, including the Moravian Brethren, Lutheran, and Baptist churches. During the twentieth century, many Czechs favoured intermarriage with individuals of Anglo-German backgrounds. Compared with Slovaks, Czechs had a higher rate of intermarriage and often moved out of ethnic neighbourhoods in an attempt to avoid being ghettoized. Prior to the Second World War, Czech immigrants often joined other national churches and organizations because their numbers were too small for them to establish their own institutions. After the Second World War, Czech immigrants also brought a higher level of education and experience to Canada, which allowed them to improve rapidly their socioeconomic status compared with that of other groups that arrived in Canada during the same period. Similar to Slovaks, postwar Czech immigrants also established weekend schools for their children, who would learn about Czech culture and history and practise their Czech language skills. With the rise of public education, Czech immigrants increasingly placed their children in public schools. Community institutions that taught the Czech language and culture to successive generations decreased as Czech parents tutored their children at home or failed to pass on their culture and language. With an increase in the number of government-supported community services since the 1970s, many Czechs in Canada seldom support Czech, Czechoslovak, or Czech and Slovak institutions and the ethnic press.[16]

Some Czechs preferred to join Slovak organizations or attempted to establish institutions that promoted a common Czechoslovak ethnic identity, which many nationalist Slovaks opposed. Relations between Czech and Slovak communities, characterized by friction and division, were often a microcosm of the political situation in Central Europe. From its inception in 1918 to its dissolution in 1992, Czechoslovakia was home to both the Czech and the Slovak nations. Since the birth of the Czech Republic and the Slovak Republic on New Year's Day in 1993, Czechoslovak groups have often referred to themselves as "Czech and Slovak."

Refugee, Émigré, or Immigrant?

In assessing the impact of sociopolitical events in Czechoslovakia on Czech immigration to Canada during the Cold War, I considered which words to use when referring to Czech individuals and families who immigrated to Canada from Czechoslovakia: *refugee, émigré,* or *immigrant?* Each word carries a unique set of political, legal, historical, and sociocultural connotations. For instance, the word *refugee* refers to someone who seeks safe haven or refuge from political, economic, and sociocultural persecution. Throughout history, refugees seeking protection have often self-identified as persecuted persons.

The first international attempt to coordinate refugee issues occurred with the establishment in 1921 of the High Commission for Refugees under the auspices of the League of Nations. As the international organization's first high commissioner, Fridtjof Nansen was tasked with assisting 1,500,000 individuals who had fled the Russian Revolution and subsequent civil war. Three decades later the United Nations Convention Relating to the Status of Refugees adopted a legal definition for any person who, "as a result of events occurring before 1 January 1951 and owing to a well-founded fear of being persecuted for reasons of race, religion, nationality, membership of a particular social group or political opinion, is outside the country of his nationality and is unable or, owing to such fear, is unwilling to avail himself of the protection of that country; or who, not having a nationality and being outside the country of his former habitual residence as a result of such events, is unable or, owing to such fear, is unwilling to return to it."[17] The convention restricted refugee status to events occurring before January 1951. The 1967 Protocol Relating to the Status of Refugees later resolved this issue. The circumstances under which the 1948ers and 1968ers fled their homeland, including communist threats and persecution and a lack of socioeconomic mobility, correspond favourably to the definition of a refugee.

Rather than being depicted as unfortunate victims of the Cold War, some Czechs chose to self-identify as émigrés. The word *émigré* refers to an individual who emigrates and often carries a connotation of social or political exile. Whereas emigrants choose to leave their homelands and resettle elsewhere, émigrés are usually forced to do so for political reasons, and they view their exiles as short term, eventually being permitted to return home. In the context of the Cold War, émigrés also espoused a desire to return home, thereby arousing suspicions about their loyalty to their country of resettlement but reassuring the host society that they were merely sojourners. Existing scholarship suggests that, compared with apolitical or disaffected refugees from Eastern Europe, anti-communist émigrés rejected their roles and identities as pawns of history and the "determinism of historical laws" used by authoritarian regimes to justify their oppression.[18] As a result, these individuals maintained lower levels of sociocultural, economic, and political integration and were largely disillusioned with their lives in Canada. This definition describes only a minority of Czechs who arrived in Canada during the Cold War. In most cases, those who viewed themselves as émigrés were the 1948ers who had experienced only the communist takeover of their homeland, not years of communist rule. Most Czechs who arrived in Canada in the decades after the events of February 1948 viewed the political situation in Czechoslovakia as rigid, if not permanent, because of the Cold War's ideological divide between East and West.[19]

Perhaps the least contentious of the three aforementioned words is *immigrant.* There is little doubt that many Czech individuals and families were admitted as immigrants and resettled in Canada under specific immigration programs, including one- or two-year manual labour contracts, under the postwar DP "bulk labour" movement, or as part of the skilled labour class, student class, family reunification class, or business/entrepreneurial class. Although immigration programs shifted throughout the Cold War period with the introduction of the 1952 and 1976 Immigration Acts and various regulations, including Order-in-Council P.C. 1967-1616, commonly referred to as the points system, many Czechs who fled their homeland arrived in Canada only after spending several months or years in European refugee camps. Therefore, using "immigrant" as an inclusive term does not adequately illustrate their circumstances. For some, the choice of resettling in Canada was largely subjective, influenced, for example, by how well they were treated by Western diplomats and immigration officials during an initial interview and medical examination, what previous knowledge they had of the country, and whether they spoke its official language(s) or understood its customs and culture. In the German, Austrian, and Italian refugee camps, Canadian officials attempted to process rapidly persons who they believed were highly desirable applicants—individuals whom they viewed as young, healthy, industrious, and experienced, and who raised no security concerns—rather than lose them to American, Australian, British, French, New Zealand, or Scandinavian officials. Although the term "immigrant" applies favourably to the Czechs who permanently resettled in Canada during the Cold War, most Czech newcomers understood why the Canadian government identified them as "refugees," especially after the establishment of the 1951 UN Refugee Convention. In turn, they responded by using the term to exemplify their fears of persecution under the communist regime in Czechoslovakia and their reasons for seeking safe haven in Canada.

The Cold War and Conformity

For Czech refugees, it was important that Canadians thought of them as subjects of the Cold War. The term "Cold War" was first used by British novelist George Orwell in October 1945 to condemn the warlike state of relations between the United States and the Soviet Union following the end of the

Second World War. Orwell criticized American imperialism and Soviet communism and their respective influence in international affairs.[20]

As Canadians saw it, the Cold War began with Igor Gouzenko, a Soviet cipher clerk in the Soviet Embassy in Ottawa. In September 1945, Gouzenko fled from the Soviet authorities with 109 documents, which he later turned over to the Royal Canadian Mounted Police (RCMP). The highly sensitive documents proved the existence of a Soviet spy ring in Canada. The Soviet cipher clerk's claim that Canadian communists were handing over secret documents to Moscow was met with national outrage. In February 1946, under Order-in-Council P.C. 411, the Canadian government established the Royal Commission to Investigate the Facts Relating to and the Circumstances Surrounding the Communication, by Public Officials and Other Persons in Positions of Trust, of Secret and Confidential Information to Agents of a Foreign Power, commonly referred to as the Kellock-Taschereau Commission. Between October 1950 and June 1951, the RCMP handled 54,000 requests to screen civil servants and private sector workers. Any deviance from postwar cultural norms of God, family, country, and democratic values was immediately viewed as suspicious and often put under state surveillance.[21]

In the first decade of the Cold War, Canada admitted close to 1 million immigrants, and concern mounted that newcomers from Eastern Europe would disrupt middle-class cultural norms. For that reason, Canadians also strove for reassurance through social conformity. Canadian officials cooperated with their American neighbours and accepted a series of ideological and political agendas that dictated which immigrants were admitted and which were restricted. The postwar consolidation of Soviet hegemony in Eastern Europe, of which the usurping of Czechoslovakia's democratic system by local communists supported by Moscow was but one example, shocked Canadian officials.[22]

As federal officials screened prospective immigrants, proponents of business attempted to thwart the immigration of noted leftists, while ethnic communities—including Eastern European groups—attempted to suppress the leftist influence in their communities. They need not have worried. In contrast to prewar immigrants who brought with them a tradition of radicalism from Europe to Canada, Cold War refugees from Eastern Europe brought liberal-conservative principles that supported democratic values and economic opportunities. In addition, immigrants from Eastern Europe brought with them an ardent anti-communism and hatred of Soviet domination of their homelands. Many of these anti-communist newcomers attached themselves to conservative causes and promoted policies that sustained the Cold War.

Across Canada, social workers and immigrant advocates encouraged "New Canadians" to abandon family structures that could be considered unconventional. Newcomers were expected to conform to the established cultural standard of a single-family household with a father as the major breadwinner and a mother as a housewife to safeguard public morality. Whether or not white, Anglo-Celtic, and Christian family norms were desirable to them, many immigrants—who had already faced discrimination and economic hardship upon entering Canada—continued to be labelled as deviant and seen as a threat to the institution of the family and the wider process of "Canadianization."[23]

Meanwhile, newcomers from Eastern Europe also faced demands for political conformity, thrust as they were into the ideological fight between democracy and communism. Differences of opinion or outright dissent were believed to undermine Canadian democratic values, while Canadian officials extolled the virtues of social cohesion and the Western way of life. Similarly, existing scholarship has shown that the Cold War in Canada imposed new social and political restraints on free speech and other civil liberties and further criminalized homosexuality and other forms of "immorality" and "deviant" behaviour because they were viewed as being outside the conservative Cold War norm of heterosexuality and a threat to the security of the country. Political dissent was depicted as treasonous and a sure sign that an individual was loyal to the Soviet Union and communism.[24] Refugees from Eastern Europe were expected to meet these sociocultural and political norms.

However, it was never that simple. My work demonstrates that, without the support of politically engaged refugees, many of whom were prominent members of Eastern European ethnocultural communities in Canada, the efforts of public and private gatekeepers to integrate refugees into Canada's conservative Cold War consensus would have been unsuccessful. Nevertheless, the efforts of gatekeepers and community elites to contain and eradicate communist threats within Cold War Canada led to widespread fear and moral panic that affected postwar immigration legislation, including the 1952 Immigration Act, which barred communist sympathizers, homosexuals, and drug users and traffickers from entering the country legally. Thus, for refugees from Eastern Europe, the fear of being labelled as communists or Soviet spies and put under surveillance was a significant factor in how they navigated the norms of their new country.

In this atmosphere of heightened vigilance, the Canadian government and ethnocultural organizations trumpeted the myth of the heroic anti-communist "freedom fighter" from Eastern Europe who had arrived in Canada to continue the struggle to liberate his or her homeland from communism. Although an asset to Canada as a skilled immigrant, the anti-communist remained preoccupied with the struggle for the old homeland rather than integrating into Canadian society. Individuals perceived as freedom fighters often succumbed to issues of personal immorality and even played both sides of the Cold War. As a result, the role of the anti-communist largely influenced how successful the state would be in gaining support from Eastern European communities for its Cold War agenda while undermining the ethnic left. The Soviet Union and its satellite states used agents in Canada to infiltrate certain ethnic groups, including the Czechoslovak community, in the hope of eliminating anti-communist activities.

In recent years, Cold War scholarship has increasingly argued that the West overreacted to the threat posed by the Soviet Union. In Canada, the Cold War often led to unnecessary panic, miscalculated reactions, and excesses, all in the pursuit of national security. Western states, including Canada, often failed to distinguish between actual threats by communists and their sympathizers inside the country and those by the Soviet Union and abroad. As a result, Canadian officials failed to react in a measured manner.[25]

Canadian authorities thus actively participated in the admission, resettlement, and integration of anti-communist refugees during the Cold War. Clearly, there was a significant level of influence that anti-communist newcomers had on Canadian officials and other non-governmental gatekeepers in undermining ethnic leftists in Canada and on foreign policy on Eastern Europe. The scope of participation, commitment, and success in fighting communism by newcomers from Czechoslovakia is the subject of this book.

Geographic Scope and Sources

This study describes Czech refugee experiences in a national context but focuses primarily on Toronto and southern Ontario for two main reasons. First, beginning in the interwar period, immigrants from Czechoslovakia began to settle in urban centres across Canada, and Toronto and Montreal attracted sizable Czech and Slovak populations. During the Cold War, nearly half of all newcomers from Czechoslovakia chose to settle in Ontario, where established Czechoslovak and nationalist Slovak communities existed. Second, the largest and most influential Canadian Czechoslovak institutions during the Cold War, the Czechoslovak National Alliance (CNA) and the Masaryk Hall (MH), were headquartered in Toronto. Although existing archival records and oral histories contain information on Czechoslovak community life across Canada, these collections focus predominantly on Czechoslovak community activities in Toronto and southern Ontario.

Government records provide us with a rich source of information on Canadian officials' role in the admission, resettlement, and integration of newcomers. Similarly, ethnic community fonds also shed light on the social, cultural, and political participation of citizens and newcomers to Canada. Institutional records donated by various Canadian Czechoslovak organizations—such as the Czechoslovak National Association of Canada (CNAC), Masaryk Memorial Institute (MMI), Canadian Czechoslovak Benevolent Association (CCBA), and Sokol Gymnastic Association of Canada (SGAC)—form a body of information from which we can ascertain the conditions and composition of membership, the level of participation in annual congresses and celebrations, and relations among Canadian Czechoslovak institutions and local, provincial, and federal authorities.

Documentation found in ethnic community fonds is often produced by "community insiders," who claim to represent their entire community, whether or not their ideological views are supported by a majority of community members. Ethnic community fonds also exclude the "silent voices" of members who do not actively participate in their community's sociocultural and political activities. Therefore, though ethnic community fonds give us a glimpse into the institutional and social history of the Czechoslovak community in Canada, often they do not include sizable constituencies within the community who are not regular participants in its activities and do not create documentation later preserved as a part of the community's archival record.

Oral history is a rich source of information on how Czech immigrants to Canada perceived themselves. Scholars might seek to gather contextual information in an attempt to reconstruct an objective past by engaging oral histories from Czech refugees who participated in community life in Canada, and from individuals whose experiences remain overlooked or ignored, but the promise of oral history is to reveal the mindset of the immigrant.

The Canadian ethnic press is also a vital source of information on Czech refugees and the existing Czechoslovak community in Canada, especially on how Canadians perceived the newcomers and more importantly on how they perceived newcomers' attempts to integrate. The Prague-sponsored "Czechoslovak weekly" *Nová vlasť* (New Homeland) was established in 1934 and published primarily in the Slovak language before ceasing its activities just prior to the communist takeover of Czechoslovakia in February 1948. The community press also included *Naše hlasy* (Our Voices) from 1955 to 1974, *Kanadské listy* (Canadian Papers) from 1973 to 2008, and the MMI's official organ, *Nový domov* (New Homeland), established in 1950 and still in circulation today. These ethnic newspapers promoted a Czechoslovak sociopolitical orientation while diminishing nationalist Slovak aspirations for self-determination and independence. During the Cold War, these newspapers espoused an anti-communist ideology and anti-Soviet bias.

Outline of the Chapters

In order to place significant events within the context of the Cold War, *Czech Refugees in Cold War Canada* is structured using a chronological and thematic approach and consists of seven chapters in addition to this introduction and the conclusion. The chapters emphasize to varying degrees questions of identity formation, ethnocultural involvement, political ideology, and relations between successive waves of Czech immigration and between Czech refugees and Canadian society. Each chapter also demonstrates how historical events profoundly influenced the significance of Canadian Czechoslovak institutions.

Chapter 1 discusses interwar immigration from Czechoslovakia and the existence of an interwar Czechoslovak community in Canada prior to the arrival of diplomats and politicians, anti-Nazi Sudeten Germans, and a transplanted Bata Shoe Company on the eve of the German invasion of the Czech Lands (Bohemia and Moravia). This chapter sheds further light on why ethnic Czech immigrants increasingly were drawn to settle in urban areas, notably in Ontario and Quebec. During the Second World War, Czechs, Slovaks, and Subcarpathian Ruthenians organized into a "Czechoslovak" alliance in order to assist in the liberation of their homeland from German occupation and to provide relief to their compatriots.

Chapter 2 focuses on the postwar plans of Czechoslovak community institutions in Canada, with a particular emphasis on the resurrection of a democratic Czechoslovak state, postwar relief, the promotion of Canadian citizenship, and the creation of ethnic heritage.

Chapter 3 describes the reactions of Canadian Czechoslovak community organizations to the communist takeover of Czechoslovakia in February 1948 and their involvement in the resettlement of political refugees, who subsequently fled to Canada in search of safe haven. This chapter also expands on what Reginald Whitaker describes as the federal bureaucracy's plea to the Canadian government on behalf of "liberalism and democratic anti-Communism" to implement a program to bring Czech refugees to Canada.

Chapter 4 examines what Franca Iacovetta describes as "Cold War encounters and ethnic battles" in which the Canadian state attempted to monitor and influence its ethnocultural communities. This chapter explains how intraethnic tensions and ideological divisions within the Czechoslovak community increased over efforts to return a Western democracy to the old homeland and the desire by the elite to instill postwar values of Canadian citizenship within the community.

Chapter 5 assesses the Canadian government's response to the Warsaw Pact invasion of Czechoslovakia in 1968 and the subsequent refugee crisis that led to the admission and resettlement of close to 12,000 refugees. Gerald Dirks notes that Canadian officials insisted that they were resettling not only the most desirable applicants but also much-needed immigrants with specific skills.

Chapter 6 discusses the role of Czechoslovak community groups in the continued struggle against communism, the promotion of human rights in Canada and abroad, and the continued effort to assist refugees who arrived in the 1970s and 1980s. It supports the idea of Ninette Kelley and Michael Trebilcock that this period was instrumental in cementing Canada's humanitarian goals for and international obligations to refugees.

Chapter 7 illustrates the efforts of Czechoslovak community organizations to create ethnocultural heritage during the emergence of official multiculturalism in Canada.[26]

▸ ▸ ◂ ◂

Successive waves of anti-communist Czech refugees arrived in Canada articulating their hope of seeing Western democracy return to their homeland and one day returning there. Over time, through a series of complex exchanges with Canadian society and the existing Czechoslovak community, Czech refugees turned their attention toward Canadian citizenship and the establishment of Czechoslovak ethnic heritage for future generations. Their experiences during the Cold War were shaped by an interplay of identities rooted in Czechoslovakia and those being forged in Canada. In order to understand this shared past better, we must first examine the role of the Canadian government and Czechoslovak ethnocultural institutions in the resettlement of interwar Czech immigrants.

CHAPTER 1

Interwar Farm Labourers, Wartime Enemy Aliens, and Allied Citizens

Martin Bursík and his sister arrived in Quebec City on 22 August 1930. They had made the twenty-two-day journey from Moravia, in what was then Czechoslovakia, in order to work as agricultural labourers. Like many Czech immigrants to Canada at the time, they did not intend to stay in Canada; their original plan was to work for a time and then return home with their accumulated savings. The Bursíks chose Canada as a destination primarily because they already had a brother and sister-in-law there able to pay for their transatlantic journey, which, as Bursík recalls, included other young adults from Czechoslovakia, Hungary, and Poland. He settled in Blenheim, Ontario, where his brother worked, and immediately began picking tomatoes and doing general farm labour for three to six dollars a day. He communicated with others in German. Bursík recalls that a typical 100-acre farm in the late 1920s and early 1930s cost between $6,000 and $10,000. Like many other Moravian Czechs, he found his plan of accumulating money and returning to the old country thwarted by the Great Depression and decided to stay in Canada. By the early 1940s, after a decade of working as a farm labourer, and with the effects of the Depression gradually lifting, he was able to purchase a farm.[1]

After resettling in interwar Canada, Czech immigrants had to navigate existing social and cultural norms. They resettled across the country and were often employed in agriculture and industry. During the 1920s and 1930s, many of these newcomers struggled in a difficult economic environment to obtain employment and acquire enough savings to bring their families to Canada or to secure a property mortgage. In order to integrate into Canadian society,

Czech immigrants had to demonstrate that they supported so-called democratic values, were not politically subversive, and remained gainfully employed. During the growth of Canadian Czechoslovak community institutions in the 1930s, Czech immigrants faced questions about their loyalty to Canada. With their old homeland under German occupation beginning in March 1939, members of the Czechoslovak community later demonstrated their support for the Allied war effort by lobbying Canadian officials for political support, raising funds, collecting clothing, and donating cigarettes to Allied troops and their fellow compatriots overseas in an effort to display their allegiance to Canada. For politically active Czech immigrants, these wartime efforts served as a mechanism by which they could become good Canadians and attain social and cultural citizenship in Canada. Ultimately, their shared experiences during the Second World War set a precedent for future Czech refugees who also sought to become engaged citizens in Cold War Canada.

Early Czech Immigration

There were good reasons why the Czech refugees of Cold War Canada drew on their ethnocultural past. Czech immigration to Canada had already begun in the decades before the turn of the twentieth century. A majority of these newcomers to Canada were agriculturalists and industrial labourers who settled in areas already inhabited by other Eastern European immigrants. The abundance of available land drew Czech immigrants to western Canada, where they were joined by compatriots who had initially settled in Illinois, Minnesota, Nebraska, Oklahoma, and Texas and now moved northward. In 1884, a Czech community was established in Kolin, Saskatchewan, and later there were settlements at Derdard, Glenside, and Dovedale; the majority of settlers in these areas were Czech immigrants from Europe. In 1900, a Czech colony was established at Prague, Alberta, by Czech immigrants from the United States. Meanwhile, in Edmonton, a small community was established that included a number of professionals and artisans.

The 1911 census gathered information on 7,204,838 persons and indicated that approximately 1,800 Czechs and 851 Slovaks resided in Canada. These numbers might be misleading, however; later records, from the interwar period, show ethnic Slovak immigration to Canada from both the United States and Austria-Hungary significantly outnumbering Czech immigration, so the 1911 census might have counted some Slovaks as Czechs or Hungarians.[2]

Prior to the First World War, a large urban Czech population in Canada resided in Winnipeg. In 1913, Czech and Slovak immigrants there founded the Czecho-Slavic Benevolent Association. After the First World War, the organization was renamed the Czechoslovak Benevolent Association to reflect the establishment of a Czechoslovak state in Central Europe.[3] By the late 1920s, Winnipeg had become the largest settlement for immigrants from Czechoslovakia, with over 400 families residing in the city. Czechoslovakia's consul general, F.V. Květoň, observed that Winnipeg's Czechoslovak community was largely comprised of tailors and shoemakers and that the city served as a "winter station" to which agriculturalists would retire once the farming season was over.[4] Farther east, in northern Ontario, small communities of Czech miners were established at Haileybury, Fort William, and Kirkland Lake. Meanwhile, industrial workers settled in cities, including Windsor, Kingston, and Toronto. Throughout the 1920s, Czech immigration patterns continued, with agriculturalists in search of available land settling in western Canada, while labourers in search of industrial employment moved to central Canada. Czech immigrants from Moravia joined a labour scheme agreed upon by the Sugar Beet Growers Association of Canada and the Czech International Institute (Česká Zahraničová Instituce), which brought over farm labourers to work in the sugar beet industry in Lethbridge, Alberta, and Chatham, Ontario. With the rise of industry and urbanization, Czechs increasingly migrated to Ontario and Quebec looking for employment and opportunity. In Montreal, most immigrants from Czechoslovakia joined either the Czechoslovak community or the nationalist Slovak community. Together these communities numbered some 3,700 individuals, while Toronto attracted close to 2,500 individuals. Czech immigrants also settled in the southern Ontario communities of Hamilton, Kitchener, Oshawa, St. Catharines, Welland, and Windsor, where many were employed in industry.[5] Czech immigrants continued to arrive in small groups from the United States, typically settling outside urban areas and seeking employment in industry, mining, and railway construction. Unlike Czechs from Europe who hoped to return to their homeland after a few years, these immigrants came to Canada with hopes of accumulating enough capital to purchase land for agricultural work.[6] Often the heads of households were forced to journey to Canada alone since they could not afford to bring their spouses and dependants during their initial resettlement.

Finances were even more problematic for immigrants from Czechoslovakia, who often could not fund their journeys to Canada without substantial bank loans. Martin Yankovic, who arrived in Halifax on 1 March 1927 and came to Canada because he could not find work at home to feed his family, had acquired a 7,000 Czechoslovak crown bank loan—on top of his personal funds of 500 Czechoslovak crowns—to help pay for his transatlantic journey. Once the bank loan was paid, Yankovic brought his wife and children to Canada. Similarly, Joe Choroš, who came to Alberta from Czechoslovakia for work in the mid-1920s, had, with his father's help, received a bank loan of 6,000 Czechoslovak crowns or approximately $500 Canadian.[7]

Once resettled in Canada, Czech immigrants quickly sought existing compatriot communities across the country. In the interwar period, Canada was home to three distinct groups of immigrants from Czechoslovakia. The first and largest group comprised Slovak nationalists, who permitted only Slovaks to join their organizations and advocated for Slovak autonomy in a federalized Czechoslovakia. The second group consisted of Czechs who joined with Slovaks and other smaller ethnic minorities, including Subcarpathian Ruthenians, to form a "Czechoslovak" community that advocated for a single Czechoslovak national identity and defended the existence of a Czechoslovak Republic. The third group, influenced primarily by their political ideology (a small group of Slovak leftists that included communists and socialists), established their own organizations.[8]

Such distinctions were inadequately reflected in official Canadian records. Census figures prior to 1920, for instance, recognized all immigrants from Czechoslovakia as citizens of the Austro-Hungarian Empire and labelled them simply as "Austro-Hungarians." From 1920 to 1923, the Dominion Bureau of Statistics classified both ethnic Czechs and Slovaks as "Czecho-Slovaks" for the purpose of recording immigrant admission by ethnic origin. For the years 1923 to 1926, with only the hyphen between their designations removed, the two ethnic groups were classified as "Czechoslovaks."[9] However, the inadequacies of the record-keeping notwithstanding, we know that, from 1918 to 1945, individuals and families who identified themselves as historically belonging to an ethnic Slovak nation accounted for approximately four-fifths of all immigration from Czechoslovakia to Canada; figures illustrate that 35,358 Slovaks came to Canada during the 1920s and a further 4,294 up to 1937. From 1926 to 1945, the Dominion Bureau of Statistics identified 5,716 immigrants as having Czech "racial" origins upon entering Canada.[10]

Ethnic divisions mattered in community institutions, as illustrated by the case of the Czechoslovak Mutual Benefit Society. Formed in Montreal in 1924, it was for many of the Czechs in the city simply a sociocultural association in which they could meet other individuals who shared a belief in a common Czechoslovak identity.[11] However, the society's membership, according to its official organ, *Nová vlasť* (New Homeland), was over 90 percent Slovak. Initially, the few Czechs in the society attempted to establish a pro-Czechoslovak organization. However, the majority of Slovak members did not support a Czechoslovak identity and political ideology and left to join or establish independent nationalist Slovak groups.[12] But the instability of the society was the result of more than the ideological divisions within it. Unemployment was widespread among its members in Montreal, and many of them were transitory, moving to the city to look for work and leaving when they could not find it. As a result, the organization ultimately failed, and the paper ceased to exist a few years later because of financial difficulty and lack of membership.

The Moravians

Although interwar Slovak immigration substantially surpassed the small group of Czechs arriving in Canada from Czechoslovakia, a substantial increase in Czech immigration did occur, and it stemmed from the province of Moravia. A group of approximately 3,000 newcomers came to Canada in search of work and eventually settled in the Chatham area of southern Ontario.[13] Like Martin Bursík, many Moravian Czechs created an image of hardworking, honest sojourners who initially came to Canada to work as sugar beet farm workers with the intention of signing short-term labour contracts, saving their wages, and returning home after two or three years of work. They received no government assistance and were left to depend on themselves and their compatriots for financial and social assistance.

One of them was fifteen-year-old František Všetula, who arrived 11 June 1925 and, as an inexperienced agricultural worker, went to work with other Czechs in the fields. Another was Frank Konečný, who arrived in 1930 at the age of twenty-two. He chose to come to North America because he already had a sister in Canada and one in the United States. In describing his initial view of Canada, Konečný noted that as a child he had been a fan of Jack London's books, which in his eyes romanticized the country. Apart from literature, Konečný could only recall that Canada was a large country. He spoke no English and used his understanding of Polish in an attempt to communicate with fellow farmers from Central Europe.

In fact, a majority of the Moravian farm labourers arrived in Canada without any previous knowledge of English. With a sizable community taking shape in the region, a meeting was held in December 1928 at Chatham's St. Joseph's Hall for all interested "Czechoslovaks." Approximately 350 people were in attendance to discuss the future of their community. Subsequently, a Czechoslovak band named after Saints Cyril and Methodius was created and later played traditional Czech and Slovak music across southern Ontario and the United States. Meanwhile, in Chatham, Moravian parents organized their children into a theatre group and taught them about their ethnocultural heritage, including ethnic songs, as a reaction to what they perceived as a lack of parental responsibility in Canadian society. Within a relatively short time, asserts fellow immigrant Antonín Vajdík, Moravian Czechs had become well established in the region, many working in the sugar beet farm industry, in which they perceived themselves as being well liked for having done a better job than some of the workers from Mexico and the United States.[14]

The Great Depression

When the doors to immigration closed, this process of integration was interrupted. A year after the arrival of Konečný and Bursík in Canada, as the effects of the Great Depression intensified, and in order to prevent further strain on the economy, the federal government issued Order-in-Council P.C. 1931-695, limiting immigration to American citizens and British subjects from Great Britain, the Irish Free State, Newfoundland, Australia, New Zealand, and the Union of South Africa who possessed "sufficient means" to maintain themselves until employment was secured.[15] Wives, unmarried children under the age of eighteen, and fiancées of men already residing in Canada were also admissible. The order-in-council also permitted agriculturalists with "sufficient means to farm in Canada" to enter the country.[16] Because of these restrictions, the number of immigrants from Czechoslovakia stabilized, with only slight annual increases or decreases.

However, even as Canada's gates were closing, Czech immigrants with capital and agricultural experience were permitted to enter Canada.[17] The Gabriel family, for instance, came from an agricultural background in Moravia and ultimately settled in Kenora, Ontario, on 26 November 1932 to pursue farming there. Marie Gabriel, only twenty-one when she arrived, raised twelve children while her husband supported the family by working in the local flour mill.[18]

Whereas the focus of many interwar Czech immigrants to Canada was primarily on improving their lot through work in agriculture and industry, Slovaks—as Consul General František Pavlásek lamented—had brought with them much of the nationalist and autonomist ideology of the Hlinkova slovenská ľudová strana (Hlinka's Slovak People's Party), including the slogan "Slovakia for the Slovaks." In 1937, Pavlásek observed that "there are only a few Czechs here, and they are mostly assimilated, and a majority of them have withdrawn from public life due to permanent attacks.... Loyal Czechoslovak thinking, ever representing the democracy and the Czechoslovak national unity, represents in some colonies but a minority."[19] Prague's consul general in Montreal astutely recognized the ideological cleavages between Canadian Slovaks and Czechs. In effect, the ethnic groups were divided among those loyal to a single Czechoslovak nation-state, Slovak autonomists who sought home rule for Slovakia, and Slovak communists.[20]

As Czechs searched for land and economic opportunity, authorities in Prague insisted that their consulate in Canada unite its former residents into a cohesive "Czechoslovak" identity, regardless of their sociopolitical or religious affiliations, in an effort to spread Czechoslovakism as an ideology to compatriot communities across Canada. Canadian Slovaks who professed a belief in a distinct Slovak ethnocultural identity avoided participating in Czechoslovak associations. Conversely, the Czechoslovak consulate in Montreal viewed nationalistic Slovaks as "anti-Czech" and even "treasonous."[21]

Czechoslovak diplomats and the ethnic press in Canada played an influential role in the politics between proponents of Czechoslovakism and proponents of a separate Slovak national identity. In 1934, a predominantly Slovak-language weekly newspaper entitled *Nová vlasť* was revived in Montreal to inform Slovaks and Czechs of Czechoslovak community news in Canada and events in their homeland. Through financial contributions from the consulate in Montreal, the publication became the semi-official organ of Czechoslovakia's representatives in Canada.[22]

Politically engaged Czech immigrants soon joined efforts to establish a Czechoslovak community in Canada. One of them was Karel Buzek, who arrived in Canada in the mid-1920s and soon found himself at the centre of compatriot politics in Toronto. As a young adult, Buzek left interwar Czechoslovakia for England with the intention of never returning home. He later resettled in Canada and worked with Horace Hume Van Wart, a First World War veteran who also served as honorary consul of Czechoslovakia but did not speak Czech or Slovak. Buzek quickly became a "vice-consul" to many immigrants from Czechoslovakia and Canadians of Czech or Slovak ancestry. In 1929, he became Czechoslovakia's consul and trade commissioner in Toronto, a position that he would hold until 1948. As such, he could not fail to be keenly aware of the political tensions between adherents of Czechoslovakism and nationalist Slovaks and Sudeten Germans, who were suspicious of Czechoslovak democracy back home and supported political autonomy for their peoples. In the contentious atmosphere that reigned in the

Figure 1. *Karel Buzek, who immigrated to Canada in the 1920s, later served as Czechoslovakia's consul and trade commissioner in Toronto until 1948, n.d.*

immigrant community, the ethnic press falsely accused Buzek of supporting Sudeten German autonomy in an effort to spread mistrust among Prague's consular representatives in Canada. Buzek later claimed that diplomatic officials and Czechoslovak community representatives were so worried about political agitation by Slovak nationalists in Canada that meetings and business dealings were often conducted in both Czech and Slovak.[23]

The Munich Agreement

Even as Prague attempted to transplant its national policies into its compatriot communities, events in Central Europe soon forced many Czechs to seek refuge in Canada. In 1938, with the emergence of Nazi Germany as a threat to Europe's security, 1.5 million Czechoslovak troops were deployed to the borders with Austria, Germany, Hungary, and Poland.[24] Leaders of the governments of France (Édouard Daladier), Britain (Neville Chamberlain), and Italy (Benito Mussolini) met with Adolf Hitler in Munich in September 1938 in an attempt to appease his desire to incorporate the Sudetenland into Germany. Although Prime Minister Chamberlain proclaimed "peace in our time," Czechoslovakia had not been invited to the conference and felt betrayed by the French, with whom Prague had signed a treaty of alliance and friendship in 1924 and a treaty of mutual assistance in 1925.[25] The British and

French governments advised President of Czechoslovakia Edvard Beneš to concede to Hitler's demand for annexation of the predominantly German-speaking Sudetenland to Nazi Germany.[26] An agreement was reached in late September 1938 in which Western Europe acquiesced to Hitler's demand in exchange for continental peace. In Canada, individuals who believed in a common Czechoslovak identity became convinced that the Munich Agreement forced upon their old homeland brought their national and ethnic durability into question.

That month the *Montreal Herald* published the story of Vladimír Hortig, a forty-one-year-old Czech immigrant and taxi driver. The paper claimed that Hortig was a good Canadian because he had been more socially engaged in his new country than many of his fellow citizens. The Czech immigrant had volunteered as a scoutmaster for five years and as a member of the St. John's Ambulance Brigade, among his other civic interests. Hortig insisted that, once a Canadian military recruitment office opened, his name would be atop the list. He went on to claim that the best thing for his fellow countrymen to do was to join the Canadian militia.[27]

The Munich Agreement marked a turning point for Czechs in search of security. Prior to it, the search for economic opportunity and better quality of life had been the driving force behind the decision of individuals from Czechoslovakia to leave their homeland. In the fall of 1938, however, fear of the emergence of fascism and a German invasion of Czechoslovakia drove 80,000 Czechs and democratic Sudeten Germans to flee the heavily German-populated Sudetenland as political refugees. When news of the outcome of the Munich conference reached Canada, public outcry led secular refugee lobbies to pressure Ottawa to find a solution to the plight of these refugees. The Canadian National Committee on Refugees and Victims of Persecution actively joined the struggle to resettle anti-Nazi Sudeten German refugees in Canada.[28] Railway immigration agents attempted to help 10,000 Sudeten Germans and 20,000 Czech refugees temporarily sheltered in camps on the outskirts of Prague. These refugees were primarily farmers, glass and textile workers, and traders. With the Depression raging at home, Ottawa refused to be seen directly examining and admitting immigrants. The federal government used Canadian Pacific Railway and Canadian National Railway agents to avoid making direct contact with prospective refugees and permitted these agents to examine and select potential immigrants.[29] As Canadian immigration authorities moved slowly to resettle the Sudeten Germans and Czechs, approximately 1,200 Sudeten German families arrived in Canada aided by diplomats from the Czechoslovak consulate in Montreal.[30] Sudeten German refugees arrived in Canada on ships, including the SS *Montcalm,* a Canadian Pacific steamship that departed Southampton, England, en route to Pier 21 in Halifax.[31] The Sudeten German refugees were taken from Pier 21 by train to Montreal before heading west toward their final destinations. A majority of the refugees were resettled in agricultural districts administered by the railway companies. In the spring of 1939, the Canadian Pacific Railway relocated 518 settlers in Tate Creek, near Tomslake, British Columbia. The Canadian National Railway concentrated its resettlement efforts around St. Walburg, Saskatchewan, where thirty families were resettled and each given a farm in disrepair and 160 acres of land.[32] Hanns Skoutajan and his parents were typical of those who had fled the German occupation of Czechoslovakia. As anti-fascist Sudeten Germans, they were deprived of their home in the Sudetenland and fled to Britain before securing transatlantic passage to Canada. On 16 April 1939, Hanns and his parents arrived at Pier 21 in Halifax aboard the RMS *Samaria.* They soon boarded a train for Montreal before heading to their final destination in Saskatchewan.[33]

Reaction to Hitler's annexation of the Sudetenland was felt in Canada, and in early October 1938 over 2,000 demonstrators from various labour unions and anti-fascist societies gathered at Fletcher's Field in Montreal to commence a parade downtown. Fearing that the pro-democracy parade was under communist influence, Mayor of Montreal Adhémar Raynault issued a proclamation cancelling the event's permit. However, the demonstrators were not deterred by the actions of city officials. Later that afternoon the Committee for the Defence of Czechoslovakia held a meeting at St. James Market Hall in support of a parliamentary democracy in Czechoslovakia. Since the demonstrators were banned from parading downtown, many of them attended the meeting to show their support and heard speeches from Czech, English, French, German, Polish, Romanian, Russian, Slovak, and Ukrainian presenters.[34]

Soon Czechs in Canada learned that the political situation in Czechoslovakia had worsened. In October, Edvard Beneš officially resigned as president of Czechoslovakia, leaving the country without a de jure head of state. In Slovakia, the ruling nationalist Hlinka's Slovak People's Party joined other Slovak political parties in Žilina to agree to terms on Slovakia's pending autonomy from Prague and later declared national autonomy in Slovakia.[35] With the support of Prague, a government was established in Slovakia under the leadership of Jozef Tiso. In mid-October 1938, Subcarpathian Ruthenia received autonomy from Prague in an attempt to quell further unrest in the state.[36] Following widespread public outrage over the appeasement of Hitler, General Jan Syrový was introduced as the de facto president of Czechoslovakia. In November, because of Slovakia's declaration of autonomy, Prague renamed the country Czecho-Slovakia to emphasize a federation between the Czech Lands and Slovakia. For the next three months, the Second Czecho-Slovak Republic was secretly undermined by Hitler and members of the conservative and nationalist Hlinka's Slovak People's Party. In late November, President of the Supreme Administrative Court Emil Hácha was elected as Czecho-Slovakia's president, and a new cabinet was officially appointed.[37]

Hitler's Invasion Spurs a Refugee Crisis

Czech anxiety over events in Central Europe intensified in the spring of 1939. In March, Prague dismissed the Slovak parliament and arrested approximately 400 individuals who it believed were conspirators against the Second Czecho-Slovak Republic. A majority of those arrested were Slovak intellectuals, students, and social leaders. Tiso later met with Hitler in Berlin, where he was instructed either to proclaim Slovak independence or to have Slovak lands partitioned by Hungary and Poland.[38] The former Slovak prime minister summoned the dismissed Slovak parliament in Bratislava to declare Slovakia's independence and its alignment with Nazi Germany. Over two dozen states, including Britain and the Soviet Union, recognized an independent Slovakia and established diplomatic relations with Bratislava. Shortly before midnight, Hácha arrived in Berlin and informed Hitler that Prague would respect Slovakia's declaration of independence. Hitler subsequently informed the Czecho-Slovak president that Nazi Germany would invade the Czech Lands the following morning. Subcarpathian Ruthenia also declared independence but was ignored by Nazi Germany. The region was subsequently occupied by Hungary.[39] Following Germany's invasion of the Czech Lands, in mid-March 1939, Hitler proclaimed the Reich Protectorate of Bohemia and Moravia.[40] Subsequently, many politicians, businessmen, clergy, and social leaders fled the country. The Second Czecho-Slovak Republic dissolved less than six months after it had been created.[41]

With their homeland under German occupation, Czechs in Canada soon turned their attention toward political efforts in Britain. In early 1939, a Czechoslovak National Committee was established in London by pro-democracy political figures who had fled the German invasion. Edvard Beneš became the committee's president, while Štefan Osuský served as foreign minister, General Jan Ingr as defence minister, and Edvard Outrata as finance minister. The Czechoslovak National Committee lobbied Western governments for recognition as Czechoslovakia's official government in exile.[42] As Czechoslovak politicians, bureaucrats, and businessmen fled fascism in their homeland, Prague's diplomatic officials also sought residency as immigrants in Canada.

The Czechoslovak consulate in Montreal initiated correspondence with Ottawa in the hope that the Liberal government could accommodate its diplomats. Dr. Frey, a senior diplomat at the consulate who had helped hundreds of Sudeten Germans to obtain new homes in Canada, was informed by diplomat Lester Pearson that there was no hope for his entry since Ottawa sought individuals with agricultural training. However, Canadian immigration authorities did permit the resettlement of Czechoslovak officials with specific business interests and capital, and Ottawa later permitted 100 Czechoslovak officials to enter Canada as temporary refugees. These individuals arrived in Canada with capital, business experience, and personal networks of prominent businessmen and Western diplomats.[43]

Czechoslovak politicians, diplomats, and industrialists were not the only individuals to leave immediately after the German invasion of their homeland. Approximately 186,000 refugees fled Czechoslovakia in the aftermath of the German invasion of the Czech Lands and the declaration of Slovak statehood and alignment with Nazi Germany. Canada became a beneficiary of this movement of people when two industrial plants were re-established there.[44] A munitions plant originally part of the Škoda Works in Plzeň, Bohemia, was built in Sorel, Quebec. Simultaneously, the Bata Shoe Company from Zlín, Moravia, was reassembled as a company town named Batawa near Frankford, Ontario. Even though the Canadian shoe industry opposed the relocation of the Bata Shoe Company to Canada, the Canadian and Newfoundland press supported the plan, claiming that the incoming business could utilize local seal skins and animal hides.[45]

Relocation of the Bata Shoe Company

Since some Czechoslovak diplomats found it difficult to obtain admission into Canada, other immigrants were sought for their business expertise and industrial background. In December 1938, Tomáš J. Baťa arrived at Canada House in London, having initially fled Czecho-Slovakia for Switzerland. After speaking with an immigration official, Baťa discovered that he would not be permitted to immigrate because Ottawa officially sought agriculturalists. However, once the official discovered Baťa's position as an industrialist, the twenty-four-year-old Czech businessman was asked to meet with Canada's high commissioner in London, Vincent Massey. In his meeting with Massey, Baťa discovered that only through an order-in-council could he be legally permitted to enter Canada. Subsequently, he was asked for his Czechoslovak passport, which the immigration official—with Massey's approval—signed with "admit the bearer as a visitor."[46] Baťa received no official stamp and later claimed that Canada's immigration bureaucracy was neither efficient nor progressive but selective and informal. He arrived in New York City aboard RMS *Queen Mary* in April 1939 and was detained on Ellis Island for possessing a Czechoslovak passport. Because American authorities could not send individuals back to a country that did not exist, especially when they did not recognize Germany's occupation of the Czech Lands, they locked up approximately 300 Czechs on Ellis Island. Baťa spent a few hours in the immigration facility's detention quarters before news of his predicament reached Washington and made the press. He was then released and later travelled to Canada via Buffalo.

Once in Canada, Baťa travelled to Ottawa to meet with Frederick Charles Blair, director of the Immigration Branch, regarding visas for 250 Bata Shoe Company employees and their families and was told that Canada would admit them. Later, in June 1939, Blair reneged on his early promise to Baťa and offered to admit only 100 families, citing political difficulties; according to Baťa, Blair indicated that his mandate from the cabinet subcommittee allowed the Immigration Branch to admit only 100 families. With the Canadian National Committee on Refugees and Victims of Persecution lobbying on his behalf, Baťa and eighty-two employees were eventually permitted to come to Canada and re-establish themselves and their industrial enterprise. After discussions with other Bata Shoe Company executives, it was decided that the company's research and development and engineering departments would be safely relocated to North America because of political uncertainty in Central Europe after the Munich Agreement. Land near Frankford, Ontario, was chosen as the site for the company town, Batawa, because it was near a major transportation route to large markets across Canada and the United States. Baťa recalled that his father was pro-American but did not know much about Canada. As a child in England, the younger Baťa had read about Canada. He later chose to relocate his company to Canada because he believed that it was a good balance between Britain and the United States.[47]

Employees of the Bata Shoe Company continued to arrive in Canada throughout 1939, some of them via the United Kingdom. Along with her fellow workers, Milada Čechová spent a few days there before sailing to

Figure 2. *Sonja Baťa, second from left, Tomáš J. Baťa, third from right, Czechoslovak Consul General Dr. František Pavlásek, sixth from right, with Czech Sokol guests from the United States during anniversary celebrations, Batawa, Ontario, c. 1940.*

Canada aboard RMS *Antonia.* Upon taking a train to Montreal before her final destination of Batawa, Čechová found that many Canadians were unemployed and on relief. The Bata workers found food and small products cheap to purchase. Čechová and her fellow workers were given twenty dollars per week in wages, of which two dollars went to pay the rent for company housing. Many of the Bata workers thought that they did not have it as hard as the immigrants who arrived after them. According to Čechová, the Bata workers had come to Canada with secure employment, whereas other immigrants from Czechoslovakia were forced to find work and acquire savings in a difficult economic environment.[48] In 1933, one-third of the Canadian population had been out of work, and the percentage of employed workers had risen slowly in subsequent years. Whether they were farm workers, manual labourers, or industrial workers employed by the Bata Shoe Company, the interwar immigrants created an image of the hardworking, honest newcomer whom Canadians could appreciate, thus allowing them to integrate into the socioeconomic fabric of Canada.

Jewish Immigration

One group of Czech refugees, of Jewish origin, had a more difficult time convincing Canadians of their work ethic and ability to integrate into Canadian society. Order-in-Council P.C. 1931-695—which severely restricted immigration and permitted only immigrants with capital to enter the country—was still in effect. In addition, F.C. Blair, the director of the Immigration Branch, was anti-Semitic and fervently supported restricting Jewish immigration; under his direction, fewer than 5,000 Jews were admitted to Canada between 1933 and 1945.[49] Still, though Jewish immigration was restricted, exceptions did exist. Seeking to flee rising levels of anti-Semitism in Czechoslovakia, Hanna and Mimi Fischl, two sisters of Jewish origin, sought safe haven in Canada, where their uncle, Louis Fischl, owned and operated a glove factory. In February 1939, the sisters were granted their long-awaited refugee permits to travel to the United Kingdom, where authorities allowed them to enter—on their way to Canada—on the condition that they not seek employment other than as domestics in private households. On 4 June 1939, the Fischls left England aboard RMS *Alaunia,* whose passengers consisted of a group of Sudeten German social democrats, a Jewish family, and British citizens. Ten days later RMS *Alaunia* arrived in Quebec City, where Canadian immigration authorities boarded the ship for medical examinations and passport verifications before the vessel could continue to its final destination of Montreal. Hanna Fischl later recalled that, in order to qualify as a Canadian immigrant, she had to declare herself nondenominational. Fischl claimed to have no problem with her self-declaration since she did not feel particularly Jewish. As a secular Jew from Czechoslovakia, she wondered what sort of anti-Semitism she would experience in Canada. On the advice of her uncle, who viewed the church as a strictly Canadian institution, Fischl became a member of the United Church of Canada.[50] The Fischl sisters were able to settle in Canada largely because of Louis Fischl's capital and his transplanted glove factory. In looking to save his nieces from looming war in Europe, Louis indicated to Canadian immigration authorities that his nieces were skilled workers and essential to his business. Director of the Immigration Branch F.C. Blair might have overlooked the Fischls' Jewish background because of Ottawa's desire for capital and new businesses and their standing as nondenominational immigrants from a defunct Czecho-Slovakia.

Another exception to Canada's official anti-Semitic discourse was Leon Koerner, who had served as Czechoslovakia's timber controller in the 1930s and, helped by Lester Pearson, arrived in Vancouver as a Czech refugee of half-Jewish ancestry in 1939. He and his wife were suffering from depression largely because of events back in Central Europe: both of Koerner's grandmothers were Jewish, and his family's property had been confiscated by the German authorities. Holding more than $1 million in capital, Koerner bought a derelict lumber mill in New Westminster, British Columbia, and hired forty-five men to saw hemlock. His business capital and expertise in the forestry industry were immediately used to purchase Alaska Pine and Cellulose Limited, which later produced 75 percent of the ammunition and ration boxes used by Commonwealth forces during the Second World War. The former timber controller's first impression of Canadian society was pessimistic. According to Koerner, Vancouver's social and business elites were unwelcoming and remained closed to him. In business, the local timber companies feared his vast wealth and experience, while the city's socialites spurned his foreign features, formal clothing, and manners. Although social integration proved to be difficult in the early years after fleeing fascism in Europe, Koerner remained humbled by the opportunity to live in Canada.[51]

Although Canadian authorities had heavily curtailed immigration during the Great Depression, according to official government estimates, 317 Czechs arrived in Canada as immigrants in 1939. Over the next three years, only 112 Czechs were permitted to enter Canada as immigrants.[52] Although Canada's door to prospective immigrants remained officially closed, individuals fleeing fascism in Europe—whether diplomats, industrialists, or workers—were able to find a safe haven in Canada through personal relationships and professional contacts. They could re-establish their political and business networks, their employment, and ultimately their lives. The immigration of the Koerners, the Fischls, and Baťa and eighty-two Bata Shoe Company employees between 1938 and 1939 strengthened the Canadian Czechoslovak community after the German occupation of the Czech Lands.

Canadian Czechoslovak Responses to the Situation in Europe

Members of the Canadian Czechoslovak community helped raise awareness of the political situation in Central Europe by publicly opposing fascism in the old country, the German occupation of the Czech Lands, and Slovakia's alignment with Germany. Indeed, they took a number of actions that promoted their anti-fascist and pro-democratic stance. In April 1939, Prague's consul general in Montreal, with the assistance of the RCMP, refused to surrender his consulate to German diplomatic representatives. Later that month Consul General František Pavlásek addressed a gathering of Czechoslovaks at the Bonsecours Market in Montreal, assuring his audience that the homeland would be freed from Nazi domination.[53] Czechs and Slovaks who professed a belief in a unified Czechoslovak identity sensed that further action by them was necessary. In May, a group of Canadian Czechs, Slovaks, and Subcarpathian

Figure 3. *Crowd gathered in Church of All Nations, Toronto, to take part in the congress of the National Alliance of Slovaks, Czechs, and Subcarpathian Ruthenians, June 1939.*

Ruthenians met in Toronto to discuss the formation of a national organization to promote Canadian Czechoslovak interests and work to liberate their Nazi-occupied homeland. In June, the National Alliance of Slovaks, Czechs, and Subcarpathian Ruthenians in Canada was formally inaugurated. Attending the organization's first meeting were 140 delegates from across Canada. Štefan Rudinský, a Slovak immigrant from Montreal, was elected as president. Karel Buzek, the Czech immigrant from Toronto, appointed Czechoslovakia's consul and trade commissioner in 1929, became the alliance's national secretary.[54] In late June, the alliance held its first annual congress in Toronto's Church of All Nations. In April 1940, Toronto's National Alliance of Slovaks, Czechs, and Subcarpathian Ruthenians (Rusyns) merged with Montreal's Czechoslovak National Alliance (CNA).[55]

"Enemy Aliens"

Across Canada, supporters of a Czechoslovak identity joined forces to coordinate the second Czechoslovak liberation movement's war and relief efforts in Canada. The newly enlarged CNA recognized the Czechoslovak National Committee in London as the legitimate political representative of the former

Czechoslovak state. Incidentally, the Canadian government was the last British dominion to recognize officially the Beneš-led national committee as the Czechoslovak government-in-exile in October 1940. During the Second World War, Czechs who remained foreign nationals in Canada (i.e., not naturalized) were subject to national security measures. The federal government viewed nationals of states that no longer existed because of German invasion, occupation, or annexation as potential security risks. As a result, Ottawa instituted the Defence of Canada Regulations, which attempted to classify foreign nationals, including Czechs in Canada, as "enemy aliens." Immigrants from the former Czechoslovakia who had yet to be naturalized as Canadian citizens witnessed their civil liberties become severely restricted. In some cases, they also lived in fear of being mislabelled as Germans. Antonín Ronza, for instance, arrived in Canada in August 1939 with other Bata Shoe Company employees. Originally settling in Frankford, near the construction of the company town, Batawa, he later moved to Picton in April 1944 to open a Bata branch. Ronza paid five dollars per month to rent an old skating rink, which housed his shoemaking business on behalf of Bata. He employed local young people and trained them in shoemaking. Because Czechoslovaks were forced to report to local police stations as enemy aliens, the ambitious Bata employee spent the final two years of the Second World War in Picton too scared to let others know that he spoke German. According to him, Canadians knew very little about Czechs or those who self-identified as Czechoslovaks, and he did not want to be mistaken for a German immigrant or as a supporter of the Axis powers. Eventually, Ronza became highly regarded in his community once the local population knew him better.[56]

Under the Defence of Canada Regulations, foreigners residing in Canada were denied habeas corpus, legal representation, and a court date. As the principal instrument of Ottawa's drive to secure the state from potentially subversive individuals, the RCMP was able to detain and arrest persons of interest and seize their property and assets. An order-in-council of June 1940 permitted individual RCMP officers to become justices of the peace in an effort to fight illegal organizations and subversion across Canada.[57] Similarly, Ottawa requested foreign legations to aid in the selection of their nationals who were trustworthy residents. On behalf of the lobbying efforts of the Czechoslovak consulate in Montreal, individuals registered as enemy aliens were permitted to receive new documents indicating their amended status as liberated enemy aliens and were entitled to receive a certificate of exemption as nationals of a friendly Allied nation.[58] Canadian Czechs who supported a common

Figure 4. *Women and girls in traditional Moravian dress stand on a truck decorated with the words "Freedom" and a "Free Czechoslovakia in a Free Europe" during a Czechoslovak Day parade, Chatham, Ontario, 2 June 1941.*

Czechoslovak identity vehemently fought against their status as enemy aliens and joined the Allied war effort by enlisting in the military, raising funds, sending relief parcels to Czechoslovak forces overseas, and lobbying federal officials for recognition as Allies. Canada would later recognize members of the Czechoslovak community as Allied citizens. In October 1940, Ottawa officially recognized the Czechoslovak government-in-exile in London. Two months later the CNA registered some of its members in an effort to demonstrate to Canadian officials that the Czechoslovak community was loyal to Canada.[59]

The Czechoslovak National Alliance

As members of the Czechoslovak community elite continued to demonstrate their support for the Allied war effort, they also brought their efforts for political recognition as loyal citizens before Canadian officials. Their efforts were part of a broader strategy to attain social and cultural citizenship in wartime Canada. Community representatives argued that Canadian-born Czechoslovaks and immigrants from Czechoslovakia were members of an Allied nation and therefore should have all wartime restrictions against them removed. In April 1941, a delegation from the Czechoslovak National Alliance testified before the House of Commons committee responsible for overseeing the Defence of Canada Regulations. The CNA's president, Štefan Rudinský, and its national secretary, Karel Buzek, were assisted by Arthur W. Roebuck, MP for Toronto-Trinity, where many members of Toronto's Czechoslovak community resided. Rudinský and Buzek called on Canadian officials to consider individuals of Czechoslovak origin as loyal Canadians. The delegation went on to claim that individuals within the Czechoslovak community could not secure employment because of the stigma of having been registered as enemy aliens.[60] The nationalist Canadian Slovak League (CSL) also lobbied federal authorities in an effort to prevent Canadian Slovaks from being registered as enemy aliens. That month Minister of Mines and Resources Thomas Alexander Crerar informed the local CSL branch in Flin Flon, Manitoba, that an amendment had been made to the Defence of Canada Regulations, which would not apply to individuals born in or nationals of Czechoslovakia as it existed on the first day of January 1938.[61] In April 1941, Ottawa issued an order-in-council recognizing Czechs and Slovaks as Allied peoples rather than as supporters of Nazi Germany. Nationalist Slovaks who defended the existence of an independent wartime Slovak state were forced to moderate their support for Slovakia since Canada was at war with Germany and its allies. Meanwhile, the CNA's lobbying efforts during this period were largely influenced by its membership, which by 1942 had grown to eighty-six branches and 6,500 members.[62]

As the CNA continued to lobby Canadian officials to demonstrate its membership's loyalty to Canada, former democratic Czechoslovak politicians, now in exile in London, sought greater cooperation with their communist-socialist colleagues in the Soviet Union. In December 1943, Edvard Beneš flew to Moscow to meet Soviet leader Joseph Stalin and prominent Czechoslovak communists who had fled east after the Nazi invasion of the Czech Lands and the Slovak proclamation of independence. The former Czechoslovak president and the Soviet leader signed a treaty of mutual cooperation between their governments. As former Czechoslovak politicians attempted to secure the future re-establishment of a Czechoslovak state, Canadian Czechoslovaks turned their attention toward the creation of an ethnocultural association in Toronto.[63] That month the Czechoslovak National Alliance agreed to commence teaching at its newly established Czechoslovak school. Nineteen students were registered, with an average age of twelve and a half years. Initially, poor attendance was blamed on a lack of public awareness of the existence of the language school. The school taught reading, writing, and speaking in both Czech and Slovak languages and included geography and the history of Czechoslovakia as subjects. After school, an hour was dedicated to physical education led by a member of the patriotic calisthenics organization the Toronto Sokol Gymnastic Union.[64] Coupled with efforts to liberate their old European homeland, the Canadian Czechoslovak community turned their attention toward establishing institutions to promote ethnocultural heritage.

Masaryk Hall

Along with the Czechoslovak National Alliance, Masaryk Hall (MH) in Toronto rallied to the cause of liberating Czechoslovakia. The hall—named after Czechoslovakia's first president, Tomáš Garrigue Masaryk—was created by charter in 1944, and as an organization it was led by a twelve-member volunteer board of directors and an executive committee with three members. Prior to the purchase of a hall in Toronto, MH had held its meetings at the Church of All Nations, where in November 1944 a meeting of Czechoslovak groups raised $9,000. In early December, Sokol Toronto was using the newly purchased hall; previously an old skating rink, it could accommodate approximately 1,000 people for its patriotic calisthenics exercises.[65] In January 1945, Masaryk Hall was incorporated and given a charter by Ontario. The organization moved into its own space and elected Rudolf Koreň, a Slovak, as its president and two Czechs—Karel Buzek and Jan Mráček—as secretary and treasurer, respectively. In its original memorandum to members, MH declared that it would use all incoming funds to improve its programs and facilities and provide a cultural and educational centre for Czechoslovak Canadians. Among its principal activities were the following: giving English-language instruction, teaching arts and crafts, instilling in its members the obligations of Canadian citizenship, offering financial relief and social assistance, providing physical training, acquiring Canadian and Czechoslovak literature and art, and establishing a Czechoslovak community centre for the region of Toronto.[66]

As a measure of its success during the 1944–45 school year, twenty-eight students attended Czech- and Slovak-language classes on Saturdays at MH's Masaryk Supplementary School. Classes were held on thirty half days on Saturdays. Of the twenty-eight students who took Czech- and Slovak-language classes, four attended only once. The oldest student was nineteen, the youngest only five, with an average age of fourteen. In his end-of-the-year letter to parents of supplementary school students, instructor Prokop V. Havlík requested that parents spend one hour per week with their children practising how to read and write in their maternal language so that they would not become *neodnárodnily* ("losers of their ethnic nationality").[67]

Figure 5. *Masaryk Hall, located in Toronto's Parkdale neighbourhood, was renamed Masaryk-Cowan Community Recreation Centre in 1987.*

Masaryk Hall also attempted to instill heritage and encourage citizenship values among its younger members with the establishment of the Masarykův klub mládeže (Masaryk Youth Club) in Toronto. In March 1946, the first meeting of the club was held inside Masaryk Hall. At this meeting, twenty-three adolescents were in attendance. Czechoslovak youth discussed a variety of activities that they wished to organize within the club, including a basketball team, ethnic dancing, trips and outings, music and singing, and an amateur talent night in which to showcase drama and music. Membership dues in the club were set at twenty-five cents per month for those sixteen and older and ten cents per month for those under sixteen.[68]

In an attempt to increase youth interest in Czechoslovak activities in Toronto, the MH's executive committee sent its president, Gustav Přístupa, to meet the members of the youth club. In his meeting that month, Přístupa informed them that, if they could find 150 members by April or May, then MH would pay for a trip to the Thousand Islands in Ontario or wherever the members of the club were interested in visiting. The youth agreed that each member in attendance had to attract five new members. According to the youth, new members did not have to be of Slavic descent, but they had to learn a few words so that they could understand what was occurring at meetings. At the same meeting, sixteen new members joined an existing group of twenty-three individuals.[69]

The executive committee responsible for MH actively engaged youth in an attempt to foster Czechoslovak identity and culture. In April 1946, the Masaryk Youth Club met to discuss the group's planned activities. It was decided that a trip to Niagara Falls would be preferable to a trip to the Thousand Islands. Czechoslovak youth also decided to organize football and tennis groups and a basketball team that would compete against other groups. The club maintained a bank account with a balance of $47.82. Its members agreed that it would be beneficial to their finances if they could hold one concert per month. Furthermore, the following month, members decided that a concert would be held on Mother's Day later that month. Each mother would receive a flower, and the club would cover the cost. The club's girls were responsible for serving food and drinks at the concert and for decorating the hall. Women from the local Czechoslovak community were engaged to provide cakes and pastries.[70] Simultaneously, the committee sought to watch over its young members as they came of age in postwar Canadian society. On one occasion, Přístupa asked the members present how many of the boys drank alcohol. The youth replied that only a few of them never drank alcohol, and all the boys except for one smoked cigarettes.[71] Přístupa responded by discouraging this type of behaviour and promoted good citizenship among the hall's youth members.

The establishment and growth of Masaryk Hall provided the Czechoslovak community in Canada with a sociocultural institution to promote Czechoslovak identity and continue to work toward the liberation of their homeland from fascism. Canadian Czechoslovaks were outraged by the demise of the Czechoslovak Republic after only two decades of independence. German occupation of their old homeland illustrated to them that the cultivation of their ethnocultural heritage remained a necessity. The introduction of a Czech- and Slovak-language school, financial and social assistance, and a patriotic calisthenics program ensured for Canadian Czechoslovaks that their ethnocultural heritage would be passed on to successive generations. After the war, the organization would continue to flourish, with an April 1946 fundraising and membership drive attracting 293 members and raising a total of $16,301.90. In December that year, members gathered to witness the symbolic burning of their hall's mortgage certificate, indicating that the outstanding mortgage of $11,925 had been paid.[72] Although the promotion of ethnocultural heritage remained an important issue for members of the Czechoslovak community in Toronto and across Canada, the Allied war effort soon took precedence, and the community's elite led efforts to contribute materials and finances as a demonstration of their loyalty to Canada. Czechoslovak contributions during the Second World War raised awareness of the community among the Canadian public and federal officials, which in turn seems to have led many Czech immigrants and refugees to pursue social and cultural citizenship in their new homeland.

Support for the Allied War Effort

During the Second World War, then, many members of the local Czechoslovak community in Toronto actively participated in both the MH and the CNA. The organizations worked together in an effort to support the Allied war effort, and the CNA was instrumental in establishing the Czechoslovak War Charities Fund (CWCF), which later became a constituent organization under the auspices of the Canadian United Allied Relief Fund (CUARF). The CWCF collected funds to be sent to the Czechoslovak government-in-exile in London and for relief, including medicine, clothing, and food, sent to Czechoslovak troops fighting across Europe and North Africa. As the national secretary of the CNA and an executive board member of the CUARF, Karel Buzek was an instrumental figure in the development of fundraising efforts to liberate the Czech Lands and Nazi-aligned Slovakia from fascist oppression and relief work for a future resurrected Czechoslovak state. Buzek informed the CNA's executive committee in February 1945 that its CWCF would be guaranteed $450,000 by the Canadian government through CUARF. In addition, the CWCF's own fundraising campaign garnered a further $72,779 for a total of $522,779. Buzek also indicated to the CNA executive committee that CUARF would order $450,000 worth of goods considered to be vital to the Czechoslovak Red Cross in London, England, spearheading a first-aid action to compatriots currently under German occupation. The CWCF funds were used to purchase milk, flour, cooking oil, dried fruits and vegetables, canned fish, cigarettes, hospital and medical supplies, bedrolls, clothing from government stores for infants and young children, and Red Cross relief packages.

Under the War Charities Act, ethnic associations across Canada were not permitted officially to establish independent fundraising campaigns for their homelands in Europe. As a result, the CNA's CWCF became a member of CUARF. The CNA's executive committee was forced to inform the Czechoslovak Red Cross in London that its fundraising duties were organized under the guidance of CUARF and the Canadian Red Cross. The CNA advised the Czechoslovak Red Cross that it would seek a grant from money previously collected to establish a Collection for National Liberation for which the CNA could send more financial support to the Czechoslovak government-in-exile led by Edvard Beneš and to the Czechoslovak Red Cross as they prepared to re-establish a postwar Czechoslovak state with funds gained from the Allied war effort.[73]

With Soviet forces gaining ground in Eastern Europe in the spring of 1945, an agreement was reached between the Czechoslovak government-in-exile and exiled Czechoslovak communists in Moscow to create a national front coalition government. Following the Soviet liberation of Slovakia, the Third Czechoslovak Republic was established in April 1945, and a government was installed in Košice, Slovakia. The coalition government comprised three socialist political parties: the National Socialists, the largest contingent; the Social Democrats; and the Czechoslovak and Slovak Communists. Two non-socialist parties, the Catholic People's Party in Moravia and the Democratic Party in Slovakia, were also included in the coalition. Soon after its establishment, the Národní fronta (National Front of Czechs and Slovaks) recognized the Slovaks as a nation and the Slovenská národná rada (Slovak National Council) as the official government of Slovakia. The newly formed Czechoslovak government published its Košice program calling for a swift end to the Second World War and the expulsion of Czechoslovakia's ethnic Sudeten German and Hungarian populations, along with all fascist collaborators. Simultaneously, land and industry belonging to German collaborators in the Czech Lands and to proponents of the wartime Slovak state were confiscated by presidential decree and appropriated to the civilian population. With Soviet troops liberating the majority of land under German control, the Czech and Slovak populations' view of the Soviet Union was largely favourable.[74]

In Canada, communist sympathizers exploited what they perceived as a sudden increase in popular support for their cause. In a meeting of the Czechoslovak National Alliance's Joint Committee held in April 1945, Cyprián Slimák, representing the Slovak-language communist paper *L'udové zvesti* (People's News), requested that the CNA lobby the Canadian government to lessen restrictions on the purchase of goods for and telegrams to a newly liberated Slovakia, even though Canada's war effort continued.[75] Slovak communists in Canada supported the liberation of Slovakia from its alignment with Germany and advocated for the reconstruction of their war-torn homeland. In Canada, the RCMP's June 1945 monthly intelligence report indicated that the force was cognizant of events in Eastern Europe and the new Czechoslovak-Soviet relationship, suggesting that "the Czechoslovak government of Benesh has sold out completely to the USSR. One need only note that while a Soviet ambassador has gone with Benesh from Moscow to

Kosice, Britain and the United States have been notified—by the Soviets, not the Czech government—that their ambassadors will not be admitted at present. Benesh is evidently no longer an independent statesman, but a puppet of the Kremlin. The significant exclusion of American forces from operating on Czechoslovak territory also tells its own story."[76] While the RCMP remained concerned about Soviet influence in Central Europe and its potential to infiltrate Canada's ethnocultural communities, Czechoslovak institutions, including the CNA and MH, focused on the Allied war effort, including sending financial contributions and relief packages to Europe.

In the spring of 1945, the CNA's executive committee received news from the Czechoslovak Red Cross that the socioeconomic situation in the Czech Lands and Slovakia was desperate. Children and the elderly urgently required clothing. The Canadian Red Cross informed the Czechoslovak National Alliance that it had prepared forty crates of clothing destined for the Czechoslovak Red Cross in London. The Red Cross officials in London were to send the shipment of clothing to the open Port of Galatz (Galati) in Romania. However, Canadian Red Cross officials were hesitant to send the shipment because its safe arrival could not be guaranteed.[77] Meanwhile, the CNA's own clothing action under the leadership of Gustav Přístupa sent forty-eight crates of clothing to Europe. Clothing donations were received from Canadian Czechoslovaks in Batawa, Owen Sound, Belleville, Oshawa, Dresden, Hamilton, and Montreal.[78]

Between February and June 1945, the CWCF collected $14,043.02 in donations. From this amount, $609.76 was used to purchase material to support the CNA's clothing action. The remaining $13,433.26 was to be used by the broader pan-Canadian CUARF for the procurement of relief goods for Czechoslovakia.[79] During the summer of 1945, CNA members across Canada donated funds to the CWCF with specific requests for their money to be donated to the Czechoslovak Red Cross in London, children in Czechoslovakia, and *partizani* ("partisans") in the midst of helping to liberate Slovakia from German domination. One of the largest donations bequeathed to the partisans occurred in Windsor, Ontario, where CNA members donated $2,900 in May 1945.[80] Donations collected for Slovak partisans were sent by the CNA to the Czechoslovak Military Mission in Ottawa, where a Fund for Partisans in Slovakia was organized.[81] Women's committees within local CNA branches also donated funds to impoverished children in the homeland. For example, the women's committee of the CNA branch in Batawa donated $143 to children in Czechoslovakia.[82] Although Canadian Czechoslovaks generously supported the

Allied war effort, many donations continued to be allocated to charities and organizations based upon the ethnic or geographic background of the donor. Donations were also sent to religious groups such as the Catholic Church and secular non-governmental organizations, including the Czechoslovak Red Cross.

No matter, a majority of fundraising continued to be sent to the CWCF as a consolidated charity under CUARF, and Czech immigrants were seen to be engaged in a noble humanitarian effort on behalf of their old homeland while they continued to support the Allied war effort in Canada. In the spring and summer of 1945, CUARF purchased $217,046.82 worth of goods on behalf of the CWCF from the $450,000 guaranteed by the Canadian government. As a result, the relief shipments grew to include 1,686 crates consisting of 834 crates of citrus extract, 351 crates of disinfectant, 313 crates of milk powder, 84 crates of cigarettes, 50 crates of warm leather boots, 48 crates of high socks, 3 crates of shaving blades, 2 crates of dried beans, and 1 crate of playing cards for hospital patients. In Montreal, these supplies were loaded onto the shipping vessel *Chertsey* and destined for the Romanian port of Constanta (Constantza) before arriving by rail in Czechoslovakia.[83] Across Canada, 1,200 clothing committees were established to seek clothing donations for Europe. The National Clothing Collection allocated 250,000 pounds of clothing to Czechoslovakia. Accordingly, the CNA requested that all of its branches across Canada cooperate with their local clothing committees in order to reach Czechoslovakia's allocation of donated clothing.[84]

Postwar Relief Efforts

As fundraising for the Allied war effort continued in Canada, Germany formally surrendered to the Allies in May 1945. Soon after, the Canadian Slovak League called for the revival of an independent Slovak state rather than the re-establishment of a Czechoslovak Republic, which would thwart nationalist Slovak demands for self-determination. Political appeals were sent to delegates meeting at the founding convention of the United Nations in San Francisco. On behalf of Canadian Slovaks, the Canadian Slovak League, Slovak Catholic Sokol, First Catholic Slovak Union, and National Slovak Mutual Benefit Society joined in calling on delegates to support the independence of the Slovak nation from Czechoslovakia. However, because of Allied recognition of the Czechoslovak government-in-exile in London as the legitimate representative of the Czech and Slovak peoples in Central Europe, the lobbying efforts of nationalist American and Canadian Slovaks were largely ignored.

Slovakia's wartime status as an Axis-aligned state severely hampered any attempts at Western recognition.[85]

In an August 1945 RCMP monthly intelligence report, Canada's national police force became increasingly aware of the cleavages that events in Central Europe had reproduced between Czechoslovak and nationalist Slovak communities in Canada. Although the RCMP depicted the relations between ethnic Czechs and Slovaks as containing "some friction," it was also conscious of the divisions within the previous waves of Czech and Slovak immigration to Canada.[86] The RCMP was aware that historically three principal groups existed in Canada. The Slovak nationalists—who permitted only Slovaks to join their organizations—did not cooperate with Slovak leftists or Czechoslovaks. The RCMP went on to assert in its bulletin that the "factions get along fairly well at present, only occasionally the class-conscious leftists criticize the 'bourgeois' National Alliance."[87] Although the RCMP understood the existing sociopolitical divisions between the Czechoslovak and nationalist Slovak communities in Canada, it overestimated the size of the Czechoslovak National Alliance, believing that the organization consisted of between 10,000 and 12,000 members and more than 200 branches across Canada. In reality, the membership peaked in 1945 with approximately 10,000 members and ninety-two branches.[88] Among them were left-leaning Sudeten Germans who established two branches in Tupper Creek, British Columbia, and St. Walburg, Saskatchewan.[89]

In terms of assessing security threats to Canada, the RCMP and Canadian immigration authorities were aware that many "undesirables" might be attempting to hide their Nazi or communist affiliations by joining the Czechoslovak National Alliance. The Security Service's "O" Division discovered that an alleged refugee from Czechoslovakia attempted to conceal his true identity as a Sudeten German with membership in the National Socialist German Workers' Party. The individual in question was a German citizen and thus subsequently interned. A wartime RCMP intelligence report noted that other Nazis were hiding in Canada disguised as Czechoslovak refugees.[90] Some Nazis, fascist sympathizers, and communist spies did succeed eventually in entering Canada in the years immediately after the Second World War.

So concerned did the Czechoslovak government become that in October 1945 František Pavlásek requested that Canadian authorities consider all passports issued by the former wartime Slovak state as invalid documents and that any alien presenting such a document should automatically be refused admission into Canada.[91] Because Slovakia had aligned itself with Germany following Hitler's invasion and annexation of the Czech Lands in March 1939, the Canadian government refused to recognize the independence of the Slovak state. The Department of External Affairs (DEA) noted that many individuals who had obtained Slovak passports had in fact escaped from Czechoslovakia through Austria in an attempt to avoid postwar trials for treason against the state. The department indicated that many of these passport holders might apply for admission into Canada; however, according to officials in Ottawa, because the Slovak passports did not meet Canada's passport requirements as held in Order-in-Council P.C. 3016, Canadian officials looked to their Immigration Branch counterparts to refuse admission to any individual with such a travel document.[92]

Word regarding the advice of the DEA concerning Slovak passports spread in October 1945 as the commissioner of immigration informed district superintendents across the country.[93] The following month a memorandum was sent from the Immigration Branch's Western District superintendent in Winnipeg informing inspectors that the DEA advised that "a number of aliens [were] travelling on passports issued by the former Slovak State or Tiso Government."[94] The Pacific District superintendent in Vancouver informed officials at the Immigration Branch in Ottawa that the advice of the DEA regarding Slovak passports would be passed along to officers at all border ports.[95] Additionally, Undersecretary of State for External Affairs Norman Alexander Robertson indicated in a letter to Minister of Mines and Resources James Allison Glen that Canadian diplomats in Washington had also received representations regarding the forthcoming admission of anti-Nazi Sudeten German refugees into Canada.[96] With the support of the Czechoslovak community in Canada, Prague's diplomatic representatives attempted to thwart the admission into Canada of nationalist Slovak politicians who had actively fought against the re-establishment of a pro-Czechoslovak state.

With the Second World War over and relief and reconstruction efforts in progress, jubilant Canadian Czechoslovaks gathered at the Czechoslovak National Alliance's Victory Congress in Toronto in November 1945. In a resolution passed at the meeting, delegates expressed their loyalty to their homeland and thanked the Allied forces, in particular their Soviet brothers, for their invaluable help in supporting the struggle to liberate their homeland.[97] In highlighting the sacrifices made across the country to support the liberation of Czechoslovakia from German domination, National Secretary Karel Buzek proclaimed in his report to the Victory Congress that, even in small towns such as Margo, Saskatchewan, where five to ten Czechoslovak families had settled during the Great Depression, two young pilots had lost their lives for both of their homelands, old and new. According to Buzek, no mobilization or draft had forced them to join the Czechoslovak Air Force in Europe; they had simply not been able to sit idle through the war. In essence, they had given their lives for freedom.[98] Buzek concluded that the approximately 40,000 Canadians of Czech and Slovak heritage had sent over 11,753,000 cigarettes to Czechoslovak soldiers serving in England, 7,250,000 cigarettes to their compatriots on the Soviet front, and approximately 2 million cigarettes to their forces in Yugoslavia via London. Among the CNA's various wartime funds to send food, clothing, and goods to troops in Europe and to victims of German oppression in their homeland, the Canadian Czechoslovak community had raised a total of $330,922 or sixty-five dollars per household.[99] The CNA's Toronto branch had donated the single largest amount of $58,676.19 to the war effort, while members in remote Farmington, British Columbia, were able to collect eighteen dollars.[100]

As a member fund of the Canadian United Allied Relief Fund, the Czech-led CWCF shared over $9 million allocated for aid to the people of twelve Allied countries under Axis occupation during the war. By November 1945, $364,420.88 of the CWCF's initial allocation of $450,000 from the Canadian government through the CUARF had already been spent on aid.[101] Under the support of the CWCF, Czechs across Canada continued to raise funds and send relief packages to Czechoslovakia. These activities garnered the Czechoslovak community greater visibility within Canadian society and the Allied war effort.

These activities also revealed a deep understanding of the issues involved in sending relief packages overseas. In a letter to Colonel P.L. Browne, director of the Voluntary War Relief section of the Department of National War Services in Ottawa, Buzek indicated that the $450,000 for 1945 was divided into six categories: food ($157,002.05), medical and surgical supplies ($121,222.44), freight charges ($85,603.33), new clothing ($56,798.92), Canadian Red Cross buying services ($22,500.00), and comforts ($6,873.26).[102] Browne advised that his department would grant the CWCF a special permit to continue to send food to Czechoslovakia. Relief parcels containing food were not permitted to contain sugar or sugar-related commodities partly because of the danger of spoilage given the length of time that packages from Canada to Czechoslovakia remained in transit. War charities such as the CWCF required special government permits in order to ship large stores of food, clothing, and medicine to Czechoslovakia after the war.[103]

With the conflict in Europe over, Czechs within the Czechoslovak community continued to focus their attention on sending aid to Czechoslovakia. In his address to delegates at the November 1945 CNA Victory Congress, Vice-President Jan Gažo, a Slovak from Windsor, Ontario, called on the members in attendance to move the organization toward a three-point plan: continuous aid to Czechoslovakia, cultivation of ethnic heritage for future generations, and promotion of Canadian citizenship. This, Gažo believed, would firmly entrench the CNA's existence in the immediate postwar years.[104] As members of the CNA across Canada, Czechs heeded Gažo's call and continued to donate funds and goods to the relief effort. Many members remained active in the dialogue regarding where their financial and material support should go. In December 1945, Moravian Catholics donated $200 to the CNA's aid efforts and requested that their donation be specifically sent to relief efforts in Moravia. Half of the funds donated were destined for the Czechoslovak Red Cross, while fifty dollars each were to be allocated to the relief efforts in the town of Hodonín and to orphanages in the towns of Hroznová Lhota and Veselí nad Moravou.[105]

The Czechoslovak National Alliance executive also wanted to assist the homeland in other ways. During an executive committee meeting in December 1945, committee member Matuš Pavlík argued that funds could be collected to honour the service of all Czechoslovak volunteers during the Second World War. Pavlík suggested that proceeds could be used to purchase food, which would then be sent to impoverished civilians in Czechoslovakia.[106] Meanwhile, Czechoslovakia's legation in Canada lobbied the federal government to have demobilized and returning Canadian Czechoslovak volunteers recognized equally with their Canadian counterparts for veterans' benefits. During the war, 782 men from Canada—314 Slovaks, 270 Czechs, 112 Canadians, 62 Sudeten Germans, 20 Subcarpathian Ruthenians, and 4 Hungarians—had applied to serve with the Czechoslovak forces overseas, with 106 of them later deemed unfit to join. After the cessation of hostilities in 1945, Colonel Karel Lukáš, Prague's military and air attaché in Canada, indicated in a letter to the CNA that of these 782 men only 230—139 Slovaks, 79 Czechs, 6 Sudeten Germans, and 6 Subcarpathian Ruthenians—eventually joined the Czechoslovak forces overseas, with 157 men enlisting in the Czechoslovak Army and 73 men in the British Royal Air Force.[107] After the Second World War, individuals who had served with the Allied Forces abroad were successful in obtaining benefits similar to those provided to members of the Canadian Forces. In order for returning Canadian Czechoslovak volunteers to be eligible for these benefits, the Canadian government required domicile in Canada at the time of enlistment or enrolment in the Allied Forces in which they served. Returning servicemen were also required to forward certified copies of a discharge certificate and a statement of gratuities or any bonus paid to them by the Allied Forces in which they served.[108] No matter these inconveniences, the service of Czech volunteers in the Allied war effort had created a favourable impression of them and the Czechoslovak community in Canada. The efforts of Czech immigrants on behalf of the Czechoslovak community during the Second World War provided them with the means to achieve sociocultural integration into Canadian society.

Moving into the Cold War

The Second World War had a profound impact on Czech immigrants in Canada. Those who had arrived prior to the war had established Czechoslovak institutions such as the Czechoslovak National Alliance and Masaryk Hall. During the war, a small group of Czech immigrants arrived in Canada and joined those organizations: 1,009 immigrants who gave their "racial" origin as Czech and 2,232 who claimed Czechoslovakian nationality.[109] Attempts by these Czech newcomers to fit into existing sociopolitical norms as a mechanism to attain sociocultural citizenship in Canada were rooted in the interwar period, when government policy determined a "desirable" immigrant to be an individual who was employable, hardworking, and medically fit, who did not hold communist or anarchist beliefs, and who refrained from seeking government assistance. Interwar Czech immigrants coupled with wartime arrivals from a defunct Czecho-Slovak state would become instrumental in welcoming subsequent waves of postwar immigrants into their "Czechoslovak" ethnocultural groups and associations. It was their hope that the newcomers would assist in promoting the three-point plan outlined by Jan Gažo at the Victory Congress: cultivation of Czechoslovak culture, promotion of Canadian citizenship among members, and continued postwar relief to Czechoslovakia. But these goals were complicated by further developments overseas. Within a few years, Canadian Czechs witnessed their recently resurrected homeland fall under communist rule. Now they were forced to navigate the tensions between promoting postwar citizenship and cultivating ethnocultural heritage in Canada while defending parliamentary democracy in Czechoslovakia and alleviating the plight of thousands of political refugees who had fled authoritarianism in their homeland.

CHAPTER 2

Postwar Relief, Canadian Citizenship, and Ethnic Heritage

In December 1946, Masaryk Hall introduced a magazine entitled *Bobřík* (Beaver) for children of "Czechoslovak origin" in Canada. The magazine taught youngsters about Czechoslovakia's history through trivia, games, and stories. As the president of Masaryk Hall, Gustav Přístupa asked young readers "to be like the small, hardworking animal—working for its new homeland, Canada—but not forgetting our old homeland, Czechoslovakia."[1] Přístupa pressed young members to show confidence, industriousness, admiration for their homelands (old and new), and desire to bring pride to the Czechoslovak community in Canada. He concluded by asking children to help "preserve" the ethnic heritage and customs that their parents had brought with them to their new country.[2]

One way in which Czechs in Canada retained this culture was by assisting in resurrecting a Czechoslovak state in 1945. During the Second World War, the Czechoslovak National Alliance reached a pinnacle of ninety-two branches and a membership of nearly 10,000 individuals. In the immediate postwar period, however, Czechoslovak organizations such as the CNA suffered from a decline in membership and financial support as many of its supporters turned their attention toward integration into Canadian society. The CNA never reached the same level of financial support and membership as it had during the Second World War. Although Canadian Czechs rejoiced at the liberation of their old homeland from Nazi domination, they recognized that postwar relief remained an immediate concern in a re-established Czechoslovakia. Following the Victory Congress of the CNA in November

1945, Czechs as members of a broader Czechoslovak group in Canada looked to Vice-President Jan Gažo's three-point plan for direction on how to improve life for their compatriots in Central Europe and continue to promote integration into Canadian society for all Czechoslovaks.

Canadian Czechoslovak institutions worked hard to address the needs of a resurrected Czechoslovak state in the immediate postwar period by means of this three-point plan. First, Czechoslovaks in Canada continued to fundraise in an effort to send postwar relief in the form of medicine, clothing, and food to their compatriots devastated by six years of German occupation. Second, Canadian Czechoslovak community leaders within the CNA and MH actively promoted the development of Canadian citizenship among their members even as many prewar immigrants began to consider returning to Czechoslovakia after six years of war and separation from relatives and friends in the old country. As non-denominational and anti-communist institutions, the CNA and MH welcomed individuals of various backgrounds, including Catholic, Protestant, and Jewish members whose origins connected them to Czechoslovakia. Many of these individuals were Canadian Czechs who regarded with suspicion the increasing communist influence in the old country. Third, these members also turned their attention toward the creation of a Czechoslovak ethnic heritage for future generations. These three pillars of the community's immediate postwar agenda entrenched the existence of the MH and CNA, solidified the Czechoslovak community's ethnocultural identity, and provided its members with a strategy to achieve sociocultural citizenship in postwar Canada.

Implementing the Three-Point Plan

Recognizing that social and economic conditions in Czechoslovakia were dire in the months after the Second World War, the CNA's executive committee was regularly updated regarding the relief situation in their homeland. In December 1945, Czechoslovakia's Ministry of Labour and Social Welfare wrote to the CNA head office in Toronto indicating that improving the nutrition of small children was the ministry's top priority. According to Prague, children up to six years of age had an average daily intake of 1,428 calories, below the required 1,600 calories. Meanwhile, those older than six consumed an average of 1,907 calories instead of the recommended 2,650 calories needed to maintain general health. Because of the increasing need for food and medication, and with relief packages to Czechoslovakia arriving only slowly, the ministry indicated that many children and youth were suffering from malnourishment and tuberculosis.[3] Sensing that the need for relief packages was great across Czechoslovak society, CNA members soon joined efforts to send much-needed foods and comfort products to their old homeland.

One product that had been in high demand throughout the Second World War and early postwar period was tobacco. In early 1946, CNA members called on their leaders to renew the wartime Cigarette Fund, which had successfully sent donated cigarettes to Czechoslovak forces in England, Russia, and North Africa as well as to Czechoslovak civilians. In an executive committee meeting held in early January, National Secretary Karel Buzek noted that approval for such a scheme had to come from Ottawa. Subsequently, Canadian authorities informed the CNA that Czechoslovak servicemen no longer qualified for cigarette parcels from Canada since the war was over. That month the Post Office Department notified the CNA that postal services between Canada and Czechoslovakia had resumed and that Canadians were now free to send parcels—subject to customs regulations for tobacco in Czechoslovakia.[4] It was also noted that the American government already permitted a cigarette service for war-torn Europe. Although the Canadian government lifted restrictions on the shipment of individual parcels with a maximum weight of four pounds and permitted the shipment of foods up to eleven pounds, Ottawa lagged behind Washington in permitting the shipment of relief goods, including cigarettes, to Europe.[5] Faced with such restrictive government regulations, the CNA struggled to meet its previous obligations and the growing demand for consumable products. Meanwhile, various organizations stepped in to assist the CNA. The Canadian United Allied Relief Fund offered to ship clothing and footwear from Canadian military stores at a rate of $5.00 per pair of footwear, $1.25 per pair of pants, and $2.50 per shirt. Canadian Commercial Enterprises of Toronto offered to facilitate the purchase of relief goods in Denmark to be sent to Czechoslovakia. The Bata Shoe Company office in Copenhagen indicated to the CNA that butter could be purchased at sixty cents per pound. As a result, 2,000 pounds of butter with a value of $1,200 were to be sent to Czechoslovakia. This plan came to naught, however, because Danish authorities refused to grant authorization for such a large shipment. With an order for Danish butter lacking the necessary clearances, the Czechoslovak Red Cross in Prague informed the CNA that it would now receive such products from the United Nations Relief and Rehabilitation Administration.

In an effort to circumvent the obstacles presented by Danish authorities, the CNA and its member branches resorted to purchasing smaller quantities of relief goods and sent them from Denmark to Czechoslovakia through the

Czechoslovak War Charities Fund, a member fund of the more broadly based CUARF. With funds from the CNA, the Canadian Red Cross purchased $26,000 worth of vitamin tablets, viosterol (oil-based vitamin D), citrus concentrate (vitamin C), sulfate, penicillin, sweaters, coats, and socks.[6] By March 1946, this arrangement was facilitating the shipment of goods to the Czechoslovak Red Cross in Prague and to the Slovak National Council in Bratislava.

In an effort to raise awareness of their relief efforts, Canadian Czech leaders reached out to the public. In a letter to the *Toronto Daily Star,* Karel Buzek, who also served as the executive director of the CWCF, expressed his gratitude to all Canadians for their donations of money, food, and clothing to the Canadian Red Cross, the National Clothing Collection, and the Czechoslovak War Charities Fund—by the end of 1945, $1,067,000 worth of relief goods had been shipped to Czechoslovakia. Buzek informed the paper's readers that, in some parts of Czechoslovakia, the destruction was so severe that government and voluntary agencies could not adequately manage the situation on the ground. The CNA's national secretary used the example of thousands of children—many of whom were homeless orphans—who remained undernourished and lacked sufficient clothing, and he insisted that parcels of food and cigarettes for families could still be ordered through the CWCF.[7] In the spring of 1946, CUARF purchased a further 5 million units of penicillin and 550 tons of flour later sent to Czechoslovakia. The Canadian consignment of goods was released among the socially disadvantaged in Czechoslovakia.[8]

Canadian Relief Aid to Europe

Significantly, as relief organizations continued to send aid packages to war-torn Europe, they corresponded to an expansion of aid such as the one announced by Prime Minister W.L. Mackenzie King, who introduced a food conservation program designed to increase Canadian shipments of vital foods to Europe. In a letter to organizations and individuals involved in collecting donations for war-ravaged Europe, the minister of national war services asked Canadians to reduce their daily requirements for these vital foods and to substitute into their diets the canned and packaged foods that would be donated to voluntary food collections. The change would allow the federal government's food boards to deliver these vital foods quickly to sources responsible for effectively distributing them overseas according to need.[9] The Canadian government hoped that its citizens would support the program by purchasing less flour, cheese, and meat and fewer wheat products and eggs, avoiding unnecessary waste, and purchasing these items only for immediate needs. Ottawa also encouraged the establishment of residential gardens that would lead to the substitution of vegetables for many of these now vital foods.[10]

These efforts were the focus of a fall 1946 delegation that arrived in Czechoslovakia to assess the destruction caused by the Second World War. The delegation began its tour of the country in Bratislava and completed its visit in Prague. It witnessed the wartime destruction of property and nationwide protests, and it visited with the injured, sick, and infirm in hospitals across the country. In eastern Slovakia, the delegation viewed first-hand how Canadian relief goods—arriving first in 1945—were put to use before American aid appeared. Upon his return from Czechoslovakia, the chair of the CNA's auditing committee, Prokop V. Havlík, informed members of the executive that it was pointless for the organization's members to send money to their relatives and friends because of the low value of Czechoslovak currency. Although one Canadian dollar was worth approximately fifty Czechoslovak crowns, Havlík argued that more could be bought with a dollar in Canada than with fifty crowns in Czechoslovakia, where the limited availability of goods meant high demand and high prices. He advised his compatriots to send clothing, footwear, and cigarettes instead. In addition, he argued that, in a newly resurrected Czechoslovakia, cigarettes continued to be a valuable gift.[11]

But sending the goods was only half of the equation. A subsequent CNA delegation to Czechoslovakia led by President Rudolf Koreň and National Secretary Karel Buzek met with a ministerial committee at Prague Castle, the official residence of President Edvard Beneš. One of the many issues discussed was the large number of missing or undelivered aid packages that members of the Czechoslovak community across Canada were sending to needy recipients in Czechoslovakia: their families and friends, the elderly, and the orphaned. In 1947, aid packages could not weigh more than six kilograms, and their shipment was processed by the CNA head office on Richmond Street in Toronto.[12] The parcels arrived in Europe via ships docking at the German port of Hamburg, or its Polish counterpart at Gdańsk, and were released for delivery by train throughout the country. Many packages were simply not arriving at their destinations. Czechoslovak officials informed the CNA delegation that they were not responsible for the loss of these parcels, claiming that many packages were improperly labelled.[13]

In a further attempt to raise funds for infirm and afflicted compatriots in Czechoslovakia, in September 1947, the executive committee of the CNA informed readers of *Nová vlasť* (New Homeland) that it was commencing a campaign to raise $10,000 to help elderly Czechoslovaks in Canada, compatriots back home, and recent arrivals in Canada. But there were tensions between the Czech and Slovak groups even in the area of relief funding. In an attempt to instigate internal political divisions, Slovak communists in Canada countered this initiative by claiming in their official organ, *L'udové zvesti* (People's News), that the CNA's campaign was a deliberate attempt to fill its own coffers.[14] The CNA countered the Slovak communist claim by indicating to readers that the organization had received annual membership dues of only one dollar per member since its founding in 1939, while all other funds collected went to various projects, such as the Cigarette Fund, or to aid Czechoslovakia's orphans and displaced persons. The CNA's executive committee noted that money collected during the Second World War effort and counted at the CNA's Victory Congress in November 1945 had equalled $330,922.00. Of this sum, $209,212.42 had been given to the CWCF, $30,983.04 had been used to purchase travelling passes for Czechoslovak troops in Europe and North Africa, and $19,735.50 had been given to the committee for all Czechoslovak groups—of which, incidentally, the *L'udové zvesti* was a member. Furthermore, the CNA raised funds to help those compatriots who did not have the financial means to insure themselves; elderly persons no longer eligible for life insurance were now able to access funds for medical reasons.[15] Although the CNA's breakdown of its finances might have put to rest this particular accusation by the Slovak communist faction, such tensions would occur repeatedly in the years to come.

In part to overcome these ethnic tensions, in November 1947, Czechoslovakia's consul general in Montreal, Josef Kotrlý, explained why the CNA was seeking donations for its various projects and why a fund for Canadian Czechoslovaks run by the same organization was necessary. Kotrlý informed Canadian Czechoslovaks in *Nová vlast'* that there were approximately 40,000 Slovaks and Czechs living in Canada, of whom only a small portion had maintained Czechoslovak citizenship. The overwhelming majority of individuals within the community were either Canadian citizens or without citizenship since they had lost their Czechoslovak citizenship and had yet to become naturalized Canadian citizens. The consul general went on to argue that not every newcomer from Czechoslovakia achieved financial or professional success after immigrating to Canada. According to Kotrlý, many individuals succumbed to accidents, unfortunate occurrences, and medical issues that left them and their families devastated.

The consul general used several examples to illustrate why such a fund within the community was necessary. He spoke of a war veteran recently released from service who had suffered an accident and could not provide for his young wife and child. Others, he said, had lost property, and some sought to return to Czechoslovakia but did not have the financial means to do so. Those recent arrivals not yet naturalized and in dire need of assistance looked to the consulate for support. Kotrlý claimed that the Czechoslovak community in Canada had the ability and resources to help compatriots in need—including individuals without Canadian or Czechoslovak citizenship and therefore not entitled to consular aid. The consul general concluded his remarks in *Nová vlasť* by arguing that it was the duty of compatriot groups in Canada to provide social services to fellow immigrants from Czechoslovakia. Kotrlý firmly believed that the CNA, along with other Czechoslovak community organizations in Canada, should collect donations openly from the public for a social fund for all Canadian Czechoslovak community members.[16]

As Czechoslovak community members considered the consul general's recommendation to establish a community fund, a campaign letter was sent out to CNA members, friends of the organization, and the public during the Christmas season in 1947 to inform them that its popular Cigarette Service would be discontinued and that any future orders would require time for proper packaging and delivery. Matuš Pavlík, treasurer of the Cigarette Service, sent a letter to the CNA head office in Toronto explaining that, according to his estimates, the service's prices of $3.20 for 600 American cigarettes and $4.00 for 600 Canadian cigarettes were actually losing the organization crucial funds. As a result of his assessment, Pavlík asked for the CNA's assistance in helping the service to pay off all outstanding costs before the final shipment date of 31 December 1947.[17] Although the Cigarette Service was terminating its activities, the CNA continued to fundraise for Czechoslovakia. For many Canadian Czechs, the transnational links among themselves, the Czechoslovak community, and the old homeland were inseparable. By sending representatives to visit Czechoslovakia, raising funds, and sending relief packages, they retained an invested interest in the future reconstruction of Czechoslovakia, further allowing them to link their old country with their new country.

Immigration Controls

During the first two years after the Second World War, Canada's immigration controls remained firm, and few Czechs arrived in Canada. Although labour organizations, in an attempt to protect their workers, largely opposed the opening of Canada's gates to immigrants from Europe, proponents of business and industry as well as humanitarian organizations advocated for a more generous immigration policy to respond to the plight of displaced people in Europe. Meanwhile, the Czechoslovak National Alliance, which continued to facilitate the purchase and shipment of relief goods to Czechoslovakia, moved to assist immigrants who did manage to reach Canada's shores. In 1946, persons who desired to immigrate to either Canada or the United States corresponded directly with Czechoslovak organizations in North America, and the CNA aided Czechs abroad in gaining entry into Canada, sometimes circumventing tight immigration controls through imaginative applications. In one case, on the strength of information from the Immigration Branch to the CNA that a provision existed in the Immigration Act "for the admission to Canada of bona fide agriculturalists who have sufficient means to commence farming in Canada," Staff Sergeant Karel Juzl of the Czechoslovak forces overseas described himself as a farmer by occupation.[18] District Superintendent J.D. McFarlane instructed the CNA to advise Juzl to visit the London office of the Canadian Immigration Branch, where officials would determine if the applicant was admissible under the regulations.[19] Ultimately, Juzl was successful in gaining entry into Canada and later disembarked from SS *Ile de France* in Halifax on 26 February 1946. Although early postwar immigration to Canada remained heavily restricted, Juzl's case demonstrates that motivated Czechs found ways to enter the country by navigating existing regulations that defined the ideal immigrant.

Soon matters became easier for prospective immigrants. A day after Juzl entered Canada, the Department of Mines and Resources—responsible for the Immigration Branch—notified the CNA that its regulations permitted the entry of visitors "in good health and in possession of an unexpired passport" issued by the country of their citizenship and carrying a visa issued by a Canadian diplomatic official in Europe.[20] In the absence of a Canadian official, a visa issued by a British diplomatic official would be accepted. Prospective non-immigrants were to have their papers examined at a Canadian port of entry. Canadian Czechs used the temporary entry regulations to bring their relatives to Canada for stays lasting from a few weeks to one year.[21] In May 1946, the Canadian government issued Order-in-Council P.C. 2071 permitting Canadian citizens to sponsor their close relatives, including parents, siblings, and orphaned nieces and nephews. At the same time, Czechs who wished to immigrate to Canada from Czechoslovakia or one of the DP camps in Western Europe continued to wait since Canadian immigration controls remained tight. The Canadian public began to put considerable pressure on the Canadian government to respond to the humanitarian crisis in Europe by opening the country's doors to immigration.

Returning to Europe

Not all movement between Czechoslovakia and Canada went in a westward direction. With the Second World War over and a Czechoslovak Republic firmly established, many Canadian Czechs entertained the idea of returning to the old country. Although many of them had come to Canada seeking economic opportunities, a better standard of living, and escape from the German occupation of their homeland, a desire to reconnect with relatives and friends or even to repatriate led an unknown number of them to return to Czechoslovakia in the early postwar years. For Canadian Czechs who wished to visit or resettle in Czechoslovakia, the DEA enclosed a document entitled "Memorandum to Persons Travelling to Continental Europe" with every passport application to future travellers from Canada. With Europe in the midst of rebuilding its vital infrastructure, including transportation networks, Canadian officials informed prospective travellers that "approval of your [passport] application does not accord any priority with regard to transportation to Europe, nor can any responsibility be undertaken with regard to return transportation."[22] Ottawa indicated that passengers from Canada could find a few seats for sea-rail service between London and Paris without a lot of difficulty. The Canadian ambassador in France, Brigadier Georges Philias Vanier, confirmed that continental travel was difficult, while accommodation was hard to secure.[23] Canadian travellers were to expect delays and difficulties.

Those wishing to travel back to the homeland applied to travel companies, including Cunard White Star Limited (Donaldson Atlantic Line), for Atlantic passage via Great Britain to Czechoslovakia. Prospective travellers were assisted in filling out their applications by the CNA head office in Toronto, which examined each application.

In many cases, applicants had been born in Austria-Hungary at the turn of the twentieth century and had never become naturalized Canadian citizens. One such applicant was fifty-five-year-old Jozef Šimkovič, a married gardener from Fort Erie, Ontario, who indicated in March 1946 on his travel application with the Cunard Line that he wished to be settled permanently in Czechoslovakia. Cunard officials indicated that his health was good and that he was prepared to leave as soon as possible. Later that month John Somr, a forty-nine-year-old married farmer from Tupperville, Ontario, indicated that he too wished to settle permanently in Czechoslovakia. Antonín Heindl, a fifty-four-year-old married labourer residing in Toronto, also sought to return to Czechoslovakia. Like Šimkovič, Somr, and Heindl, many applicants were middle-aged men who had arrived in Canada looking for economic opportunities but later yearned for their families back in Central Europe. In some instances, they were farmers and labourers from Czechoslovakia who had never intended to remain permanently in Canada.

Although many applicants resettled in the old country, others simply desired to reconnect with family back in Czechoslovakia. One of them was Steve Kulkoský, a fifty-nine-year-old married coal miner from Bellevue, Alberta, who had become a naturalized British subject. In his travel application, Kulkoský revealed that he longed to visit his wife and family in Czechoslovakia.[24]

Communism Gains Ground

As democratic Canadian Czechs continued to reconnect with relatives and friends in Czechoslovakia or bring their loved ones to Canada for visits, they also watched with apprehension the popular emergence of the communist movement in their homeland during the elections of May 1946. In the Czech Lands, the Communist Party of Czechoslovakia under Klement Gottwald garnered just over 40 percent of all votes. In Slovakia, the Democratic Party under Jozef Lettrich achieved 62 percent of all votes. Altogether, the Communist Party of Czechoslovakia—including the Communist Party of Slovakia —gained 38 percent of all votes cast throughout the country and was the largest party in the parliament. The Communist Party won ninety-three and twenty-one seats, respectively, for a total of 114 seats in the 300-seat interim National Assembly in Prague. Universal suffrage did not extend to ethnic German and Hungarian citizens of Czechoslovakia, disenfranchised after the Second World War.[25] The Communist Party was more popular with Czech voters, whereas Slovaks favoured the Democratic Party as a broad coalition of non-communists. The May 1946 election results in favour of the Communists in the Czech Lands reflected bitter disillusionment among many Czechs about the West and the Munich Accords of 1938. After approximately six years of fascist occupation, many Czech voters were grateful to the Allies, in particular the Soviet Union, for their liberation.[26] Beneš remained in office as president of Czechoslovakia, while Gottwald became prime minister. The May 1946 election results brought together four political parties into a National Front coalition government. The Communists retained the premiership and nine cabinet posts, while the other parties shared the remaining seventeen ministries. The Communists consolidated their power over influential ministries, including Interior, Information, Agriculture, Social Welfare, Internal Trade, and Finance. In Ottawa, Canadian diplomats noted that the Communists under Gottwald left little doubt that they were in a strong position since they also maintained control over the police and the internal security service.[27] Many Canadian Czechs became increasingly alarmed by their homeland's flirtation with communism.

The Iron Curtain Descends

Canadian Czechs would become directly affected by political events in Czechoslovakia. In January 1948, the Canadian chargé d'affaires in Prague, Ronald Macalister Macdonnell, noted in his correspondence with Ottawa that Communist Parties everywhere viewed control over police forces as a fundamental objective in their attempts to obtain political power.[28] This was no different in Czechoslovakia, where the Communists had seized control of the police forces in order to drive the struggle for power in their favour.[29] Canadian diplomats in Prague were well aware of the early manoeuvrings of the Communists for a police state. Diplomatic reports sent back to Ottawa by Canadian officials in Prague were consistent and insightful, and the officials remained tentatively hopeful that the political situation in Czechoslovakia could be resolved with a local compromise; otherwise, the Communists would seize the moment to act. The Canadian chargé d'affaires went on to note that there were "many alarming rumours flying about Prague to the effect that the Communists are ready for a coup. On the other hand, the Communists judged by the standards which their party has followed in other Eastern European countries . . . have been restrained or at any rate have not been as violent in their language as they could have been."[30]

In Prague on 20 February 1948, twelve cabinet ministers submitted their resignations in protest over Communist Party intransigence and control of the national police. Unlike the National Socialists and the People's Party, the left-leaning Social Democrats took a neutral position and criticized the tactics of both sides. President Beneš refused to accept the twelve resignations and remained steadfast against subsequent demands for new elections.[31]

Not only did these events occur quickly, but also they affected Czech immigrants and the Czechoslovak community as the Canadian public learned about them. The 21 February edition of *Saturday Night* carried an article written by Alec Harrison entitled "Can Beneš Save the Czechs from Iron Curtain?"[32] Harrison depicted Beneš as a passionate defender of his country. On 24 February, Macdonnell wrote to Ottawa that, with a rise in arrests, strikes, accusations, and the further arming of police, the best possible outcome on the eve of the Communists' takeover of Czechoslovakia was that the non-communists could retain enough political strength and courage to act as a weakened but real opposition. In Macdonnell's view, any future election would find non-communists supporting the communist movement in an effort to avoid retribution.[33]

The next day, fearing sociopolitical unrest, President Beneš reversed his initial decision and accepted the twelve resignations and acknowledged a new Communist Party–led cabinet with Gottwald as prime minister. In all, the Communist Party held thirteen of the twenty-four cabinet posts.[34] As president, Beneš had been responsible for Czechoslovakia's capitulation to Nazi Germany without a fight in 1938, and now he was responsible for accepting the Communists' demands in 1948. He erroneously believed that closer ties between Prague and Moscow, between himself and Stalin, would allow Czechoslovakia's democratic independence to coexist with the Soviet Union after the Second World War.[35] In a dispatch to Ottawa on 26 February, Macdonnell indicated that "the iron curtain has begun to descend."[36]

Canadian newsprint outlets reported daily events during the Communists' seizure of power. The Associated Press acknowledged that, after twenty years of independence and nine years after the German invasion, Czechoslovakia was now completely under communist rule.[37] Members of more democratic parties resigned in an attempt to catch the Communists off guard and later called for a general election. The Communists demanded that Beneš let them form a new government. Their threat of a general strike—the first in the country's history—and a 50,000-strong demonstration in central Prague forced Beneš to acquiesce.

Despite its coverage, the North American press downplayed the significance of the change. The Associated Press noted that the Communists' seizure of power was a relatively non-violent event with no barricades or bloodshed, though a few fists were thrown.[38] Similarly, the Canadian Press reported that the Czechoslovak Embassy in Ottawa was shrouded in silence. Reporters could not reach Prague's minister in Canada, František Němec, who avoided making official comments on events back home. After dining with Major James Coldwell, a staunch anti-communist and leader of the Cooperative Commonwealth Federation, Němec asked his close friend if he would be willing secretly to store the papers of the wartime Czechoslovak government-in-exile in London. Němec informed Coldwell that he was being watched by Communist Party authorities, who had stationed an operative on his staff at the legation. The Ottawa police later placed a cordon around the legation after the Communists' takeover in Prague.[39] Canadian diplomats also refused to comment on events in Central Europe but noted that Ottawa was unlikely to withdraw its recognition of the Czechoslovak government following the takeover.[40]

The *Ottawa Evening Citizen* published an editorial entitled "Strangling Czech Liberty" in which it argued that the Communist Party takeover of Czechoslovakia with less than 40 percent of the popular vote was a "political crime beyond condemnation or even excuse."[41] The paper defended the coalition government formed after the May 1946 election in which socialism through democratic means was slowly being achieved. The paper accurately noted that to view the seizure of power as a Soviet plot merely oversimplified the situation in Czechoslovakia.[42] Beneš formally installed the Communist Party government but did not immediately resign. As tension throughout the country turned to apathy, Edvard Beneš resigned from office in early June, thus clearing the way for Klement Gottwald and the Communists to complete their domination of Czechoslovakia.

Reaction in Canada

Throughout Canada, members of the Czechoslovak community were affected by the Communist Party seizure of power. Noting political events in Czechoslovakia, between 1946 and 1948, Slovak members of the pro-communist Independent Mutual Benefit Federation of Toronto frequently visited the office of the Czechoslovak consul general in Montreal, Josef Kotrlý, demanding to be recognized as official advisors of the consulate. The federation's secretary and member of the Labour-Progressive Party of Canada, Cyprián Slimák, insisted that he be permitted to screen all persons claiming Czechoslovak nationality and demanded that decisions on their identities be deferred to him. Slimák requested that Czechoslovak passports be provided to individuals without any identification papers. Kotrlý noted that in one case individuals of German and Hungarian descent arrived at the consulate demanding passports. When asked for references to ascertain their identities, the individuals gave the name of Tim Buck, national leader of the Labour-Progressive Party—a successor to the Communist Party of Canada.

As representatives of the Czechoslovak government in Canada, diplomats and their offices were often witnesses to intra–immigrant group conflict. This was also the case following the 1948 Communist Party seizure of power. During his tenure as Czechoslovakia's consul general in Montreal, Kotrlý reported to Vladimír Clementis, the Communist Party deputy minister of foreign affairs in Prague. In a 26 March *Halifax Chronicle Herald* article entitled "Former Czech Consul Tells of Red 'Web,'" Kotrlý claimed that Clementis personally interfered in foreign legations and consulates. Subsequently, domestic communist sympathizers attempted to subvert the consulate and turn it into a front for communist propaganda. The Czechoslovak consul general alleged that Slimák attempted to turn his office into a space for the dissemination of communist literature, films, and other materials that the Labour-Progressive Party of Canada received from Prague. Following Kotrlý's protests, Communist Party authorities sent their propaganda via diplomatic mail to Czechoslovakia's legation in Ottawa, thus avoiding any opposition from Kotrlý in Montreal. On 26 February, only a day after the Communist Party takeover of Czechoslovakia, Slimák left Canada by air for his homeland. Four months later, on 25 June, his wife, Mary, and children Milan and Helen left for Czechoslovakia aboard SS *Radnik*. Canadian officials were made aware of their emigration through a British United Press dispatch, dated 19 March 1948, which indicated that Slimák had been appointed as editor-in-chief of the communist newspaper *Pravda* in Bratislava. In 1949, Slimák was given a consular appointment in Budapest, Hungary.[43]

Members of the Canadian Czechoslovak community remained divided over the new communist government in Czechoslovakia. In detailing his experience with communist sympathizers in Canada and Communist Party authorities in Prague, Kotrlý observed in the *Chronicle Herald* that there existed in Canada a small group of honest individuals who supported communism. According to the consul general, these persons supported communism largely because of their minority complex. They had arrived in Canada without any knowledge of English or French and thus could not integrate themselves into the civic, national, cultural, intellectual, or artistic life of the country. Although Kotrlý alluded to the insecurity of these individuals, he was quick to conclude that Communist Party agents had found a clever approach to incorporate persons who had trouble adapting to life in Canada into communist groups and associations.[44]

"The Problem of Immigration"

Meanwhile, the Czech community would not be unaffected by Canada's new concern about "the problem of immigration," as Senator Arthur W. Roebuck described it in a speech that he delivered on the floor of the Senate in April 1946.[45] Questioning whether Canada was to remain indefinitely a third-rate power with a secondary influence in the world or open its doors to immigration in order to become one of the most powerful states, the senator introduced a motion to establish a committee of inquiry. The newly established Senate

Standing Committee on Immigration and Labour considered several issues, including the desirability of admitting immigrants to Canada; the type of immigrant preferred, with reference to his or her origin, experience, and other characteristics; the availability of immigrants for admission into Canada; the national capacity to resettle, find employment for, and maintain new immigrants effectively; and future regulations for entry into Canada.[46]

As the Senate examined the future of Canadian immigration policy, a Cabinet Committee on Immigration Policy convened in May 1946 decided that the RCMP would become responsible for screening prospective immigrants overseas. The committee noted that the RCMP should investigate the records and backgrounds of applicants. With growing anti-communist sentiment throughout the Western world, the committee sought to prevent Communist Party agents, communist sympathizers, and leftist agitators from entering the country against the labour needs of the business community and the market. However, in March 1947, Liberal Minister of Mines and Resources J.A. Glen informed cabinet that "there was no provision of law for rejection" on the ground that an individual was a communist.[47] The Liberal cabinet agreed to ignore this measure and decided instead that the Immigration Branch should refuse admission to any prospective immigrant who, after a security review, was deemed a communist. Another impediment to easing the restrictions on immigration was the fear that an increase in immigration could prevent returning Canadian soldiers from finding employment, a fear eased only gradually because of the aforementioned security pressures, introduced despite the lobbying of Minister of Reconstruction Clarence Decatur Howe. As a result, the cabinet committee was slow to view an increase in immigration as advantageous to Canadian society and its economy.[48]

Not only was there a new fear of immigrants, but also the RCMP's operations were overseen by an interdepartmental group known as the Security Panel, whose mandate it was to advise the federal government. It soon recommended that the government begin vetting procedures for prospective civil servants.[49] The RCMP issued 5,466 names to the Security Panel in the first three months of its operation. Of the 217 reports requiring further assessment, only 27 cases were deemed "legitimate security risks."[50] In the summer of 1946, RCMP officers were stationed in Canadian immigration offices across Europe and charged with refusing entry to any individual "who . . . from their own history and background would be unlikely to adapt themselves to the Canadian way of life and to our system of democratic government."[51]

Still, as Canada's postwar economic recovery began to take shape, businesses and ethnic associations increasingly lobbied the federal government to allow for more immigrants to resettle in Canada. The government opened the country's doors to forestry workers, garment industry workers, and farm labourers. Admissible immigrants who did not fit into these categories—such as entrepreneurs and professionals—were required to sign one-year agricultural labour contracts in order to enter Canada. The Department of Labour's priority was to relocate to Canada young, single, and physically healthy DPs—individuals forced to migrate because of socioeconomic or political displacement caused by the Second World War.[52] Under the department's labour schemes, workers were admitted into the country for one- or two-year work contracts. Those who sponsored incoming DPs had to guarantee that they had the financial and residential means to support them for the length of their labour contracts.[53] Not only did Canadian Czechoslovak organizations, including the CNA and MH, become sponsors of hundreds of DPs living in European camps, but also they lobbied parliamentarians to increase the number of family reunifications and private sponsorships so that the Czechoslovak community could better assist refugees who sought permanent resettlement in Canada.

The Senate Standing Committee on Immigration and Labour

The CNA would be put in the spotlight, where it could share its recommendations for immigration policy. In June 1946, Senator Arthur W. Roebuck wrote to National Secretary Karel Buzek requesting that the CNA appear for a hearing before the Senate Standing Committee on Immigration and Labour; the committee had set aside one hour to hear the CNA's representatives submit their brief. Roebuck indicated to Buzek that the committee had contacted progressive and conservative Ukrainian and Polish groups. In his letter to Buzek, Roebuck—keenly aware of domestic ethnic political sensitivities—asked whether the CNA represented almost all Czechs and Slovaks in Canada or if there would be any protests from individuals if only the CNA was invited to present a brief before the committee. Roebuck believed the CNA to be an "appropriate" Canadian ethnic association and wanted to hear its brief.[54] In his reply to Roebuck's questions, Buzek indicated that, should the committee wish to hear from members with various political orientations, it should contact the Czechoslovak Joint Committee, an umbrella organization of various groups cooperating in postwar relief matters. However, the CNA national secretary failed to mention that a majority of Slovaks were represented by nationalist Slovak associations in Canada, the most influential of which was the Canadian Slovak League. Buzek sent to the committee the names of successful Czech Canadian farmers available to speak, including Alfred Mráček of Dodsland, Saskatchewan, and Joseph Gaschnitz of Nacmine, Alberta. The names of successful industrial workers were also submitted and included Stan Kvarda of Batawa, Ontario.[55] The committee later requested that the Czechoslovak delegation discuss the widening of categories of relatives permitted to enter Canada.

At every turn, the CNA insisted that its central mandate was to provide assistance to Czechoslovak refugees who requested it. It soon made this point before federal officials when, in July 1946, the Senate Standing Committee on Labour and Immigration invited informed parties dealing with immigration to testify. The committee heard presentations on the selection and resettlement of immigrants from Lieutenant-Colonel Arthur J. Hicks, a retired staff officer with the Allied military government in Europe; President Rudolf Koreň and National Secretary Karel Buzek of the Czechoslovak National Alliance in Canada; Sven Stadius of the Association for the Advancement of Finns in Canada; and Gustef Sundquist of the Finnish Organization of Canada. Buzek testified that the CNA sought to help newcomers in adapting to Canada while emphasizing their psychological resettlement. He lamented the severed contact between Czechoslovaks in Canada and their families back home, especially since transatlantic transportation companies had yet to begin bringing to Canada individuals for whom a voyage had already been paid. Although keenly aware that transportation had to be reserved first for Canadian troops returning home, Buzek argued that Canada could lose many recent immigrants because similar efforts had not been made to resettle their relatives in Canada for over fifteen years or more. The CNA's national secretary claimed that husbands and wives already in Canada would likely return to Czechoslovakia to reconnect with their families.

On behalf of the CNA's membership, Buzek urged the standing committee to pressure Canadian authorities to initiate measures to reunite recently arrived DPs with their family members still waiting to leave Europe. Specifically, the CNA called on Ottawa to give priority to immigrating families once the families of returning Canadian servicemen had been repatriated. Buzek indicated that Canadian immigration authorities should also be stationed in Prague to expedite the process.

The CNA delegation then sought to increase the quota set for parents and individuals seeking to enter Canada. Buzek acknowledged that many of the organization's members required donations of foreign capital to reunite with families and friends in Canada. In his testimony, Rudolf Koreň insisted that the CNA was aware that in some cases officials representing the undersecretary of state and the naturalization division attempted to discover why some recent immigrants in Canada had not yet brought their families from Czechoslovakia. The answer, Koreň claimed, was simple: they could not afford the deposit required to do so. In some cases, fathers had yet to see their children for the first time or had spent a considerable number of years in solitude away from their families. If they were not reunited, Koreň concluded, then many of these individuals would be forced to return to Czechoslovakia.

The CNA then called on Canadian immigration authorities to discontinue the division of prospective immigrants into privileged and non-privileged groups based upon ethnicity. Buzek informed the committee that he found this method of classifying immigrants disgusting and exploitative. The CNA could not understand how Germans were considered privileged but members of the CNA, which consisted of individuals with a similar Central European cultural background, were considered inferior.

In its final recommendation, the CNA called on the Canadian government to appoint impartial administrators to oversee the admission of prospective immigrants and to implement a consultative committee to act as an information service within the Immigration Branch.[56]

Returning to Czechoslovakia

Meanwhile, the Czechoslovak consulate in Montreal put in place new regulations pertaining to the flow of immigrants back to Czechoslovakia. In the 16 January 1947 issue of *Nová vlasť*, the paper informed readers that individuals who had fled Czechoslovakia after 1 September 1938 would be permitted by the United Nations Relief and Rehabilitation Administration to repatriate to their homeland. However, those who had left before this date would not be recognized and considered for repatriation.[57] Prague was attempting to fill vacancies left in the economy by those who had fled in 1939 and by the postwar mass expulsion of Sudeten Germans and Hungarians that had begun in 1945.[58] Individuals seeking to return to Czechoslovakia could request registration forms from the Czechoslovak consulate in Montreal. The CNA head office also stored the forms and provided advice to prospective returnees.[59] In the 2 January 1947 issue of *Nová vlasť*, editor Martin Dudák claimed that 300 compatriots once active in the Czechoslovak community in Canada had returned to Czechoslovakia the year before. Dudák expected that the community would lose another 100 individuals who desired to be reunited with their families back home. According to the editor, while continuing its efforts to provide help to orphans and families back in the homeland, it was incumbent on the existing community to shore up its membership.[60] In an effort to bolster support for immigration, Dudák argued that new Canadians from Czechoslovakia would quickly transplant their loyalty to their country of resettlement and build a future in Canada with their children.[61]

In February 1947, Czechoslovakia's new ambassador to Canada, František Němec, arrived to assume his post, replacing František Pavlásek, who had left in July 1946.[62] With Němec's guidance, the consulate in Montreal advised fellow compatriots in Canada that only the wives and children of Czechs who were naturalized Canadian citizens would be permitted to leave Czechoslovakia for Canada and be reunited with their families. Consul General Josef Kotrlý noted that officials would grant travelling documents only to individuals with relatives who were already Canadian citizens.[63] Three months after Němec's arrival, Czechs watched closely as the Canadian government began to initiate reforms to immigration policy in order to meet the political and economic needs of the country.

Immigration Policy under Mackenzie King

In an attempt to assuage demands for a liberalized immigration program, in May 1947, Prime Minister Mackenzie King outlined his Liberal government's immigration policy to the House of Commons. In his speech to fellow members, he revealed that his government would promote population growth by encouraging immigration. Ottawa would continue to select immigrants carefully according to the absorptive capacity of Canada's economy. Moreover, Mackenzie King indicated that Canada's policy on immigration had to be related specifically to the social, political, and economic situation resulting from the Second World War; immigration to Canada would fall into two categories: measures designed for immediate application and a long-term program. Canadian immigration policy was to assess critically the urgent need to resettle individuals displaced and left homeless by the war.

Mackenzie King admitted that the resettlement of political refugees and DPs constituted a unique problem. Although Canada was a member of the United Nations (UN) and the International Refugee Organization (IRO), and actively participated in the Intergovernmental Committee on Refugees, it was not obligated to accept any specified number of refugees or displaced persons (the latter was a distinction used by the IRO to establish a specific category of refugees forced to leave their countries during the Second World

War and refused repatriation to those homelands now under authoritarian regimes. However, Mackenzie King thought that Canada was morally obligated to partner with other states and international organizations to resettle permanently individuals displaced as a result of the war or fleeing political persecution by Soviet authorities. Ottawa was willing to aid its Western allies in resettling millions of displaced persons who remained in camps across war-ravaged Europe. Because of the limitations of transportation, the federal government decided that immigration from Europe would consist primarily of individuals with close relatives already living in Canada, with the government providing resettlement assistance to DPs and political refugees. Crucial to the Liberal government was that prospective immigrants be carefully selected and that the number of admitted persons be adjusted to the absorptive capacity of the country. As a result, though the prime minister argued that entry into Canada was not a fundamental human right but subject to the control of Parliament, he did note that discriminatory provisions within immigration legislation should be removed.[64]

Czech immigrants and the Czechoslovak community in Canada would be directly affected by the new postwar immigration policy. Also in May 1947, the government issued an order-in-council outlining requirements for immigration to Canada. Under the new regulations, relatives of Canadian citizens or legal residents—including fiancés/fiancées, spouses, and unmarried children—could apply for entry into Canada. For applicants wishing to work in agriculture, the CNA noted that families or single men with a minimum of $2,000 in capital could be admitted into Canada and resettled on their own farms. If applicants had guaranteed work on relatives' farms, it was only necessary to possess a minimum of $1,000 in capital. The CNA's head office in Toronto welcomed the submission of documents—including a Canadian citizenship certificate, a landing card, a bank statement, and a letter indicating residential status—that its staff would review in an attempt to help its members' relatives achieve entry into Canada.[65] Although the Canadian government was willing to assist European DPs in settling in Canada, its process of selection and restriction was guided by economic, ethnic, and political considerations. Department of Labour officials were sent overseas to select applicants for settlement, and Immigration Branch representatives routinely rejected prospective immigrants based upon ethnic and political prejudices, including Jews and left-wing or communist sympathizers additionally labelled as "undesirables" and "security risks." In this climate of heightened vigilance, Canadian Czechoslovak organizations, including the CNA, continued to assist

Czechoslovak nationals who wished to immigrate to Canada. Meanwhile, many members of the Czechoslovak community began to turn their attention toward creating an ethnocultural heritage in Canada.

The Community across Canada

With new immigration policies in place and postwar relief activities decreasing in frequency and intensity, cultural organizations such as Masaryk Hall in Toronto focused their attention on the promotion of ethnic heritage among younger generations. Meanwhile, the CNA sent out *dotazníky* ("questionnaires") to its branches throughout Canada in the hope of gaining further information on the size and activities of each Czechoslovak community. For 1947, members in Winnipeg wrote that their community consisted of 750 individuals, of whom 400 were of Slovak origin and the other 350 of Czech origin. Teaching either the Czech language or the Slovak language was deemed unsustainable because of the small number of Czechoslovak youth in Winnipeg. Community members in Winnipeg believed that their separate Czech and Slovak ethnic identities were respected by the local press and prominent city officials.[66] In Kingston, members indicated that fifty-three persons of Slovak origin and five individuals with Czech background resided in the city and were primarily employed as factory workers. Relations with the greater Kingston community were deemed *velmi dobré* ("very good").[67] In Oshawa, the questionnaire revealed that many of the members were employed as factory workers and that relations with fellow citizens, identified as 60 percent English and 40 percent mixed (the latter consisting of Slovaks, Poles, Ukrainians, Italians, and Germans), were *obstojné* ("tolerable"). The responses suggested that interethnic relations among individuals from Central and Eastern Europe were marked by hostility because of transplanted Old World tensions. However, CNA members in Oshawa believed that their relations with municipal officials and the press were relatively good.[68]

By far the largest concentration of Czechs and Slovaks in the 1940s was in Montreal, home to 250 Czech Canadians (many of whom were employed as industrial and construction workers, craftspeople, and entrepreneurs) and 3,000 Slovak Canadians, divided between "Czechoslovaks" and what the questionnaire bitterly termed "nationalist Slovak *separatisti.*" Only a small group of Slovaks participated in ethnocultural activities with their Czech neighbours. Members of the Czechoslovak community operated a Slovak-language supplementary school with a teacher hired from Czechoslovakia.

This educational institution was tasked with promoting a pro-Czechoslovak history of the homeland and instilling the Slovak language in youth.[69]

The Demise of *Nová vlasť*

Keeping the Czechoslovak community together during these times faced significant hurdles, one of which was the demise of *Nová vlasť*. A more challenging issue for the community was comprised by the ethnic and political dynamics among its members. In Montreal, for example, three ethnic newspapers reflected the ethnic divisions among immigrants from Czechoslovakia. Nationalist Slovaks followed the Canadian Slovak League and its official organ, the weekly *Kanadský Slovák* (Canadian Slovak), with a national circulation of close to 2,000; meanwhile, Slovak communists—who until 1937 had supported Czechoslovakism—claimed that their weekly, *Ľudové zvesti*, garnered nearly 2,500 readers. In reality, the Slovak communist press represented a small faction within the Canadian Slovak community. The paper never published the number of its subscribers. It is likely that members exaggerated the paper's readership in an attempt to portray themselves as a much larger group. As members of a Czechoslovak community, Slovaks and Czechs in Montreal and across Canada sustained the pro-Czechoslovak *Nová vlasť* newspaper, established in 1934, with a weekly national circulation of approximately 2,500 readers.[70]

But the Czechoslovak community was witnessing many changes, as noted by Editor-in-Chief Martin Dudák, who asserted in his final end-of-year editorial in *Nová vlasť* in 1947 that the wave of returnees to the old country was decreasing the community's number in Canada. He claimed that middle-aged immigrants were preoccupied with attaining greater property and standing for themselves, whereas the community's youth were being left behind in terms of knowledge of their Czechoslovak heritage. In his editorial, Dudák argued that young people were nowhere to be seen at national holiday celebrations or other cultural events, nor did they attend Czech- and Slovak-language schools.[71] True, many immigrants had now returned home to Czechoslovakia, but his claims were exaggerated: the arrival of postwar DPs more than made up for the loss of individuals who had returned to Europe.

Nonetheless, after fourteen years of service to the Czechoslovak community in Canada, *Nová vlasť* was forced to cease activity, publishing its final issue on 5 February 1948.[72] There were two main reasons for this demise. First, despite the community's growth, individual subscriptions began to decrease drastically after the war, resulting in financial difficulties for the paper. Second, and possibly more significant, the paper became a victim of community politics. In early 1948, the CNA sought to bring the Montreal-based publication to its headquarters in Toronto. The organization subsequently withdrew $1,400 from the newspaper's reserves to fund the transfer to Toronto, where it could have greater control over content and publication. The CNA executive committee later informed Dudák that it would repay the loan once the newspaper was re-established in the city and had resumed publication. In the final issue of *Nová vlasť,* however, Dudák claimed that the CNA had reimbursed the newspaper only forty-two dollars. Although the paper had no debts for the years 1946 and 1947, the CNA's failure to repay its loan meant that the paper no longer had funds to continue.[73]

With the demise of *Nová vlasť,* Czechoslovaks lost a significant pillar of their community. It had regularly reported on sociopolitical events in Czechoslovakia and kept Czechoslovaks in Canada aware of community activities across the country. The ethnic newspaper had also vigorously supported the cultivation of Czechoslovak cultural heritage and Czech- and Slovak-language retention.

Masaryktown

Fortunately, in these heady days, another important institution to establish and promote Czechoslovak culture in Canada would soon emerge. Within months of the demise of *Nová vlasť,* Masaryk Hall members laid the groundwork for a cultural and educational centre for Czechoslovak community life on the outskirts of Toronto. Although the idea for such a centre had been articulated at the end of the war, the Communist Party takeover of Czechoslovakia in February 1948 lent increased urgency to the project. In a meeting held the following month, Masaryk Hall members condemned the "rape of the Czechoslovak Republic" by the Communists.[74] Many of the members were also active in the patriotic calisthenics organization Sokol Toronto, which held its meetings inside MH. On the recommendation of Masaryk Hall executive committee member Prokop V. Havlík, Sokol Toronto became the first group in Canada to abandon relations with Communist Czechoslovakia. The members of Masaryk Hall agreed that they would work to raise awareness that a tragedy had taken place in Czechoslovakia while attempting to strengthen Czechoslovak life in Canada.[75]

To that end, in June 1948, MH purchased a sixty-four-acre farm in the Highland Creek area of Scarborough, on the eastern outskirts of Toronto. The purchase of the parcel of land that would one day incorporate Masaryktown was unanimously approved by MH members in a meeting held in October 1948. Masaryktown's founding purpose was to "provide [a] recreational centre for games, entertainments, cultural education, and summer holidays for all Canadian citizens of Czechoslovak origin and their friends."[76] Members also sought to build a facility whereby it would be possible to house and care for senior citizens and those unable to work within the Czechoslovak community. The northern half of Masaryktown was divided into individual lots of 60 x 100 feet, for which an individual would pay $200 as rent on a ninety-nine-year lease. Each lot could eventually be willed to a lessee's children. Each lessee was expected to erect on the property a cottage with an area of 320 square feet, with two windows and one door, to be painted every three years, and containing a working toilet and septic tank. During the summer of 1948, the committee responsible for maintaining the newly acquired land sent out letters to MH members informing them that farmland had been purchased. The committee noted that it had bought sixty-two acres of land for $14,500 so that its members could have a place to rest and relax away from the stresses of city life.[77] Although it was not built specifically in response to the Communist Party takeover of Czechoslovakia, Masaryktown became a meeting point for anti-communists and pro-democrats as a centre of Czechoslovak community life in the greater Toronto area.

In the hope of building ethnocultural identity and promoting Canadian citizenship, Masaryk Hall held its first annual Czechoslovak Day in July 1948 on the grounds of the newly purchased Masaryktown. Individuals and families from Kitchener, Guelph, Hamilton, and Niagara Falls came to the celebration of Czechoslovak heritage and culture. Sokol branches from Batawa, Toronto, Cleveland, and Detroit attended and demonstrated various calisthenic exercises, while local, provincial, and federal guests gave speeches.[78] Masaryktown was open to all visitors, and MH members were requested to volunteer two or three hours of work to prepare the land. They were asked to bring an axe, a hoe, and a rake with them on their next visit. Similarly, MH's executive committee sought the services of a farm worker for the entire property for a monthly wage.[79]

The establishment of Masaryktown was not without challenges. Although community members in Toronto looked to their newly acquired land as a "little Czechoslovakia," many non-Czechoslovak residents who lived in the vicinity of Masaryktown opposed its establishment. In the 15 July 1948 issue of a local newspaper, *Enterprise,* residents complained to the local city council about

Czechoslovak children raiding nearby orchards and gardens. In a letter to the newspaper, a regular visitor to Masaryktown noted that intolerance and hatred could be heard and seen from local residents who opposed a Czechoslovak institution near them. One resident was heard shouting "I'll send the dog after them!"[80] The letter asked readers to treat Czechoslovak children with respect since they would eventually grow up to be proper Canadian citizens. The letter noted that, even though the youngsters were the children of immigrants, they also had the right to enjoy the sun, fresh air, and water.[81]

A significant component of Masaryk Hall's agenda was to promote Czechoslovak identity and use of the Czech and Slovak languages among the youth. Ethnocultural schools were one structure in which ethnic organizations could attempt to create cultural heritage. According to Aloysius Balawyder, ethnic schools were integral to the strengthening of culture and language among the youth because they instructed children of Slavic heritage about their ancestral language and history and helped to establish and promote ethnocultural concerts, festivals, and presentations. As a result, ethnic schools encouraged nationalistic sentiments in children and adults alike as they listened to traditional songs, attended dances and presentations, and ate traditional foods. At the same time, ethnic organizations promoted Canadian citizenship among their members. The teaching of English (and French in Quebec) was urged to embed Canadian traditions in ethnic communities. Canadian Slavic groups frequently organized national days and invited distinguished representatives of Canadian society such as local MPs, mayors, government ministers, bishops, and even prime ministers.[82] At Masaryktown in Scarborough, calisthenics were organized by the local patriotic Sokol unit. Important dates such as 7 March, the birthday of Czechoslovakia's first president, Tomáš Garrigue Masaryk, and 28 October, the birth of the First Czechoslovak Republic, were celebrated annually. In a circular letter to all branches, the CNA informed its members that it would work in cooperation with MH to build further Masaryktown, the Masaryk Youth Club, the supplementary school, and the library. As well, it would continue efforts to expand the Czech- and Slovak-language school to other locations across Canada wherever members wished to establish such an institution. The CNA viewed the Masaryk Youth Club as an important venue in which the community's youth would recognize their citizenship obligations. It was deemed vital that Czechoslovak youth across Canada organize a national congress.[83] However, the Communist Party takeover of Czechoslovakia soon loomed over community events as Canadian

Czechs and the broader Czechoslovak community turned their attention toward the emergence of a totalitarian regime in Communist Czechoslovakia.

▶ ▶ ◀ ◀

After six years of devastation, immigrants arriving in Canada from the ruins of postwar Czechoslovakia came in search of the economic well-being that they had lost in their homeland and a quality of life that they defined in middle-class terms. During 1946 and 1947, 572 immigrants claimed their nationality as Czechoslovakian upon arriving in Canada, and with this identity they built immediate bridges to previous immigrants from Czechoslovakia and Canadian-born members of the Czechoslovak community.[84] These early immigrants influenced the newcomers in the creation of their Czech Canadian identity. But the wartime experiences of these postwar arrivals also influenced Canadian Czechoslovak institutions, which increasingly came to promote their pro-democracy and anti-totalitarian values. The Communists' seizure of power in Czechoslovakia in February 1948 and the subsequent wave of political refugees fleeing their homeland exerted a profound influence on the CNA and Masaryk Hall. The well-established interwar immigrants at first viewed the successive waves of Cold War refugees from Czechoslovakia with empathy. But the newcomers were distinct from the well-established forerunners; these "1948ers" were offered government support for resettlement in Canada, and they were virulent promoters of an anti-communist identity. Both factors laid the groundwork for ideological conflict within the community. The interwar immigrants supported anti-communist values but prioritized Canadian citizenship, whereas the 1948ers remained intent on lobbying the Canadian government and using community institutions to liberate their old homeland from communism. The 1948ers' anti-communist rhetoric fit the sociocultural and political norms found in postwar Canada. This identity would help to shape the Czech newcomer's social position within the Canadian Cold War consensus espoused by public and private gatekeepers, all in an effort to attain social and cultural citizenship as good Canadians.

CHAPTER 3

Aftermath of the Communist Takeover: Canada and the 1948ers

In 1949, František and Marie Flosman, and their two sons Josef and Jiří, left Czechoslovakia after the Communists confiscated their mill property and deemed them to be enemies of the working class. Marie's brother was a senator who faced severe political pressure when he refused to join the Communist Party. The Flosmans left Czechoslovakia without their possessions in an attempt to demonstrate that they were not in the process of illegally leaving the state. They thought of themselves as émigrés, planning to resettle temporarily in France until communism was defeated in their homeland. But first they were sent by West German authorities to the Ludwigsburg DP camp under American administration, where they resided for about a year. Marie worked in a children's kitchen at the camp, while her husband cleaned bathrooms and hallways. During their stay at the DP camp, the Flosmans changed their plans to move to France and began to think of themselves as immigrants. At first, they requested to immigrate to Australia. However, when they learned that the DP camp would be closed and its inhabitants forcibly absorbed into the postwar West German economy, the Flosmans applied to immigrate to Canada. They declared their vocation as agriculturalists in order to meet existing Canadian immigration regulations, which permitted entry to individuals with agricultural backgrounds and the financial means to maintain themselves. In turn, immigration officials classified them as a "farm family" and permitted them to resettle permanently in Canada. With a successful application, the family changed their plans, switching an émigré identity for an immigrant badge.

When the Flosmans arrived in Canada in 1950, they found employment and accommodation on a farm near London, Ontario. Soon after, however, the farm was sold, and the Flosmans were forced to relocate and find employment elsewhere. In Chatham, Marie found work in a kitchen, while her husband was employed as a farm labourer for sixty-five cents per hour. The Czech couple's eldest son, Jiří, was employed in a Toronto hotel earning twenty dollars per week to help support the family. Within the same year of resettling on a farm near Chatham, the family had to move again when that farm was sold. They decided to relocate to a farm near Burlington, where Marie picked fruits and vegetables, while František worked as an office assistant at a Czech Canadian construction company for one dollar per hour. Despite this moving about, the Flosmans found their way into the Canadian Czech community. Lacking a knowledge of English, they formed connections with other Czechs and Eastern Europeans. They relied on the local branch of the CNA, the "Czechoslovak colony," and Marie's co-workers, established interwar immigrant farm labourers and their families, many of whom had initially worked in western Canada prior to moving east. These ethnic ties were certainly bolstered by the fact that the family received no financial assistance from the Canadian government in finding accommodation or employment.[1]

The Flosmans were typical of the approximately 55,000 to 80,000 individuals who fled from Czechoslovakia to the West in the first two years after the Communists seized power. The Communist Party government press referred to them as the *utíkali,* or those who "ran away."[2] In Canada, the CNA was instrumental in establishing the Canadian Fund for Czechoslovak Refugees (CFCR), whose mandate was to assist displaced persons and political refugees from Czechoslovakia with obtaining employment and housing and facilitating their settlement and integration into society. Many of the CNA's members also played active roles in Toronto's Masaryk Hall and continued to provide short-term financial assistance to newcomers and signed affidavits for prospective DPs and—after February 1948—refugees to enter Canada on one-year farm labour contracts.[3]

Refugees who left Czechoslovakia in the wake of the Communist Party takeover—including individuals from DP camps in Allied-occupied Austria and Germany, and Italy—found the pre-existing Canadian Czechoslovak community sympathetic to their plight. These political refugees became commonly referred to as "1948ers" or simply "48ers," for their emigration was ultimately tied to the Communists' takeover of power. Many of these anti-communist refugees had been members of pro-democracy political parties in Czechoslovakia, and once in Canada they joined Czechoslovak institutions such as the CNA and MH seeking to focus their agendas on humanitarianism and the liberation of their homeland from communism. These individuals began to represent Czechs and a small group of Slovaks as their legitimate "Czechoslovak" constituents.

Still, their agenda was opposed by a minority of conservative and nationalist Czechs and by the nationalist Slovak community.[4] Meanwhile, older members of the Czechoslovak community, informally referred to as "oldtimers" or "old-fashioned," emphasized domestic issues, including Canadian citizenship, English- and French-language instruction, and cultivation of ethnic heritage. So, though established members of the Czechoslovak community were sympathetic to the situation of the newcomers, the conflicting agendas within the community ultimately led to intergenerational and ideological differences among its members.[5] The recently arrived Czech refugees found in this conflict a space in which to defend their anti-communist beliefs, anti-Soviet sentiments, and Western democratic values. These refugees used ethnocultural institutions to position themselves as community representatives to public and private gatekeepers and demonstrate their political commitment to the conservative Cold War consensus in Canada.

The events of February 1948 and their consequences for the Czech newcomers were significant. The 1948ers consisted primarily of pro-democracy and anti-communist politicians, diplomats, intellectuals, clergy, professionals, workers, and students whose reasons for leaving their homeland were not homogeneous. Karol Stark, a Bata worker who had fled Czechoslovakia prior to the German occupation, recalled that the 1948ers came to Canada with a higher level of education than that of previous waves of immigrants from Czechoslovakia.[6] Although some individuals fled the possibility of torture and imprisonment, and a lack of social mobility, others chose to leave out of a sense of adventure and opportunity, no matter their different professions or levels of education.[7]

Refugees fleeing the country on the heels of the Communists' takeover were left in utter dismay by the turn of events. Upon being told that Edvard Beneš had officially installed the Communist Party government, Sudeten German refugees Wenzel Kuttig and his wife were shocked and believed that their country was ruined. The Kuttigs arrived at Dorval Airport in Montreal as part of a group of eighty-five immigrants from London and were en route to their son's farm in British Columbia. The cigarettes and beverages handed to them and other immigrants by airport officials in an attempt to ease their arrival in Canada did little to alleviate their fears. Events in Czechoslovakia left the couple skeptical when airport officials informed them that a peaceful and quiet life was available in Canada.[8]

Czechoslovak Diplomats Resign Their Posts

In Canada, the political events in Czechoslovakia were followed by a spate of resignations of Czechoslovak representatives. In Ottawa, František Němec resigned his diplomatic post in early March 1948, declaring that he was an ardent anti-communist who subscribed to the freedoms of speech, worship, and press.[9] Following in the footsteps of the Czechoslovak minister, four other embassy officials resigned from their diplomatic posts to coincide with the resignation of the Czechoslovak ambassador to Washington.[10] Prague's consuls in Toronto (Karel Buzek) and Winnipeg (Maitland B. Steinkopf) later followed Němec's lead and also resigned their diplomatic posts. Canadian officials could only conclude that Němec had acted in his own best interest rather than waiting for his recall to Prague and allowed him and his wife to remain in Canada as Czechoslovak citizens. Undersecretary of State for External Affairs Lester Pearson went so far during a press conference as to indicate that Němec would "be considered in the same way as we would consider a Czech applying for immigration visas from Czechoslovakia."[11] Indicating the closeness of the relationship between Canadian authorities and Němec, the Czech diplomat later telephoned Prime Minister Louis St. Laurent, who personally took up his case in cabinet.[12]

Unlike Němec, Consul General Josef Kotrlý in Montreal was more direct in his assessment of Czechoslovakia, and he resigned in protest over communist and dictatorial politics there. In his communication with the Canadian press, Kotrlý claimed that during the Second World War he had fought in the underground against Nazi tyranny, and now he saw another enemy in Communist Party oppression. Furthermore, without financial support from anyone, Kotrlý claimed that he and his staff were poor and obligated to work in order to maintain themselves and their families. It was his hope that they would all be permitted to stay in Canada.[13]

Despite the Communists' seizure of power, the Canadian government maintained the status quo in its relations with Czechoslovakia.[14] With legations in other Soviet Bloc capitals, Canadian officials viewed their diplomatic missions in Eastern Europe as official "listening posts" able to relay vital information back to Ottawa.[15] As a result, the Canadian government continued to monitor the situation in Czechoslovakia.

Illegal Emigrants or Political Refugees?

Matters would become difficult for anyone seeking to leave Czechoslovakia. After entrenching one-party rule in the country, the Communist Party authorities used propaganda politically to humiliate and disclaim individuals who had recently left or were in the midst of fleeing the oppressive regime. The party produced a new class of criminal disloyal to the state: the illegal emigrant, "an individual who left the country without permission."[16] Communist officials refused to define those who fled in the aftermath of February 1948 as "exiles" because doing so would have implied that they had left their homeland for political reasons, such as having been expelled for democratic leanings. Conversely, "émigrés" left their country in order to improve their socio-economic positions.[17] Family members left behind were blacklisted by the communist regime for their ties to "enemies of the state" and "criminals" and forced to live with their relatives. Children were denied access to university studies because of their bourgeois or democratic family backgrounds and only later were permitted to learn a trade.[18]

Canada responded to this unpredictable situation in the spring of 1948, with cabinet approving a proposal to provide unofficial assistance to anti-communist and pro-democracy refugees from Czechoslovakia. In May, the Canadian government became aware that over 10,000 individuals had crossed Czechoslovakia's border into the American and British Zones of Occupied Germany. Close to 10,000 of these predominantly Czech political refugees were temporarily settled in the American Zone, followed by another 300 refugees in the British Zone. About thirty Czech refugees made their way into Allied-occupied Austria. The government viewed the resettlement of these refugees in Canada as advantageous since this movement of individuals "would bring to our shores a considerable number of people who share our ideals and who, over the years, would contribute richly to our national life."[19] Canadian representatives in Europe viewed the Czech refugees as the "cream of the crop."[20]

Under the direction of the International Refugee Organization, Czech refugees were registered in receiving camps and given shelter, food, and financial support before being permanently resettled in the West. The IRO defined individuals who fled Czechoslovakia between 1 February 1948 and 1 October 1950 as political refugees.[21] In the American Zone of Occupied Germany, 3,057 refugees were situated in six permanent camps under the jurisdiction of the United States Army: Dieburg, near Dammstadt (385); Burg, near Giessen

(447); Wegscheid, near Bad Orb (380); Wasseralfingen, near Aalen (460); Unterjettingen, near Boblingen (583); and Schwabach, near Nuremberg (802). In these camps were refugees with various professional occupations, while children constituted 12 percent of the entire refugee population. Canadian officials also discovered that approximately 3,000 Czech refugees were living outside the camps, for whom there were no registration records. Czech refugees continued to arrive in West Germany at a daily rate of forty individuals. It was unclear to Canadian immigration officials whether the new arrivals resided in the refugee camps or elsewhere.[22]

At this stage, Czech Canadian industrialist Tomáš Baťa, who had advocated on behalf of Czech immigrants to Canada before the war, once again engaged with Canadian officials, seeking support for his compatriots. In a meeting held in June 1948, he informed them of his recent trip to Europe, estimating that there were approximately 500 to 700 desirable immigrants among the refugees from Czechoslovakia in Allied-occupied Germany. Since Order-in-Council P.C. 1931-695 restricted immigration during the Great Depression to individuals with agricultural backgrounds and sufficient capital to maintain themselves, Baťa made the case that a majority of the individuals had previous agricultural experience and should be admitted into Canada. However, some of the refugees held occupations as entrepreneurs, engineers, chemists, and draughtsmen, and a few were artisans. But, noting that not all applicants were who they claimed to be ("among the refugees are those who are deserting their wives and families, some have made off with the cash box and there are undoubtedly some who have been placed by the Communists"), Baťa implored Canadian officials to give careful attention to refugee selection and screening.[23] Canadian officials who acknowledged that many of the Czech refugees were not agriculturalists, but of the "professional and clerical type [and] therefore [a] low percentage would qualify for existing group movements" to Canada, accepted the refugees nevertheless.[24]

St. Laurent remained concerned that the Americans would attempt to resettle the most sought-after individuals within this wave of refugees, thereby leaving Canadian officials with a less desirable group to assess for possible resettlement in Canada. Demonstrating his sympathy for the plight of the refugees, St. Laurent declared that the Czechs "who have fled from the Communist dictatorship in Czechoslovakia . . . are people who have demonstrated that they are free men and are on our side of the line in the fight against Communism."[25]

The Canadian government continued to stall in its reception of refugees from Czechoslovakia as it awaited a report from Canadian immigration officers in Europe; preliminary reports noted that the health of the refugees appeared to be good and that many were interested in settling in Canada.[26] Furthermore, the refugees were predominantly white-collar workers, trade unionists, civil servants, teachers, and professionals, and they shared a common characteristic: they had chosen to flee their homeland for uncertainty and privation rather than submit to communist oppression. The Canadian Immigration Mission considered these refugees to be sturdy individuals.[27]

In the years following the February 1948 Communist Party takeover, nearly 20,000 refugees from Czechoslovakia settled in the United States and a few thousand in Canada. Among this group of political refugees were pro-democracy social and political elites, including former party leaders, members of parliament, clergy, intellectuals, and military officers.[28] North America, in particular the United States, was seen as the final destination for many of the exiles, who sought official recognition and financial support for their struggle to liberate Czechoslovakia from Communist Party rule.[29]

The Community Welcomes the Newcomers

At the same time, the American government solicited displaced democratic exiles for information on the Communist Bloc and sought "auxiliaries" for its countless intelligence activities. However, not all immigrants were willing to participate in the Americans' anti-communist agenda. As a right-wing member of parliament who witnessed the early purges of the democratic political class, Jiří Škvor believed at first that Communist Party rule would eventually succumb to the strong democratic tradition in Czechoslovakia. However, when it became clear that the Communists were solidifying their grip on the country, he decided to leave his wife and young son and flee across the border into the American Zone, where he eventually obtained political asylum. His initial feeling of relief at having found safety was later replaced with depression as thoughts of his family and homeland began to consume him; he realized that, as a former democratic parliamentarian, he would have received better treatment at "Alaska House," an old nursery on the outskirts of Frankfurt where many prominent democratic figures from Czechoslovakia were housed by the United States.[30] Nonetheless, Škvor chose to immigrate to Canada, which he preferred over the United States, where he would have been pressured into joining the Czechoslovak democratic resistance. Once in Canada, the Czech political refugee signed a labour contract and immediately departed for Medicine Hat, Alberta, where he became a cowboy, earning one dollar per day. After his initial labour contract expired, Škvor moved to

Montreal, where he later became a professor of Slavic languages and literature at the Université de Montréal.[31]

Many Czech refugees found Canada more accessible than the United States. From its headquarters in Karlsruhe, the Canadian Immigration Mission had dispatched four teams to Germany and another two teams to Austria.[32] As these immigration and labour teams travelled across the DP camps of Europe to assess and select prospective immigrants, many Czech refugees were permitted entry into Canada based upon their skills and abilities: university education, high level of technical training, and willingness to sign one-year farm labour agreements. The refugees were also required to submit to a physical exam that included sit-ups and a distance run.[33]

From 1948 to 1949, 3,984 newcomers to Canada identified their nationality as Czechoslovakian. Similarly, 3,626 individuals claimed Czech as their racial origin. Meanwhile, 4,713 gave Czechoslovakia as their last country of residence.[34] Their levels of education and skill notwithstanding, they were largely forced to accept unskilled and menial jobs and, in some cases, to sign agricultural labour contracts for a term of one or two years—as in the interwar years, Canada continued to seek immigrants for agricultural work.[35] However, many of these 1948ers arrived in Canada without the necessary agricultural skills for their manual labour contracts. Understandably, a significant portion of them later moved to cities in the hope of finding other types of employment and receiving assistance from the local CNA branch and Czechoslovak community.[36]

Hamilton, with its steel plants, was one such urban centre, and newly arrived Czechs found their first accommodations as boarders in the homes of European immigrants who had settled in Canada prior to 1939. The Lanc family, for instance, who had been in North America since the 1900s, opened their home to newly arrived Czech, Polish, Romanian, Slovak, and Ukrainian refugees and helped many of the newcomers to find work in the local factories and steel plants. Another oldtimer who helped was Karol Stark, who had fled Zlín, Czechoslovakia, prior to the German invasion of the Czech Lands in March 1939. He settled with the Bata Shoe Company in Batawa before moving to Kitchener, where he was able to save his earnings and acquire a mortgage for a six-room home for his family. As chair of the local CNA branch from 1948 to 1954, Stark travelled frequently to Toronto and Hamilton.

Local branches throughout the country were instrumental in promoting Czechoslovak culture, with activities that included regularly scheduled dance and theatre events, classes for language retention, and book publication in the

Czech and Slovak languages. The CNA was well represented in Hamilton, with up to 100 individuals regularly attending branch meetings. Although many of the existing CNA members were recent immigrants themselves and could not afford financially to assist other newcomers from Czechoslovakia, prewar immigrants such as Stark provided many newly arrived refugees with assistance in finding accommodation and employment.[37]

Two such refugees were František Braun and his wife, who arrived in Canada in 1949 with only $300 and some clothing. With the help of a Czech Canadian farmer from southern Ontario, who sponsored them as contract farm labourers, the Brauns arrived in Hamilton unsure of what their new lives would bring and torn between hope for the future and desire to return home. Overall, though, the couple's first impression of Canada was that it was a place of happiness. During the Second World War, Braun had fought for the Czechoslovak forces and believed in defending democratic values. After deciding to settle in Hamilton, without speaking a word of English, he acquired employment as a labourer working seven days a week, while his wife began working in a chocolate factory. The couple were able to bring home fifty-one dollars per week in wages. On Sundays, Braun picked fruit to make another three to four dollars. The couple believed that their early struggles in a new land were reasonable since they still had their freedom. Braun recalled that, "if you were honest and you did the work, then people treated you well."[38] He noted that Canadian society did not understand the hardships of newcomers. According to him, the refugee experience was difficult because Canadians did not recognize that newcomers like him and his wife were helping to build the country. Over time, the Brauns worked hard, saved their earnings, and eventually sold their business to their son.[39]

The Canadian Fund for Czechoslovak Refugees

While the Brauns felt fortunate to have permanently resettled in Canada, their fellow compatriots back home struggled to acquire the necessary documentation in order to leave their country, now under a communist regime. Occasionally, they were required to pay 50,000 Czechoslovak crowns, or $1,000 Canadian, to acquire legal documentation permitting them to leave Czechoslovakia. In other cases, R.M. Macdonnell, Canadian chargé d'affaires, indicated to Ottawa, visa applicants "merely hint[ed] at this type of corruption."[40] From January to April 1948, the Canadian legation in Prague issued only 326 immigration visas and twenty-seven visitor visas.[41] In August 1948, Macdonnell informed Ottawa that the Czechoslovak government continued to permit emigration to Canada without any recourse, but legal documentation proved to be too costly for most citizens. Consequently, only those individuals who could afford to pay corrupt officials for travel documentation were able to leave. In many instances, these individuals were forced to settle in refugee camps in Allied-occupied Austria and Germany, and Italy.[42]

Department of External Affairs officials, considering the plight of anti-communist refugees from Czechoslovakia as early as March 1948, now took steps to form an organization. It would be an unofficial group of humanitarians supported by prominent refugees who had already settled in Canada, including the last democratic Czechoslovak ambassador to Canada, František Němec. But Assistant Undersecretary of State for External Affairs Escott Reid thought that other high-profile Canadians should join, arguing that "the communists and fellow-travelers did a magnificent job in the thirties in organizing public sympathy and support for anti-fascist refugees. If liberalism is to demonstrate that it is a dynamic creed, liberals should show at least the same degree of enthusiasm and ability on behalf of democratic anti-communists."[43] A month later an application for incorporation of the Canadian Fund for Czechoslovak Refugees was sent to Louis St. Laurent by a group of petitioners led by CNA National Secretary Karel Buzek, Senator Cairine Wilson, and Bernard Keble Sandwell, editor-in-chief of *Saturday Night* magazine. The newly established fund's objectives were to assist displaced persons and refugees of "Czecho-Slovak origin" legally admitted into Canada to obtain employment and housing and to facilitate their settlement and integration into Canadian society. The fund also sought to aid newcomers who required financial assistance. The CFCR was also instrumental in locating relatives and friends of the newcomers in the hope that reunification would further help the refugees in resettling in Canada. But the fund was more than a humanitarian impulse, for it carried a political agenda that attempted to "assist with information and educational materials so that the democratic heritage of such persons can be combined and integrated with that of Canada at the earliest possible date."[44] Upon its establishment, the CFCR indicated to government officials its desire to promote the democratic values of individuals who had fled the Communists' takeover after February 1948. The fund solicited financial contributions, including subscriptions, donations, and money to procure food, clothing, blankets, and medicine for the health and well-being of individuals in Austrian, German, and Italian DP camps.[45]

As members of the Canadian Czechoslovak community sent funds and relief to refugee camps in Europe, refugees from Czechoslovakia continued to arrive on Canadian shores. On 23 April 1949, under the guidance of IRO Escort Officer Arne Hansen and Captain MacMillan, the turbine steamer USAT *General Leroy Eltinge* carrying 841 refugees arrived at Pier 21 in Halifax. The ship supported the International Refugee Program by transporting refugees from Bremerhaven, Germany, to Canada. Among the newly arrived group were 113 refugees from Czechoslovakia. These individuals were recruited as contract labourers on Canadian farms.[46] In their ten days aboard the *General LeRoy Eltinge,* the refugees published a newsletter, *The Voice of New-Canadians,* declaring that Communist Party authorities had maligned the refugees. They had claimed that the "capitalist pirate, Captain MacMillan, supported by the Norwegian bandit Arne Hansen, captured 841 fascist refugees in Bremerhaven so that instead of repatriating them to their homeland, where under communism there was better living and happiness, directed the ship to Halifax in Canada."[47] There was no doubt in the minds of the passengers that they were no longer welcome in Czechoslovakia. Less than a week after the arrival of the refugees, officials in Ottawa approved incorporation of the CFCR without any security objections. Canadian officials viewed the new organization as semi-official since Senator Cairine Wilson was a director.[48]

Along with the newly established refugee fund, the CNA continued to aid the settlement of refugees from Czechoslovakia. In one case, it supported Mike Nikodem of Smithville, Ontario, who applied to the Canadian Pacific Railway's Department of Colonization seeking to relocate Jozef Brunovský and his family to Canada. Nikodem's application was initially denied on political grounds because Brunovský had fought for the Slovak state, part of the Axis coalition during the Second World War.[49] Because of a lack of English-language skills, Nikodem solicited the assistance of CNA National Secretary Karel Buzek. He in turn informed the Immigration Branch that Brunovský had in fact been drafted into the wartime Slovak Army, later deserting to join the partisan movement and take part in the 1944 Slovak National Uprising against the Germans. After receiving a letter from A.H. Creighton, district superintendent of colonization for the Canadian Pacific Railway, Buzek informed Nikodem that a "provision existed that granted admission to persons in this class where it can be established that such service was under compulsion."[50] Buzek advised Nikodem that definitive evidence be submitted to the immigration authorities in order for the decision to be reversed.[51]

As Canadian Czechoslovak organizations concentrated their efforts on family reunification and refugee resettlement, officials in Ottawa were charged with selecting refugees who would become Canadian citizens and make positive contributions to the Canadian economy. Successive Liberal governments under Prime Ministers Mackenzie King and St. Laurent viewed the movement of Europe's DPs and anti-communist refugees to Canada as a significant contribution to the postwar development of the country. Subsequently, Ottawa implemented an Immigration-Labour Committee to which representatives from the Departments of Mines and Resources, Labour, External Affairs, and National Health and Welfare were appointed. This committee assessed the necessary labour requirements and defined what type of refugee should be resettled in the country. Canadian industry was to guarantee that it could offer one-year labour contracts to prospective DPs, ensuring that the standard wage for this type of labour was respected, and provide accommodation upon the newcomer's arrival.[52]

With both the CNA and the new Czechoslovak-funded resettlement activities gaining wider public attention, Canadian Czechs began to correspond with Karel Buzek regarding the feasibility of admitting close relatives and friends into Canada. Buzek informed his compatriots that they would need to fill out forms for prospective immigrants to enter Canada as farm labourers with assured farm employment. The CNA thus worked to arrange signed affidavits from farmers who sought contract labourers. It also worked closely with former Czechoslovak Ambassador Němec in the hope that his political contacts could help to accelerate the process of admitting successful political refugees.[53] While Němec focused his efforts on the resettlement of anti-communist refugees from Czechoslovakia, another prominent member of the Czechoslovak community in Canada turned his attention toward promoting democratic values among fellow compatriots.

The Pro-Democracy Ethnic Press

On 1 June 1949, a Czech-language newspaper titled *Čas* (The Time) published its first issue in Trenton, Ontario. The newly established paper hoped to serve the pro-democracy and anti-communist Czechoslovak community in Canada. Editor Jan Dočkálek, having served with the Czechoslovak forces overseas for three years, wrote that he had come to Canada to publish a newspaper for fellow pro-democracy refugees. He was especially grateful that the influential émigré organization Council of Free Czechoslovakia (CFC), based in Washington, had agreed that a pro-democracy newspaper was necessary in Canada.[54] Further support came from the mayor of Trenton, Ken J. Couch, who claimed in the inaugural issue that a thriving Czechoslovak community existed in his city. The mayor expected that the members of the community would become good Canadians and believed that the culture and skills that these new Canadians retained from their old country would help them to integrate into the local community. Couch asserted that *Čas* would aid these individuals and Trenton in better understanding each other.[55] The staunchly pro-democracy newspaper became the means by which Dočkálek could demonstrate his loyalty to Canada and seek social and cultural citizenship within an anti-communist Cold War consensus that supported his efforts.

Anti-communist Czechs continued to promote their democratic ideals and protest against communist oppression in their homeland. In June 1949, the CNA held its seventh congress and adopted a resolution barring individuals from membership in the organization if they supported the communist movement, acted on behalf of the Czechoslovak government, or maintained relations with Prague. Many of the delegates in attendance were recently arrived refugees who had joined the congress's call on the United Nations to use its powers to establish free democratic elections in Czechoslovakia under its supervision.[56] A month later the organization closed its Montreal branch for alleged activities sympathetic to the communist cause. Then, in its 27 July 1949 issue, *Čas* complained that communist sympathizers in the Montreal branch refused to vote for anti-communist measures, did not support recently arrived refugees, and maintained relations with Czechoslovak government representatives. Consequently, the paper noted, these individuals were publishing communist propaganda in compatriot Czechoslovak papers to the detriment of the community.[57]

As an anti-communist ethnic newspaper, *Čas* called on the Czechoslovak community in Canada to support their compatriots fleeing the communist regime. The pro-democracy weekly argued that many of these refugees were skilled agriculturalists who could only be an asset to Canada. Community members were subsequently asked to follow the example of other ethnic groups and aid the resettlement of Czech refugees by providing them with labour contracts. *Čas* argued that such support would constitute a patriotic duty on behalf of Canadians.[58]

DP Students Arrive

One group of refugees from Czechoslovakia who did not require labour contracts to enter Canada were students. They soon arrived to resume education at universities and colleges across the country. In late August 1949, twenty-four university students from across Europe left Naples, Italy, and boarded SS *Charlton Sovereign* and USAT *General Stuart Heintzelman* as part of a group of

302 DPs classified as Catholic orphans, close relatives, students, and minors. These students were permitted to enter Canada on one-year International Students' Service Scholarships to institutions across the country. After an eleven-day transatlantic journey, the students arrived at Pier 21 in Halifax and spent three days in the city. On 9 November, they arrived by train in Montreal, where they were greeted by the local press. Five students were to remain in Montreal to attend McGill University, Université de Montréal, and Macdonald College. The remaining nineteen DPs were to attend other schools. Although immigration regulations required adults to commit to one-year labour contracts, the university students were the first group of refugees to have this requirement waived. They were "good" refugees: three of the twenty-four students had been incarcerated as political prisoners in Czechoslovakia. As promising students, Miroslav Dosedĕl and Václav Opřátko, for example, were to study natural sciences and chemical engineering, both at the Université de Montréal. Nicholas Thuroczy, an ethnic Hungarian of Czechoslovak origin, was to study agronomy at Macdonald College.[59] During the Cold War, Canadian immigration authorities considered anti-communist refugee students desirable immigrants and admitted them into the country.

Diplomacy in "Transcurtainia"

Aiding the continued flow of Czech refugees was a decision by officials from the DEA to maintain Canadian diplomatic missions in Prague and Warsaw. In a confidential memorandum, officials within the European Division of the DEA argued that consular work pertaining to immigration accounted for the majority of the legations' workload, so replacing the mission in Prague with a consulate might make sense. Yet doing so would not reduce costs and could seriously reduce its influence among diplomats and Communist Party authorities. Officials in Ottawa warned that the Prague and Warsaw offices could lose their diplomatic "protection, rations, customs and other privileges . . . necessary to maintain any sort of tolerable living in 'Transcurtainia.'"[60] Canada's legations in Prague and Warsaw continued to serve as diplomatic "listening posts" and provide consular services.

Their plan, however, came with certain difficulties when, in January 1950, DEA officials learned that the Communists in Prague were implementing increasingly hostile tactics against Western government representatives. In the case of the Canadian legation, locally engaged staff were arrested on suspicion of espionage or prevented from working. Unsubstantiated charges of spying and consorting with anti-communist elements were filed against two Canadian non-commissioned officers, Sergeant Reginald Danko and Corporal J.G. Vanier.[61] In order to protect Canadian representatives, Ottawa arranged with the chief of the air staff for the return of Danko and Vanier to Canada and then retaliated by expelling bookkeeper Richard Bergmann and assistant clerk Hugo Bohounak, two members of the Czechoslovak legation in Ottawa, as *personae non gratae*.[62]

Canadian diplomats stationed in Eastern Europe informed Ottawa of evidence that a "concerted drive, probably part of a general Russian strategy," was under way to interfere in the activities of Western diplomatic missions.[63] The strategy effectively sought the arrest and false accusation of Western diplomatic personnel in order for local Communist Party authorities to blacken their reputations. As a result, Western diplomats, including Canadian representatives stationed in Prague, worked in "a growing atmosphere of fear, suspicion, frustration, and isolation in which the westerner simply has no place. He becomes in short an enemy alien."[64] Canadian representatives in Prague informed DEA officials in Ottawa that legations in Eastern Europe should remain open since they were important in safeguarding Canadian legal and financial interests and the immigration of relatives of Canadian citizens.[65]

Canadian Czechoslovak leaders were increasingly frustrated by the tactics used by Communist Party authorities. Czechoslovak citizens seeking to obtain passports in order to travel abroad had to collect far more documents than were required by the Canadian legation for an entry visa to be granted. Three types of passport were attainable from the communist regime: diplomatic, business relations, and "emigration" (*vystěhovalecství*).[66] After February 1948, the acquisition of a valid passport for travel abroad became increasingly hard to attain. Excluding Communist Party officials, passports were rarely granted to the average family in Czechoslovakia in order to prevent emigration.[67] In his correspondence with officials in Ottawa, Canadian Chargé d'Affaires in Prague John Arnold Irwin mentioned the case of a fourteen-year-old orphan, Anna Sukelová. Since September 1948, she had attempted to obtain a passport from the Communists in order to be reunited with her uncle in Canada. In two years, Sukelová had collected twenty-two official documents from various Communist Party government offices and agencies. Once she had received a "promise of visa" from Canadian officials, the government in Prague summarily refused her application for a passport.[68] Initially, individuals were required to submit, along with their passport application, an identity card, proof of citizenship, a police registration card, and a marriage certificate, if applicable.[69]

Czech refugees reported that Communist Party officials intentionally made emigration from Czechoslovakia as difficult as possible and not only in terms of paperwork. Various government offices and ministries dictated the number of personal effects that each individual was permitted to take. The Valentin family, for instance, who had left Austria and resettled in Žilina, Czechoslovakia, shortly after the Second World War, were informed that they would be permitted to take only three pairs of underwear and two shirts per family member.[70] In the face of these obstacles, legal emigration from Czechoslovakia to Canada slowed drastically by March 1949, when only sixty-eight visas were issued to Czechoslovak citizens, and a year later only ten visas were issued.[71] Irwin noted that the voluminous correspondence between ordinary citizens and the Canadian legation had begun to decrease steadily as the Communist Party authorities clamped down on official emigration.

Canada Vets the Immigrants

Czech refugees faced not only hurdles in leaving their homeland but also obstacles in entering Canada. In a memorandum entitled "Czechoslovak Immigration," Canadian immigration officials were hesitant to support a plan by the Washington-based Council of Free Czechoslovakia to vet the backgrounds and desirability of prospective immigrants submitted to Canadian officials by the council.[72] Former Czechoslovak Ambassador to Canada František Němec informed immigration officials that the council was offering the services of former Czechoslovak Brigadier General František Dastich to aid immigration officers in vetting prospective immigrants. Immigration bureaucrats noted that it was becoming increasingly difficult for Canadian security officers to obtain reliable security information on refugees from Czechoslovakia. Officials in Ottawa ultimately refused Němec's request to send a representative to assist in the selection of Czech refugees for immigration. Conversely, Canadian officials believed in steering suitable and desirable immigrants to Canadian visa offices in Germany.[73]

To this end, the Immigration Branch worked with the Royal Canadian Mounted Police to implement an immigrant security vetting process known as Stage B. This additional security step entailed an interview with a visa officer and a medical test in Europe. In 1948, the RCMP stationed Stage B officials across Europe hoping to keep Communist Party agents and their sympathizers from entering Canada. By 1950, 20 percent of immigrants whose entry into Canada was rejected because of a suspicion of communist sympathies appealed to the minister of citizenship and immigration. Of those who appealed, only 20 percent were eventually permitted entry into Canada. As a result, 96 percent of individuals labelled as security risks by immigration officials and RCMP officers never entered Canada.[74]

Fears of Communist Infiltration

During this period, Canadian military intelligence indicated that the threat of a Soviet-led attack on the West remained probable. In its assessment of possible forms and scales of offensive operations against Canada, the Department of National Defence indicated ten situations in which the Soviet Bloc could attack Canada. The first scenario considered subversive activities, from anti-war propaganda to strikes and acts of sabotage, as the most likely threats.[75] At the same time, though, the Joint Intelligence Bureau in Ottawa concluded that, because Czechoslovakia imported raw materials from the West, it remained a viable partner in Eastern Europe, and any attack would hurt the country. As the bureau noted, there was "ample evidence to show that Soviet ideology on the one hand and the cold logic of industrial necessity on the other may rapidly become conflicting elements in the formation of future policy."[76] Clearly, if Prague severed its ties with the West, then Czechoslovakia's standard of living would be diminished.[77] Canadian intelligence authorities were aware that Prague was suffering from a deficiency in manpower with the expulsion of the Sudeten German and Hungarian minorities. As a result, the agricultural, mining, and technological industries were in decline, and Prague began a campaign to attract Czechs living abroad to return to their native country.[78] Further, Prague's Ministry of the Interior sent Army Security Intelligence Office and Ministry of National Defence agents overseas in a concerted effort to blackmail Czech refugees in Canada to return home.[79]

Czech migrants would be assisted when, in the summer of 1951, the United Nations Conference of Plenipotentiaries on the Status of Refugees and Stateless Persons adopted the Convention Relating to the Status of Refugees, guaranteeing asylum as an international human right. The convention defined the term "refugee" to be applied to DPs who fled their countries because of a genuine fear of persecution. Since the term "displaced person" remained open to interpretation, the convention established that a refugee was any individual who, "as a result of events occurring before 1 January 1951 and owing to well-founded fear of being persecuted for reasons of race, religion, nationality, membership of a particular social group or political opinion, is outside the country of his nationality and is unable or, owing to such fear, unwilling to avail himself of the protection of that country; or who, not having a nationality and being outside the country of his former habitual residence as a result of such events, is unable or, owing to such fear, unwilling to return to it."[80]

It was a wide definition, however, and Canadian immigration authorities feared the infiltration of Communist Party agents, and the RCMP feared that the convention would hinder Ottawa's ability to deport persons considered security threats. Hence, the Canadian government did not become a signatory to the convention. Instead, Canada used the convention merely as a framework for the admission or denial of entry of individuals and continued to use an ad hoc approach whereby orders-in-council were used to grant refugees' entry into Canada.[81] Therefore, even with the establishment of the convention, Czech refugees in Austria, West Germany, and Italy remained at the mercy of Canadian immigration officials and the RCMP, who enforced security screening over the refugees' right to asylum.

Furthermore, Canadian Czechoslovak organizations continued to receive grievances from refugees who made it into Canada. In May 1951, President of Masaryk Hall Gustav Přístupa wrote to the Department of Labour insisting that recently arrived Czech refugees were claiming that they were being insufficiently fed at the government hostel at Ajax, Ontario, and remained hungry after mealtimes. The main complaint of the newcomers was that food servings were too small. Přístupa recommended that, instead of allotting each refugee two slices of bread, a loaf could be left on the table for everyone to eat according to his or her appetite. The MH president noted that, in a country such as Canada, no individual should go hungry, especially when it came to daily food such as bread.[82] The Department of Labour replied that it was surprised by the letter and claimed that Ottawa had operated the hostel for over four years without any complaint. The department noted that its official policy guaranteed that meals served to newcomers be of good quality and quantity.[83] No doubt it was of little comfort that, if refugees' physical needs were inadequately tended to, their spiritual needs were not neglected. Newly arrived refugees in Ajax, and elsewhere in greater Toronto, were later welcomed by Reverend Jaroslav Zeman and a group of parishioners from the Czechoslovak Baptist Board and each given two dollars, a Czech-language Bible, and other religious literature.[84] For many Czech refugees, the path of migration involving admission to and resettlement in Canada remained complicated. Whereas some refugees struggled to secure entry into Canada, others were welcomed with enthusiasm.

Freedom Fighters

Although many Czech refugees found their initial experience in Canada disappointing, other newcomers were heroically welcomed as anti-communist freedom fighters. The bold escape of thirty-two people on 11 September 1951 certainly underscored the desperation of those wanting to flee to the West. Czech engineer František Jarda cut the brake lines of Czechoslovak state railways train 3717 departing from the town of Cheb and raced it through the border town of Aš and into Selb, West Germany. Of the train's 111 passengers, mostly students and spa patients, 79 later returned home, including several railway employees, six children, two soldiers, and a policeman unaware of the Czech engineer's plan to flee to the West. According to Jarda, he brought his wife and two children to the West because it was "no longer bearable to live in an Eastern European state. We made plans for our flight for a long time. We bought food and clothing—everything we could."[85] The American legation in Frankfurt helped to process the refugees from what the Canadian press dubbed the "Freedom Train."[86] Czech Canadian shoe production magnate Tomáš J. Baťa later cabled Jarda to inform him that he appreciated his courage, resolution, and ingenuity and offered him employment with the Bata Shoe Company.[87]

Still, though, the path to Canada was complicated. Twenty-five of the thirty-two train passengers were temporarily housed at the Ludwigsburg and Valka refugee camps in West Germany, with the other seven passengers slated to arrive in Canada at a later date.[88] The escapees housed in the refugee camps viewed prolonged stays there as dangerous, perhaps because Communist Party agents were known to infiltrate holding centres and attempt to repatriate individuals to Czechoslovakia. And, though the United States remained the preferred destination, American authorities expected the escapees to become active in propaganda activities against their communist homeland, which these refugees often had no desire to do. Canada, which made no such stipulations, thus became a more desirable destination. Canadian officials in West Germany informed the passengers that they would only be subjected to a health exam, after which they would be classified for labour contracts.

The train incident illustrated to Canadian Czechoslovak institutions—including the CNA and Masaryk Hall—the importance of helping refugees. Many more Czechs wanted to flee communist oppression in Czechoslovakia and were forced to attempt daring and life-threatening escapes. The refugees from the so-called Freedom Train not only garnered praise from and increased the morale of Czech refugees already in Canada but also fascinated a Canadian public that increasingly began to understand the efforts of these refugees against the communist regime in their homeland.

Indeed, one of the Freedom Train passengers, Karel Ruml, chose to settle in Canada because the federal government offered to accept him more quickly than other Western countries since it conferred on him the status of *dřevorubec* ("lumberjack"). When Jarda, Ruml, and some of the other Freedom Train refugees arrived in Halifax, in October 1951, they were given a hero's welcome by a throng of journalists and local citizens.[89] They were hurried onto a train departing for Toronto, where they arrived thirty-two hours later to yet another news conference. Their arrival in Canada had captured the hearts of many Canadians. Matters soon became more difficult as Canadian authorities transported some of the refugees to temporary housing in Ajax before permanently resettling them in Toronto. Many of them had difficulty facing the harsh Canadian climate and were ill equipped to handle their first Canadian winter. Moreover, their financial prospects were often dismal.

Ruml, for instance, though he had entered the country as a "lumberjack," began his career in Canada by sorting documents in the basement of an insurance company for twenty-seven dollars per week. Ruml lived in a small bedroom; breakfast and accommodation cost him twenty-five dollars per week, leaving the single Czech refugee with two dollars to spend on all other necessities. As a result, he ate plenty of porridge each morning in an attempt to stave off hunger later in the day. In the first few months, he purchased lots of bread and sardines but often remained hungry. The Czech refugee also avoided the city trams and buses by walking everywhere, all in an attempt to save money. Unprepared for the harsh Canadian winter, and with no money to purchase much-needed winter clothing, he often had to work in the cold basement with soaked shoes and sullied pants.

Even the local Czechoslovak community disappointed him. Although Czech refugees who resettled in urban centres often found friendship, cooperation, and goodwill within their local communities—in Toronto's Masaryk Hall, for instance, located in the European quarter south of Queen Street—Ruml found that intraethnic animosity prevailed. Many older members (pre-1948 arrivals) within the Czechoslovak community donated time and money to assist postwar immigrants and were aware that these newcomers had languished in European holding camps—sometimes for years. However, Ruml claimed that these earlier immigrants often did not extend their hands in friendship but remained inhospitable, largely ignoring the recently arrived newcomers.[90]

Although some Czech refugees, like Ruml, were seen by Canadian officials as desirable immigrants, they later struggled to find the same level of acceptance in the Czechoslovak community. For others, bureaucratic notions of refugee desirability often prevented them from gaining entry into Canada. In this predicament was Bohumír Říbek, a twenty-two-year-old trained toolmaker from Czechoslovakia. In March 1949, he fled his homeland for a DP camp in West Germany. From there, he applied for refugee status with the International Refugee Organization. A month later Říbek was sent a "Notification of Ineligibility" because he had been deemed "not within the mandate of the organization" because of his "insufficient proof to claim refugee status."[91] In May, the young Czech refugee wrote a letter to the IRO's Review Board outlining why he should be given status as a political refugee. In his letter, Říbek described his life in Czechoslovakia, stating that during his apprenticeship as a toolmaker he had been threatened because of his political affiliation and uncompromising anti-communist viewpoint. As a member of Edvard Beneš's National Socialist Party, he had spoken out publicly many times about communist terror, and he was later pressured to sign a Communist Party membership card or face retribution. In October 1949, the Review Board agreed with his claim regarding fear of political persecution and found him to be within its mandate. Soon after, he signed a one-year manual labour contract with the Canadian government to work as a hard-rock miner in Val-d'Or, Quebec. In October 1950, Říbek landed in Halifax aboard the *General R.M. Blatchford* to begin his new life in Canada.[92]

Other Czech refugees who could not provide proof of persecution or had difficulty finding sponsors appealed to compatriot organizations in Canada rather than directly to international organizations. They hoped that these ethnocultural institutions could guarantee their reliability as desirable refugees for resettlement in Canada.

Masaryk Hall was often inundated with requests for assistance from overseas. In one case, Czech refugee Zdeněk Střelec wrote to MH from Casablanca, Morocco. Having fled first to a DP camp in Germany, he had been accepted as an immigrant in Morocco but hoped to make Canada his new home if a democratic and independent Czechoslovakia could not be resurrected.[93] Střelec's information was later passed on to Canadian immigration officials for possible selection overseas. In another case, Antonín Sevelka, his wife, Věra, and their three sons Jiří, Michal, and Antonín Jr., contacted relatives in the United States for help in leaving their DP camp in West Germany for the West. On their behalf, a letter was sent to Masaryk Hall, which then sent

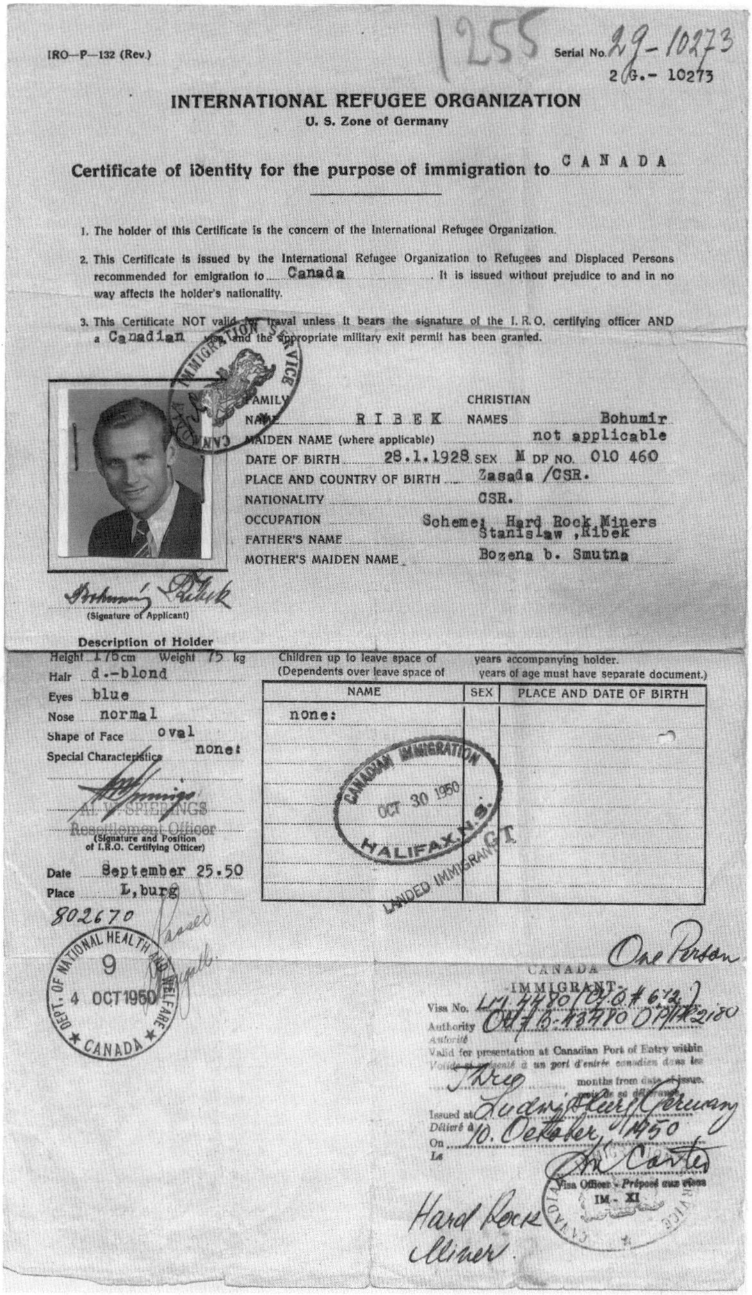

1255

IRO—P—132 (Rev.) Serial No. 29-10273
2G.- 10273

INTERNATIONAL REFUGEE ORGANIZATION
U. S. Zone of Germany

Certificate of identity for the purpose of immigration to CANADA

1. The holder of this Certificate is the concern of the International Refugee Organization.

2. This Certificate is issued by the International Refugee Organization to Refugees and Displaced Persons recommended for emigration to Canada. It is issued without prejudice to and in no way affects the holder's nationality.

3. This Certificate NOT valid for travel unless it bears the signature of the I. R. O. certifying officer AND a Canadian visa and the appropriate military exit permit has been granted.

FAMILY NAME R I B E K CHRISTIAN NAMES Bohumir
MAIDEN NAME (where applicable) not applicable
DATE OF BIRTH 28.1.1928 SEX M DP NO. 010 460
PLACE AND COUNTRY OF BIRTH Zasada /CSR.
NATIONALITY CSR.
OCCUPATION Scheme: Hard Rock Miners
FATHER'S NAME Stanislaw ,Ribek
MOTHER'S MAIDEN NAME Bozena b. Smutna

(Signature of Applicant)

Description of Holder
Height 175 cm Weight 75 kg
Hair d.-blond
Eyes blue
Nose normal
Shape of Face oval
Special Characteristics none:

AL. W. SPIERINGS
Resettlement Officer
(Signature and Position of I.R.O. Certifying Officer)

Date September 25.50
Place L,burg
802670

Children up to leave space of years accompanying holder.
(Dependents over leave space of years of age must have separate document.)

NAME	SEX	PLACE AND DATE OF BIRTH
none:		

CANADIAN IMMIGRATION OCT 30 1950 HALIFAX, N.S.
LANDED IMMIGRANT

DEPT. OF NATIONAL HEALTH AND WELFARE 9 4 OCT 1950 CANADA

CANADA IMMIGRANT One Person
Visa No. LM 4480 (CAG # 672)
Authority OH # 5-43480 DP# 2180
Autorité
Valid for presentation at Canadian Port of Entry within
Valide pour présentation à un port d'entrée canadien dans les
Three months from date of issue.
Issued at Ludwigsburg Germany
Délivré à
On 10. Oktober 1950
Le
Visa Officer - Préposé aux visas
IM - XI

Hard Rock Miner.

Figure 6. *IRO Certificate of Identity issued to Bohumír Říbek, for the purpose of immigration to Canada, 25 September 1950.*

applications for admission to the Immigration Branch. Here, too, the hall's intervention was successful. In both cases, Canadian officials informed MH that the proposed immigrants would be included on immigration lists furnished to officers overseas, where arrangements could be made for their examination. In February 1952, after having spent four years in West Germany, where their youngest son, Antonín, was born, the Sevelkas landed in Halifax aboard the MV *Anna Salén* before resettling in Toronto.[94]

Masaryk Hall also provided financial assistance to Czechs who had already been living in Canada for some time. In one case, Zdeněk Němeček of the Czechoslovak Desk at Radio Free Europe in New York City wrote a letter, in December 1951, that a fellow compatriot, Ladislav Libý, living in Chicoutimi, Quebec, had lost his vision after a chemical explosion at the ornament factory where he worked. Němeček hoped that financial assistance from MH could be secured for his medical care and reintegration into society.[95] In other circumstances, MH provided compatriots with financial loans of varying amounts, for example $500 or $1,000 with an interest rate of 6 percent payable twice per year.[96] However, given the dire situation of Czech refugees in Austrian, West German, and Italian camps, MH continued to make their resettlement a priority. By the fall of 1951, President Přístupa had personally signed 652 affidavits for overseas refugees seeking to be admitted into Canada.[97] For some Czech refugees abroad, MH was a vital source of assistance in their desired resettlement in Canada.

Emigration Standstill

By the early 1950s, Czech refugees who arrived in Canada had spent years in holding camps or on daring escape routes to the West. Making matters worse, Communist Party authorities stopped granting passports or exit visas for Canada-bound emigrants. In 1951, the Canadian legation issued only twenty-one entry visas, and in January 1952 the Ministry of Foreign Affairs in Prague effectively ended any access to official emigration. Chargé d'affaires Benjamin Rogers noted that only one entry visa was issued that year to an individual with a Czechoslovak passport for emigration to Canada.[98] Communist Party authorities even refused to grant exit permits to prospective emigrants who had close relatives in Canada. Initially, Canadian officials were led to believe that each decision to refuse an exit permit was based upon merit; however, given that passports for travel to West Germany were easily acquired, they began to suspect that Communist Party authorities were discriminating against applicants for travel to Canada.[99]

Meanwhile, Canadian officials were in the process of affirming what had been standard practice in Canadian immigration policy. The 1952 Immigration Act granted the minister of immigration far-reaching powers to set regulations that enforced the legislation. As a result of ministerial discretion, individuals and groups could now be refused entry into Canada based upon factors such as nationality, geographic origin, custom and tradition, unsuitability to climate, or inability to assimilate into Canadian society. Communist sympathizers, homosexuals, and drug addicts and traffickers were added to the prohibited classes. The act instituted appeal boards composed of federal officials who presided over deportation cases, but it also strengthened cabinet's ability to refuse entry to "undesirables."[100] It is understandable, then, how the Canadian public could view Czech refugees as staunch supporters of democratic values or as "suspicious" immigrants from behind the Iron Curtain.

Rifts within the Community

Even as some refugees from Czechoslovakia were viewed as freedom fighters, others were suspected of communist sympathies. In March 1952, the right-wing *Toronto Telegram* alleged that the Czechoslovak National Alliance had some previous association with the Labour-Progressive Party. The CNA executive vehemently denied the allegation and their connection to communism. In a letter to the newspaper, executive members, led by President Karol Stark, asserted that the CNA was strongly anti-communist. The executive went on to note that every CNA member had publicly pronounced loyalty to Canada and pledged to fight communism. After the allegations were published, the executive feared that CNA members could be wrongly associated with communist activities in Canada and deemed disloyal Canadians or even spies.[101] Canadian Czechoslovak organizations continued to fight allegations within the Canadian press that they were associated with communism.

But the threat of this association paled compared with other defamations a year later. In 1953, Toronto's Czechoslovak community became embroiled in a controversy at City Hall as Czechoslovaks and nationalist Slovaks openly contested the value of each community's commemoration of the past. In May, controversy erupted when members of the nationalist Slovak community dressed in traditional clothing placed a wreath at the Toronto City Hall cenotaph to honour the memory of First World War General Milan R. Štefánik and President of Slovakia Jozef Tiso, who held office during the Second World War. Czechs and Slovaks who supported a "Czechoslovak" orientation and were critical of the independent wartime Slovak state claimed that its leaders, including Tiso, had collaborated with Germany and been complicit in the deaths of thousands of innocent civilians. The following day the *Toronto Daily Star* published an image of the ceremony and incorrectly cited Tiso as formerly a president-martyr of Czechoslovakia.[102] The CNA publicly denounced the wreath and argued that its presence wrongly coupled Štefánik and Tiso; the association considered one as a Czechoslovak patriot and the other as a traitor. In the letter, President Stark argued that, because Tiso had been president of the Slovak Republic, he had de facto been a German collaborator. The CNA believed that it was defending the honour of those who had perished for the cause of freedom.[103]

In an attempt to counter the CNA's accusations, executives of eight Canadian Slovak organizations—the Canadian Slovak League, First Catholic Slovak Union, First Catholic Slovak Ladies' Union, Slovak Catholic Sokol, Slovak Liberation Committee, Slovak National Council Abroad, Slovak Legion, and Union of Slovak Journalists Abroad—assembled in Toronto on 16 May to craft a resolution to send to Mayor Allan Lamport. They asserted that Tiso had in fact been a de jure president because he had been elected by members of the Slovak parliament in October 1938. The executives noted the "malignancy of a small group which wishes to continue in its domination and oppression of the Slovak people."[104] They considered the CNA's allegations as "racial discrimination" and contrary to the United Nations Declaration of Human Rights.[105] In light of the cenotaph controversy and efforts to appease both groups, city officials agreed to prevent the memorial from becoming a site for transplanted European ethnic divisions in the future. Refugees who fled the 1948 Communist Party takeover of their homeland soon had to face a harsh realization about their resettlement in Canada: the interethnic tensions between Czechs—as members of a broader Czechoslovak community—and nationalist Slovaks would persist.

A Change in Focus

As communism became ever more firmly entrenched in Czechoslovakia, Czech refugees to Canada were forced to re-evaluate their position. Many 1948ers, convinced that communism would be defeated, believed that they would return to their homeland within a few years when parliamentary democracy was restored; after all, their country had a strong democratic tradition. This mindset prevented many refugees from rapidly assimilating. As Vít Wágner, a 1948er who arrived in Canada in 1951 and worked in a lumber camp in Heron Bay, Ontario, put it, if Czech refugees "had known that they would

Figure 7. *Vít Wágner, left, and an unidentified man working at the Ontario Paper Company's lumber camp, Heron Bay, Ontario, c. July 1953.*

stay permanently then they would have assimilated more rapidly."[106] In the coming years, as the communist regime in Czechoslovakia strengthened its grip on political power, the recently arrived Czech refugees learned that their stay in Canada would be permanent.

Many of the 1948ers sought to entrench their anti-communist and pro-democratic beliefs in the Czechoslovak organizations that they joined in Canada. In their encounters with previous immigrants from Czechoslovakia and Canadian-born members of the Czechoslovak community, they came up against divergent political beliefs and ideological differences, and tensions among community members were inevitable. Repulsed by instances of spying by Communist Party agents, recently arrived Czech refugees steered community organizations to adopt anti-communist stances. They even attempted to influence Canadian foreign policy to oppose Communist Czechoslovakia. Most of the Cold War refugees soon saw themselves not as exiles but as immigrants, and they turned their attention toward becoming good Canadians. This step helped to ameliorate the ideological divisions between themselves and the oldtimers. The newcomers were no longer simply anti-communist émigrés but hopeful members of Canada's middle class.

CHAPTER 4

Community Tensions and Ideological Divisions

"How an Immigrant Girl Fell in Love with Canada" garnered much attention when *Maclean's* published the story in April 1960.[1] In the article, Czech refugee Marika Robert described her experience of coming to a new country and her integration into Canadian society. Upon arriving in Montreal aboard SS *Columbia* in 1951, Marika pondered how many years it would take her to assimilate and become a part of Canada's future. She described her initial problems finding accommodation as a single woman and newcomer to Canada. In the weeks after her arrival in Canada, Marika met dozens of well-established Czech "landladies" wary of the issues that newcomers such as an unmarried woman could bring into their traditional environment. Many of these property owners with whom Marika boarded informed her that no male visitors would be permitted in her room and harassed her with questions about pet ownership, religious affiliation, and sleeping habits. Further, her landlords forbade her to cook, smoke, bathe, or stay in the room during the day. Her pathway into Canadian society would not be easy.

Indeed, many newcomers to Canada in the postwar era initially struggled to find employment and became destitute, often causing difficulties for their landlords. Marika eventually found accommodation in a house with multiple rooms, or "cells," and a communal bathroom while she looked for employment.

In the *Maclean's* article, Marika also lamented the complexity of the immigrant setting in which intraethnic dynamics heavily influenced her experience. She noted that immigrant communities and society at large could be divided between old and new immigrants, political and economic immigrants, and

Western immigrants and immigrants from behind the Iron Curtain and that each group envied the immigration experiences of the others. Although many refugees from Eastern Bloc countries continued to recognize and maintain their ethnic identities through adherence to a common nation, language, religion, history, and territory, they also became Canadians. During the Cold War, Czech refugees like Marika Robert began to self-identify with Canadian society and its culture and customs after realizing that they had acquired a new way of thinking, vocabulary, habits, tastes, and interests, all while cultivating their ethnic heritage.[2]

During the early 1950s, Czech refugees continued to arrive, accounting for 3 percent of all European refugees who resettled in Canada.[3] Profoundly influenced by the events of 1948, later refugees were often determinedly anti-communist. In the following years, as few individuals were granted travel documents and officially permitted to leave the communist regime, many were forced to attempt dangerous and life-threatening border crossings to the West. Not surprisingly, Czech refugees who arrived in the years after the Communist Party seizure of power in 1948 continued their efforts to liberate Czechoslovakia into the 1950s and 1960s.

During the 1950s, many 1948ers turned their attention toward resolving ideological divisions and personality conflicts between them and oldtimers within the Czechoslovak community in Canada. Prague's surveillance and infiltration of Canadian Czechoslovak organizations, its communist repatriation propaganda, and the tragic events surrounding the failed Hungarian Revolution of 1956 demonstrated to 1948ers that communism in Czechoslovakia would not be easily defeated. Eventually, many 1948ers joined the pre-existing Czechoslovak community and began to emphasize Canadian citizenship and promotion of an ethnic heritage, the latter ironically in order to attain social and cultural citizenship in Cold War Canada. In this period, two major Canadian Czechoslovak organizations—the Czechoslovak National Alliance and Masaryk Hall—were incorporated, with the former receiving a charter from the Canadian government. Both organizations advocated for the liberation of Czechoslovakia and the reunion of Czechoslovaks in Canada with their relatives in the old homeland. Because many 1948ers had left close relatives behind in Czechoslovakia, reunion with loved ones was paramount but hampered by Communist Party authorities in Prague. They viewed the 1948ers as illegal émigrés and the emigration of their relatives to Canada as an "internal matter."[4] During the 1950s and 1960s, very few individuals and families would arrive in Canada.

Appeal to Czech Refugees to Return Home

Not only did Czechoslovakia disallow emigration, but also it sought to lure emigrants back home. In May 1955, the head of Czechoslovakia's legation in Ottawa, Bedřich Hruška, purchased advertising space in Canadian newspapers imploring recently arrived refugees from Czechoslovakia to return home. The advertisement stated that individuals guilty of a criminal offence for leaving Czechoslovakia illegally under the influence of propaganda would be pardoned if they returned within six months after the 9 May amnesty.[5] The question of return was contentious within the Canadian Czechoslovak community. Although some individuals did return, they were fewer than 100, and their reasons seem to have been largely ideological rather than financial or personal. The Communist Party quickly turned its propaganda machine against émigrés in the broader West. Soon after, agents for the StB (Státní bezpečnost or State Security) invited these individuals to return to Czechoslovakia and defend themselves against these attacks. Prague's actions were defined in a 1953 document entitled "The Indicative Report on Subversive Activities of the Czechoslovak Emigration against Czechoslovakia."[6] The document identified all émigré activity against the communist state as hostile. Communist Party authorities used disinformation as a tactic for spreading lies and creating divisions among the anti-communist 1948ers. In Ottawa, legation officials later claimed that eighty individuals returned to Czechoslovakia from Canada during the amnesty campaign, while the RCMP and anti-communist Czechoslovak leaders in Toronto believed that the figure was much smaller, with fewer than ten individuals returning to Czechoslovakia.[7] Many of those who returned to Czechoslovakia after the Second World War were Canadian Slovaks politically active in left-wing organizations, including the Slovak Benefit Society of Canada, the Independent Mutual Benefit Federation, the Communist Party of Canada, and its successor the Labour-Progressive Party of Canada.[8]

Refugees from Czechoslovakia who entered Canada after the 1948 Communist Party takeover did so at a cost to their families, relatives, finances, and properties. Their networks of family members, friends, and business contacts back home were subjected to police surveillance, interrogation, and even torture. In an effort to repatriate those who had fled and subsequently embarrassed the communist regime, diplomatic officials and the StB were employed to coerce, blackmail, sabotage, and spy on refugees in Canada. In October 1955, the *Toronto Daily Star* published the sensational story of a Soviet-led espionage network operating in Toronto. The piece featured an interview

Figure 8. *Jiří Štembera pointing to Czechoslovakia's coat of arms and the words "Truth Prevails" in front of the Czechoslovak legation, Ottawa, 26 October 1955.*

with Jiří (George) Štembera, a twenty-nine-year-old Czech refugee and anti-communist newspaper editor living in Toronto who claimed to have been commissioned by the Czechoslovak Embassy to work as a secret Communist Party agent. His task had been to spy on 6,000 recently arrived refugees from Czechoslovakia as well as on the personal interests, acquaintances, finances, and political participation of twenty prominent members of the Czechoslovak community in Canada. They were listed as dangerous enemies of Prague, and Štembera's intelligence was to be used to lure or blackmail them to return to their homeland.[9]

First on this list was Ota Hora, a former democratic member of Czechoslovakia's postwar parliament who had fled his homeland in the wake of the Communist Party takeover. As a 1948er, Hora resettled in Ottawa and was employed as an accountant with the Canadian government. He was later reunited with his wife and son in 1950. In Canada, Hora became an influential member of the Council of Free Czechoslovakia and regularly broadcast to Czechoslovakia on Radio Free Europe.[10]

Also included on the list was Jiří (George) Corn, a former mayor of Kostelec nad Černými lesy and a member of the Edvard Beneš–led National Socialist Party. While still in Czechoslovakia, Corn was notified of his imminent arrest and went into hiding in Prague. In 1949, with the help of the anti-communist underground, he was smuggled out of the country to a refugee camp in West Germany. His wife, Jaroslava, was imprisoned in Prague for six weeks, and her movements were restricted. Once the Communist Party authorities were convinced of her innocence in Jiří's emigration, she was released from prison. Jaroslava and the couple's two children, Jiří Jr. and Jaroslava Jr., later fled the country. In January 1951, while working for the IRO, Jiří Corn signed a manual labour contract, indicating that his wife and two children would later join him, to work on a sugar beet farm near Iron Springs, Alberta. Two months later Corn immigrated to Canada. The family eventually resettled in Toronto, where they later became active in the CNA and Sokol movement.[11] When interviewed by the *Toronto Star,* Corn indicated that as a democrat he was honoured to be included on the list of prominent anti-communists from Czechoslovakia to be spied on by Communist Party agents.[12]

Other prominent community figures on the Czechoslovak Embassy's "spy" list included Gustav Přístupa (president of Masaryk Hall), Maria Gajda (community radio broadcaster from Toronto), Jaroslav (Jerry) Janda (secretary general of the Middle Class Party of Czechoslovakia), Jiří (George) Hlubuček (*Our Voices* publisher), Josef (Joseph) Čermák (University of Toronto law

Figure 9. *Czechoslovak national identity certificates issued to Jiří Corn and Jaroslava Cornová, c. 1947.*

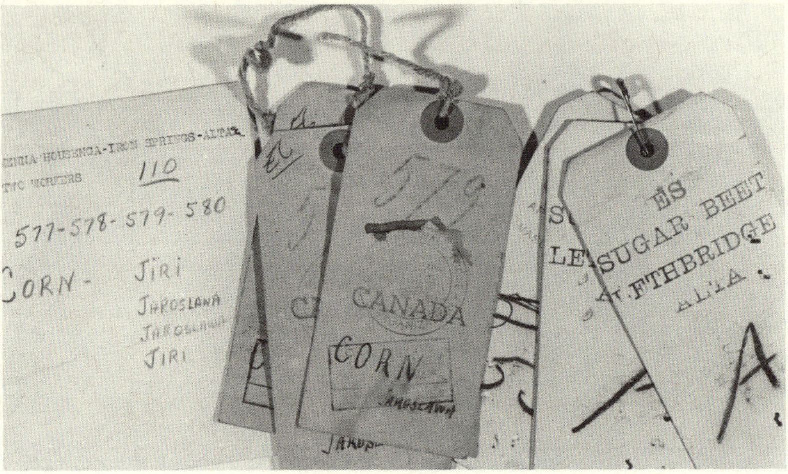

Figure 10. *Identification tags worn by the Corn family, indicating their status as DP recruits and intended placement at Iron Springs, Lethbridge County, Alberta, c. March 1951.*

student and anti-communist newspaper publisher), František (Frank) Třešnák (secretary of the Union of Journalists-in-Exile), Ivan Jelek (CNA secretary), and Karel Buzek. The list included several other individuals also involved in anti-communist compatriot politics.

Ironically, Jiří Štembera himself was one of the twenty refugees spied on in the greater Toronto area. Štembera submitted information by meeting an StB courier at the northeast corner of King and York Streets in downtown Toronto. In his initial interview with an StB intelligence official in Ottawa, Štembera used a false identity (Milan Jina) and was offered cigarettes and cognac. He claimed to have met with Third Secretary Antonín Dvořák and attaché Lubomír Sefrna in the Czechoslovak legation's basement in Ottawa. During this meeting, Štembera was informed that Canadians were barbarians who lacked culture and did not care about refugees from Czechoslovakia. He began his deception of Dvořák and Sefrna by asking for information on how to return to Czechoslovakia. In response to his request, these Communist Party officials informed the Czech refugee that Canada had nothing to offer his fellow compatriots except a lack of employment and starvation.[13]

While Czechoslovakia's Communist Party authorities were attempting to recruit members of the Czechoslovak community to spy on each other in Canada, they were also keen to acquire access to sensitive information pertaining to Canadian defence plants and government agencies. Legation officials informed Štembera that Prague sought access to highly sensitive information from sources including the A.V. Roe plant in Malton, Ontario.[14] In October 1955, an outraged group of nearly 200 anti-communists from the Canadian Czechoslovak community gathered in Toronto to draft a memorandum for the Department of External Affairs in Ottawa. On behalf of anti-communist Czechoslovaks, Karel Buzek, the former Czechoslovak consul, Václav Peřina, a Czechoslovak war veteran, Josef Čermák, a University of Toronto law student, and Jaroslav Sehnoha, a former Czechoslovak ambassador to France and India, presented a memorandum that pressured the Canadian government to expel Czechoslovak diplomats Dvořák and Sefrna.[15]

Although many recently arrived refugees from Czechoslovakia approved of Štembera's outing of a Communist Party spy ring, others—including Prokop Havlík, a community "oldtimer" and a former treasurer of the CNA—questioned Štembera's intentions. In an editorial entitled "Vyzvědačství" ("Spying") in the Canadian Czech-language paper *Nový domov* (New Homeland), Havlík argued that, because Communist Party authorities vetted the background of every person whom they considered for espionage work, the accuracy of Štembera's story was suspect.[16] Havlík argued that the *Toronto Daily Star* had fallen prey to sensationalism when it published photos of some of the twenty prominent Czechoslovak anti-communists. He also pointed out that publication in the paper of images of some of the twenty compatriots was ill advised since all of the information in Štembera's story had yet to be fully corroborated by Canadian authorities.[17]

The initial news of an alleged spy ring within the Czechoslovak community in Toronto divided individuals. Oldtimers in Masaryk Hall opposed expulsion of the diplomats because they feared that relations between Ottawa and Prague would suffer as a result and cause undesirable diplomatic tensions. They further noted that Štembera's claims were not substantiated. In its letter to Minister of External Affairs Lester Pearson, Masaryk Hall argued that the organization was composed of ardent anti-communists who did not wish to exacerbate tensions between Ottawa and Prague. Divisions among members of MH continued to simmer in the summer of 1955 when it became public that many of the 1948ers were allegedly attempting to influence others with their party ideologies and seize control of Czechoslovak organizations in order to align them with their anti-communist agenda. Consequently, MH severed ties with many of these recent political refugees.

Figure 11. *Jiří Štembera, left, and an unidentified man discussing the* Toronto Daily Star's *front-page headline "Hired as Secret Agent Toronto Czech Bares Communist Spy Plot," 28 October 1955.*

As president of Masaryk Hall, Gustav Přístupa informed Pearson that it was vigilantly helping Canada to fight communist oppression, giving individuals the opportunity to live in a democratic state. In representing the view of many oldtimers, Přístupa condemned the irresponsibility of the group of 200 anti-communist Czechoslovaks and the Canadian Press for publishing a story that brought unnecessarily negative attention to the Czechoslovak community in Toronto.[18]

Although members of the Czechoslovak community across Canada disagreed over the authenticity of Štembera's claims, officials at the Czechoslovak Ministry of Foreign Affairs protested what they perceived as a breach of diplomatic immunity. According to Prague, the subsequent press campaign that criticized its diplomats in Canada was false. The alleged recruitment of Štembera as a spy forced Prague to assert that it was only providing normal consular assistance to its former residents. Canadian officials minimized

Prague's complaints by stifling further publicity and expressing their desire to maintain good relations. The repatriation campaign resulted in the return to Czechoslovakia of approximately three dozen refugees from Canada. Soon after arriving in Czechoslovakia, a minority of these returnees applied to return to Canada and were summarily denied.[19]

In the meantime, other Soviet satellite states continued their efforts to lure anti-communist refugees back home. In the summer of 1956, Undersecretary of State for External Affairs Jules Léger reported that such attempts were meant to silence the émigrés.[20] The *Globe and Mail* indicated that only a few individuals fell victim to this communist operation. However, the Communist Party authorities successfully employed a scheme whereby first-class mail was sent from Europe often purportedly written by relatives of those who had escaped to Canada. Léger argued that Ottawa could not prevent this type of communist scheme from occurring, but he noted that any interference by foreign governments in Canada should be brought to the attention of the federal government. Pearson indicated, however, that there was no course of action for Canadian authorities to take since mail censorship did not exist in Canada.

In the months following Štembera's claims, the RCMP counterespionage branch began to investigate claims that the Soviet Embassy in Ottawa was intimidating its former citizens into returning behind the Iron Curtain.[21] Meanwhile, Canadian officials and anti-communist 1948ers remained vigilant to the threat posed by the Communist Party government in Czechoslovakia.

Canadians Speak Out against Communism in Czechoslovakia

In July 1956, Masaryktown held its ninth Czechoslovak Day, and members of MH discussed the reunification of families separated by the Iron Curtain. They resolved that the Canadian government should negotiate with the Communist Party authorities in Czechoslovakia to release all persons who wished to leave the country to be reunited with their families in the West. Individuals who chose to leave were also to be fairly compensated for their property. Canadian Czechoslovak organizations demanded that valid passports be issued for those who desired to emigrate to Canada or to be released from their Czechoslovak citizenship. The resolution included a request that the Communist Party authorities not persecute emigrants seeking to leave the country and/or individuals who applied to leave the country but whose poor health prevented them from doing so.[22]

After the Masaryktown resolution, the Department of External Affairs instructed the Canadian legation in Prague to write letters on behalf of those who had sought immigration to Canada and were found to be admissible. The prospective immigrant then presented the letter to the Communist Party authorities informing them that a Canadian visa would be granted to the applicant provided that an exit permit and medical screening were successfully completed. Negotiations between the DEA and Prague centred on Czechoslovaks with dual citizenship and "pure Czechoslovaks" whose relatives had resettled in Canada prior to the Communist Party takeover in 1948.[23] After further discussion with officials, the Canadian legation in Prague forecasted little hope of family reunification for persons who left Czechoslovakia illegally after February 1948. The communist regime in the country actively prevented 1948ers—who, it believed, worked to embarrass Prague—from being reunited with their families.[24]

Several months later, in the fall of 1956, the CNA held its annual congress in Montreal. At the gathering, CNA executive member Josef Broušek informed delegates that an agent of the StB had spent the past five years collecting information on fellow compatriots in Toronto. An executive member of the local CNA branch in Toronto, fifty-five-year-old Dr. Bruno Dostál, infiltrated Canadian Czechoslovak institutions in an attempt to subvert the work of anti-communist refugees. As part of his operation, Dostál was employed by the University of Toronto as a librarian. After suspicions were raised about his suspected spying on behalf of the communist regime, Dostál returned to Czechoslovakia in October 1956. Information regarding his departure was confirmed when the communist paper *Hlas domova* (Voice of Homeland) in Prague published an interview with him following his return to Czechoslovakia.[25] Subsequently, outraged delegates representing thirty anti-communist and pro-democratic groups in Canada issued a statement warning their compatriots "to be on guard against Red agents who may try to intimidate you."[26] Communist infiltration was increasingly seen by recently arrived refugees as highly dangerous to Czechoslovak community institutions and to Canada's national security. Although community members disagreed on the future activities of their respective institutions, they remained steadfast in their efforts to demonstrate their anti-communist and pro-democratic values in Canada.

Delegates at the 1956 CNA congress in Montreal also discussed the rift among members. On the agenda of the two-day meeting was how to heal the divide between those who wanted to turn toward the promotion of Canadian citizenship and those who wanted to focus on returning a democratic system of government to Czechoslovakia. The discovery of another attempt by Prague to spy on its former citizens in Canada put further pressure on CNA members to deal with communist infiltration of the Canadian Czechoslovak community. Newly elected as the CNA president and the last democratic Czechoslovak minister in Canada, František Němec identified the situation as deplorable and damaging to the good name of the community and its members. The annual meeting unanimously approved a motion that called on the CNA to re-establish unity among its members. The association subsequently passed a resolution expressing the loyalty of its members to Canada and their willingness "to give our lives in the defence of our new homeland against any enemy."[27] For some members, communist participation within their organization led them to renounce their membership. Upon hearing of Dostál's activities, Josef Ludvík, a member of the CNA's Toronto branch, requested that the organization's head office immediately revoke his membership and strike his name from its member listing. Ludvík informed the CNA that, as a Czech political refugee and anti-communist, he found the idea that a communist was able to infiltrate the organization and then return to Czechoslovakia reprehensible, and thus he could no longer remain a member.[28]

A week later plans to celebrate the anniversary of the birth of the Czechoslovak Republic were affected by a demonstration in support of the Hungarian Revolution. Local members of the CNA joined Hungarian Canadians to protest the Soviet invasion of Hungary. The demonstration engaged old immigrants and recent Eastern European arrivals to present a resolution to Lester Pearson demanding that Canada assist the Hungarian refugees.[29] In the *Globe and Mail,* Karel Buzek, former CNA executive member and Czechoslovak consul, asked if the recent uprisings in Hungary and Poland meant that Czechs should now strike for freedom against the communist regime in their homeland. His answer was that refugees from Eastern Europe should first demonstrate to Canadian society that their compatriots overseas would not tolerate Soviet domination. Buzek informed the *Globe and Mail*'s readers that they should support the Canadian Red Cross and send aid to Hungary. Buzek wanted local ethnic groups to cooperate and solicit more assistance for individuals who actively fought communist oppression or planned to in the near future.[30]

Most Czechs, however, could do little to change the political situation in their country. The Communist Party maintained a substantial following across all sectors of society and controlled all aspects of daily life. Since Czechoslovakia remained a communist satellite state with a relatively higher standard of living than that of its counterparts in Eastern Europe, opposition to the regime from within was often more measured. As a result, the uprisings that swept through Poland and Hungary in 1956 did not occur in Czechoslovakia. However, they served to awaken the country's intellectuals, who would later commence a process to reform the communist system from within.[31]

Canadians of Eastern European origin were shocked by communist infiltration in their organizations and dismayed by the failure of the Hungarian Revolution. For many anti-communist Czech refugees, promoting the return of parliamentary democracy to Czechoslovakia was a struggle. In some instances, Canadian Czechoslovak organizations were upbeat and indeed revitalized in their efforts against communism; in Winnipeg, for example, the local CNA branch meeting in the hall of the Canadian Czechoslovak Benevolent Association grew from nineteen to 105 members amid reports of daily Soviet repression in Hungary.[32] Elsewhere, though, organizational memberships in Canada tended to decrease as community members focused on ethnocultural identity on the one hand and Canadian citizenship on the other. Czech immigrants were beginning to lose hope for their homeland.

The Sokol Movement

During the first decade of the Cold War, relations between Canada and Czechoslovakia suffered because of political events in Eastern Europe. The increase in international tensions resulted in part from the 1953 uprisings in Plzeň, Czechoslovakia, and East Germany; the 1956 revolt in Poznań, Poland; and the 1956 Hungarian Revolution. With Soviet assistance, these rebellions were crushed and led to the subsequent emergence of hardline communist control. Still, Canadian diplomats informed officials back home that Prague maintained a "cautious policy" of developing better relations with the West.[33] Within the Czechoslovak community, the failure of the 1950s uprisings illustrated to many 1948ers that their attempts to help return parliamentary democracy to Czechoslovakia would last longer than a few years. Many 1948ers thus began to turn their attention toward settling ideological differences between oldtimers and recent arrivals within the Czechoslovak community.

Many of the differences between the groups in the Czechoslovak community revolved around the leadership and direction of the patriotic Sokol calisthenics movement in Canada and the appropriation of its title. As a patriotic voluntary organization established in Prague in the nineteenth century, the Sokol movement promoted patriotism and calisthenics for their educational, spiritual, and physical benefits. The movement's annual meetings were known as *slets* ("festivals"). In interwar Czechoslovakia, the movement was firmly rooted in democratic principles and remained non-partisan. Sokol members were instructed to be at the front line in the defence of freedom and democratic values in their homeland and across the world. Members were to use their physical strength and moral power to promote peace and freedom and defend democratic values. Prior to 1939, Czech immigrants established branches across Canada, with the first formed in Michel, British Columbia, in 1911, and an urban branch which opened in Winnipeg in 1928.[34] With the Communist Party takeover of Czechoslovakia in 1948, the Sokol movement, banned in the old homeland for its anti-communist stance, nevertheless took off as the Czechoslovak Sokol Abroad, with five-member districts in Western Europe and North America. In July 1952, the Sokol Gymnastic Association of Canada was founded as a district of the Czechoslovak Sokol Abroad, and the Canadian Czechoslovak community took part in promoting calisthenics, informing the public of conditions in Czechoslovakia and the struggle against communism, while assisting in the resettlement of refugees from Czechoslovakia in the West.[35]

In 1949, the Sokol movement gained more momentum when postwar political refugees fleeing communism established Sokols in Exile. Still, there was upheaval. Although former MH president Gustav Přístupa and his fellow members in Toronto briefly joined the group, they soon resigned since they considered themselves Canadians of "Czechoslovak extraction" rather than Czechoslovaks in exile. Canadian officials noted that "one group considers themselves to be Canadian citizens and the purpose is to perpetuate Czechoslovakian customs so as to embody these customs in the Canadian way of life, whereas it is alleged that the newer group wishes to preserve Czechoslovakian customs and culture in the hope of their eventual return to their native land."[36] Přístupa informed Canadian officials that in his opinion, once the 1948ers began to identify with Canadian society, conflicting interests within the community would be reconciled.[37]

Přístupa was right, and soon the conflict between oldtimers and community leaders did subside. His successor as MH president, Prokop V. Havlík, lamented these divisions and worried that not enough compatriots were joining the Kanadská Obec Sokolská (Canadian Sokol Organization [KOS]); he feared in particular that numbers were dwindling because youth in the community were turning instead to other Canadian pursuits.[38] Nevertheless, both the 1948er-led Sokol Gymnastic Association of Canada and the Canadian Sokol movement joined the Czechoslovak Sokol Abroad group to fight Communist Party rule in Czechoslovakia and worked to involve their children as young members. At the local level, too, the Sokol movement continued to grow. In May 1958, for example, the 1948ers opened their own Sokol facility in Toronto and, boasting 158 members, took part in calisthenics, cultural activities, and sports, including a highly touted competitive men's volleyball team and a table tennis team.[39] Signalling their good standing with the government, the opening celebration was attended by several officials, including Minister of National Health and Welfare Jay Waldo Monteith, Ontario Minister of Education W.J. Dunlop, and Vladimir Kaye, national liaison officer for the federal Department of Citizenship and Immigration.[40] The Sokol movement was off to a good start, and soon both federal and provincial political parties courted members for their votes.

Politicians Seek the Czechoslovak Vote

As the Sokol movement healed old divisions, federal and provincial politicians did their part to diminish the influence of the old ethnic left-wing voters across Canada and to promote efforts against communism by courting the ethnic vote. This courtship helped to integrate "New Canadians" into society and, more importantly, civic life, where they were increasingly co-opted into joining political parties, lobby groups, voting blocs, patronage appointments, and patron-client relationships.[41] Given their ardent anti-communism, a large portion of Canadians who arrived after the Second World War tended to align themselves to the political tenets of the Progressive Conservative Party and the Liberal Party. The Conservatives, in particular, left their British Canadian base and actively sought the anti-communist ethnic vote in an attempt to displace the vote for the left, which had dominated prewar ethnic politics in Canada. Postwar refugees brought with them fresh memories of their persecution by the Communists in their home country. The postwar anti-communist Czech refugees, in particular, came to identify predominantly with the Progressive Conservative Party brand since some immigrants viewed the Liberal Party as somehow linked to social democracy movements in Europe.[42]

In the hope of raising support for the Liberal Party, in power at the time, Minister of Citizenship and Immigration John Whitney ("Jack") Pickersgill, Minister of Finance Walter Edward Harris, and Parliamentary Assistant to Minister of Defence Paul Hellyer joined the Czechoslovak Day celebrations and Sokol festival at Masaryktown in 1956. After attending the festivities, Pickersgill published his thoughts about the Sokol movement in Canada in MH's official organ, *Nový domov,* stating that the movement promoted democratic principles and physical education, which moulded new Canadians

Figure 12. *Men and women participating in a Sokol* slet *before a platform of community leaders and public officials, Masaryktown, July 1956.*

and their children into democratic citizens with sound bodies and minds. According to Pickersgill, the Sokol movement was making a vital contribution to the development of Canada.[43] Illustrating his support for the activities of MH and Sokol members, Walter Harris wrote a letter to MH, also published in *Nový domov,* congratulating Sokol Toronto on the twenty-fifth anniversary of its founding. Harris informed the newspaper's readers that he first visited MH and Sokol Toronto on the grounds of Masaryktown in December 1954. In his letter, he asserted that the Sokol movement's members and their children benefited from its programs. According to the minister of finance, the organization illustrated to society that both interwar Czech immigrants and recently arrived political refugees had brought with them from their old homeland sought-after qualities in Canada: physical activity, morality, democratic values, and perseverance.[44]

Hoping to gain the political support of the Czechoslovak community in Toronto, Harris and his wife became the first non-Czechoslovak members of Sokol Toronto. In extending his best wishes to the members of Sokol Toronto on their milestone anniversary, Minister of National Health and Welfare Paul Martin Sr. indicated in *Nový domov* that he was also well acquainted with the programs of the Sokol movement across Canada. He noted that in 1955 he and his wife had become members of the local Sokol branch in Windsor. Martin went on to argue that the significance of the efforts of the Sokol movement in Canada were twofold: first, helping new Canadians to build healthy bodies and sound minds; second, making an important contribution to the well-being of its members and Canadian society as a whole. The minister believed that the Sokols were instrumental in preserving and strengthening health activities in Canada.[45]

As transplanted party politics and ideological differences continued to shape relations between 1948ers and the pre-existing Czechoslovak community and its institutions, Canadian diplomats in Prague agonized over communist intransigence on family reunification and Canadian consular affairs. Communist officials in Prague persisted in preventing the emigration of Czechs to Canada or their visits to the West. As a result, Canadian officials could not process the high demand for visas.[46] In September 1958, the DEA was advised by the RCMP that it had received information indicating that Prague intended to permit the reunification of three or four children with their parents in Canada, who had fled the country without them. Officials in Ottawa indicated that in this case the StB had corresponded with the Czech parents in Canada and that a rare reunification would occur.

This was also the case for Dagmar and Zdeněk Zimmer. The Czech couple were married in October 1945 and later left their home in Moravia to resettle in western Bohemia. In the town of Cheb, they established a small but prosperous business with close to 500 steady customers. In February 1948, their business was nationalized by the Communists, and the couple decided to emigrate to the West. Zdeněk emigrated illegally, while Dagmar and their son returned to her hometown of Valašské Meziříčí in Moravia to be closer to relatives, though as the wife of a political émigré she was unable to find work. After Zdeněk successfully reached England, he quickly became lonely, and thus Dagmar—rather than see her husband return to Czechoslovakia and face certain imprisonment—made the difficult decision to leave their young child behind with her parents and also flee her homeland. In March 1949, she escaped through the woods and eventually made her way to the Augsburg refugee camp. She soon joined Zdeněk in England, where in 1951, having saved approximately $300, they boarded a ship in Southampton for the week-long journey to Canada. Landing at Quebec City, they travelled to Hamilton, where an old Czech friend resided. Within a few years, Zdeněk and Dagmar learned English and joined the CNA branch in the city. However, they found their early years in Canada difficult because of their separation from family and their son.

Thus, in November 1957, the Zimmers applied to the International Committee of the Red Cross in Geneva in the hope of finding international support for their fight to be reunited with their child. However, when the Red

Cross petitioned Prague, it was informed bluntly that children should not be without their parents but that such reunification was possible only if the parents returned to Czechoslovakia.[47]

It remained a closed country. In 1958, for example, it permitted thirty-three individuals to emigrate to Canada compared with only thirteen the previous year. Although approximately 400 Canadians were able to visit Czechoslovakia compared with only 275 the year before, many of them were officials, business representatives, and persons with friends and family members in Czechoslovakia.[48] Moreover, individuals who left Czechoslovakia following the events of February 1948 remained separated from loved ones. In some cases, prominent anti-communist refugees attempting to secure a close relative's immigration to Canada found permission only with impossible conditions. In January 1958, for example, Bořivoj Čelovský, a 1948er who worked for Statistics Canada, approached the Czechoslovak legation in Ottawa to inquire about bringing his aging mother to Canada. The legation's third secretary, Milan Kleník, who also served as the local StB officer and was code-named Kolda, informed him that his mother could be brought over only if Čelovský infiltrated and monitored Czechoslovak organizations in Canada, ceased engaging in exile politics, and swore that he viewed his immigration unfavourably.[49] After visiting the legation, where he was given the StB code name Red, Čelovský informed the RCMP Special Branch of his meeting with the Czechoslovak diplomat and agreed to become a double agent. He was given the code name František Svoboda (Francis Freedom). He thus began filing regular reports, meeting Kleník in places in the Ottawa Valley and the Outaouais region of Quebec. Čelovský remained a double agent for three years. Two months after commencing his deception, the StB visited his mother in Ostrava and asked her to request a visit to Canada. The Communist Party authorities used the visit as part of a scheme to follow Kleník in order to make sure that his agent was clean. When Kleník returned to Czechoslovakia for a vacation in 1958, he was never seen in Canada again, and the RCMP concluded that he had been recalled for unprofessional behaviour in public. In July 1958, when his mother arrived in Canada, Čelovský continued his work with the StB but now pretended to be an alcoholic and a traitor to Canada in order to deceive the organization. When it discovered his deception, it sent him a bogus letter from his ex-wife demanding spousal support, an initiative meant to cause tension between him and his family and further dependence on the StB. It was three years of immense difficulty for Čelovský. His story of forced cooperation with the StB was repeated among other 1948ers who attempted to bring their close relatives to Canada or among those hoping to secure financial support, better accommodations, or loans for their relatives to purchase automobiles in Czechoslovakia.[50]

Beginning in 1960, Czech refugees in Canada were also introduced to a new form of blackmail by Communist Party officials in Czechoslovakia. The RCMP informed the DEA that in one case the StB had developed a unique technique for inserting illegal agents into Western countries. According to the RCMP, the illegal agent had submitted a letter to the Canadian Embassy in Prague claiming to be the illegitimate child of a Canadian woman living in Czechoslovakia. Thus without Czechoslovak citizenship, he was now applying for citizenship in Canada.[51] Dismayed by such communist tactics in their homeland, members of the CNA enthusiastically supported the implementation of a Canadian Bill of Rights by the Progressive Conservative government of Prime Minister John Diefenbaker in August 1960. The CNA's Ottawa branch endorsed the new law and argued in a letter to Diefenbaker that "we—New Canadians from behind the Iron Curtain—fully appreciate the importance of the new Act, safeguarding the human dignity and political rights of each citizen."[52]

The CNAC Is Incorporated

As noted above, unsettling stories of Prague's subversive activities were met by increased activities among Czechoslovak organizations in Canada. Coinciding with the incorporation of Masaryk Hall into Masaryk Memorial Institute in July 1960, the CNA was given a federal charter under the seal of the Office of the Secretary of State and incorporated as a not-for-profit organization the following September. The organization's name was changed to the Czechoslovak National Association of Canada. The operations of the organization were to be carried out across Canada without financial gain to its members, and any profits were to be used for the promotion of its projects.[53] Among the newly chartered organization's goals was the development of the highest standards of citizenship for Czechoslovak Canadians through establishment of and participation in ethnocultural and patriotic activities. This agenda served to further Canadian citizenship in several ways: in all matters, members were to act to further the rights and welfare of Czechoslovak Canadians and Czechs coming to Canada; to aid in the improvement of socioeconomic and cultural conditions of Czechoslovaks in Canada and the rehabilitation of immigrants and refugees from Czechoslovakia; and to promote goodwill, tolerance, and understanding among all ethnic groups in Canada while maintaining and defending freedom and democratic values in Canada and elsewhere in the world. Finally, the CNAC was also responsible for instilling cultural and linguistic traditions among its members and the broader Czechoslovak community in Canada. The CNAC's standing committees included the Committee on Refugees, Reconstruction, and Rehabilitation tasked with operating the association's assistance program for Czechoslovak refugees and other asylum seekers. The committee was also responsible for aiding Czechoslovaks outside Canada if assistance was deemed necessary for their rescue and rehabilitation. The other committees included the Public Relations Committee; the Research, Press, and Archives Committee; and the Organization Committee. In March 1961, Minister of Citizenship and Immigration Ellen Fairclough presented the federal charter to the newly incorporated CNAC at a ceremony in Hamilton.[54]

Not all recent arrivals from Czechoslovakia approved of the federal charter and incorporation of the CNAC with a mandate to represent Canadians of Czechoslovak origin. Individuals who opposed the federal charter did so because of personality clashes and refugee politics originating in the party politics of interwar Czechoslovakia. Clerical, right-wing, moderate, and centre-left parties were re-established in exile by prominent individuals who had been members of these parliamentary parties in democratic Czechoslovakia. In Canada, these groups reassembled and began to speak for "Czechoslovaks" as their true representatives. Although many of the 1948ers joined the CNAC, they were opposed in their political objectives by conservative Czech groups and nationalist Slovak organizations that had accused Edvard Beneš and his followers of cooperating with the Soviet Union during and immediately after the Second World War.[55] Nationalist Canadian Slovaks opposed the CNAC's federal charter because it gave the organization a mandate to represent all ethnic Slovaks and Czechs.

As the largest ethnic Slovak organization in Canada, the Canadian Slovak League had been reincorporated and granted a federal charter in June 1954.[56] In March 1960, the organization protested to the Department of the Secretary of State that Canadian Slovaks were already represented on a similar mandate with the reincorporation of the CSL and that the incorporation and federal charter of the CNAC would further confuse the Canadian public regarding the differences between "Czechoslovaks" and Slovaks. The CSL concluded that its members no longer lived in Czechoslovakia, and therefore there was "no ground for using the name of a foreign state for 'protecting or educating' Canadians of Slovak origin."[57] Nationalist Canadian Slovaks did not want the CNAC to use "Czechoslovak" as part of its name.

Intraethnic tensions were also prevalent within the Czechoslovak community as ideological differences continued to come to the fore. As proponents of a Catholic and conservative faction of 1948ers, Václav Vostřez and František Hašek opposed the CNAC's mandate and contested its executive's claim to represent Czechs and Slovaks as "Czechoslovaks" in Canada. In 1957, a split between members of the CNA's Hamilton branch culminated with the ouster of Vostřez. Along with fellow CNA members František Hašek and Zdeněk Zimmer, they subsequently founded the Czechoslovak Association of Czechs, Slovaks, and Sub-Carpathian Ruthenians, based in Hamilton. Vostřez published the Czech-language bulletin *Brázda* (The Furrow), and six years later he ran for the Social Credit Party in the riding of Hamilton East against the Progressive Conservative incumbent and Postmaster General Ellen Fairclough.[58]

Ideological clashes also continued among members of the Sokol movement in Canada. In May 1961, representatives of the Sokol Gymnastic Association of Canada and the Canadian Sokol Organization, who had been at odds with each other for years over the direction of the Sokol movement in Canada, met in Toronto. Ervin Sypták and Prokop V. Havlík, president of the MMI, represented the KOS and were joined by Jan Waldauf, Karel Jeřábek, Jiří Corn, and Louis Vávra of the SGAC. In the meeting, Čorn raised four issues that he believed needed to be addressed: first, joint attendance in public; second, joint representation on athletic unity and gymnastic issues in Canada; third, objections to a federal charter and incorporation for both organizations; and fourth, resolution of the differences in the names for both groups. Havlík replied by informing the SGAC representatives that the Sokol unit based at the MMI and Masaryktown would continue to operate there and not relocate its activities. Consequently, Vávra noted that the 100th anniversary of the Sokol movement was to occur in 1962 and that it was in the interest of all Czechoslovaks to hold a united *slet.* Vávra envisioned a *slet* that included old-timers who supported the Sokol movement's calisthenics and the promotion of a Czechoslovak cultural heritage and 1948ers who also emphasized Sokol's patriotic and democratic values. Havlík replied that the annual Czechoslovak Day and *slet* would continue because they comprised a tradition that could not be disobeyed. The groups agreed to continue discussions on how to find a *modus vivendi* within Toronto's Czechoslovak community.[59] Although the parties sought reconciliation, SGAC and KOS remained separate groups.[60]

Two years later, in December 1964, KOS published its first magazine, *Sokol—Toronto News Letter.* As the original Toronto Sokol unit housed at the

Figure 13. *Community members from Canada and the United States participating in a Sokol* slet *during Czechoslovak Day, Masaryktown, 5 July 1963.*

MMI, the group sought to inform its members and the greater public about its physical fitness and social programs. KOS hosted dances, Halloween parties, and its annual *slet* in July at Masaryktown.[61] Faced with increasing cooperation among rival Sokol institutions in Canada, KOS ceased to exist two years later. Sokol units across the country joined the SGAC, which became known as Sokol Canada. Finally, all Canadian Sokol groups were united under one organization.

As the oldtimers and the 1948ers began to resolve ideological tensions within the Sokol movement, many of these individuals were also members of the CNAC and the MMI. The CNAC's various committees worked alongside the MMI because of its experience in financially supporting immigrants from Czechoslovakia. The Women's Council of the CNAC regularly corresponded with the MMI to guarantee that newcomers were accommodated in Canada.

Established in 1960, the Women's Council secured accommodations, clothing, food, employment, language courses, and access to new schools for refugee families. Incidentally, newcomers were grateful for the early support offered by these groups. However, many refugees—while thankful for community support—thought that they had overused community resources and refused additional support.[62] In many instances, the Women's Council was the intermediary between newcomers and the existing Czechoslovak community across Canada. Volunteers from the council individually assessed each refugee family on its own merits to determine whether it required clothing, employment, and residence or simply financial support to send the children to summer camp at Masaryktown.[63] The council was also instrumental in sending donations and clothing to individuals and families in refugee camps in Austria, West Germany, and Italy.[64]

The MMI was instrumental in providing assistance to newcomers from Czechoslovakia. In December 1962, MMI members were captivated by news of a young Czech stowaway's escape to Canada. After spending three days in the freezing fuselage of an outbound Cubana Airlines plane from Prague, fifteen-year-old Miloš Navrátil disembarked in Gander, Newfoundland, where Canadian immigration officials noticed that the adolescent did not possess any travel documents. The officials inquired whether he wished to remain in Canada and seek asylum or continue to Havana. Navrátil replied that he had a great-uncle in Ottawa and wished to remain in Canada.[65] News of the teenage stowaway spread quickly as several mainstream newspapers reported his story to Canadians. Immigration officials took Navrátil from Gander to Pier 21 in Halifax, where he was processed. Later the United Nations High Commissioner for Refugees requested further information to determine whether Navrátil could be considered a UN convention refugee.[66] The president of the MMI, Prokop V. Havlík, informed immigration officials that an anonymous Czech Canadian had donated $100 to Navrátil and that, since he had escaped from Czechoslovakia, he should be categorized as an opponent of communism and be permitted to remain in Canada. Havlík claimed that, should the young stowaway's relatives not be located, the MMI would assume responsibility for him.[67] Two months later Navrátil was taken in by Jaroslav Tichý and his wife in Dartmouth, Nova Scotia.[68] The story illustrated that the MMI was able to lobby Canadian authorities successfully to have Navrátil legally admitted into Canada as an individual who had fled from communism in his homeland. The MMI also guaranteed his safety and provided assistance in locating accommodation and basic necessities upon his arrival.

In an effort to assist recently arrived refugees, non-Czechoslovak groups often donated funds to the MMI for its activities at Masaryktown. The Reorganized Church of Jesus Christ of Latter Day Saints made a small donation later allocated to Jan Machálek, a fifteen-year-old boy who had recently arrived in Canada with his widowed mother after residing in West Germany as a refugee. In gratitude for the contribution, Havlík invited the church to send a child of eight to twelve years of age to spend two weeks at Masaryktown during the annual children's summer camp.[69] As a charitable organization, the MMI carried out many of its activities at its centre of Czechoslovak community life, Masaryktown, in Scarborough on the outskirts of Toronto. Although established to provide financial, cultural, and educational support to "Czechoslovak people," it did not restrict its programs to individuals and families of Czech or Slovak origin.[70] Masaryktown held annual children's summer camps for which families paid a small fee, while orphans and underprivileged children were admitted free of charge. The MMI permitted other groups to use the grounds at Masaryktown, including the local Scarborough police club, the Catholic Children's Aid Society, and the Toronto Young Men's Christian Association Camping Branch. The last group often voluntarily contributed to the MMI building fund for property maintenance and the future construction of a community residence for elderly members. Similarly, individuals and families were welcomed by the MMI to use Masaryktown's grounds and swimming pool for a fee of five dollars. Guides were provided to supervise children's activities and to train adolescents in gymnastics and other physical pursuits.[71] An important facet of the MMI's assistance to Czech refugees was its ability to meet the needs of individuals and families who did not live in the vicinity of Toronto.

Czech refugees in remote communities across Canada solicited the MMI for short-term financial support or long-term charity because of unemployment, disability, illness, or lack of funds. A questionnaire sent by the institute asked whether the individual in need was employed, his or her salary or wage, behaviour on the job, level of honesty, and whether he or she was married and had children. In one case, the MMI sent a questionnaire to the local postmaster in Renabie, Ontario to verify whether Frank Effenberger, employed by Renabie Mines Limited, was a good risk for a short-term loan. The postmaster, replied that he was a very good worker, did not miss shifts at work, and never drank alcohol. Effenberger was deemed to be honest and conscientious. When asked if there was any illness or accident that made it necessary for assistance, the postmaster replied "no—s.o.s. children's teeth—Mrs. Effenberger is a very good wife and housekeeper—but they have never enough money for a dentist (for example)."[72]

With the MMI assisting Czech refugees across the country on an individual basis, some members soon questioned the organization's effectiveness in meeting the needs of the local community in Toronto. In his 1964 annual report to members of the MMI, Assistant Treasurer Edward Ovsenný discussed the organization's future and its cultural purpose: "Why does MMI continue to exist? Are not most of us assimilated into the 'Canadian way of life' . . . especially the second generation? Why are we of the board of directors . . . striving so strongly to keep a bit of the old world culture alive in this modern New World community? What good is it? Who now needs it?"[73] Since the treasurer's annual report contained only financial information about the corporation, Ovsenný sensed that communal reflection was necessary in order to decide on the institute's future role in Canada as a centre of Czechoslovak community life. Ovsenný argued that European culture contributed to individual members' experiences in Canada, but time and assimilation had made it more difficult for the institute to attract second-generation youth as members. He proposed that the MMI adapt to the changing interests of young parents. If it did not directly engage youth and young adults, then its purpose would be "doomed to a slow degeneration."[74]

As MMI members questioned the future role of their institution because of a lack of participation by second-generation Canadian Czechoslovaks who rapidly integrated into Canadian society, federal officials were also examining sociocultural integration across Canada. In July 1963, the Canadian government announced that it would examine the state of biculturalism and bilingualism across Canada and recommend any necessary actions to improve the relationship between English Canada and French Canada. The Liberal government of Prime Minister Lester Pearson established the Royal Commission on Bilingualism and Biculturalism to recommend how the federal government could develop the country based upon an equal partnership between anglophones and francophones. As part of its mandate, the commission also took into account the cultural contributions of other ethnic groups in Canada. In October 1963, the commission co-secretaries, Neil M. Morrison and Paul Lacoste, welcomed ethnic groups to submit briefs.[75] As the local MP for Parkdale, in which Masaryk Hall was situated, Stanley Haidasz, parliamentary secretary to the minister of national health and welfare, invited individuals from Toronto's Czechoslovak community to submit a brief to the commission and to participate in its public hearings.[76]

As a national ethnic organization that claimed to advocate on behalf of the Czechoslovak community across Canada, the CNAC—represented by Antonín Daičar, president; Jiří G. Corn, secretary general; and Jaroslav A. Bouček, chairman of the CNAC special committee—submitted a brief to the commission detailing its observations and recommendations. Like those of other ethnic groups, the Czechoslovak contribution to the commission was later labelled "generally cautious, even-handed and largely supportive of the Commission's role."[77] The brief indicated that the association believed that "the maintenance and strengthening of a united . . . though not necessarily uniform Canada to be a goal towards which they are prepared to work and contribute their share."[78] Although the CNAC recognized the special position of the English and French languages in Canadian society, it thought that Canada in the early 1960s was a product of a multitude of ethnic groups. The CNAC remained sympathetic to the political and cultural aspirations of French Canadians, but it argued that these ambitions had to be compatible with Canadian unity and the work of the federal government. As a result, CNAC members approved of any necessary constitutional changes to support French Canadian demands if they did not jeopardize Canada's integrity. The CNAC brief went on to note that "it is our opinion that much more now depends on the efforts of the French Canadians themselves to enjoy fully the advantages of their existing autonomy within a larger political and economic unit, rather than on constitutional changes."[79] In discussing the role of French Canadian minorities outside Quebec, the CNAC recommended that rights be given to minority schools, that involvement in government be encouraged, and that use of French be guaranteed when dealing with federal authorities. The brief noted that "the European experience in linguistically mixed areas is that the acquisition of an additional language is the result of either economic necessity or the close daily contact of two interdependent ethnic groups, and that attempts to increase the knowledge of the second language by force or propaganda are generally unsuccessful."[80]

When it came time to discuss multiculturalism, the CNAC appreciated that Canada did not force its ethnic communities to integrate rapidly and supported a much slower process of assimilation. In Canada, children of Czechoslovak origin could learn English or French as a second language to their benefit. However, instruction in ethnic languages other than English and French was to be left to the initiative of parents or the ethnic community and supported by public funds. The CNAC supported government funding of multiculturalism but sought to remain responsible for its implementation at a local level—in the home and the ethnic community. Consequently, the CNAC argued that Canada's cultural evolution would be strengthened if individuals with diverse ethnic backgrounds were represented in public organizations, including the Canadian Broadcasting Corporation, the National Film Board, and federal and provincial departments with portfolios in cultural and educational affairs.[81]

The MMI's Financial Struggles

As the CNAC shared its recommendations on cultural pluralism in Canada, the MMI found itself in a difficult financial position as it struggled to pay its bills and provide assistance to recently arrived refugees from Europe. Prior to incorporation as an institute, MH sold half of Masaryktown by tender in 1956, and its financial difficulties temporarily disappeared. The charitable organization continued to fund its weekly newspaper *Nový domov,* a community library, a local Sokol unit, and the annual children's summer camp at Masaryktown. In a letter to provincial officials, MH noted that expenses at Masaryktown for 1958 were $10,624.28, whereas the organization's income was only $5,333.35. The letter noted that Masaryktown was kept in perfect condition, which made it one of the most identifiable landmarks in the area and enhanced the surrounding township. In the fall of 1959, MH contacted provincial officials regarding its level of property tax. On behalf of MH, counsel Yaroslav Hueber requested that township officials review the property tax that the charitable organization paid. According to Hueber, lower taxes would allow MH increasingly to divert its revenues into activities beneficial for all of Scarborough's residents.

The hall received a small income from various activities held at its location on Cowan Avenue. Its board of directors was aware that, without proper kitchen facilities, profits would remain small. The board discussed the possibility of applying for a liquor licence, which would dramatically increase revenue, but ultimately decided against selling liquor on its premises. The executive chose to concentrate its funding on holding dances and renting the hall to various churches to play bingo. Between 1959 and 1964, $416,813.46 was raised from bingo games to be used to maintain services for the Czechoslovak community in Toronto. Approximately 39 percent of bingo funds was used for relief and assistance—support for the needy, elderly, or disabled and for the future construction of a home for the aged in Masaryktown. A quarter of all funds was allocated for cultural, recreational, and entertainment activities, including the annual children's summer camp at Masaryktown. Meanwhile, nearly 22 percent

Figure 14. *Crowd observing a Sokol* slet *during Czechoslovak Day, Masaryktown, 5 July 1964.*

was put toward physical training involving the local Sokol unit. Approximately 11 percent of funds was used to support Canadian citizenship by organizing Dominion Day and Victoria Day celebrations; purchasing Czech, Slovak, and Canadian literature; and holding art exhibitions.[82]

Within the Czechoslovak community, education was also viewed as an important component that would shape young members into engaged Canadian citizens. In early 1964, the MMI informed its members that it was allotting $1,250 to a scholarship fund. The institute envisioned that students would receive prizes if they met the following conditions: Czech, Slovak, or Carpathian Ruthenian ancestry; high school matriculation with first- or second-class honours; and enrolment in university studies. Applicants would submit a written composition on the theme of "Constructive Citizenship—A Conscious Responsibility" pertaining to the family, Czechoslovak identity, or a town, city, country, or the world.[83] Submissions were to be between 250 and 750 words and could be written in Czech, Slovak, Carpathian Ruthenian, English, or French. Seven prizes would be allocated for the competition. A first prize of $500 was established, and the seventh prize winner would receive twenty dollars. Submissions would be judged by a scholarship committee composed of the institute's executive officers and supplementary school language instructors and the editorial staff of *Nový domov.*[84]

Community members became increasingly concerned about cultivating their ethnocultural heritage as younger members of the community were assimilating into Canadian society and no longer participating in community activities. As the Canadian Czechoslovak community worked to cultivate its ethnocultural heritage for younger generations, its members engaged the Canadian government to increase family reunifications and to undermine the Communist Party government in Czechoslovakia.

Canadian-Czechoslovak Diplomacy Continues: Expo '67 and Spies

Canadian Czechoslovak institutions were heartened that early in the 1960s diplomatic relations between the Canadian and Czechoslovak governments remained cordial. In June 1962, cabinet decided to raise its legation in Prague to the status of an embassy and to extend the Czechoslovak government the same privilege in Canada. In part, the communist regime in Czechoslovakia began to rewrite its emigration regulations in order to facilitate the reunification of families. Individuals who had left Czechoslovakia illegally after February 1948 were permitted to return for visits without difficulties as long as they did not engage in activities detrimental to the country.[85] Officials in Ottawa asked legation staff in Prague to confirm whether the DEA's practice of submitting individual cases to the Communist Party authorities was harming each applicant's chances of success and whether submitting a list of names was preferable.[86] Karel Vojáček from the Czechoslovak Ministry of Foreign Affairs informed Western diplomats that Prague had eased its visa restrictions and allowed former residents travelling with Canadian passports to enter Czechoslovakia. As a result, Czech parents residing in Canada could reunite with the children whom they had left behind, while couples could legally emigrate and be married abroad. Czechoslovak diplomats hoped that the lessening of emigration and travelling restrictions would bring about friendly relations between East and West. In assessing the new consular conditions, Canadian Ambassador John Alexander McCordick noted that Prague came "to the conclusion that their former policy was costing them much in the image they created abroad and was not compatible with the campaign they were mounting to attract large numbers of tourists to this country, especially from among Czechs who had settled elsewhere in the last 30 years or so."[87]

In August 1965, a Canadian parliamentary delegation landed in Czechoslovakia for an inaugural visit. Prague's earlier step to allow Czechs with Canadian citizenship to visit their old country and for families to be reunited had turned out to be a hollow gesture. The parliamentary representatives raised the issue of family reunification with Communist Party officials, indicating that since 1961 only 260 Czechoslovak citizens had been able to immigrate legally to Canada. The officials informed Canadian representatives that Prague viewed emigration as an internal matter in which Canada should not interfere. In May 1966, a Canadian delegation submitted a list of thirty applicants to the Czechoslovak Ministry of Foreign Affairs in the hope of reuniting Canadian citizens with their relatives in Czechoslovakia. An additional list of twenty-five names was sent a month later. Prague viewed the gesture negatively and thought that Ottawa had no right to interfere.[88] As Canadian officials lobbied Prague for the reunification of families, the Department of Manpower and Immigration released a White Paper calling for the introduction of new liberalized immigration regulations that eliminated racial and geographic discrimination. However, refugees who held ideological beliefs in opposition to those of the Canadian government—including communism—would continue to encounter difficulty in gaining entry into Canada.[89]

Matters did not proceed, however, as hoped. Not only did the Czechoslovak government ignore Canadian demands for family reunification, but also it cynically promoted the repatriation of Czech refugees as it increased espionage activities in Canada. The RCMP observed that the Soviets were using evasive countersurveillance techniques by arranging to meet their agents outside urban centres. In October 1965, Victor Myznikov, a Komitet gosudarstvennoy bezopasnosti (Committee for State Security or KGB) officer in the Soviet Embassy in Ottawa, used hitchhiking as a means to meet one of his agents, thirty-three-year-old Canadian-born Mike Mihalčín Jr., in Brockville, Ontario. Once there, Myznikov handed Mihalčín two papers. The KGB officer returned to Ottawa, while Mihalčín departed for Toronto and later flew back to Edmonton via Thunder Bay. Mihalčín had been born in Canada to Slovak parents and then moved back to Czechoslovakia in his youth. Because his father was an active member of the Slovak Benefit Society of Canada, participated in the Independent Mutual Benefit Federation in Hamilton, and was believed to be a member of the Labour-Progressive Party in Fort William, Ontario, the StB considered Mike Jr. an ideal spy. In 1961, he returned to Canada with his wife and young child as an StB spy, and the family resettled in Edmonton under their real names. Upon learning about Mihalčín, the RCMP Special Branch believed that it had made a significant discovery, because he showed the "signs of a deep penetration agent."[90] The RCMP Special Branch nicknamed its surveillance of Mihalčín "Operation Kitbag" and code-named him Elf.[91] Canadian security officials waited for the StB sleeper agent to make his first move in Canada.

While Canadian authorities watched out for communist spies and Canadian diplomats continued to pressure Prague for the reunification of Czechoslovak nationals with their Canadian relatives, the CNAC held its eighteenth congress in Hamilton in April 1966. A particular focus of the congress was the problem of compensation to Canadians for property nationalized in Czechoslovakia. Members in attendance resolved to request that the Canadian government insist that Prague pay compensation to persons who were Canadian citizens when their property was nationalized by the Czechoslovak government. In a letter to Secretary of State for External Affairs Paul Martin Sr., CNAC president Antonín Daičar and Secretary General Jiří Corn argued that international law "afflicts an injustice on persons who were not citizens of the espousing state at the time when the property damages were suffered. It would appear that these persons do not enjoy the same protection as other Canadian citizens."[92] Delegates at the congress were concerned about Prague's refusal to transfer estate inheritances and proceeds from the sales of assets in Czechoslovakia to their beneficiaries in Canada. Subsequently, attendees urged Ottawa to adopt a policy of reciprocation by denying the transfer of proceeds from sales of property in Canada to inheritors in Czechoslovakia.[93] A year later CNAC members met in Ottawa to discuss further lobbying efforts regarding compensation claims for nationalized property and the renunciation of Czechoslovak citizenship.[94]

Perhaps sensing that the world's attention would soon be focused on Canada and learning of Czechoslovak President Antonin Novotný's upcoming visit to Montreal in May 1967, the CNAC informed Canadian officials that it would not take part in or support any protests that could damage or embarrass Canada. CNAC president Antonín Daičar and Secretary General Jiří Corn indicated that under normal circumstances they would have asked members to protest Novotný's visit to Canada. However, they desired to "do our duty as loyal citizens of Canada on the occasion of its centenary and so we appeal to all Slovaks and Czechs to be composed and dignified and permit a correct reception of Mr. Novotný and his entourage."[95]

In May, Governor General Roland Michener welcomed President Novotný to Canada for his five-day official visit to Ottawa, Quebec City, and the International and Universal Exposition (Expo 67) in Montreal to discuss bilateral trade, cultural affairs, and technology. The trip went smoothly enough until, in a press conference in Ottawa, Novotný was asked whether political prisoners had built some of his country's displays at Expo 67, and he replied that it was entirely possible. A small commotion erupted when Lubor Zink, a 1948er and a *Toronto Telegram* correspondent, asked him whether Ottawa and Prague had concluded a secret agreement to suppress defections among Expo 67 personnel who wanted to stay in Canada. Novotný denied any knowledge of any secret agreement and labelled Zink a spy. Zink responded by asking about the status of individuals in the "so-called free socialist society" of Czechoslovakia.[96] The exchange made national headlines and was followed by the international press. Zink later received dozens of letters from Canadians and compatriot organizations overseas, including *České slovo* (Czech Word), whose editor praised Zink's direct questioning of the Czechoslovak president.[97] Two days later Novotný arrived in Montreal and visited his country's pavilion at Expo 67, where he was enthusiastically greeted by a fifty-five-year-old Czech, William Valeš, who alongside Novotný had been imprisoned at the Mauthausen concentration camp during the Second World War. Novotný was also confronted by Gerry Kernc, a Czech resident of Montreal, who slipped the president a letter seeking help in getting his twenty-three-year-old twin daughters, Ludmila and Marie, from Prague to Expo 67.[98]

In an attempt to steer public attention away from the press controversy initiated by Zink, Miroslav Galuška, ambassador and general commissioner for Czechoslovakia at Expo 67, informed Canadians that it was Prague's ambition to develop broader mutual contacts in future years. In reality, Czechoslovakia wanted to increase trade with Canada to aid its stagnant economy. Prague was interested in importing wheat, metals, chemicals, asbestos, hides, and seeds from Canada. Conversely, Czechoslovak officials sought to export ham, beer, jewellery, glass, sports equipment, and furniture, among other goods. The Communist Party government hoped that trade would increasingly lead to peaceful coexistence between the countries.[99]

Relations between Czech refugees in Canada and the Czechoslovak government were tense when, in May 1967, the Department of External Affairs informed Canadian citizens that Ottawa was entering negotiations with the Czechoslovak government over outstanding claims by individual Canadians against Prague. Potential claims were limited to issues involving nationalized property, rights, interests, and debts with the Czechoslovak government after February 1948.[100] The CNAC lobbied Ottawa to pressure President Novotný and delegation officials during their visit to Expo 67. The association demanded that the Canadian government ask Prague to permit Czechoslovak nationals to visit Montreal for Expo 67, especially individuals whose expenses were to be paid by Canadian residents. The CNAC also demanded that Canadian claims for property nationalized by the Czechoslovak government be settled and called on the Canadian government to include claims from persons who became Canadian citizens after the nationalization of their property. The reunification of Canadian families with their relatives in Czechoslovakia, and Prague's acceptance of the renunciation of Czechoslovak citizenship by naturalized Canadian citizens, were included in the CNAC's lobbying efforts in Ottawa.[101]

When StB spy Mike Mihalčín was apprehended by the RCMP, relations became even more difficult. Meeting Anatoli Shalnev, a Soviet citizen attached to the Soviet pavilion, on Park Avenue in Montreal, Mihalčín received a shortwave radio and tuner to be able to listen to coded Soviet intelligence broadcasts. But soon the RCMP brought Mihalčín in for questioning. During his interrogation, Elf admitted that he was a Soviet spy who received coded information. Mihalčín claimed that his shortwave radio broke soon after he acquired it, and therefore he ignored all Soviet information and espionage activity. Whether the RCMP found his story credible is debatable, but he was later released on the belief that too much time had elapsed for him to have been a useful double agent. During his interrogation, Mihalčín informed the RCMP Security Service that he had become disillusioned with Soviet communism after his return to Canada, and he had simply chosen to ignore further Soviet information and activity.[102]

Still, the CNAC remained hopeful and thus submitted its recommendations to Ottawa for new immigration regulations and introduction of the points system, which removed geographic and racial discrimination and focused on linguistic ability, previous education, and employment experience in the selection of immigrants. The CNAC argued that membership in the Communist Party should not preclude an applicant from gaining entry into Canada from Eastern Europe. The association noted that in many cases individuals were coerced into joining the party out of fear of losing their employment and the persecution of close relatives. Known democrats and their relatives were denied promotions and access to higher education, and this discrimination often included subsequent generations. The CNAC recommended that the federal government permit Eastern Europeans to seek asylum and be recognized as refugees regardless of whether they were admissible according to the proposed points system.[103]

For Czechoslovak nationals granted passports to travel to Expo 67, many were finally able to visit their families in Canada.[104] Approximately one-fourth of persons legally permitted to travel outside Czechoslovakia headed to the West.[105] Some individuals chose to request asylum once in Canada. A majority of these individuals chose to resettle in Toronto, where they became known as the "Expo Émigrés." The MMI assisted the newcomers as they were processed by the local office of the Department of Manpower and Immigration in Toronto. Each newcomer was loaned a maximum of $140 per week from the Czechoslovak Credit Union to meet basic living expenses. Because the waiting period for landed immigrant status was long, the MMI contacted Canadian officials and arranged for individual work permits on behalf of their recently arrived compatriots. As chairman of the MMI's Immigration and Public Relations Committee, František Novotný negotiated with Canadian immigration officials on behalf of these newcomers and signed guarantees for individuals requesting political asylum.[106] In certain cases, Canada attempted to deport some of the asylum seekers back to Czechoslovakia because of their political backgrounds as Communist Party members. After lobbying the federal government, the MMI was able to prevent their deportation.[107]

Canadian Czechoslovak community institutions were buoyed in the months following Expo 67 and the arrival of the Expo Émigrés, and members of Toronto's Czechoslovak community began discussing the feasibility of establishing a "Czech and Slovak" literature course at a Canadian university. Three Czechoslovak organizations agreed in principle to work together to make a postsecondary university course a reality. The MMI, CNAC, and CFCR approached the University of Toronto, in part because the city was home to a sizable community from Czechoslovakia. The university was chosen to host the undergraduate course for the "promotion of knowledge of our literature in Canada among university students planning to enter an academic or diplomatic field."[108] In addition, the proposed course was to enable subsequent generations of Czechoslovak Canadians to study the language and literature of their cultural heritage. All three pro-Czechoslovak organizations in Canada undertook fundraising efforts to contribute $12,000 per year for three years to support the salary of an instructor. After 1970, the University of Toronto agreed to finance the course from its own financial reserves for another three years.

The three Canadian Czechoslovak organizations reached out to community members in the hope that they would provide financial support for a Czechoslovak literature course in Canada. As members of the CNAC executive, Daičar and Sypták noted that, since Polish, Russian, and Ukrainian were already being taught at the University of Toronto, Czech and Slovak language and literature classes should not be missing from this group. Simply, such a course was necessary for the creation of a Czechoslovak cultural heritage in Canada.[109] In 1968, the University of Toronto partnered with the MMI,

CNAC, and CFCR to subsidize a Chair for Czechoslovak Studies for three years. Nationalist Canadian Slovaks opposed establishment of a chair in Czechoslovak studies and the language and literature course because of its promotion of a unified "Czechoslovak" identity. With the beginning of classes in 1968, a majority of students enrolled in the course were second-generation Canadian Czechs and Slovaks with a "Czechoslovak" orientation, many of whom had arrived with their parents after 1948 and could already speak or write in their native language. As a result, classes primarily focused on Czech and Slovak literature and grammar.[110]

▸ ▸ ◂ ◂

In the 1950s and 1960s, the immigration of Czech refugees who espoused anti-communist and pro-democracy sentiments was encouraged by Canadian officials who continued to be wary of communist sympathizers and Soviet agents. Meanwhile, Czech refugees provided the Canadian government's anti-communist agenda with greater legitimacy since many of these individuals had witnessed first-hand the political persecution initiated by the Communist Party in Czechoslovakia.[111] Still, many Czech families remained divided between West and East, democracy and communism, freedom and oppression. But they also suffered from the rising and then dashing of hope for the old homeland. The early 1968 reform movement in Czechoslovakia, removing press censorship and reintroducing personal freedoms, was squelched several months later by the Soviet-led Warsaw Pact invasion. The resulting refugee crisis eventually led to a significant wave of immigration to Canada. This new group of Cold War refugees from Communist Czechoslovakia soon reinvigorated Canadian Czechoslovak institutions. They once again made the struggle for a democratic system of government in their old homeland a central focus, one that enabled the refugees to achieve social and cultural citizenship in Canada.

CHAPTER 5

Warsaw Pact Invasion: Canada and the 1968ers

Libor and Jiřina Roštík married in April 1968. They had already achieved many of their dreams, including close relationships with their family and relatives, good-paying jobs, and a lakeside cottage. The young couple believed that they had a bright future together in Czechoslovakia. While Jiřina was employed as a technical illustrator and draftswoman, Libor worked as an electrical engineer. Yet they decided to begin new lives in the West and enlisted the help of Libor's brother-in-law, an engineering expert who worked in the sugar industry in Cuba, asking him to invite them for a visit. The Roštíks received a two-month exit visa from the Czechoslovak government and went to Havana, leaving their family, friends, and material possessions behind. During their eight weeks in Cuba, they agonized over whether to return home or seek political asylum in the West. Believing that they would never be fully accepted in another European country, Libor and Jiřina chose Canada because of its vast resources and acceptance of immigrants.

Their return flight from Havana to Prague included a stopover in Gander, Newfoundland, and in early December 1968 the Roštíks (along with three other refugees, Josef Kocián, Miroslav Kantarský, and Miroslav Tadla) disembarked there and immediately requested political asylum in Canada. The Roštíks, dressed for the tropical climate of the Caribbean, began their new lives in Canada in the middle of winter with only ten American dollars and some personal effects from Cuba. Canadian immigration officials took them to a local hotel, where they received vouchers for breakfast. After their transportation to Pier 21 in Halifax, the Roštíks were medically cleared and interviewed by Canadian immigration officials, who later accepted the couple as political refugees and allowed them to leave the detention centre in Halifax and begin a government language program in the city. After successful completion of weekly language tests, the Roštíks were guaranteed a weekly allowance of thirty-five dollars.[1] Soon the Czech couple rented a small apartment in the city while they continued to attend English-language classes. In the middle of their six-month course, Libor was hired by Dominion Engineering Works in Montreal as a project engineer. Shortly after relocating there, Libor and Jiřina began to learn French. Why would a young couple leave family and friends and a promising professional future to take on such hurdles?

In contrast to the 1948ers, who had fled communism as an ideology, those who fled the Warsaw Pact invasion of Czechoslovakia in 1968 were fleeing communism as a lived reality. Two decades under Communist Party rule had brought not the promised societal and economic equality but a two-tier class system. Whereas privileged Communist Party functionaries had access to Western material goods and could travel with relative freedom, regular citizens endured long lineups for everyday goods and services of inferior quality, crumbling buildings and infrastructure, and travel restrictions that meant that they could not leave the Communist Bloc. For many Czechoslovak citizens, their religious, political, or bourgeois backgrounds forbade them and their children from attaining promotions in the workplace or attending university. Meanwhile, in the West, the spirit of freedom was in the air: the civil rights, women's liberation, and anti-war movements; hippiedom; rock 'n' roll; and student riots were gaining momentum. The rise of counterculture and radical political agitation in all facets of life in the West collided with existing Cold War norms of the conservative nuclear family, staunchly anti-communist, with a male breadwinner as head of the household. The emergence of progressive and anti-war politics occurred at a time when anti-communist hysteria was widespread in the West and when espionage by Western and Eastern European intelligence agencies was extensive. Given this sociopolitical climate, Canadian authorities responded cautiously to immigration from behind the Iron Curtain. Individuals who fled from persecution in the Eastern Bloc were often viewed by the Canadian public as "freedom fighters" but also distrusted as potential spies.[2]

Federal officials and the Canadian public came to learn that most of these newcomers were ardent anti-communists who espoused democratic values and sought safe haven from totalitarianism and sociopolitical repression. Public and private gatekeepers viewed the Czech refugees who fled their homeland in 1968 as individuals who could bolster their conservative Cold War consensus against the "left" in Canada, which opposed Western imperialism and American-led efforts in the Vietnam War. Many of the Prague Spring refugees, politically engaged, joined Canadian Czechoslovak organizations to lobby federal officials to defend Canada from the spread of communism and to return democratic government to Czechoslovakia. Some of the recent arrivals also became community representatives who brokered relations between the Czechoslovak community and the Canadian government. These ethnocultural liaisons strengthened the social and cultural citizenship of previous waves of Czech refugees but also demonstrated to Czech newcomers that achieving a similar form of civic engagement was possible after having fled an authoritarian and repressive regime in their homeland.

Prior to the Warsaw Pact invasion of Czechoslovakia, it was impossible to shield completely the Eastern Bloc from Western influences. Young people were particularly inspired by Western culture. As individuals tried to flee to the West, ever-tighter border controls led to daredevil escapes and failed attempts—either fatal or punishable by imprisonment. Ever more repressive controls on society—including restrictions on freedom of movement and association, press censorship, and surveillance of citizens by Eastern Bloc security services, Securitate (Romania), Stasi (East Germany), and StB (Czechoslovakia), for example—were all parts of daily life behind the Iron Curtain. Opposition to state-sponsored measures preventing reform or revolution against communist governments does not have a successful history. In the first two decades after the Second World War, communist governments in Eastern Europe crushed four significant attempts at rebellion, including the 1953 uprisings in Czechoslovakia and East Germany; the 1956 uprising in Poznań, Poland; and the 1956 Hungarian Revolution, from which Canada resettled approximately 37,500 refugees. Across Eastern Europe, attempts to escape by individuals, families, or groups often ended fatally. However, attempts to flee to the West continued. In August 1961, the iron fist of Soviet rule tightened with the building of the Berlin Wall, which divided Berlin between West Germany and East Germany. Across Eastern Europe, potential reformers within communist systems behind the Iron Curtain were faced with a dilemma: how to effect significant change when recent history illustrated that attempts at reform or outright rebellion were quickly quashed by the Soviet authorities. The emergence of a communist reform movement in Czechoslovakia can be traced to the early 1960s, when a significant cross-section of society—including party members, students, workers, agriculturalists, intellectuals, and clergy—became increasingly dissatisfied with the hardline Communist Party government and advocated for change to the political and socioeconomic systems in Czechoslovakia.

The Prague Spring

Throughout the 1960s, Communist Party–led organizations were in a state of decline. Membership in the Communist Party became unpopular across society. Increasingly, many Czechoslovak citizens thought that reform of the political system and stagnant economy was a priority to combat the deceptions, rigidness, and authoritarianism of communist rule in their country.[3] Liberal elements outwardly criticized the party and First Secretary Antonín Novotný for failing to reform Czechoslovak society and economy.[4] Within the Communist Party itself, reformers decided to seize an opportunity to confront years of hard censorship and economic decline. In January 1968, Novotný was replaced as first secretary of the Communist Party by the Moscow-educated Slovak reformer Alexander Dubček. Faced with the reality that overt revolt was hopeless, Dubček strove to implement liberal reforms within the structure of Czechoslovak communism.

In April 1968, Dubček declared that, under "socialism with a human face," communism in Czechoslovakia would be liberalized.[5] His efforts had been bolstered when in late March, Novotný was replaced as president by General Ludvík Svoboda. After purging Stalinist hardliners from the leadership of the party, reformers in the upper echelons of the party attempted to combine democratization of individual rights with liberalization of the economy. That same month, the Communist Party of Czechoslovakia released its Action Program detailing how the country would institute its own form of socialism instead of following the Soviet model.[6] In the following months, press censorship decreased, writers who opposed the regime were rehabilitated, and political reforms were instituted. In May 1968, press censorship was completely abolished, religious groups were free to exercise their faith traditions, and personal freedoms were entrenched.[7] In the middle of June, a group of intellectuals urged Ludvík Vaculík, a writer and prominent reformist member of the Communist Party, to draft a declaration in support of socialism through democratic means. The manifesto, titled "Dva tisíce slov, které patří dělníkům, zemědělcům, úředníkům, umělcům a všem" ("Two Thousand Words that Belong to Workers, Farmers, Scientists, Artists, and Everyone"), argued that the socialist system had to learn from its failures and that reform would humanize the communist regime.[8] This period of communist liberalization in Czechoslovakia became known as the Pražské jaro (Prague Spring).[9] The reforms were met with growing concern in capitals across the Eastern Bloc, whereas Western governments quietly supported democratization of the political system in Czechoslovakia.

Meanwhile, Czech refugees in Canada watched with anticipation as events unfolded in their old homeland. In Prague, Canadian diplomats viewed the communist regime's changing of the guard as a revolution from within the upper echelons of the Communist Party. In correspondence shared among Commonwealth governments, Alan Renouf, the Australian ambassador in Belgrade, argued that with Dubček in power "Czechoslovakia is finally throwing off the remnants of Stalinism and is moving into a new era where the younger, more modern Communists will set the pace."[10] Canadian diplomats were hopeful that a reformist leadership would be able to negotiate terms for family reunifications, which remained a contentious issue between Ottawa and Prague. After multiple meetings between parliamentarians on both sides, 142 individuals were permitted to emigrate from Czechoslovakia to Canada in the first quarter of 1968. Similarly, Canadian and Czechoslovak officials were in negotiations over outstanding Canadian property claims against Czechoslovakia, which totalled more than $200 million. Ottawa did not release this figure to the Communist Party authorities.[11]

Although supporters of communist reform in Czechoslovakia were hopeful that the Prague Spring would bring about much-needed change, neighbouring communist states—including East Germany, Poland, and the Soviet Union—viewed the changes with fear since they could spread and weaken the stability of their hardline and conservative regimes.[12]

Operation Danube

Fearing that Prague's liberalization would spread, the Communist Party governments of Bulgaria, East Germany, Hungary, Poland, and the Soviet Union met in the Polish capital in mid-July and decided to issue a "Warsaw Letter," which demanded that Prague reinstitute censorship and suppress independent political groups or face a military intervention. Subsequently, the five Communist Party governments conducted a press campaign against Czechoslovakia's reformist leaders and stationed Warsaw Pact troops along the country's border with East Germany, Poland, Soviet Union, and Hungary. In Western capitals, the prospect of an invasion of Czechoslovakia by Warsaw Pact member states was seen as unlikely, and any intervention in Czechoslovakia by Western governments was ruled out.[13]

Despite this view among Western countries, Czechoslovakia's Communist Party leaders met in late July with Soviet leader Leonid Brezhnev in Čierna nad

Tisou, Slovakia, where the Soviets impressed on their counterparts that further reforms would come with grave consequences.[14] The Soviets demanded that Prague remove reformers from key party positions, reinstitute press censorship, and ban all political clubs, including the Klub angažovaných nestraníků or KAN (Club of Committed Non-Party Members) and the Klub bývalých politických vězňů or K 231 (Club of Former Political Prisoners). The Club of Committed Non-Party Members was founded during the Prague Spring by 144 prominent intellectuals and members of society as an independent organization that promoted social justice, human rights, and reform of the communist system in Czechoslovakia. The Club of Former Political Prisoners was also established during the Prague Spring and comprised approximately 80,000 members across Czechoslovakia. The club's supporters were individuals sentenced under paragraph 231 of the criminal code for (anti-socialist) crimes against the state. The organization represented former political prisoners and fought for their social and political rehabilitation under the communist regime.[15]

With the emergence of diverse political associations that advocated on behalf of their members before the reformist Czechoslovak government, Communist Party officials from Bulgaria, East Germany, Hungary, Poland, and the Soviet Union met in Bratislava and agreed to defend communism from reform.[16] With Dubček advocating for patience, the Soviet Union could no longer accept public attacks by the local population against Czechoslovakia's Communist Party and ordered the Warsaw Pact to invade the country.[17] Overnight on 21–22 August, approximately 170,000 soldiers and 4,600 tanks from Bulgaria, Hungary, Poland, and the Soviet Union crossed into Czechoslovakia as part of Operation Danube and sought to quell the Prague Spring.[18] Operation Danube's main objective was to assist conservative Communist Party officials in seizing power from reformist members in order to reinstitute a hardline Communist Party government in Czechoslovakia.[19]

The 1968ers Leave

The occupation of their country by Soviet and Warsaw Pact troops provided a strong motivation for Czechs to leave their country in search of better lives. Some were able to acquire exit visas on the basis of letters of invitation written by contacts in the West. Others were already outside their country's borders at the time of the invasion. Czechs also left for the Šumava Mountains and walked for more than six hours before reaching the border. In the weeks after the Soviet-led invasion, emigration was relatively simple: Czechoslovak border officials simply permitted individuals and families to cross the border into West Germany or Austria, where they were registered and given accommodations and food tickets—necessary help since, in many cases, Communist Party officials had seized most of their funds at the border.

Prague Spring refugees arrived in the West with only their personal effects and clothing—often in only two pieces of luggage—in an effort to demonstrate to the Communist Party authorities that they were ostensibly leaving the country only for a "vacation." Subterfuge extended to personal relations: out of fear for the safety of close relatives and friends, many refugees did not inform them of their emigration.[20] Friends and contacts in Western Europe also wired money to Czech refugees as they slept in school gyms and later government-provided accommodations while waiting to learn whether they would remain in Central Europe or resettle in Australia, Canada, New Zealand, the United States, or Western Europe.[21] Referred to by the Czechoslovak government press as the *vycestovali* or those who "travelled out," approximately 150,000 individuals resettled in the West after the Warsaw Pact invasion. The *vycestovali* formed a majority of approximately 225,000 individuals who fled their homeland for the West since the Communist Party seizure of power in February 1948.[22]

Scholars remain divided over the reasons for Canada's decision to resettle close to 12,000 Prague Spring refugees. Some scholars have argued that economic considerations and self-interest played a major role in the government's decision to resettle young and well-educated professionals who could make an immediate socioeconomic impact. Others have claimed that Cold War politics led Ottawa to suspend temporarily its immigration regulations in an attempt to embarrass the Soviet Union for ideological reasons.[23] Advocates for the rights of refugees criticized the federal government for playing into Cold War politics in choosing to permit individuals and families fleeing from communism in Eastern Europe to enter Canada, whereas persons escaping from right-wing regimes were often ignored.[24] However, recent scholarship suggests that Ottawa believed that it had to intervene on humanitarian grounds, bringing well-educated refugees to Canada who did not pose a security threat to Canadian society. Similarly, Ottawa did not want to embarrass the Soviet Union and unnecessarily heighten Cold War tensions. Viewed by federal officials as "good material" for their professional backgrounds and sought-after experience, Prague Spring refugees were considered desirable immigrants who could make an immediate impact on the Canadian economy.[25] Canadian Czechoslovak organizations lobbied the government to push for a Soviet withdrawal from Czechoslovakia and to resettle a large number of their compatriots in Canada.

Canadian Foreign Policy before and after the Invasion

During the Prague Spring, the CNAC carefully followed political developments in Czechoslovakia. The organization's executive members informed Canadian Secretary of State for External Affairs Mitchell Sharp that they welcomed the liberalization movement taking place within the Communist Party of Czechoslovakia. Antonín Daičar and Jiří Corn argued that while liberalization was occurring, individuals in Czechoslovakia were benefiting from greater individual rights and freedoms. The CNAC hoped that the liberalization of Czechoslovakia would result in the democratization of its institutions and that personal freedoms would be fully returned to the populace. Subsequently, the CNAC, well aware of Moscow's continued intervention in Czechoslovakia's affairs, requested that Canada apply pressure on the Soviet Union through diplomatic channels to prevent Moscow's influence.[26] However, Canadian officials simply watched as events in Czechoslovakia unfolded and remained silent on the Prague Spring in an effort not to heighten tensions with Moscow. According to Undersecretary of State for External Affairs Marcel Cadieux, it was not in Prague's best interest for Canada to make an official public statement.[27]

As news broke of events in Czechoslovakia on 20 August, Sharp informed the press that the movement of Warsaw Pact troops into the country was disappointing and that there would be diminishing confidence in Europe on an East-West détente. Sharp remained confident that the invasion was not a threat to world peace since Czechoslovakia was not resisting the Soviet-led advance.[28] A day later, with the Canadian prime minister enjoying a vacation on the beaches of Spain, Soviet Ambassador to Canada Ivan Shpedko informed Acting Prime Minister Paul Hellyer of the Soviet-led invasion of Czechoslovakia. Shpedko indicated to Hellyer that the Soviets had sent troops into the country in order to rescue socialism.[29] Meanwhile, a delegation of nine Czechoslovak community leaders representing the CNAC, the MMI, the Permanent Conference of Slovak Democratic Exiles, and the Czechoslovak Society of Arts and Sciences issued a joint statement on the events of 20–21 August. The statement expressed that Canadians of Czechoslovak origin were "deeply shocked by the rape of Czechoslovakia by the Soviet and Warsaw Pact armies."[30] The four organizations argued that, after the Munich Conference of 1938 and the Communist Party takeover of 1948, Czechoslovakia deserved the international community's support. Representatives of the four organizations met with Hellyer and Sharp and presented a memoir on events in Czechoslovakia.[31] The representatives demanded that strong measures be taken by the Canadian government, including formulating a declaration condemning the invasion of Czechoslovakia and its brutality against the local population; submitting a protest before the United Nations over the aggression of Warsaw Pact states in Czechoslovakia; proposing a resolution at the United Nations Security Council to create an international peace force to be deployed in Czechoslovakia; using diplomatic channels to secure the freedom of individuals arrested by the Soviets during the invasion; and ensuring the safe departure of individuals and families with Canadian citizenship and their return to Canada while also facilitating the admission of refugees from Czechoslovakia.[32] After their meeting, representatives of the CNAC informed the press that the remarks of the secretary of state for external affairs were exceptionally bland.[33] On behalf of its fifty-seven branches across the country, the nationalist Canadian Slovak League also sent representatives to meet Canadian officials and share their views on the Soviet invasion of Czechoslovakia. In an interview with the *Montreal Gazette,* president of the CSL John Dvorský indicated that the Soviets had viewed the Slovaks as brothers but had now come into Czechoslovakia as enemies. Canadian Slovaks also insisted on taking a stand against the Soviet-led invasion to demonstrate their opposition to Moscow's policies.[34]

Canadian press outlets also voiced their concerns about the direction of Canada's foreign policy following the Warsaw Pact invasion. *La Presse* argued that the invasion provided the government with a perfect opportunity to demonstrate in which direction its foreign policy would go. The paper contended that the government's policies had been anemic and passive but could now become proactive in the face of an international crisis. Addressing concerns from both the public and the press about the government's position regarding the invasion, on 21 August Sharp issued a statement in which he explained that the Canadian government was shocked and dismayed by the invasion of Czechoslovakia. The government also condemned the Soviet Union's use of force. The secretary of state expressed that all Canadians were deeply concerned about the people of Czechoslovakia.[35] Sharp went on to suggest that the Soviet invasion and subsequent occupation of the country comprised a flagrant breach of the principle of non-intervention to which Moscow claimed to subscribe. Sharp concluded the statement by indicating that Ottawa remained in contact with its embassy in Prague and would ensure the safety of all

Canadian citizens in Czechoslovakia.[36] The minister argued that refugees from Czechoslovakia would receive the same welcome as had Hungarians in 1956. The Canadian press wondered whether his condemnation would bring about action.[37] Members of the press in attendance inquired whether Dubček would be granted political asylum in Canada, to which Pierre Trudeau replied that the question was premature. The prime minister acknowledged that Canada's ability to act in Eastern Europe would be limited but that supporting the reformist leaders of Czechoslovakia would remain a priority.[38]

Since the Canadian government's ability to act in the aftermath of the invasion was limited, its Permanent Representative to the United Nations George Ignatieff—along with colleagues from Brazil, Denmark, France, Paraguay, Senegal, the United Kingdom, and the United States—introduced a draft joint resolution at the UN Security Council condemning the Soviet-led invasion of Czechoslovakia. The resolution called on the four Warsaw Pact countries that had participated in the invasion—Bulgaria, Hungary, Poland, and the Soviet Union—to withdraw their forces and cease their intervention in Czechoslovakia. The draft resolution mirrored the measures advocated by the CNAC. The Soviet Union opposed consideration of the resolution question—withdrawal of the Warsaw Pact forces from Czechoslovakia—but was defeated 13-2 when the Security Council voted to put the question on its agenda. Despite this result, as a permanent member of the council, the Soviet Union vetoed the draft resolution.[39] The symbolic political gesture by the Canadian government and several Western countries to denounce the Soviet-led invasion was later met with an outpouring of support for the Czechoslovak community in Canada.

Ethnic Organizations in Canada Respond

In the aftermath of the Warsaw Pact invasion, the CNAC received condolences from the Trans-Canada Alliance of German Canadians expressing their shock and dismay by the Soviet occupation of Czechoslovakia. The alliance also condemned the involvement of the German Democratic Republic in planning Operation Danube. East German authorities feared that the Prague Spring could lead to a popular uprising in their country. However, just a few hours before the invasion, Moscow ordered East German forces not to cross the Czechoslovak border.[40] On behalf of German Canadians, the alliance expressed its wish for Germans and Czechoslovaks to live together as good neighbours.[41] Similarly, the Central Organization of Sudeten Germans in Canada, which represented former citizens of Czechoslovakia, condemned

Figure 15. *Toronto-based Czech demonstrators gathering at Masaryk Memorial Institute to board buses to Ottawa, 22 August 1968.*

the Soviet occupation. The organization asserted that people's belief in freedom would remain strong and that democratic government would return to Czechoslovakia.[42]

In the early morning of 22 August, over 200 members of the Czechoslovak communities in Toronto and Hamilton left the MMI in a convoy of buses and cars decorated with Canadian and Czechoslovak flags. Before the convoy left southern Ontario for the nation's capital, president of the MMI Ervin Sypták informed the *Globe and Mail* that the Canadian Czechoslovak community was in complete turmoil, and he feared that, while women and children were permitted to leave Czechoslovakia, the Communist Party authorities would prevent men from leaving with them.[43] Other members of the Czechoslovak community did not discount the use of force to protect Canadian citizens or to free their homeland from Soviet occupation. Jarmila Jelínek of Hamilton informed the *Toronto Star* that the Canadian government should support armed intervention.[44] Arriving at Parliament Hill in the afternoon, Sypták, Jelínek, and their fellow compatriots demanded that recently returned Prime Minister Trudeau provide assistance in ending the Soviet occupation of their old homeland. Protesters held flags and placards that stated "Nazis 1938,

Figure 16. *A woman is interviewed by a man with a microphone while Czech demonstrators protest against the Soviet-led Warsaw Pact invasion of Czechoslovakia, Toronto, 22 August 1968.*

Russians 1968,""Russians Leave Czechoslovakia," and "Soviet Murderers Are Capable of Killing Every Good Idea." The demonstrators were later joined by Trudeau, Sharp, Hellyer, and Paul Martin Sr.[45]

In Winnipeg, a silent vigil was also held on 22 August at the cenotaph in Memorial Park to show solidarity with the people of Czechoslovakia. Underscoring the group's commitment, one of the vigil's organizers, Jack Stevenson, a professor of philosophy at the University of Manitoba, indicated to the press in attendance that the vigil would continue for twenty-four hours—which it did.[46] Over 300 individuals formed a procession up Memorial Boulevard to place a wreath with the words *Freedom at All Cost* at the cenotaph. Although fifteen different ethnic communities were represented in the procession, a majority of the individuals were members of the Ukrainian Canadian Committee. Winnipeggers carried placards, including "Warsaw Pact—Russian Control," "End Soviet Aggression," and "Today Czechoslovakia—Tomorrow the World." Premier of Manitoba Walter Weir addressed the crowd, stating that it was fitting that the protesters chose the city's cenotaph to demonstrate against the Soviet invasion of Czechoslovakia since the monument was a site for Winnipeggers to pay tribute to those who had given their lives in the name of freedom.[47]

In Ottawa, the protests begun in the evening of 21 August outside the Soviet Embassy by individuals from Ontario and Quebec continued for two days. A majority of the approximately 200 protesters were Czech and Slovak immigrants who carried placards and signs expressing to the Soviets to "Go Home," "Give Us Back Our Liberty," "What Happened to Humanity, Soviet Imperialists?," and "Soviet Murderers Get Out from Czechoslovakia," while others illustrated that "Truth Prevails, Even Soviet Murderers Won't Come to Kill an Ideology." The protesters marched and sang Czechoslovakia's national anthem while hurling insults at those inside the embassy. Soviet Press Secretary Vladimir Makhotin was heckled and spat on as he left the grounds. The protest lasted almost two hours before poor weather ended it.[48] During the afternoon of 22 August, demonstrators left the Soviet Embassy and congregated before the Czechoslovak legation, once again singing their old homeland's national anthem before two diplomats came to greet them. The demonstrators hoped to bring attention to their cause and to lobby the Canadian government to admit refugees from Czechoslovakia. Chargé d'Affaires Alois Drhlík and Third Secretary Erhard Salomon were inundated with questions regarding their personal political beliefs and the situation in Czechoslovakia. Both diplomats stated to the crowd that they supported the Prague Spring and its reforms.[49]

In Montreal, approximately 800 individuals gathered at the cenotaph in Dominion Square to lay a wreath for deceased freedom fighters. The crowd then proceeded to shout "Dubček! Dubček!" as they made their way to the Soviet consulate, where they attempted to present a petition to an official demanding the immediate withdrawal of Soviet troops from Czechoslovakia. In illustrating their opposition to Soviet imperialism, the demonstrators remained at the consulate for days, even breaking the legation's windows. A short walk away Montrealers gathered at the Czechoslovak consulate, where they were greeted by two officials who thanked them for their support.[50] Not everyone in the Czechoslovak community supported an anti-communist identity. Some adhered to socialist-communist values from their involvement in labour movements, unions, and the politics of the interwar left in Canada.

Within the Czechoslovak community in Canada, only a few individuals were adherents of communism. Throughout the twentieth century, communists within the community had established groups promoting social justice,

Figure 17. Czech demonstrators protest against the Soviet crackdown of the Prague Spring reform movement and communist aggression in Vietnam, Toronto, 22 August 1968.

progress, and peace, all in the hope of attracting members to the communist movement. A lifelong communist, Jozef Duriančík published the pro-communist Slovak-language weekly *L'udové zvesti* (People's News). He had come to Toronto from Czechoslovakia in 1926 at the age of seventeen and later joined others who advocated for workers' rights during the Great Depression. In 1933, he began printing the socialist weekly, which espoused progressive and democratic socialist ideals. For thirty-five years, the paper had remained loyal to the Prague government, never disagreeing with its policies, including the promotion of Czechoslovakism in Slovakia. But now the editor found himself profoundly disturbed by the Soviet invasion of Czechoslovakia, and in an interview with the *Toronto Daily Star* he admitted that he no longer knew what he was or what to do; the invasion had shaken his communist values to the core. In preparing his first issue since the invasion, the communist Slovak editor attacked the Soviet Union for its aggression and brutality. Duriančík concluded that the people of Czechoslovakia would overcome their new reality and continue their struggle for personal freedom and national independence.[51] Meanwhile, the official organ of the nationalist Canadian Slovak League, *Kanadský Slovák* (Canadian Slovak), condemned the Soviet-led invasion and argued that "not to have one's own state was a question of life and death."[52]

With many community members dismayed by the demise of the Prague Spring and the subsequent Warsaw Pact invasion of their old homeland, in the following weeks Canadian officials followed the situation in Czechoslovakia closely. In late August, Secretary of State for External Affairs Mitchell Sharp informed the CNAC that he was monitoring it on an hourly basis and reassured the organization's executive members that Ottawa would take every useful action within its power.[53] Meanwhile, CNAC branches continued to hold protests in urban centres across Canada. The largest demonstrations were held in Montreal and Toronto. In the latter city, the 29 August demonstration was organized by prominent members of the Canadian Czechoslovak and nationalist Slovak communities. Despite interethnic tensions, both groups came together in their mutual opposition to the Soviet-led invasion of Czechoslovakia. Under the chairmanship of George Ben, a Slovak and an MPP for the constituency of Humber in Toronto's West End, a march took place from the Ontario legislature to Nathan Phillips Square at Toronto City Hall. Premier of Ontario John Robarts and Mayor of Toronto William Dennison spoke before a crowd of over 5,000 individuals. A resolution was signed by Canadian ethnic organizations representing twenty-five nations under Soviet domination in demanding justice for Czechoslovakia. The CNAC was joined by the CSL in its defence of democratic reforms in Czechoslovakia. The Czech-language weekly *Naše hlasy* (Our Voices) published an editorial entitled "Our Answer to the Soviets: No More Talks! Get Out! Save Dubček, Save Czechoslovakia," and promoted the public demonstration.[54] The anti-communist paper argued that Czechoslovakia was fighting for its life and that readers should help by lobbying federal officials to sever all political, economic, and diplomatic ties with Moscow.

With the cooperation of twenty-five ethnocultural organizations—including the CNAC, the MMI, and Sokol Canada—the protest was successful in uniting support for a democratic Czechoslovakia.[55] The groups signed a declaration condemning the Soviet-led Warsaw Pact invasion of Czechoslovakia and called on Ottawa to continue to voice the country's displeasure with recent events. The declaration also called on Canadian officials to "resist Czechoslovakia being reduced to colonial status by requesting the General Assembly of the United Nations to: (a) condemn unequivocally Soviet aggression in Czechoslovakia; (b) insist upon an immediate and unconditional withdrawal of foreign troops from Czechoslovakia; (c) assist in establishing an independent representative government in Czechoslovakia through free elections; (d) advocate application of sanctions to enforce the foregoing; and (e) ask all nations of the free world to open their borders to victims of the Soviet imperialistic aggression and domination."[56] The protest in Toronto also pressured Ottawa to advocate for the implementation of free elections in all Soviet satellite states under the auspices of the United Nations and to demonstrate support for self-determination and the sovereignty of nations in Eastern Europe.[57]

The Canadian Government Responds

It has been estimated that over 80,000 Czechoslovak citizens were already abroad during the events of August 1968. Many were professionals on business in the West or vacationing in Yugoslavia, whose borders were open to travellers with valid documents, when the Soviet-led invasion occurred. Many Czechoslovak nationals preferred to wait and see how the political situation would evolve in their homeland before seeking asylum in another country. Most of the individuals carried valid passports and had the financial means to remain where they were for extended periods of time.[58] With Czechoslovakia's border open, many individuals and families chose to flee to the West rather than stay in the aftermath of the invasion. With hundreds of Czechoslovak nationals crossing into Austria and West Germany, the UNHCR hesitated to label them refugees because of a fear that they could create an "artificial refugee problem."[59] The international organization was concerned that identifying Czechoslovak nationals as refugees could become problematic should they later choose to return home rather than resettle permanently elsewhere. In Canada, officials were quick to avoid categorizing individuals who fled Czechoslovakia as "freedom fighters" since many of them would later be admitted for their socioeconomic potential as predominantly middle-class professionals who spoke multiple languages and were university educated. Department of Manpower and Immigration officials demonstrated no hesitancy in referring to Czechoslovak nationals as refugees in an effort to expedite their admission into and resettlement in Canada. Since Canada did not have an active refugee policy, and was not a signatory to the UN refugee convention, immigration officials used ad hoc measures and relaxed admission criteria, including medical screening, in order to facilitate rapidly the permanent resettlement of "good material" in Canada.[60]

Responding to pressure from the UNHCR and the Austrian government, Canadian immigration officials drew on their previous experience: the emergency resettlement program initiated for Hungarians fleeing to the West after the 1956 Soviet invasion of their homeland. At the time, the Canadian government believed that the Hungarian refugees would be the sole exception to its immigration practice.[61] But twelve years later, sensing that a humanitarian response was once again necessary, the government instituted a special program—from September 1968 to January 1969—that would ultimately resettle close to 12,000 refugees from Czechoslovakia and be applauded by a Canadian public that supported a humanitarian response to their plight.

In early September 1968, a special interdepartmental committee was formed with representatives from External Affairs, Manpower and Immigration, National Health and Welfare, and the Solicitor General—who represented the security concerns of the RCMP—to implement a resettlement scheme.[62] The special program for refugees from Czechoslovakia allowed immigration regulations to be relaxed as the requirement for the possession of a travel permit was waived and medical examinations and criminal record checks were concluded in Canada. The government sponsored chartered flights to bring refugees to Canada. Once in Canada, these newcomers would be assisted by the Department of Manpower and Immigration through financial assistance for accommodations and living expenses, medical and dental coverage, and English- and French-language training under the auspices of the Canada Manpower Training Program to support refugees as they entered the workforce.[63]

To implement the special program rapidly and efficiently, in early September 1968 officials in Ottawa instructed their immigration teams in Vienna and Belgrade to give refugees in Austria and Yugoslavia the same special treatment that the Hungarians had received in 1956. By the end of the first week of September, Canadian immigration officials in Belgrade had received approximately 500 inquiries and 100 immigration visa applications from refugees in camps.[64] However, despite Ottawa's instructions to its diplomats and immigration officials, those in Belgrade had difficulty obtaining permission from Ottawa to hire a bus to transport refugees from camps to Vienna for further processing. Furthermore, the Canadian Embassies in both Belgrade and Vienna suffered from a lack of instructions from Ottawa on how to deal with the refugees. Tim Creery, a journalist from the *Ottawa Citizen,* arrived in Belgrade in early September only to remark that the warm welcome extended to refugees to resettle in Canada was a shameful hypocrisy; some of the refugees had been forced to abandon their efforts to resettle in Canada because they had used up their personal funds while waiting to be processed. The situation called for improvisation. In early September, officials at the Canadian Embassy in Belgrade were able to find accommodations for twenty-three refugees, using the funds allocated for the legation's rent to cover the cost. Creery noted that, at the time of the Warsaw Pact invasion, approximately 50,000 refugees from Czechoslovakia called Yugoslavia home. Several weeks later, because of high unemployment in the country, only 5,000 remained. Many refugees had left for Austria, while others were trying their luck with embassies in other countries of Western Europe.[65] Astonishingly, given the urgency of the situation, Canada had yet to fill one of the two visa officer positions at its embassy in Vienna. With the informal cooperation of embassy staff, John Zawisza was forced to implement local solutions as quickly as possible. He soon realized that, to handle all of the incoming applications, a case-processing plan had to be developed. Zawisza distributed a generic Czech-language translation with the English and French versions of the Immigrant Application Form so that applicants could understand its details.[66] During the first three weeks after the Canadian announcement on 6 September of a special program for refugees from Czechoslovakia, Zawisza and his colleagues received 2,474 inquiries about permanent resettlement in Canada.[67]

With the special program well under way by the end of the first week of September, in Canada the CNAC held its annual congress in Batawa, Ontario. The association's central council resolved to invite all members to donate a minimum of five dollars on behalf of their families to one of the three major Canadian Czechoslovak organizations—the CNAC, MMI, and CFCR—and requested that they fundraise among their Canadian friends. On learning that the Canadian government would open its doors to refugees from Czechoslovakia, the CNAC advised its members that each refugee should be registered as an "open immigrant" to shorten the waiting period for his or her application to be processed.[68] The government also immediately supplied health insurance to individuals in this category, whereas normal immigrant applicants had to wait six months before becoming eligible. Ottawa informed the CNAC that it would attempt to process refugees within two weeks of receiving their applications for resettlement in Canada. Refugees who wanted to be sponsored as immigrants by relatives or friends in Canada would have to wait longer because applications for their sponsorship would have to be filed in Canada.[69]

The Refugees Arrive

Soon the first group of refugees from Czechoslovakia landed in Canada, on 8 September, after being processed by Canadian officials overseas.[70] Three days later, a group of fifty-four refugees arrived in Montreal from Vienna. The Department of Manpower and Immigration housed the refugees at Queen's Hotel in the city. Shortly thereafter, the group was assisted by federal officials in finding accommodations and employment.[71] On 15 September, a group of 203 refugees aboard the first charter flight arranged by the Canadian government arrived in Toronto after a nine-hour journey from Vienna. *Globe and Mail* reporter Peter Whelan noted that the refugees were as well dressed as any airline passengers arriving at airports in Montreal or New York. Canadian immigration officials believed that the country was receiving "a small gold mine of talent."[72] Many of them were multilingual, with some knowledge of English, French, German, or Russian. Additionally, most of them were members of the professional and technical classes comprised of academics, doctors, dentists, judges, architects, engineers, journalists, designers, lawyers, scientists, and tradespeople.[73] The chartered flight that carried 203 refugees to Toronto included many such professionals.

Canadian officials struggled to identify where to send the refugees. After placing each immigration visa applicant through a twenty-minute interview to assess his or her level of education and work experience, the applicant was informed about Canada and that employment in his or her chosen field could not be guaranteed.[74] One of the fortunate 203 refugees was Bedřich Procházka, a fifty-nine-year-old Czech who had been a judge and diplomat. Along with his wife, Emilie, and daughter, Hana, they left everything behind and fled Prague by train to Vienna, where they eventually boarded a chartered Air Canada flight to Toronto. A day later Procházka visited a Canada Manpower Centre to find housing and employment as a technical translator. He had worked at the Canadian Embassy in Vienna as a translator. The Procházkas spoke four languages, and their reasons for choosing Canada were simple. They had friends and family in the country, and Canadian officials had welcomed them and their fellow refugees.[75]

The refugees arriving from Austria, France, Italy, Switzerland, West Germany, and Yugoslavia were rapidly processed through immigration and customs and sent out to several hundred compatriots waiting in the airport to help them resettle in their new country. Immigration authorities accommodated refugees with temporary stays at three local Toronto hotels before

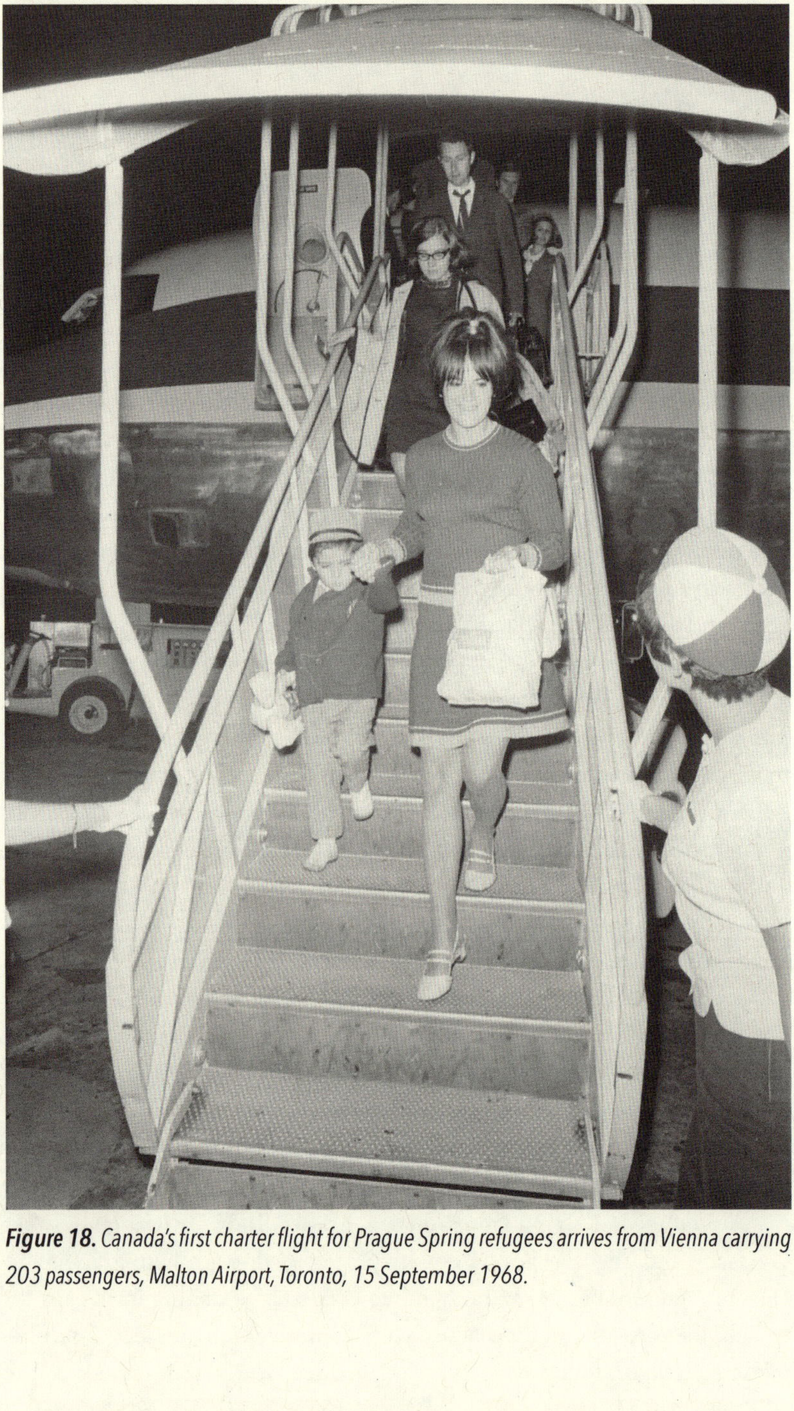

Figure 18. *Canada's first charter flight for Prague Spring refugees arrives from Vienna carrying 203 passengers, Malton Airport, Toronto, 15 September 1968.*

Figure 19. *A crowd of compatriots welcomes passengers from Canada's first charter flight for Prague Spring refugees, Malton Airport, Toronto, 15 September 1968.*

they were sent to various locations, including Hamilton, Oshawa, Kitchener, and Sudbury; Halifax; and Montreal.[76] The MMI organ *Nový domov* claimed that its institute had worked alongside Canadian officials to secure accommodations and employment in positions similar to their chosen fields in Czechoslovakia for approximately 80 percent of the 203 refugees prior to their arrival in Toronto in mid-September.[77] As Canadian officials in Europe continued to process applicants on a priority basis, the federal government relaxed its immigration procedures to expedite the resettlement of these refugees. Once in Canada, they received assistance from the Canada Manpower Centres along with universities and private organizations for language training, employment, accommodations, and other services. Resettlement support came not only from federal and provincial authorities but also from Czechoslovak community organizations.

The Canadian Czechoslovak community re-established the Canadian Fund for Czechoslovak Refugees and worked alongside the Czechoslovak National Association of Canada, the Masaryk Memorial Institute, and various federal and provincial departments to help the refugees from Czechoslovakia. Once in Canada, the 1968ers yearned to continue in their professions without communist interference. Compared with other immigrants who arrived in the late

Figure 20. *A Prague Spring refugee holding flowers is embraced after arriving in Canada, Malton Airport, Toronto, 15 September 1968.*

1960s, the 1968ers were quickly employed in their respective fields though underemployed in certain professions, including medicine and law, requiring recertification. Several years after their arrival, Prague Spring refugees maintained longer employment and higher income than did other immigrants who had arrived in Canada during the same period. Although highly adaptable as skilled workers and experienced professionals, some of the Prague Spring refugees continued to struggle to meet their economic needs in their new country.

Czech refugee women, for example, tended to be underemployed more frequently than their male counterparts. In some instances, immigration officials even refused to admit them to English- or French-language courses. The lower rate of suitable employment and income among Czech women resulted in part from Canada's occupational structure of unequal opportunity and pay for women compared with men.[78]

Similar to the 1948ers, who had fled the Communist Party takeover of Czechoslovakia, the 1968ers constituted a large wave of educated and skilled refugees. Unlike the 1948ers, however, the 1968ers had spent approximately twenty years living under communism and had experienced first-hand the effects of totalitarianism, including imprisonment. Not surprisingly, once established in Canada, many of them would actively promote the dissemination of dissident publications in the West, including the Czech refugee couple Josef Škvorecký and Zdena Salivarová, who established Sixty-Eight Publishers in Toronto.[79] Newly found political freedom and economic opportunity for entrepreneurship in Canada permitted many of the Prague Spring refugees to begin new careers or resurrect old professions as Canadian officials continued to resettle hundreds of Czech refugees daily during the special program.

Parliament Debates the Crisis

The Canadian government's response to the Warsaw Pact invasion of Czechoslovakia and its implementation of a special program to resettle refugees were sources of much debate in federal political circles. In mid-September 1968, the twenty-eighth Parliament was summoned to meet for official business. The Liberal government began to answer questions from the official opposition regarding the Prague Spring refugee crisis. Minister of Manpower and Immigration Allan MacEachen handled questions during Question Period pertaining to Canada's response to the Soviet-led invasion. MacEachen replied to a query from Progressive Conservative MP for Fundy-Royal, Robert Gordon Lee Fairweather, that Canadian officials overseas had been instructed to relax existing procedures and handle refugees from Czechoslovakia on a priority basis. Refugees interested in resettling in Canada would be processed as quickly as possible. Subsequently, Progressive Conservative MP for Calgary, Douglas Scott Harkness, asked MacEachen about the cost of resettling refugees, to which MacEachen replied that there was no way to ascertain the amount spent on each refugee. The minister went on to note that each incoming refugee would be treated as an individual case, and the Canadian government would help to pay the transportation and settlement costs. MacEachen informed Leader of the Official Opposition Robert Stanfield that instructions to relax immigration procedures had been sent to Europe a week earlier.

Stanfield argued in his reply to the prime minister's Speech from the Throne that the minister of manpower and immigration had reacted rather slowly to the crisis in Czechoslovakia. In a show of partisan politics, the opposition leader opined that Ottawa's response had left Canadians with the perception that their government was detached from the problems faced by refugees and that, as a result, Canadians could not be proud of their government.

Prime Minister Trudeau disagreed with Stanfield and indicated that his government's efforts were successfully resettling Prague Spring refugees in Canada. Trudeau told the House of Commons that, over the previous weekend,

280 refugees had arrived in the country, 267 of them requiring government sponsorship, and in the coming days two more chartered flights would arrive with another 266 individuals. Embassy staff in Vienna, now increased, conducted over 150 interviews daily in order to process refugees quickly. MacEachen noted that 2,374 Czechoslovak nationals had inquired at the embassy about entering Canada and that 901 individuals had summarily applied.[80]

The next day MacEachen announced that a team of four experts would be sent to Vienna to select highly skilled and valuable refugees such as artists, musicians, scientists, and intellectuals and assist in their resettlement in Canada.[81] The government sent Arnold Walter, the former head of the Royal Conservatory of Music in Toronto; J.D. Babbitt, the secretary for international relations at the National Research Council; Guy Gagnon, the coordinator of bilingualism for the Department of Manpower and Immigration; and Andrew Rossos, a professor in the Centre for Eastern European Languages at the University of Toronto.[82] This group of professional experts assisted Canadian officials in selecting desirable individuals and families who would make an immediate contribution to Canadian society and economy. Soon word of Canada's special program spread among Prague Spring refugees and led to an increase in requests for permanent resettlement in Canada.

An Unprecedented Opportunity

By late September, immigration officials at the Canadian Embassy in Vienna estimated that they had received approximately 2,400 applications for immigration visas since 21 August, averaging roughly eighty applicants per day. The officials were inundated with requests to come to Canada since the United States did not have a special program in place for refugees fleeing Czechoslovakia. According to the international news agency Reuters, an American diplomat in Vienna stated that the embassy was handling refugees with the same procedures established twenty years before the Warsaw Pact invasion. Incidentally, many of the refugees did not have clear options for resettling in the West. For instance, Ivan and Marta Stražnický visited the Australian, Canadian, and New Zealand Embassies hoping that officials would help to make the decision easier for them. In the end, the Stražnický family chose Canada because of how they were treated at the Canadian Embassy. According to Ivan, the Australians and New Zealanders left him and his wife with the impression that they might be permitted to enter their countries. However, Canadian officials welcomed the family without reservation.[83] As the Americans sought to take 600 refugees without emphasizing Prague Spring refugees crossing the border into Austria, a Canadian immigration official noted that Canada had an unprecedented opportunity to acquire well-educated and experienced individuals from diverse fields.

That opportunity would soon be turned into an attack on government policy. In late September in the House of Commons, MacEachen rejected a claim by Progressive Conservative MP for Prince Edward–Hastings, George Hees, that—in sending a special four-member immigration team to Vienna specifically to select certain refugees—Canada was simply choosing to resettle the most desirable refugees from various professions.[84] The minister of manpower and immigration argued before the House of Commons that the government's special program for refugees from Czechoslovakia provided free air transportation and temporary financial assistance to all refugees regardless of their backgrounds. He went on to note that the four-person team was to provide Canadian officials in Vienna with expert advice on employment opportunities for scientists, musicians, artists, and other professionals.[85]

Government Support for the Newcomers

As the federal government and provincial authorities worked to establish an effective and comprehensive resettlement scheme as a component of the special program, the CNAC moved to secure temporary accommodations for recently arrived refugees in Toronto. In early October, Alex Havrlant, a Czech lawyer and vice-president of the association, asked the Toronto Board of Education about the use of expropriated properties slated for demolition the following year. The CNAC then leased two properties on Marmaduke Avenue for fifty dollars per month each.[86] The MMI published an informational brochure entitled *První směrnice pro nové příchozí* (First Guide for Newcomers), which informed recent arrivals from Czechoslovakia where to find accommodations, employment, government programs, and social assistance. The guide advised newcomers to Toronto not to stay at a hotel for more than two or three days so that the MMI could assist them in finding apartments. Single adults and couples without children were informed that, if they secured apartments on their own, Canadian authorities would find that unfavourable since they were allocating public funds toward their initial resettlement and would be forced to cover any previous rental agreement. However, couples with young children would have their first month's rent paid by the federal government and receive a loan to cover their last month's rent. The government provided additional allowances of approximately twenty-five dollars for single adults and thirty-five dollars for married couples.

Figure 21. *Prague Spring refugee Bedřich Procházka speaks with staff at the Canada Manpower Centre, Dundas Street, Toronto. He and his wife Emilie (seated next to him) speak four languages–Czech, German, French, and English. His daughter Hana (pictured standing) also speaks Russian, September 1968.*

To secure employment, newcomers were instructed to visit a local Canada Manpower Centre and to register with the Technical Service Council. New arrivals were expected to have their personal documents translated and foreign work experience certified.[87]

Initially, many refugees from Czechoslovakia struggled to acquire employment in Canada, their professional qualifications notwithstanding. For a minority of individuals, including fifty-three-year-old Igor Helfert, though work came quickly, it was not in his chosen field. The former lawyer and diplomat was employed as a plant worker assembling vinyl-sashed windows. He understood that he was fortunate to acquire work and accommodation within two weeks of arriving in the country and claimed that he and his fellow refugees received excellent treatment.[88]

Many refugees from Czechoslovakia were aided in their resettlement by friends and family members already living in Canada. For others, the process was slow and unsettling. Thirty-two-year-old electrical engineer Jiří

Taranovský and his wife, from Prague, knew no one in the country and were put up by the Department of Manpower and Immigration in local hotels, such as the Ford Hotel in Toronto's Chinatown and the Waldorf Hotel in Hamilton's Jackson Square. In Hamilton, Jarmila Lenk and her children, arriving several weeks after her husband, moved into his one-bedroom unit in a boarding house; the landlord gave them a hotplate so that the family could cook meals. Once they were able to pay rent, they moved into a one-bedroom apartment at $110 per month and bought a bed and some furniture.[89] After leaving the Ford Hotel in Toronto, Marie Vejvalková and her husband received train tickets from Canadian authorities for their final destination of London. There the Manpower and Immigration Centre found them accommodation, cheap furniture, linens, plates, and cutlery—leaving the couple overjoyed.[90]

Some refugees found their own accommodations after staying in a government-funded hotel. In one instance, a Czech couple found a place to stay in the home of a Ukrainian couple in which use of the kitchen and washroom was communal. Ludmila Kotáčková and her husband paid ten dollars per week in rent and attended English-language classes in the evenings. The couple hoped to secure employment prior to the arrival of their first child. With their first child, the couple moved into a new apartment. While Ludmila stayed at home to raise their daughter and learn English, her husband secured employment with Westinghouse Electric Company.[91]

Canadian immigration officials also furnished recently arrived refugees with a list of rental units—in many cases, however, they included rundown properties such as undesirable basement apartments. The government provided the refugees with twenty-four dollars per week, and those who did not have pre-established contacts in Canada were assisted by local Czechoslovak organizations such as the CNAC and MMI in obtaining furniture and clothes. The MMI often attempted to persuade newcomers to stay temporarily with Anglo-Saxon families (rather than in ethnic Czech or Slovak homes) because they could quickly learn Canadian culture, customs, and the English language.[92] Although it remains unclear how many Czech refugees accepted offers to live with non-Czech Canadian families, recent arrivals appreciated efforts by community institutions to help them with resettlement.

Donations from the Community

An important part of the Canadian Czechoslovak community's efforts to help the refugees was raising funds. The MMI, for example, solicited several thousand dollars, and the CFCR (recently re-established because of the refugee crisis) amassed over $10,000 to assist individuals arriving in Canada. Businesses owned by Czech Canadians were also solicited for financial assistance on behalf of the refugees. The Bata Shoe Company issued 500 vouchers to the CFCR. Each voucher was worth seven dollars to be used to purchase footwear and other items from the company. In cooperation with the CNAC, the fund distributed the vouchers to local branches across the country.[93] For example, in Winnipeg 100 vouchers from the corporation with a total value of $700 were allocated to newly arrived refugees there. Similarly, the Star Slipper Company managed by Czech immigrant Vojtěch Škubal donated forty-five pairs of men's winter boots, and the Fortune Shoes Company donated sixty pairs of women's boots, twenty-two bathroom towels, and eight wool blankets.[94] In Edmonton, forty-eight pairs of men's boots, sixty pairs of women's boots, and fifty-five vouchers were delivered to the most deserving newcomers.[95] In all, the CFCR received $8,600 in footwear vouchers from the Bata Shoe Company; $5,000 from Antonín Ronza of Susan Shoe Industry Limited of Hamilton for footwear, towels, blankets, and bedding; $5,000 from J. Škubal of Fortune Footwear Limited; and $1,000 each from Joza Weider of Collingwood, Ontario, and lumber magnate Leon Koerner of Vancouver.[96] Although fundraising was an important component of assisting the newcomers, community institutions also turned to public commemoration to increase awareness of the Czechoslovak community in Canada and the political situation in Czechoslovakia.

Members of the Czechoslovak community held celebrations across the country to commemorate the fiftieth anniversary of the establishment of Czechoslovakia in October 1918. In Toronto, the celebrations were held a day early and attended by prominent members of local, provincial, and federal governments and ethnocultural associations. Even though Liberal Senator Andrew Thompson—who served as an ethnic liaison between ethnocultural communities and the federal government—did not attend the festivities, he sent the MMI a telegram congratulating the organization on its work in resettling Prague Spring refugees.[97] Former mayor of Toronto Nathan Phillips and his wife were in attendance along with representatives of the Canadian Polish Congress, the Court of Canadian Citizenship, Immigrant Settlement Services within the Canada Manpower Centre, and the City of Toronto.[98] In Hamilton, which initially received approximately 270 refugees, Mayor Victor Copps proclaimed 28 October as "Czechoslovak Day" in the city, and the national flag of Czechoslovakia was raised at Hamilton City Hall for one week.[99]

During these national celebrations and public displays of political support across Canada, the flow of refugees from Czechoslovakia continued. In early

November, over 3,000 refugees were already resettled in Canada. Fifteen charter flights organized by the government had brought over 2,625 of them. In the same period, 1,534 refugees reported to the Canada Manpower Centres across the country. In the ten weeks since the Warsaw Pact invasion, 600 refugees had secured employment, with fewer than half finding work in their professions. All refugees who reported to the Canada Manpower Centres were eligible to receive resettlement assistance from the federal government.[100]

Canadian authorities were aware that the flow of applications from Prague Spring refugees had declined since the middle of October, when approximately 1,500 individuals had arrived in a single week. A month later only 472 refugees arrived in Canada. The special program for refugees from Czechoslovakia remained in effect long enough for refugees to decide whether to resettle in Canada or remain in Europe. For many Czechoslovak nationals, the decision to leave in the months after the Soviet-led invasion and the closure of the border depended on whether they could secure invitations to visit business partners or family members in other socialist countries, thereby receiving exit visas from the Communist Party authorities in Prague.

The Canadian government estimated that between 10,000 and 11,000 refugees would be permanently resettled in Canada before the special program ended on 10 January 1969. Throughout the scheme, Ottawa had spent over \$4.7 million to resettle the refugees, who in turn owed \$1.3 million in transportation loans to the government.[101] The *Globe and Mail* noted that Ontario was the principal destination for more than half of all the newcomers from Czechoslovakia. Quebec was the second choice followed by Alberta, Manitoba, and British Columbia. A majority of the arrivals resettled in urban centres in these provinces.[102]

When the special program was terminated in January 1969, refugees from Czechoslovakia who had applied to enter Canada were considered under normal immigration regulations. However, they continued to be eligible for government assistance if they could meet the required conditions. For example, in order to participate in the Department of Manpower and Immigration's Occupational Training Program for Adults, individuals had to have been members of the Canadian workforce for an uninterrupted period of three years. But the change in regulations also left some refugees without any support. Such was the case for Vladimír Malík, who had arrived with his parents in Malton, Ontario, in late October 1968. They had been permitted entry into Canada as visitors for six months and less than two months later had applied to stay permanently in Canada. Although his parents had decided to return to Czechoslovakia, Vladimír was granted landed immigrant status on 6 March 1969. But because he was sponsored after the end of the special program, he was not eligible for financial, residential, and language training assistance.[103] Prague Spring refugees not admitted into Canada under the special program continued to be welcomed into the Canadian Czechoslovak community. Along with their compatriots who had arrived weeks or months earlier, they soon helped to reinvigorate community organizations, many with aging members.

Prague Spring Refugees across Canada

Over 12,000 Prague Spring refugees, including individuals who arrived after the special program, were successfully resettled across Canada by late spring 1969. Winnipeg received approximately 1,000 refugees, and the local CNAC branch later held a Christmas pavilion for the newcomers that 380 individuals attended and for which the branch paid $620. Throughout the year, 389 individuals received new clothing and bedding. While Calgary gained 700 individuals, Edmonton welcomed 200 newcomers, who received assistance from the CNAC branch. The local Canada Manpower Centre, in cooperation with the provincial Department of Education, enrolled the newcomers in a ten-week English-language course. Traditionally strong centres of immigration such as Toronto, Hamilton, and Montreal—where sizable Czech and Slovak populations resided—received the bulk of the newcomers, with Toronto receiving approximately half of all recently arrived refugees.[104] In the city, the Women's Council of the CNAC raised $2,700 and assisted refugees with finding employment, housing, clothing, and any issue pertaining to resettlement. In Ottawa, the local CNAC branch acquired winter clothing for refugees and ensured that they were enrolled in twenty-four-week English-language classes. Cornwall, Ontario, received twenty refugees and supported their resettlement by providing employment and housing as well as winter clothing and footwear. Similarly, a small number of refugees were settled in summer cottages in northern Ontario, where women's organizations outfitted the newcomers with winter clothing and other necessities. The Montreal branch furnished refugees with blankets, bedsheets, utensils, kitchenware, furniture, footwear, and children's accessories. The branch also organized an information service for newcomers and aided in translating their documents, and local Canadian Czech doctors provided medical assistance. The CNAC was one Czechoslovak Canadian institution that benefited greatly from the arrival of thousands of refugees from Czechoslovakia.

Along with the CNAC, the MMI in Toronto and the CCBA in Winnipeg witnessed an increase in memberships. In 1968, the CNAC with branches across the country comprised 825 members, with 214 in Toronto and 182 in Montreal. These two branches accounted for 48 percent of all members. By March 1969, the organization boasted a membership of 1,303 individuals. New CNAC branches were established in Halifax and St. Catharines. In Kingston, the arrival of 170 refugees also brought about the establishment of a new branch.[105] Many of the 1968ers joined local CNAC branches for assistance in finding employment and accommodations and for a sense of community. In a letter to CNAC branches, executive members Jiří Corn and Emil Talacko requested that members across the country meet and create a plan to assist refugees in finding employment after they completed their language training. The CNAC also advised its members to work with other local groups, such as the Rotary Club, the Lions Club, and the Kiwanis Foundation. In early May 1969, the CNAC held its twenty-first annual congress with Minister of Manpower and Immigration Allan MacEachen in attendance. Corn and Talacko requested that each branch send as many delegates as possible in order to make the event a success. Among the many issues discussed was the political situation in Czechoslovakia, the immigration of 1968ers to Canada, cooperation between the CNAC and other organizations (including the Canadian Fund for Czechoslovak Refugees and the Czechoslovak National Council of America), the Czechoslovak community's place among Canadian ethnic groups, and the state of bilingualism in Canada.[106]

Amnesty, a UN Convention, and a Senatorial Delegation

The issues discussed at the annual meeting were soon overshadowed by new political developments in Czechoslovakia. Less than a month after the annual congress, in late May 1969, the communist regime in Czechoslovakia announced a general amnesty for individuals who had fled the state illegally after the Warsaw Pact invasion or whose travel permits had expired. Czechoslovak citizens had until mid-September to return home or normalize their status at a Czechoslovak embassy or consulate.[107] A week later the general amnesty was followed by Canada's ratification of the UN Convention Relating to the Status of Refugees—eighteen years after its adoption in Geneva. Canada had maintained a stance of non-commitment when it came to providing the world's refugees with asylum. The Canadian government did not wish to be forced by international law to accept all convention refugees. Although asylum became an international right under the convention, Canada chose to protect its right to refuse or deport asylum seekers because of security concerns. With no active refugee policy in place, federal officials used the convention as a framework for Canada's selection and resettlement of refugees.[108] Similar to the resettlement of the 1956 Hungarian refugees, the special program that brought Prague Spring refugees to Canada was also ad hoc. Czechoslovak community organizations and recently resettled refugees watched with interest as Paul Martin Sr., leader of the government in the Senate, reported to the upper chamber on the mid-June visit by a Canadian senatorial delegation to Czechoslovakia. The senators had spent three and a half days in discussions with Czechoslovak government ministers, members of the National Assembly, and heads of the governments of the Czech and Slovak states. In Martin's view, Czechoslovak nationals were forced to address a change in the sociopolitical climate of their country after August 1968. A new *modus vivendi* would allow the people to save their liberalizing reforms without threatening their partnerships in the Warsaw Pact and with the Soviet Union. The delegation condemned the Soviet-led aggression and refused to accept the notion that a country or group of states had the right to intervene in the domestic affairs of another state. The senatorial delegation recognized Czechoslovakia's delicate position and attempted to express its views without worsening the situation.[109]

Less than three weeks after the Canadian senatorial delegation visited Czechoslovakia, in early July, the twentieth celebration of Czechoslovak Day was held at Masaryktown. Approximately 5,000 individuals in the Canadian Czechoslovak community attended the festivities, including the annual Sokol *slet* in which over 200 individuals participated. The gathering included an address from Mitchell Sharp, secretary of state for external affairs, who claimed that the Czech and Slovak peoples "stand as an example to all nations of the indomitable spirit of man that enables him to maintain the ideas of freedom and individual dignity in the face of overwhelming force."[110] Sharp argued that the Prague Spring and its slogan of "Socialism with a Human Face" was the direct result of twenty years of Stalinization and the brutal repression of freedoms. The liberalization of Czechoslovak communism was "not the work of Western so-called imperialist infiltrators, it was a genuine outpouring of the very soul of the people of Czechoslovakia."[111]

With increased lobbying by Czechoslovak representatives, the Canadian government paid greater attention to community events in an effort to strengthen cooperation among individuals who were ardent anti-communists, supported the Cold War consensus, and wanted to become "good Canadians." Because of this existing relationship, officials also concentrated on the successful socioeconomic integration of Prague Spring refugees. In the fall of 1969, a Canada Manpower Centre in Toronto informed the Ontario Department of the Provincial Secretary and Citizenship that refugees from Czechoslovakia were encountering difficulties in securing employment in their chosen fields. In particular, nurses and medical professionals struggled because of long delays in having their qualifications certified. In many instances, clearances were dependent on reports from Czechoslovakia, and the Communist Party authorities often replied that the applicant did not exist in their files. The centre expressed concerns that federal and provincial authorities were sending confidential information to Prague that the authorities there could use for their own questionable purposes.[112] Despite these bureaucratic concerns, cabinet promoted the resettlement of Prague Spring refugees as a sociopolitical and economic success before Parliament.

Standing in the House of Commons in early November, Minister of Manpower and Immigration Allan MacEachen informed his fellow MPs that the government had resettled more than 11,200 individuals during the special program for refugees from Czechoslovakia, costing Canada over $11 million. Of this total, approximately $3 million was spent on English- and French-language training for over 7,000 refugees. Over 80 percent of the refugees were placed in gainful employment, resulting in what the minister identified as a successful combination of compassion and good economics. MacEachen went on to note that Prague Spring refugees were successfully contributing to the country's economy and culture.[113]

The 1968ers' Adaptation

With the resettlement of Prague Spring refugees considered a success by the Canadian government, bureaucrats soon turned their attention toward evaluating the success of the refugees in adapting to Canada's society and economy. In the mid-1970s, the Department of Manpower and Immigration conducted a study of the economic and social adaptation of refugees from Czechoslovakia. The study included 2,734 of 6,639 refugee heads of households from Czechoslovakia. Within the sample, 813 respondents—of which 791 were men and 22 were unmarried women—answered three questionnaires during the study. The respondents were not fully representative of the sample since a majority were educated and technically skilled middle-aged men. Since women were underrepresented, the study largely reflected the views of male heads of households.[114] Refugees from Czechoslovakia were identified as somewhat older, well educated, largely married, and predominantly comprised of professionals and craftspeople. Eighty-five percent of the respondents had been enrolled in language courses upon their arrival in Canada in comparison with only 50 percent of all immigrants in the same period. Eighty percent of the respondents indicated that they had taken English-language training, whereas 41 percent had taken French-language classes (primarily in Quebec). Only 29 percent participated in social clubs and service groups. Among those who did participate, 67 percent were members of groups patronized by Canadians from all backgrounds. The study concluded that refugees from Czechoslovakia were beginning to identify with being Canadians and relinquishing their European identity. Two-thirds of the 813 respondents indicated that they felt more attached to Canada than to Czechoslovakia.[115] In terms of economic adaptation, many of the respondents had required extensive language training and had fought a public perception that they lacked the proper qualifications for employment in their chosen fields. Over the three-year period of the study, Prague Spring refugees were able to increase their monthly earnings by 40 percent from $518 per month in 1968–69 to $726 per month in 1971–72. Their average yearly income also increased from $6,620 to $10,349, and their rate of unemployment remained at only 10 percent.[116] The federal study demonstrated that many of the respondents were successfully adapting to Canada's culture and economy.

The study also noted that individuals who entered Canada during the special program were able to attain longer terms of employment and higher levels of income than did the average immigrant. Over 70 percent of the households were in the age range of fifteen to forty-four, with more than twelve years of formal education, and one-third were in the skilled or professional fields. However, because the study sample included less than 10 percent of all refugees from the special program, its conclusions remained incomplete.

Nonetheless, the study illustrated that refugees from Czechoslovakia openly espoused Canada as their new home and Canadian identity more than did the average immigrant in the same period. Consequently, the 1968ers were more readily incorporated into the socioeconomic structures of their local communities.[117] Although a majority of the refugees married other compatriots, Canadian immigration officials noted that some refugees intermarried with Canadian-born partners and became increasingly assimilated. They soon wondered to what extent the refugees from Czechoslovakia would cultivate their cultural identity or assimilate further with other Canadians. Immigration officials concluded that, whichever course the newly resettled refugees chose, they would continue to integrate successfully into Canadian society.[118]

▶ ▶ ◀ ◀

Between 1968 and 1969, Canada permitted 14,374 individuals who claimed Czechoslovakia as their country of citizenship to enter the country. Many of these newcomers were Prague Spring refugees who arrived in Canada from other countries where they had sought safe haven from the Soviet invasion of August 1968. The largest groups of refugees came from Austria (7,902), Czechoslovakia (2,595), West Germany (1,635), Switzerland (744), France (599), Great Britain (235), and Italy (204).[119] Over the next two decades, many of the 1968ers who supported a Czechoslovak identity followed earlier refugees from Czechoslovakia and joined Canadian Czechoslovak institutions. Both the CNAC and the MMI were revitalized with new members, many of whom had earlier supported the 1948ers' anti-communist and anti-Soviet agenda. The Warsaw Pact invasion of Czechoslovakia in August 1968 strengthened the anti-communist identity of many 1948ers and Canadian-born members of the Czechoslovak community. The events of 1968 also heightened anti-Soviet sentiment as witnessed by the post-invasion demonstrations held at the Soviet Embassy in Ottawa and in major cities across Canada. The arrival of the 1968 wave of refugees from Czechoslovakia also reinforced the 1948ers' efforts to influence Canadian foreign policy on the Soviet Union and Czechoslovakia. In the years after the arrival of the 1968ers, Canadian Czechoslovak institutions continued to advocate for family reunification, the return of democratic government, human rights, and the elimination of censorship in their old homeland. Ultimately, the virulent anti-communist and anti-Soviet sentiment displayed by many Czech refugees not only influenced their post-immigration culture in Canada but also shaped the lobbying efforts of Czechoslovak institutions as they continued to oppose the communist regime in their old homeland.

CHAPTER 6

Opposing the Communist Regime

In 1978, the Rouses and Šolcs, in separate circumstances, packed their belongings and left by car for Hungary and later for Yugoslavia. Both couples were affected by the entrenchment of Soviet rule in Czechoslovakia, making emigration a complicated and potentially dangerous undertaking. Both found that visas for travel to non-communist countries were virtually impossible to obtain but that travel within the Eastern Bloc was permitted. Thus, their route took them through Hungary and then into the less restrictive Yugoslavia. In addition to these problems, Iva Rous (or more specifically Rousová) faced criticism from her loved ones because of her decision to emigrate. They warned her that in the West she would be treated as a foreigner and ostracized for not speaking English. Ladislav Šolc and his wife wanted to visit Austria and were considering emigration to the West.

After reaching Yugoslavia, both couples requested asylum as refugees from Czechoslovakia. However, under an agreement between Belgrade and Prague, Czechoslovak nationals were to surrender to Yugoslav officials their government-issued grey passports, valid only for travel to Yugoslavia. Iva and her husband were forced to sign a document stating that they would return to Zagreb by a certain date and time. If this condition was met, they were told, then their passports would be returned to them. They never saw their passports again.

In many cases, Czech refugees visited the UNHCR's Belgrade office in the hope of securing official status as convention refugees. Unsuccessful applicants were soon left with a difficult decision: remain in Yugoslavia for the foreseeable future, return home to Czechoslovakia and face possible imprisonment, or cross the Yugoslav border into Austria without further inspection from Yugoslav border guards.

Iva and her husband hid their savings in their clothes, fearing that they would be sent back to Czechoslovakia if their savings were found in their luggage. During a long weekend, the couple spent a night in prison since visa offices were closed and they could not be relocated in time to a refugee camp. The couple were later visited by a Yugoslav Ministry of the Interior official who photographed them and demanded their signatures. The Rouses were given twenty-four hours to report to the Traiskirchen refugee camp on the outskirts of Vienna. With little money left, the family crossed the border into Austria and stayed for two weeks in Traiskirchen, where they were assisted by local Catholic organizations. Eventually, Iva and her husband were granted work permits, and Austrian authorities provided them with basic accommodations, food, clothing, and $100 per month.

Iva recalled that many refugees waited more than eight months to come to Canada because of a lack of guaranteed employment or a sponsor. However, after only four months in early 1978, the couple were admitted into Canada as immigrants by immigration officials in Vienna.

In November that year, the Rouses arrived in Montreal and were medically examined and cleared to work. They were accepted by the Canadian government much sooner because Iva's husband knew English and German and had guaranteed employment with Havlik, a machine parts company in Preston, Ontario. The government furnished the Rouses with hotel accommodations and food in Toronto prior to their relocation to Preston.

Much to her surprise, Iva found that Canadians were more helpful than her compatriots back home, whom she identified in public as envious, dishonest, and distrusting. Residents of Preston assisted the family in finding an apartment and furniture. After two years in Canada, Iva recalled, she earned everything that she needed to survive, whereas back home in Czechoslovakia she would have lived in poverty. The Rouses saved thirty dollars per month to pay Canadian authorities for their resettlement. In reminiscing about their immigration experience, Iva believed that Canada did not owe them anything, and they were thankful for having been granted admission. According to her, the couple owed Canada. The Rouses quickly became Canadians.[1]

The Šolc family also reached Austria and stayed at the Traiskirchen refugee camp, where Austrian authorities provided the family with accommodation and food. Since Canada was their first choice for permanent resettlement in the West, the family was later flown to Canada once the refugee camp was full. In the spring of 1978, the family arrived in Montreal and spent the night in a government-provided hotel room. The following day the family flew to Hamilton, where a Manpower and Immigration official took the Šolcs to a local hotel and assisted in their initial resettlement by providing funds for food, rent, and household items. The Canadian government provided them with funding for their first five months in Canada, and Ladislav enrolled in English-language classes. Meanwhile, the local Canadian Czechoslovak community found employment for his wife.

Recalling his immigration experience, Ladislav claimed that in Canada everything seemed to be foreign. He found it hard at first and wanted to leave Canada, but the thought of learning a new language or culture elsewhere was daunting. In the months following his immigration to Canada, he found adequate employment for himself and accommodation for his family. After a few years in Canada, they considered themselves Canadians.

The Rouses and Šolcs exemplified a third wave of Czech immigration to Canada: those who fled from the communist regime during the last two decades of the Cold War. Unlike the 1948ers and 1968ers, these newcomers left their homeland not after a specific crisis but during a period of normalization.[2] The Czechoslovak government press referred to them as having *se vypařily* ("self-evaporated"). This wave of emigration from Czechoslovakia included academics, professionals, and skilled tradespeople in construction, manufacturing, and service industries.

Canadian Czechoslovak organizations, including the CNAC and MMI, were revitalized by this third wave of Cold War refugees, who strengthened the anti-communist and pro-democratic identity of these prominent organizations. Politically active newcomers joined the 1948ers and 1968ers in denouncing the "left" in Canada because of their opposition to American-led efforts in the Vietnam War. As members of the Canadian Czechoslovak elite, who represented a small European ethnocultural group in Canada, Czech refugees sympathized with Quebecers' desire to assert their national rights in the 1960s and 1970s. However, they denounced the emergence of the Marxist-Leninist paramilitary group Front de libération du Québec (FLQ), which they believed threatened Canadian democracy and its multicultural identity. Across Canada, politically active Czech refugees continued to assert an anti-communist ideology to defend democratic values and the Cold War consensus espoused by federal officials. During the 1970s and 1980s, this strategy heightened the Canadian public's awareness of the Czechoslovak community, and its lobbying efforts before federal and provincial officials, and brought Czech refugees closer to social and cultural citizenship in Cold War Canada.

Pressuring the Canadian Government to Assist Family Reunification

During the 1970s and 1980s, the Czechoslovak National Association of Canada became increasingly concerned as a significant portion of the Canadian public demonstrated against American foreign policy on Vietnam, which many Czech refugees within the broader Canadian Czechoslovak community believed was combatting global communism. The CNAC protested against the Czechoslovak government's elimination of individual freedoms and human rights and against the Soviet occupation of Czechoslovakia. The association lobbied the Canadian government, and MPs continued to oppose the Soviet occupation of Czechoslovakia. The CNAC was concerned that Ottawa's expanding relationship with the Soviet Union could give the Canadian public the perception that communist states contained acceptable political systems and safeguarded human rights and individual freedoms. Although many Czech refugees in Canada retained vivid memories of life under fascism and later communism, the international community's promotion of détente troubled many anti-communist Czechs, who believed that Canada would be pressured into legitimizing Moscow's intervention in Czechoslovakia. The CNAC pressed the Canadian government to expedite family reunification cases, lobbied for the removal of restrictions on the visits of relatives, and demanded that Prague remove Czechoslovak citizenship from individuals who later received Canadian citizenship to prevent their detention when visiting Czechoslovakia. Whereas a majority of 1948ers refused to normalize relations with the Czechoslovak government, many 1968ers—who had spent more than two decades under communism—remained apolitical. In some cases, the 1968ers wanted to regularize their status as illegal émigrés, who had fled the country without permission, in efforts to visit family members and friends left behind.

For some Czech refugees, a return home was less desirable given their experiences with the Communist Party authorities. As victims of political persecution in Czechoslovakia, they soon focused on raising awareness of human rights abuses and the totalitarian and repressive nature of their homeland. In Canada, the Prague Spring had given rise to the founding of the Sociální sdružení bývalych Čsl. Politickych věznů (Kanada) (Welfare Association of Former Czechoslovak Political Prisoners in Canada or WAFCPP), which brought together victims of communist persecution who had resettled in

Canada. The arrival of the 1968ers energized the association, which immediately sought cooperation with compatriot organizations in Canada. In January 1970, the association formed a working committee to make decision making a collective effort.[3] Soon after, the WAFCPP elected members to a provisional committee that directed the association's agenda.[4] With the arrival of many refugees who had been victims of political persecution in Czechoslovakia, the WAFCPP engaged both organizations to promote its agenda of supporting former political prisoners and commemorating the victims of the communist regime in Czechoslovakia. The organization also supported efforts to resettle Czech refugees permanently in Canada.

The Brezhnev Doctrine

Just as refugee resettlement continued to be an important issue within the Canadian Czechoslovak community, so too were its efforts to raise public awareness of the suppression of individual freedoms, human rights abuses, and the totalitarian nature of the communist regime in Czechoslovakia. In the spring of 1970, the CNAC held its twenty-second annual congress in Winnipeg. A resolution was adopted by delegates in attendance demanding that all foreign troops withdraw from Czechoslovakia and that free elections be held under international supervision. The congress also declared that the Soviet Union's Brezhnev Doctrine was incompatible with international law since it permitted Moscow to intervene in the internal affairs of Czechoslovakia. Soviet leader Leonid Brezhnev first declared this new foreign policy at the Fifth Congress of the Polish United Workers' Party in November 1968. The policy was used to limit a Soviet satellite state's independence from Moscow and to eliminate efforts at democratization or liberalization of the society, economy, and political state. The doctrine was used retroactively to justify the Soviet-led invasions of Hungary in 1956 and of Czechoslovakia in 1968.[5] Similarly, the CNAC resolution demonstrated the association's concern about public reaction to events in Czechoslovakia and the communist world. As an anti-communist organization, the CNAC was concerned that a significant portion of the Canadian public was demonstrating against American imperialism. Although the Soviet occupation of Czechoslovakia did not draw the same amount of outrage compared with events in Vietnam, the CNAC later argued that these protests were not reactions to the endangerment of democratic values but planned actions aimed at disrupting democratic society.

Vietnam War Protests: Anti-Imperialism versus Anti-Communism

During the late 1960s and early 1970s, escalation of the Vietnam War led many Canadians who opposed American intervention in Southeast Asia and elsewhere to demonstrate across the country. In an era of increasing social protests, marches, peace conferences, and university sit-ins, many Canadians voiced their concerns about Western imperialism and Canada's involvement in it. Between 1965 and 1974, up to 125,000 American war resisters arrived in Canada seeking refuge from American authorities. Many of these individuals and their family members were skilled and university educated, and they joined efforts that opposed American involvement in conflicts around the world. Canadian authorities permitted American war resisters and their families to enter Canada but remained concerned how this wave of newcomers would influence relations between Ottawa and Washington. In an effort to defend the country against communist sympathizers and individuals engaged in anti-American social protests, Canadian officials tasked the RCMP with gathering information and conducting surveillance of influential war resisters.[6]

As former citizens of a country under communist domination, many CNAC members were suspicious of anti-war protesters and remained supportive of American-led attempts to defend democratic values in their homeland and elsewhere.[7] Disturbed by misleading reports on the Vietnam War published in Canadian newspapers, Vladimír Krajina, a Czech refugee, CNAC member, and professor of botany at the University of British Columbia, wrote to Prime Minister Trudeau suggesting that these media reports carried a "deliberate overemphasis of antiwar protests mostly organized under the influence of Communist or pro-Communist elements either in Europe or in North America."[8] As a former leader in the Czech underground resistance during the Second World War and an elected member of the postwar democratic Czechoslovak parliament, Krajina fled Czechoslovakia after the communist takeover. In 1949, he sought refuge in Canada. He was sentenced to death by both Nazi Germany and Communist Czechoslovakia. After resettling with his wife, Maria, in Vancouver, the Krajinas opened their residence to recently arrived refugees and joined the local branch of the CNAC.[9] On behalf of CNAC members in Vancouver, Krajina indicated that they were worried about the "continuous brain-washing of the Canadian public" as opposition to American foreign policy grew and as sympathy for the Soviet cause led Moscow to continue to support the Vietnam War and hamper any attempt at peace.[10] Krajina requested that the Canadian government pressure media outlets to ensure that a balance in news coverage be maintained; he feared that a rise in anti-American press coverage could lead to a communist victory in the Cold War. Along with Krajina, CNAC members could not understand why so many individuals opposed the American presence in Vietnam—which they viewed as temporary—as opposed to the Soviet occupation of Czechoslovakia. Krajina used the example of the condemnation by the World Council of Churches of American involvement in Cambodia to illustrate his point about the level of brainwashing that similar organizations had reached and to show who would suffer the most if a communist victory occurred.[11] Many of the Czech refugees had endured communist persecution and vehemently opposed anti-American and anti-war protests in order to oppose leftist political action often sympathetic to communism.

As political prisoners who had experienced communist brutality first-hand, members of the WAFCPP joined the CNAC in supporting Western efforts to defend democratic and human rights in Czechoslovakia and the communist world. Several months after the annual congress in Winnipeg, the WAFCPP requested use of the MMI's facilities to host its own national congress. The institute acknowledged the request in a letter and asked for a facility use fee of twenty-five dollars and a list of the association's delegates. The event coincided with the annual Czechoslovak Day held on the grounds at Masaryktown. The group of former political prisoners was permitted to participate officially as a member compatriot organization and laid a wreath to the memory of tortured, executed, and deceased political prisoners of the communist regime in Czechoslovakia.[12] Three months later, on the second anniversary of the Soviet-led invasion, the organization released a proclamation demanding that Soviet and Warsaw Pact forces withdraw from Czechoslovakia immediately and that a democratic election be held to form a new government.[13]

Quebec's Quiet Revolution and the FLQ

Meanwhile, Canada was dealing with turmoil of its own. In 1960, after nearly two decades under the staunchly anti-communist and conservative Union Nationale led by Maurice Duplessis, Quebecers had elected the Liberals led by Jean Lesage. Election of the provincial Liberals was followed by a rapid process of modernization and secularization known as the Quiet Revolution. Until the 1960s, Quebec had been dominated by conservative political elites and the Catholic Church, which played a vital part in Canada's Cold War consensus. The Quiet Revolution led many Quebecers to question the role of the Catholic Church in society and the federal government in the province.

By the end of the decade, many Quebecers had become increasingly critical of American-led intervention overseas and the proliferation of nuclear weapons. While the Quebec government called on Ottawa for greater control over the province's affairs, separatists demanding independence were divided into two factions: individuals who sought to use the existing democratic system to achieve their aims and joined the Parti Québécois and paramilitary factions that turned to armed struggle.[14]

In the fall of 1970, the CNAC turned its anti-communist lobbying efforts toward events in Canada because of a fear that the democratic system of government was under attack. In October, the kidnapping of British Trade Commissioner James Cross and the assassination of Quebec Minister of Transportation Pierre Laporte by members of the FLQ forced the Canadian government to implement the War Measures Act and suspend habeas corpus, giving police far-reaching powers of arrest. In its correspondence with the Prime Minister's Office, the CNAC indicated its support for the government's position on domestic terrorism. The organization supported Ottawa's temporary powers to protect Canadian democracy under the War Measures Act but demanded that the government remain sensitive to citizens' rights. The CNAC further advocated for the enactment of legislation that would "deal with actions of any radical groups in Canada whose aim is to create chaos, destroy democracy and introduce dictatorship."[15] Heavily influenced by past events in Czechoslovakia, the CNAC argued that "the destruction of a democratic society can be achieved by small, usually well-organized minority groups. These groups, using intimidation, accusations and terror are usually assisted by professional revolutionaries and supported from abroad."[16] As a result, the Canadian Czechoslovak organization viewed the FLQ as a movement that espoused Marxist ideology and used violence to attack democratically elected governments.

Communist Extortion Tactics

The CNAC believed that ensuring public safety against leftist radicals while maintaining the rights of citizens was crucial. This view was influenced by the consistent threat of communist intimidation that many Czech refugees in Canada faced. In November 1970, the Free Central European News Agency based in London reported that Communist Party authorities in Prague were in the midst of blackmailing 70,000 former Czechoslovak residents. In citing an official Czechoslovak government document in the possession of the British government, the anti-communist news agency claimed that Prague had established a Legal Advisory Centre to address the departure of refugees to the West—overwhelmingly to Australia, Canada, France, Great Britain, New Zealand, Switzerland, and West Germany. The news article stated that Prague had officially acknowledged the departure of approximately 51,000 individuals since the 1968 Warsaw Pact invasion. Similarly, the news outlet argued that KGB advisors were behind a plan to raise foreign currency for Eastern Europe.[17] The communist scheme to blackmail refugees from Czechoslovakia consisted of letters indicating that "prosecution has been initiated against you for the criminal act of abandoning the Republic according to . . . the Criminal Code." In addition, the letters sent to unsuspecting refugees by lawyers representing a "Legal Advisory Centre" stated "that established facts do sufficiently justify the conclusion that you have been . . . staying abroad illegitimately with the intention to take up permanent residence there."[18] In the letter, state-appointed legal counsels subsequently noted that the costs of the legal proceedings and those of a defence in court were the sole responsibility of the defendant, required to send a deposit of 700 Czechoslovak crowns in Canadian funds within fifteen days. Should the defendant fail to send the required deposit, the letter warned, a lawyer was "entitled to accept payments by your close relatives in Czechoslovakia."[19] Although the *in absentia* trials were a farce, they were continually followed by threats and pressure.

Upon learning of a new scheme to blackmail Czech refugees in Toronto, twelve Czechoslovak groups in the city issued a letter in December 1970 calling on fellow compatriots not to become victims of the communist scheme and to leave letters from state-appointed Czechoslovak lawyers unanswered. The Toronto Area Coordinating Committee of Czech and Slovak Democratic Organizations recognized that a small minority of recent arrivals might succumb to communist pressure because of fear that a close relative in Czechoslovakia would be persecuted.[20] Similar measures against those who had fled after February 1948 were never instituted, and the news agency believed that the plan by Moscow and Prague to obtain foreign currency was devised to seek political retribution in a Czechoslovakia undergoing normalization after the Warsaw Pact invasion.[21]

The committee hoped that, with the Canadian government's involvement, the situation could be remedied. The twelve Canadian Czechoslovak organizations believed that two issues justified Canadian government involvement. First, the committee argued that refugees from Czechoslovakia were being subjected to moral and economic pressure by Communist Party authorities that made their resettlement in Canada difficult. Second, Prague's scheme to blackmail the newcomers could remove several million dollars from the Canadian economy. Although the second issue was unrealistic, it might have been meant as a pressure tactic by the twelve groups to force Ottawa's involvement. The coordinating committee hoped that its demands would prevent further moves by Prague against the Canadian Czechoslovak community and recently arrived refugees from Czechoslovakia.[22] A month later the CNAC branch in Vancouver sent a letter to Secretary of State for External Affairs Mitchell Sharp requesting assistance against Prague's blackmail scheme.[23]

Amid Prague's attempts to pressure its compatriots, the CNAC held its twenty-third annual congress in May 1971 in Niagara Falls. During the congress, delegates resolved to defend the identity and sovereignty of the Czech and Slovak peoples. Similarly, delegates agreed to continue to protest the Eastern Bloc's elimination of individual freedoms and human rights, the Soviet military domination of Czechoslovakia, and the controversial Brezhnev Doctrine. Delegates demanded that the Canadian government and MPs continue to oppose the Soviet occupation of Czechoslovakia. Members attending the annual congress were concerned that Ottawa's expanding relationship with the Soviet Union could give the Canadian public the impression that communist states contained political systems that protected human rights and individual freedoms. The CNAC pressed Canadian parliamentarians to continue to expose the propaganda of totalitarian regimes and to preserve democratic values around the world. Fearing that many student groups and labour organizations held pro-communist sympathies, the Niagara Falls congress called on the federal government to limit the amount of press given to labour and university groups who attempted to raise awareness of social justice issues only to increase social unrest and weaken Canadian unity and democratic institutions. Similarly, the congress concluded by demanding that Ottawa terminate access to postal services by communist states that attempted to blackmail refugees from Czechoslovakia. The CNAC would later argue that any Eastern Bloc diplomat harassing refugees in Canada should lose his or her accreditation and be removed from the country.[24]

Beginnings of Détente

Although the CNAC was suspicious of closer ties between Canadian and Soviet officials, in May 1971 Pierre Elliott Trudeau became the first Canadian prime minister to visit the Soviet Union officially. That month Trudeau and Soviet premier Alexei Kosygin signed a protocol obligating both countries to hold annual meetings on sociocultural, economic, and political developments.

Much to the dismay of Eastern European communities in Canada, the Liberal government sought greater cooperation between the two countries. Fearing Soviet demands and opposed to any rapprochement between Ottawa and Moscow, the CNAC called on the Canadian government to demand full reciprocity in its dealings with the Soviets. The organization reminded the prime minister that it would be a mistake to assume that Soviet leaders would ignore communist doctrine, permanent revolution, and world domination. The association argued that détente could not occur until Moscow acknowledged that the Warsaw Pact invasion in 1968 was in violation of the United Nations Charter.[25]

The Canadian Czechoslovak community was deeply concerned about Trudeau's official visit to the Soviet Union. Many individuals within the community believed that Canada's rapprochement with the Soviets could lead to an appeasement of Moscow's occupation of Czechoslovakia and suppression of individual freedoms and human rights.

In addition to its lobbying efforts in Ottawa, the CNAC initiated a postcard campaign in the summer of 1971 to remind officials and prominent Canadians of the Soviet occupation of Czechoslovakia. Approximately 16,000 postcards with the phrase "21 August, Invasion of Czechoslovakia, Day of Soviet Shame" were sent to all Canadian parliamentarians, premiers, Supreme Court justices, national press outlets, television and radio stations, and members of the UN Security Council.[26] Individual CNAC branches were instructed to send postcards to locally elected officials and media outlets in early August to ensure that they reached their destinations prior to the third anniversary of the Soviet-led invasion of Czechoslovakia. All remaining postcards were sent to politicians and officials in Communist Czechoslovakia and across the world.[27]

In August 1971, as it had done in the two previous years, the CNAC published a proclamation on the anniversary itself. On behalf of its members, the organization demanded that all Canadians condemn the Brezhnev Doctrine since it was dangerous to international peace. The CNAC subsequently demanded that any understanding between Ottawa and Moscow could not be based upon acceptance of the 1968 Soviet-led invasion. As a result, the organization argued that Canada should not negotiate with the Soviets unless full reciprocity was assured. As part of its struggle against communism, the CNAC continued to promote before the Canadian government free elections and the immediate withdrawal of Soviet troops from Czechoslovakia.[28]

In an attempt to reassure the community, Undersecretary of State for External Affairs Albert Edgar Ritchie informed the CNAC that Ottawa would not renounce its condemnation of the Warsaw Pact invasion. Upon learning that Soviet premier Alexei Kosygin would lead an eight-day official visit, first arriving in Ottawa in October 1971, to hold talks with Canadian officials, the CNAC lobbied the Prime Minister's Office and Secretary of State for External Affairs Mitchell Sharp not to recognize the Soviet-led occupation and to advocate for the Soviet withdrawal from Czechoslovakia.

Kosygin's visit to Canada generated considerable protest by communities with roots in countries now behind the Iron Curtain. That month approximately 2,000 individuals representing Canadians of Czechoslovak, Estonian, Hungarian, Polish, Latvian, Lithuanian, and Ukrainian origin held a demonstration in Vancouver against the visit. Approximately 300 members of the Canadian Czechoslovak community participated. The following day representatives from the CNAC's Vancouver branch visited the University of British Columbia and participated in a discussion with students on the implications of Kosygin's visit.[29] In November, a month after the visit, Sharp replied in a letter to the CNAC that Ottawa had not altered its position on Czechoslovakia since the Soviet invasion of Czechoslovakia. The success of these protests was moderate: although the Canadian government, in its discussions with Premier Kosygin and the Soviet delegation, did not support or excuse the Warsaw Pact invasion of Czechoslovakia in 1968, it also did not denounce it.

Citizens of Which Country?

Despite the moderate support for their lobbying efforts before the Canadian government, in the fall of 1971 the CNAC became concerned about how refugees from Czechoslovakia were being treated by Czechoslovak representatives in Canada. At the embassy in Ottawa and the consulate in Montreal, Canadian residents were increasingly being harassed by Czechoslovak diplomats with supplementary questioning. The CNAC appealed to Sharp to intervene, for many of these Canadian residents simply wished to acquire tourist visas in order to visit their relatives and friends in Czechoslovakia. In January 1972, Sharp informed the CNAC that the Department of External Affairs had discussed the issue with Czechoslovak representatives in Ottawa and received assurances that, in the case of refugees from Czechoslovakia who were now Canadian citizens, only one visa application form was necessary. Czechoslovak diplomats claimed that supplementary questions were asked in only specific cases and were not considered normal routine. However, since the Czechoslovak government did not recognize dual citizenship, legation officials aggressively interviewed visa applicants who had never officially rescinded their

Czechoslovak citizenship after settling in Canada and acquiring Canadian citizenship. Sharp urged CNAC members to ascertain their status in their old country given that many 1948ers and 1968ers had been found guilty of leaving the country without permission and were thus considered illegal émigrés; any who wished to visit the old country would be subject to a certain amount of risk since the Communist Party authorities did not recognize their Canadian citizenship or residency. In his letter to the CNAC, Sharp wrote that "any person of Czechoslovak birth who has not obtained a release from his Czechoslovak citizenship, or otherwise obtained the blessing of the Czechoslovak authorities for his emigration abroad, is at least theoretically vulnerable, should he choose to visit his homeland, since Czechoslovak law does not recognize the concept of dual nationality. In other words, the simple possession of a Canadian passport is not enough."[30] During the period of normalization, Czechoslovak authorities continued to view Czech refugees as individuals who had left the state illegally and without permission. Moreover, they considered them to be Czechoslovak citizens and therefore subject to Czechoslovak laws and prosecution.[31]

The October Crisis Continues to Reverberate

In this tense environment, Czech refugees in Ontario and Quebec who were CNAC members continued to lead efforts to lobby federal officials and to raise awareness among the Canadian public about the sociopolitical situation in Czechoslovakia. They were soon joined by their compatriots in western Canada, who also exposed existing conditions in their old homeland. In April 1972, the CNAC's western Canadian branches held a Congress of Western Provinces in Edmonton. Delegates from Calgary, Edmonton, and Vancouver were joined by representatives of the Alberta Department of Culture, Youth, and Recreation and the Canadian Department of the Secretary of State to discuss relations between the West and the Eastern Bloc. The delegates resolved that any negotiations between Canada and the Soviet Union should not recognize any sphere of influence as permanent. The delegates resolved that independence and liberty were guaranteed to even the smallest states, and Czechoslovakia's independence and human rights had to be safeguarded from Soviet intervention. CNAC members demanded that the international community help to restore these values.[32] A month later delegates to the CNAC's twenty-fourth annual national congress in Kitchener accepted the western Canadian branches' conclusions.

Although events in Eastern Europe preoccupied delegates at the congress, they were also concerned about the preservation of Canada's democratic system of government. Eighteen months after the October Crisis in Quebec, the CNAC continued to believe that Marxist and separatist radicals, including the FLQ, still posed a threat to Canadian democracy. Using Czechoslovakia as an example, CNAC president Jiří Corn, a Czech 1948er, drafted a letter to the editors of Quebec newspapers arguing for the preservation of democratic values, social progress, and cultural diversity in Canada. He observed that recent revolutionary elements in Quebec had attempted to destroy the country's sociopolitical system while a majority of Canadians had remained silent. The CNAC president argued that most Quebecers were also apathetic and warned them to remain vigilant to prevent being misled or threatened by an organized minority. According to Corn, recent events in Quebec were similar to those in Czechoslovakia, where outside agitation had removed freedom and a democratic system of government. He concluded by urging Quebecers to safeguard Canadian democracy and hoped that francophone Quebec would one day attain its national and socioeconomic goals in peace as part of a united Canada.[33]

To support Corn and the CNAC executive's lobbying efforts in Quebec, the organization's Montreal branch, in partnership with eleven other ethnic organizations, sent a memorandum to Premier Robert Bourassa. In it, the organizations illustrated their concerns about the events of the October Crisis and the anarchy created by subversive elements. In joining with the CNAC, ethnic organizations representing Balts, Croatians, Greeks, Hungarians, Italians, Latvians, Lithuanians, Poles, Romanians, Slovaks, and Ukrainians in Quebec argued that the province was in danger of being toppled by revolutionaries who would destroy its political institutions before assuming power themselves. Promoting an anti-communist agenda that included a distrust of unions, the twelve groups called on Bourassa to re-establish public order so as to prevent an undemocratic seizure of power and impede the rising influence of labour unions and leftist politics. They also proposed that the Quebec government bring to justice all individuals who committed crimes against the state, other individuals, property, and the press; illustrate for Quebecers new threats and expose their ultimate goals; revoke the right to strike for all civil servants under provincial jurisdiction; ban all unions from partisan politics and force union leaders seeking political office to resign from their unions; ban unions from funding political parties; inform Quebecers of the salaries of union executives; bluntly inform Quebecers when legislation supported by unions was not in the best interests of union members; educate the population about the Canadian democratic system of governance; and instruct members of the National Assembly who took part in public consultations to explain the results of negotiations with unions.[34] The anti-communist ethnic organizations hoped that their memorandum would assist provincial officials to safeguard Quebec from subversive leftist groups.

The lobbying efforts of many individuals within the Canadian Czechoslovak community to protect Canadian democratic institutions and see a democratic system of government return to their old homeland were further galvanized in 1973 by the fifth anniversary of the Warsaw Pact invasion of Czechoslovakia. The anniversary illustrated to many community members that communism in Czechoslovakia would not be easily defeated and that the Soviet occupation would continue for the foreseeable future. In August, the CNAC issued a letter to international leaders convened in Ottawa for the Commonwealth Heads of Government Conference. The organization viewed the Commonwealth as a family that promoted democratic values. In the letter, Jiří Corn indicated that the process of Soviet-led normalization after the Warsaw Pact invasion had been successfully completed: Czechoslovakia was now a "twentieth-century Soviet colony."[35] Corn called on the Commonwealth leaders to use their influence in world affairs to help millions of Eastern Europeans regain their democratic rights and each communist satellite state to become independent of the Soviet Union.[36] In its efforts to raise awareness of the struggle for democratic government and human rights in Czechoslovakia, the CNAC printed postal seals to inform Canadians that "the efforts of the Czech and Slovak people to gain personal freedom and more political independence were crushed. Five years later, the people of this unfortunate country are still suffering under Soviet domination."[37] Canadians could purchase a set of eight seals for one dollar. The association hoped that the seals would promote international solidarity with its cause.

Across Canada, the fifth anniversary of the Warsaw Pact invasion was also marked by masses, vigils, and processions. In St. Catharines, Ontario, a motorcade involving sixty-two automobiles and 100 individuals protesting the invasion culminated in a half-hour ceremony at the city's cenotaph. Local residents representing Czech, Estonian, Hungarian, Latvian, Polish, Slovak, and Ukrainian communities were led in a prayer "for all captive peoples behind the Iron Curtain" by the Very Reverend Mykola Komar of Saints Cyril and Methodius Ukrainian Catholic Church.[38] In Ottawa, a holy mass was celebrated at the Church of the Dominican Fathers to remember all Czechoslovak nationals who had died resisting the Soviet-led invasion and those who continued to be persecuted by the communist regime for their political and religious

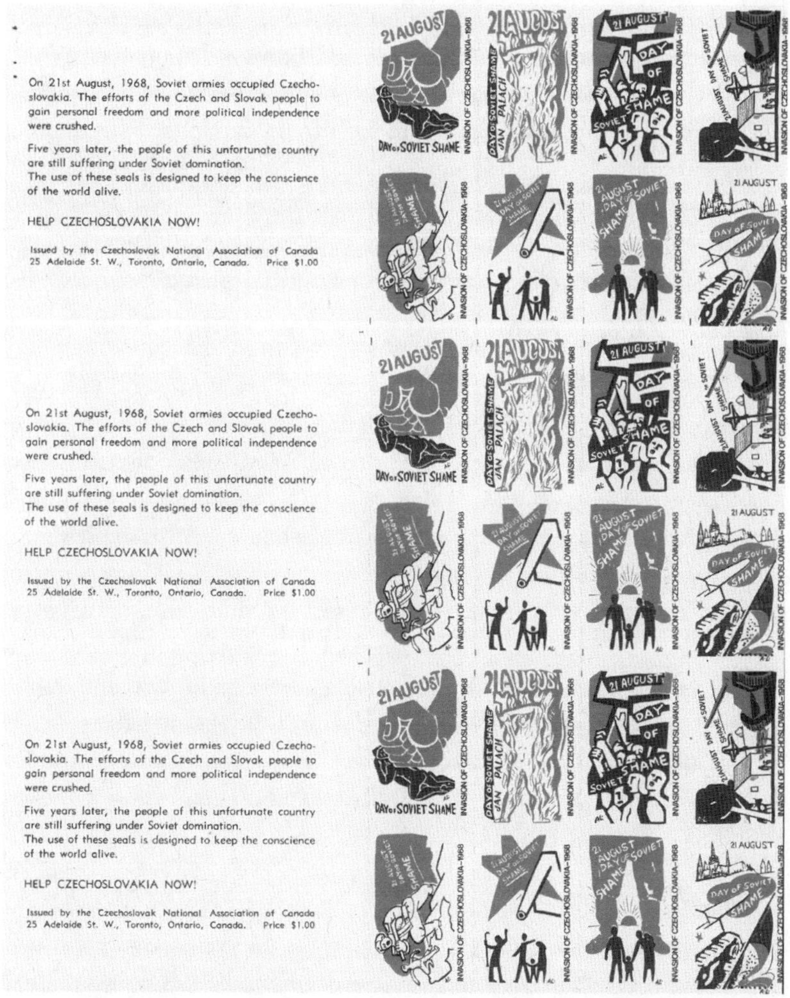

Figure 22. *Printed sheet of postal seals with the words "Help Czechoslovakia Now!" for the CNAC's campaign commemorating the fifth anniversary of the Warsaw Pact invasion of Czechoslovakia, 1973.*

beliefs. Later that morning the CNAC's central council held an emergency meeting with representatives of other Eastern European nations to draft a resolution later presented to the federal government. The resolution called on Canadian parliamentarians to consider the consequences of the Soviet Union's Brezhnev Doctrine. In previous years, the branch had demanded that Ottawa attempt to obtain a Soviet withdrawal of this new doctrine and the restoration of independence and personal freedom in Czechoslovakia. Canadians of Czech, Estonian, Hungarian, Latvian, Lithuanian, Polish, Slovak, and Ukrainian descent demanded that the Soviets withdraw from Czechoslovakia, respect the concept of self-determination for the nations of Eastern Europe, allow the free movement of people, and adhere to reciprocal agreements pertaining to cultural, legal, financial, and trade exchanges in the international community. On the evening of 21 August, individuals representing Ottawa's Eastern European communities joined a motorcade-led procession toward the Soviet Embassy.[39]

Desperate Measures

Five years after the Soviet-led invasion of their homeland, Czech refugees in Canada were reminded of the event's impact on their compatriots in the West. The Czech-language monthly *Kanadské listy* (Canadian Papers) published details of the death of a young 1968er in Melbourne, Australia. Twenty-seven-year-old J. Kulstrunková jumped from the sixth floor of an apartment building after throwing her five-year-old son and three-year-old daughter from there. The Czechoslovak consul general in Montreal, Dr. Andruš (who retained jurisdiction across Canada for issuing travel visas for Czechoslovakia), antagonized the local Czechoslovak community by suggesting that community organizations and the ethnic press were responsible for émigré suicides. Andruš went on to argue controversially that the ethnic press scared its readers with threats that often led refugees to conclude that immigration to Canada had been a mistake. As a result, they wished to return to Czechoslovakia. As president of the CNAC's Montreal branch, Victor Žícha replied to Andruš by stating that the statutes of the CNAC called for the promotion of goodwill, understanding, and tolerance among compatriots. Žícha also argued that the CNAC protected the rights of Canadians of Czechoslovak origin and recent arrivals; advanced the social, economic, and cultural conditions of Canadians of Czechoslovak origin; and cooperated with similar organizations that assisted newcomers. The branch president claimed that the CNAC was a non-partisan organization and thus above politics. Accordingly, Žícha noted that newcomer suicides were indeed a tragedy but that they were not the results of compatriot organizations or politics since Czechoslovak organizations in Canada assisted newcomers in adjusting to life in their new country.[40] In Montreal, the local CNAC branch tried to combat the assertions made by Andruš by informing readers that it provided recently arrived Czech refugees with assistance in finding accommodations, employment, and basic necessities. Additionally, the branch held weekly citizenship courses in its cultural centre, where newcomers learned about Canadian geography, history, and citizens' rights. For those who desired to become Canadian citizens, the branch offered advice on how to proceed.[41]

Understandably, refugees from Czechoslovakia were shocked and dismayed by Kulstrunková's suicide. Then, in the summer of 1974, a twenty-five-year-old ship's cook from Czechoslovakia made national headlines when he jumped ship and requested asylum in Canada. Jan Morcinek had been serving as a cook aboard the vessel *Bratislava,* which regularly crossed the Atlantic Ocean, stopping at various American ports prior to a final stop in Port-Cartier, Quebec, from where it was to head back to Leningrad in the Soviet Union. Realizing that this was his last chance to obtain freedom, Morcinek jumped into the St. Lawrence River, swam ashore, and requested political asylum. Unfortunately, he encountered an unexpected legal obstacle: Canadian authorities did not recognize his status, arguing that since he had arrived aboard the *Bratislava*—considered Czechoslovak territory—he should be deported. An interdepartmental committee met in August 1974 to consider his claim to refugee status. After the committee denied his request, Morcinek appealed to the Immigration Appeal Board, which decided that his claims were not valid. Refugees were expected to claim asylum in a second country after fleeing persecution in their homelands. Once they had made their claims for asylum, refugees would then apply for permanent resettlement in a safe third country. Morcinek had claimed asylum in Canada in the hope of securing permanent resettlement. However, he would need to seek permanent resettlement elsewhere in a third country. On his behalf, the CNAC appealed his case to the Supreme Court of Canada. The organization sought donations from the Canadian public to cover his daily expenses and legal costs, in excess of $5,000. The CNAC branches in Toronto, Montreal, and Hamilton were able to raise $2,000. CNAC president Louis Urban, a 1948er, informed members that unless they supported the young man—a fellow refugee who, like them, had made a decision not to live under the communist regime—he would likely face a prison sentence back in Czechoslovakia.[42] The CNAC continued to raise awareness of his plight in the hope that the federal government would alter its decision to deport the young cook to likely imprisonment in Czechoslovakia. The *Toronto Sun* informed readers that his family had been blacklisted for supporting Alexander Dubček's reforms during the ill-fated Prague Spring. Nonetheless, in March 1975, Canadian authorities ordered Morcinek to be deported after he lost his appeal before the Supreme Court.[43]

Late in 1975, during International Human Rights Day held annually on 10 December, *Toronto Sun* columnist Peter Worthington drew further attention to Morcinek's plight. Worthington argued that, because of the Morcinek family's support for the Prague Spring, the young cook's incarceration in his homeland would be guaranteed if deportation proceedings were allowed to go forward. The journalist concluded that it was wrong for the Canadian government to send individuals who requested asylum back to their homelands only to face certain imprisonment and punishment. Worthington noted that, while Canadian officials were attempting to send Morcinek home, the Canadian public had failed to voice their opposition. According to Czechoslovak law, Morcinek was liable to be found guilty of section 103 (detracting from the dignity of the republic) of the Penal Code, for which he could receive a five-year prison term, and section 283 (absenting himself without permission to a foreign country), for which he could receive a seven-year prison term.[44] In the spring of 1976, the *Toronto Star* reported that neither the Canadian government nor the courts found the young Czechoslovak citizen to be a genuine refugee because he was not threatened with persecution back in his homeland. The newspaper argued that Morcinek did not possess a criminal record, was physically healthy, and was gainfully employed. Although the Canadian press attempted to demonstrate that repression in Eastern Europe forced many individuals to seek political asylum in the West out of a genuine fear of persecution if they returned home, Canadian authorities viewed Morcinek as inadmissible.[45] In April 1976, before the House of Commons, Otto Jelínek, a 1948er and Progressive Conservative MP for High Park–Humber Valley, asked Robert Andras, the minister of citizenship and immigration, about Morcinek's imminent deportation. Andras informed Jelínek that, since a deportation order had already been issued, he could no longer submit a ministerial permit for Morcinek to stay in Canada. Andras noted that, since Morcinek had claimed asylum in Canada, as his second country, he would need to apply to a safe third country. From that country, the Czechoslovak national could then apply to come to Canada under existing admissions criteria. In an attempt to prevent his return to Czechoslovakia, or at least to delay it, Morcinek, who expected to be deported from Canada at any moment, sought to leave on his own terms and requested political asylum in West Germany in an attempt to apply later for permanent resettlement in Canada.[46]

The Détente Debate Continues

Although CNAC members were unsuccessful in preventing Morcinek's deportation by Canadian immigration officials, in the spring of 1975 delegates attending the organization's twenty-seventh annual congress in Toronto resolved that Canadian policies were increasingly susceptible to communist infiltration under the guise of détente—which delegates argued supported Soviet imperialism and totalitarianism. They were also disturbed by the Western desire to decrease political tensions in Europe, which they believed would lead countries such as Canada to recognize the status quo in Eastern Europe. Similarly, CNAC members attending the annual congress condemned all opposition to the role of the United States in safeguarding democracy in Eastern Europe and other parts of the world. Although the CNAC was opposed to violence as a means to achieve the independence of Czechoslovakia, the organization argued for continuous support for NATO to counterbalance the Warsaw Pact and its increasing military capability. Delegates also agreed to promote an immigration policy that permitted entry to individuals who would strengthen Canadian democracy as opponents of not only communism but also individuals who agitated against Canada's democratic political system. The delegates concluded their congress by resolving that the CNAC was concerned by the "downfall of the world's political morals and by indifference to our devotion to defend freedom and democracy."[47] According to the association's members, faith in democratic values would ultimately maintain each individual's rights and freedoms.[48]

Although CNAC members were opposed to the use of military force to achieve political sovereignty for their old country, détente remained a controversial issue. Fearing that the Canadian government would be pressured by the Soviets to accept Moscow's right to interfere in the affairs of Czechoslovakia, the CNAC proclaimed its support for the Canadian government's policy of détente with the Soviet Union provided that the agreement represented the coexistence of peoples, nations, political ideologies, and cultures in a spirit of reciprocity. The CNAC also pressed the Canadian government to expedite family reunification cases, lobby for the removal of restrictions on visits of relatives, and demand that Prague automatically annul the Czechoslovak citizenship of individuals who had acquired Canadian citizenship, so as to prevent their probable detention when visiting Czechoslovakia. On behalf of all Cold War refugees from Czechoslovakia, the CNAC requested that Ottawa pressure the Communist Party authorities in Prague for material reciprocity with regard to government benefits, pensions, and inheritances at exchange rates beneficial to 1948ers and 1968ers.[49] The Czechoslovak government agreed to pay $3.25 million to settle claims against the state from its former citizens whose properties had been nationalized after February 1948. In 1975, the funds were deposited with the Foreign Claims Commission in Ottawa.[50]

As détente began to alter relations between the West and the Eastern Bloc, in July and August 1975 thirty-five states, including Canada and Czechoslovakia, signed a declaration to formalize détente and improve relations between the West and the Eastern Bloc. The resulting Helsinki Accords indicated that state sovereignty, non-intervention in a state's internal affairs, and respect for human rights were formally agreed to by all signatories. With the signing of the Helsinki Accords on 1 August, the International Covenant on Civil and Political Rights and the International Covenant on Economic, Social, and Cultural Rights came into force in March 1976.[51] Six months later the Helsinki Accords were legalized in Czechoslovakia.[52] Throughout the 1970s, the issue of human rights in Czechoslovakia was increasingly discussed by opponents of the communist regime there and by Czech refugees and journalists in the West.[53]

Individuals who fled Czechoslovakia during the period of normalization brought stories of daily repression of human rights and civic freedoms by the communist regime. Similar to the "Expo Émigrés" who arrived in Montreal in 1967, a small group of Czechoslovak citizens arrived in Canada during the 1976 Summer Olympics, also held in Montreal. They were officially permitted to leave Czechoslovakia on tourist visas and expected by the Czechoslovak government to return home after the Olympic Games. One of them was Břetislav Marek, who did not speak a word of English or French and after arriving at Mirabel Airport lost his way travelling on the city's underground metro network. Curious to see what life in Canada was like, Marek used the staging of the games to visit the country and decide whether he would attempt to stay permanently in Canada. Upon visiting a friend in Sudbury, Ontario, he informed him of his intention to immigrate to Canada. Marek later visited the local immigration bureau in Sudbury, where Canadian officials informed him that it would be difficult for him to immigrate since he had arrived in the country on a tourist visa. Nevertheless, Canadian officials were sympathetic to his plight and extended his stay and found him employment. His earliest employment experiences in Canada included working two days per week in a restaurant making food for a buffet and as a night janitor in a school in Sudbury. Marek later moved to Hamilton, where members of the local Czechoslovak community helped the Czech newcomer to navigate the various government offices before Canadian immigration officials allowed him to stay in the country as a landed immigrant. He received Canadian documentation after waiting for a period of six months. Since Marek did not return to Czechoslovakia, he was blacklisted by the communist authorities for illegally emigrating to the West.[54]

Charta 77

Increasingly, harassment of opponents of the communist regime in Czechoslovakia, abuse of political prisoners, and intimidation and blackmail of former compatriots in the West were documented. In Slovakia, the Slovenska organizácia na ochranu ľudských práv (Slovak Organization for the Protection of Human Rights) was established to defend the human rights of the local population.[55] In January 1977, a charter was publicly released in Czechoslovakia criticizing the Communist Party authorities for their human rights abuses and for failing to enforce human rights conditions found in the Helsinki Accords and two aforementioned international covenants. The charter had 242 signatories ranging from former reformist Communist Party members such as writer and journalist Ludvík Vaculík, who wrote a manifesto, "Two Thousand Words," during the Prague Spring, to dissident artists and intellectuals, including playwright Václav Havel and actor Pavel Landovský. The informal Charta 77 (Charter 77) movement was a loose collection of predominantly Czech individuals who defended individual human rights in Czechoslovakia. In early January, Vaculík, Havel, and Landovský were arrested by the Czechoslovak secret police for attempting to present their document to the Federal Assembly in Prague. Shortly after their arrests, the charter appeared in the Western press, with West Germany's *Frankfurter Allgemeine Zeitung,* Great Britain's *The Times,* France's *Le Monde,* and Italy's *Corriere della Sera* publishing the opposition document.[56] While the Communist Party authorities viewed both Charta 77 and Slovenska organizácia na ochranu ľudských práv as illegal movements hostile to state-sponsored socialism, refugees who had fled the country and Western media outlets closely followed the human rights movements, helping to raise awareness of and public support for human rights in Czechoslovakia.[57]

Another Extortion Tactic: "Amnesty"

As Communist Party authorities suppressed a growing dissident movement in Czechoslovakia, their efforts to exert further pressure on former compatriots in Canada continued. Throughout the 1970s, the Canadian government remained watchful of attempts by the Czechoslovak government to intimidate former citizens who now resided in Canada. Czech refugees were alleging that Prague had offered amnesty to them and their compatriots if they chose to return to Czechoslovakia. Prague's amnesty plan amounted to blackmail since most of the refugees in Canada declined the offer to return to their homeland—whereupon the Communist Party authorities sought retribution against their relatives and friends in Czechoslovakia. Prime Minister Trudeau attempted to reassure the refugees, stating that they could not be forced to act against their will because "the Czech[oslovak] embassy has no power over Canadians." As he further stated, "I think this is unacceptable treatment of Canadian citizens. I don't think they should be subject to blackmail."[58] There was little that the Canadian government could do to prevent attempts by officials in Prague to extort former nationals in Canada. Yet most of these efforts failed because they were met with cynicism and outright refusal by Czech refugees. Soon this lack of success forced Czechoslovak authorities to alter their course, but their attempts to pressure former compatriots and extort much-needed foreign currency from them continued.

In the mid-1970s, the Czechoslovak government reversed its policy preventing refugees from visiting the country to see relatives and friends. Including the 1948ers, many of those who emigrated after the events of 1968 were now Canadian citizens under the legal jurisdiction of Canadian representatives overseas. Many 1948ers and 1968ers increasingly suffered from psychological stress from not having seen their loved ones for years and in some cases decades. As 1948ers and 1968ers successfully settled in Canada, many individuals became divided over their willingness to seek legalization of their immigration to the West from the Communist Party authorities in Prague. A majority of 1948ers refused to cooperate with Prague because any relations would strengthen the Communists' political legitimacy, influence, and authority. Conversely, some 1968ers considered themselves apolitical and were willing to pay the Czechoslovak government's fees to have their names normalized under Czechoslovak law for leaving the country without permission.

Under the Czechoslovak government's plan labelled "normalization of relations," Canadian citizens paid between $300 and $2,500 to be able to travel to

Czechoslovakia without the threat of prosecution. To normalize their relations with Prague, Czech refugees needed to request officially a presidential pardon for their "crime" and seek permission to reside permanently abroad. In some cases, before their requests for "normalization" could be processed, 1948ers and 1968ers in the West were pressured to repay the costs of their earlier education in Czechoslovakia, initially funded by the state.[59] The Czech refugees then received documentation permitting them to visit Czechoslovakia legally.

Most Czech refugees in Canada viewed the Czechoslovak government's plan as a scheme to extort much-needed foreign currency for a faltering national economy.[60] With similar objectives, Communist Party authorities also sent StB (Státní bezpečnost or State Security) agents to visit compatriots in Canada in order to inform them maliciously that a close relative was ill and required their return to the old homeland. The StB agent produced a form to normalize relations with the regime that the compatriot then signed under pressure. Unknown to the Canadian, the StB agent returned to Czechoslovakia with proof that the refugee was a communist spy. The StB pressured refugees in the West to become spies or information gatherers and even extorted money from them.[61] Communist Party officials in Prague continued their attempts to repatriate former citizens who they believed had left the state illegally, without permission. In an effort to suppress negative portrayals of the communist regime in Czechoslovakia by many 1948ers and 1968ers, StB agents and Czechoslovak diplomats were sent to the West to engage in propaganda and "normalization of relations" campaigns through the use of blackmail.

Many individuals within the Canadian Czechoslovak community continued their anti-communist activities in spite of Prague's efforts to pressure their compatriots in the West to regularize their standing with the communist regime. A major initiative was the continued resettlement of refugees residing outside Czechoslovakia. In 1979, the Canadian government established three designated classes of refugees for Indochinese, Latin Americans, and Eastern Europeans. Individuals who did not fit the UN refugee convention definition could still be admitted into Canada through one of the three classes. The most open criteria applied to the Eastern European self-exiled persons class, which dictated that individuals only had to prove that they were outside their country of citizenship and wanted to settle permanently in Canada.[62] In the summer of 1980, the CNAC and Minister of Employment and Immigration Lloyd Axworthy signed an agreement establishing a quota for all refugees from Czechoslovakia who resided outside the Iron Curtain and wanted to resettle in Canada. The Canadian government agreed to set the quota at 3,400 individuals per year. The basis of the agreement permitted the CNAC to sponsor political refugees with the assistance and cooperation of the department. Subsequently, Ottawa guaranteed that the sponsorships would be accepted.[63] However, fewer individuals from Czechoslovakia arrived in Canada than the federal quota permitted. During the 1970s, only 2,172 individuals claimed Czechoslovakia as their country of last permanent residence upon entering Canada. A majority of these newcomers—1,189 or 54.7 percent—chose to resettle in Ontario, followed by Quebec, British Columbia, and Alberta.[64]

In the early 1980s, Canadian immigration officials in Europe witnessed an increase in the number of refugees from Czechoslovakia residing in temporary accommodations in Austria, France, Italy, and West Germany. The Canadian government maintained an annual quota of 500 immigration visas for all refugees in West Germany. As a result, a majority of refugees from Czechoslovakia faced an obstacle since there were many more applicants than available spaces for resettlement in Canada. Individuals who could prove that they had close relatives living in Canada, or had the ability to speak English or French and had secured employment, would become the fortunate few admitted into Canada. From July 1982 to June 1983, Canada increased its quota, offering 750 visas to Eastern European refugees in West Germany. Refugees from Eastern Europe who initially requested political asylum in West Germany and wished to resettle there permanently were not eligible to come to Canada. They were expected to claim asylum in their second country prior to travelling to their country of permanent resettlement, which served as a safe third country. In this case, West Germany was to serve as a second country from which individuals and families could apply for asylum in Canada.[65]

Defection: A Routine Matter?

Securing a Canadian visa in West Germany was only one of several ways in which Czech refugees could find safe haven in Canada. In the mid-1980s, the Canadian press increasingly highlighted the many defections occurring during routine flight stopovers in Canada. Once on Canadian soil, Czechoslovak citizens requested political asylum after leaving their planes at Montreal's Mirabel International Airport and Gander International Airport in Newfoundland. Quoting Canadian immigration officials, the *Montreal Gazette* claimed that approximately one defection occurred every week. Československé státní aerolinie (Czechoslovak State Airlines) advertised direct flights to Cuba from Prague. The aircraft used on these flights had a maximum range of 4,900 miles, short of the 5,300 miles necessary for a direct flight between Prague and Havana.

If poor weather occurred, the plane often landed in Gander.[66] Given the distance between Havana and Prague, the fact that no communist state existed in North America, and the fact that the American government prohibited direct flights to Cuba, aircraft originating in Czechoslovakia were forced to refuel in Canada. Czechoslovak State Airlines used Mirabel or Gander for its stopovers. Czechoslovak citizens wanting to board a plane to Cuba for a vacation were often vetted by Communist Party authorities. Many of those permitted to leave the country were ordinary members or apparatchiks who were pressured to show their allegiance to the state and joined the Communist Party of Czechoslovakia.[67]

During the 1980s, the number of defections at Gander and Mirabel was virtually equal. According to the *Toronto Star,* Canadian immigration officials and RCMP officers at Mirabel were so used to weekly defections from Czechoslovak State Airlines Flight 576 that they would walk through the transit area specifically searching for passengers seeking to defect. The local Czechoslovak community affectionately referred to the defectors as the *Kubanci* ("Cubans").[68] In 1984, the CNAC changed its name to the Czechoslovak Association of Canada (CAC). As president of CAC's Montreal branch, Victor Žícha met defectors at Mirabel to offer immediate assistance, including translation, Canadian currency, and transportation to a local hotel where other defectors were temporarily staying. Žícha and the branch also aided newcomers in securing housing, employment, and language classes.

Many of these newcomers arrived in Canada as immigrants in the independent class or as refugees.[69] To assist them, the CAC maintained a special fund for resettlement and continued its efforts to resettle refugees from Czechoslovakia throughout the 1980s. Czech Canadian shoe magnate Tomáš Baťa continued his efforts to assist the CAC and newcomers by providing funds, winter clothing, and footwear. For relatives wishing to bring their family members to Canada, they had to agree to a sponsorship with the CAC for a period of one year. The organization was also willing to assist the community in resettling entire families if a ten-year sponsorship agreement was concluded.[70] With a steady flow of defections and the continued sponsorship of refugees to Canada, the Czechoslovak government implemented another scheme to entice former compatriots back to their old homeland.

Another Amnesty

In 1985, Prague celebrated the fortieth anniversary of the Soviet liberation of Czechoslovakia to end the Second World War. In their continued efforts to entice Czech refugees back to their homeland, Communist Party authorities declared a general amnesty for all refugees in the West to return without prejudice. However, very few individuals returned to Czechoslovakia for ideological reasons. Among their main reasons were a sense of nostalgia, poor health, lack of employment or economic success, and personal or family issues.[71] The Canadian Czech-language newspaper *Kanadské listy* argued that Czechs in the West could foreseeably return home as citizens of Western states since they were protected by their adoptive countries' diplomatic representatives. Controversially, the newspaper argued that refugees who had left Czechoslovakia recently for the refugee camps in West Germany and Austria had done so without pressure from the communist regime. The paper claimed that these refugees had not left a desperate situation and therefore did not warrant asylum or immigration in the West. Refugees who had fled Czechoslovakia in the 1940s and 1950s had been pressured and persecuted or unable to coexist with the authorities of the communist regime.[72]

Czechs young and old continued to flee that regime. For many individuals and families leaving their homes for the West, absolute secrecy was a vital part of their preparations. Often close relatives were not informed of a family member's emigration in order that they could truthfully deny any knowledge of the event before Czechoslovak government officials. Many Czechs continued to struggle with the moral ramifications of leaving behind siblings, parents, and even children. In the case of families with young children, many applied for exit visas because crossing the border illegally with children in tow was too risky. In the summer of 1985, Marta Procházka decided to leave Czechoslovakia with her young children. Communist Party authorities approved exit visas for them to take a vacation in Yugoslavia. In July, the Procházkas crossed the border into Hungary and then into Yugoslavia. In their attempt to reach Austria, they were turned away and forced to visit the UNHCR office in Belgrade in the hope that they could be legally accepted as convention refugees. After several weeks of waiting in Yugoslavia, the Czech family received their UN documentation and were able to reach the Traiskirchen refugee camp south of Vienna. Marta recalled that fellow Czechs in the camp were not helpful but that Canadian Embassy officials accommodated the Procházkas, who later began new lives in Canada.[73]

Ivo Moravec had a somewhat different experience that left him wondering how many individuals would in fact be admitted into Canada from the refugee camps in Austria. Initially, he was issued a grey passport by the Communist Party authorities in Prague, valid only for travel to Yugoslavia. After making his way to a refugee camp across the border in Austria, he pondered an important question: how selective would Canadian immigration officials be? Moravec found that Canadian officials preferred families and decent individuals but did not favour any specific profession. He was left feeling disadvantaged, for his higher education, skills, and experience seemed to matter little to Canadian officials in Vienna. He claimed that individuals with skills and experience in the trades received preferential treatment compared with applicants with university degrees. Yet Moravec and his family were later informed by letter from the Canadian Embassy that they would be permanently resettled in Canada.[74]

An Embarrassment for the Communists

As a major component of its struggle against communism, the CAC continued its efforts to resettle Czechoslovak citizens in Canada in order to embarrass further the Communist Party authorities in Prague and to provide safe haven to individuals and families. In bringing attention to defections to Canada, the *Christian Science Monitor* claimed that, from 1982 to 1986, approximately 350 Czechoslovak nationals had defected on Canadian soil.[75] In its official *Věstník* (Bulletin), the CAC sought assistance from the Canadian Czechoslovak community to sponsor more refugee families and single adults. In a March 1987 issue, the organization solicited sponsors to help resettle a twenty-four-year-old seamstress, a twenty-eight-year-old electrician, and a thirty-three-year-old jeweller-watchmaker, all living in refugee camps in Italy. Additionally, the *Věstník* sought sponsors for a young couple: a twenty-three-year-old electrician-mechanic and a twenty-two-year-old laundry maid. The *Věstník* claimed that the refugees in Italy were willing to take any employment offered to them in Canada. The CAC added that, without the help of its members, the refugees would languish in European camps for several years.[76] By the end of 1988, CAC branches across the country had answered the request and sponsored 182 refugees from Czechoslovakia. Some of the aforementioned refugees were due to arrive in the new year.[77]

Defections by Czechoslovak nationals continued to play an important role in the activities of CAC branches across Canada, which provided much-needed resettlement support to newcomers. In the first six months of 1989, 251 people requested refugee status in Canada, an increase of eighty from the same period a year before. Sensing that the number of cases was rising substantially, the Canadian government sought to curb the number of defections in an effort to prevent any public political controversy arising from what appeared to be an uncontrolled immigration system. In the summer of 1989, Canadian immigration authorities at Montreal's Mirabel International Airport intervened to prevent further defections from Czechoslovakia by imposing stricter processing procedures. Immigration officials required airline passengers flying from Eastern Europe to have in their possession fuller documentation or cause the airline to incur large fines. The length of a stopover was also carefully watched, and passengers found it difficult to access Canadian officials. However, stricter procedures and stiffer financial penalties did not prevent Czech refugees from hiding in airport bathrooms or rushing to the nearest federal official or RCMP officer to claim asylum. Despite the implementation of more stringent controls, the Montreal office of the Immigration and Refugee Board granted refugee status to approximately two-thirds of all cases, permitting the newcomers from Czechoslovakia to stay in Canada.[78] During the 1980s, 9,855 individuals claimed Czechoslovakia as their country of last permanent residence upon entering Canada. Nearly half—47.6 percent or 4,690 people—chose to relocate to Ontario. From 1983 to 1989, 5,660 Czechoslovak nationals were admitted into Canada as refugees. During the same period, 558 individuals were admitted as independents, 472 under the family class, 105 under the assisted relative class, and 3 under the entrepreneur class. Those admitted under the refugee class represented 83.3 percent of all newcomers from Czechoslovakia during this period. In 1990, Canada eliminated the Eastern European self-exiled persons refugee class first established in 1979.[79]

For Canadian Czechoslovak organizations, providing immediate resettlement support to refugees often overshadowed other community priorities, including raising awareness of the victims of communist persecution. The latter was often manifested by public commemoration events. Within the Welfare Association of Former Czechoslovak Political Prisoners in Canada, the conflict between these priorities led to an internal rift. Several of the association's members established their own group, K-231 in Exile, to continue their agenda of honouring and preserving the memory of political prisoners and victims of the communist regime in Czechoslovakia. As members of the newly formed group, former Czechoslovak political prisoners in Canada commissioned the creation of a monument to honour the victims of communist persecution in their old homeland and to commemorate victims of communism throughout the world. In July 1989, a statue of a tortured man crucified on a sickle and hammer symbolizing Soviet oppression was unveiled. The monument, *Crucified Again,* was created by Czech sculptor and 1968er Josef Randa of Winnipeg and erected on a donated parcel of land at Masaryktown. Over $32,000 was raised from compatriots in the West to commission the statue in Toronto.[80]

The End of the Communist State

Four months after the unveiling of *Crucified Again,* Czech refugees watched as political events unfolded in Czechoslovakia. In mid-November 1989, riot police suppressed a student-led protest against the communist regime there. Two days later a broad spectrum of Czechoslovak society joined in a series of popular demonstrations against one-party rule. A crowd of approximately 200,000 individuals in Prague swelled to half a million only twenty-four hours later. The popular demonstrations that swept the country were led by students and dissidents who formed Občanské forum (Civic Forum) in the Czech Lands and Verejnosť proti násiliu (Public against Violence) in Slovakia. Later that month a two-hour general strike was held across the country followed a day later by an announcement from the Communist Party government that it would formally dismantle the one-party state. During the protests sweeping across Czechoslovakia, members of the CAC returned to their old homeland in an effort to assist the reform movement. Three representatives, including John Hašek (a 1948er who fled communist imprisonment with his family to the West), arrived with approximately $25,000 raised by the Canadian Czechoslovak community to assist the homeland in its transition to a parliamentary democracy.[81] Only a few weeks later, in mid-December, President Gustáv Husák appointed the first non–Communist Party government since February 1948 and resigned from office three days later. Shortly thereafter, Civic Forum and Public against Violence announced that intellectual and playwright Václav Havel would be their candidate for president. The choice sparked outrage in Slovakia, which wanted to install a Slovak (Alexander Dubček) as president of the federal republic. In late December, Dubček was elected speaker of the parliament, and soon after Havel became the first democratic president of Czechoslovakia since 1948. The sweeping changes in Czechoslovakia in the fall of 1989 were referred to in the Czech Lands as the *Sametová revoluce* (Velvet Revolution) and in Slovakia as the *Nežná revolúcia* (Gentle Revolution).[82] The events of November and December that year returned parliamentary democracy to Czechoslovakia after four decades of one-party rule.

In early 1990, officials within the Czechoslovak president's office held discussions with Canadian diplomats in the hope that former compatriots in Canada could play a decisive role in Czechoslovakia's reorientation from communism to democracy. Both groups agreed that, as Czechoslovakia's first democratic head of state since 1948, Havel had to spend at least one night in Canada during his first visit to North America. In February 1990, the recently elected Czechoslovak president arrived in Canada for a two-day visit, spending an evening in Ottawa before departing for Toronto. His objective was to encourage the special relationship between Canada and Czechoslovakia before departing for Washington. Vital to this relationship were the Czech refugees who had permanently resettled in Canada during four decades of communist rule. Canadian diplomats asserted that these individuals served as an important human link between the countries. In the case of the 1968ers, who had spent two decades under communist domination, a Canadian diplomat stationed in Prague during the Velvet Revolution noted that they had sought asylum from communist persecution. Often no longer able to coexist with the regime, they had left their families and friends behind to resettle in a country about which they knew very little. Czech refugees had often been denied contact with their homeland. Some refugees had actively fought against the communist regime, and almost all believed that the situation would remain unchanged during their lifetimes. In Canada, many Czech refugees were surprised by the sudden change in their old homeland during the events of November 1989.[83]

After meeting the local Czechoslovak community in Ottawa, Havel flew to Toronto, where he received an honorary doctorate of law. Before a capacity crowd of approximately 2,000 at the University of Toronto's Convocation Hall, the dissident-turned-Czechoslovak president declared that a "democratic federation" would exist between Czech and Slovak nations in a post-communist Czechoslovakia.[84] Havel argued that Czech statehood had to be separated from Czechoslovak statehood in order for an equal federative union to take hold between the Czech and Slovak nations.[85] During his official visit in Toronto, individuals within the Canadian Slovak community voiced their aspirations for greater autonomy for Slovaks in Czechoslovakia. Among jeers and whistles from a capacity crowd, Reverend Dušan Toth—who represented the World Slovak Congress, a prominent international body representing Slovaks who lived abroad—argued for Slovak equality and minority rights in Czechoslovakia. The crowd in attendance was largely divided between Czechoslovaks and nationalist Slovaks. While members of the Canadian Czechoslovak community wished to hear from the playwright-turned-president, nationalist Slovaks wanted to voice their concerns for the future of Slovakia. The *Globe and Mail* concluded rather astutely that the Czechoslovak and nationalist Slovak communities remained argumentative compared with their brethren in Czechoslovakia, consumed by a newfound parliamentary democracy.[86] Several months later, in June 1990, Czechoslovakia held its first free elections in forty-four years. That same year, the Canadian government admitted 1,151 UN convention refugees from Czechoslovakia who had left the former communist state prior to the return of a democratic system of government. Newcomers from Czechoslovakia formed the eighth-largest refugee group by country of origin admitted into Canada that year. From 1990 to 1992, 2,965 immigrants from Czechoslovakia were permanently resettled in Canada. During this period, persons admitted under the refugee class represented 54.2 percent of all newcomers from Czechoslovakia. Of the 2,965 individuals permanently resettled in Canada, 1,608 were admitted as refugees, 683 under the family class, 338 as independents, 325 under the assisted relative class, and 11 as self-employed.[87] During the summer of 1992, Czech and Slovak politicians held negotiations over the future of Czechoslovakia. Czech politicians favoured a continued federation between the Czech Lands and Slovakia, whereas Slovak leaders sought greater sovereignty over Slovakia's affairs. Although a majority of Czechoslovakia's citizens initially disapproved of any breakup of the state, Czech and Slovak politicians mutually agreed to a Velvet Divorce in the fall of 1992. On 1 January 1993, the Czech Republic and the Slovak Republic became independent states. In May 1995 the CAC, a national ethnocultural organization that represented the Canadian Czechoslovak community, recognized this political shift in Central Europe and was renamed the Czech and Slovak Association of Canada.[88]

▸ ▸ ◂ ◂

Politically active Czech refugees in Canada remained divided between those who believed that the most important issue within the Czechoslovak community was the resettlement of refugees from their old homeland and those who believed that raising awareness of the crimes perpetrated by the communist regime in Czechoslovakia was of the highest importance. The conflict over which issue would be atop the Czechoslovak community's agenda continued since members had diverse backgrounds and interests and held varied opinions about the future of their community. In a 1991 study of immigrants from Czechoslovakia, the Quebec Ministry of Cultural Communities and Immigration noted that Czech refugees who had arrived in Canada in the two decades following the Warsaw Pact invasion were considerably more diverse in their backgrounds compared with earlier waves of refugees from Czechoslovakia.[88] Whereas the 1948ers and 1968ers were predominantly educated and skilled professionals, the more recent Cold War arrivals were not only professionals but also skilled tradespeople in the construction, manufacturing, and service industries.

The third wave of Cold War Czech refugees embedded their anti-communist and democratic agenda in Canadian Czechoslovak organizations, including the CAC (formerly CNAC) and MMI. As a result, both the CAC and the MMI continued to maintain an anti-communist Cold War identity and actively supported Canada's Cold War agenda. As Canadian Czechoslovak organizations, the CAC and MMI actively lobbied the federal government in an attempt to influence Canadian foreign policy on their old homeland and domestic politics in Canada. As human rights abuses and the repression of civil liberties continued to be exposed by Western media outlets and by recently arrived refugees, Canadian Czechoslovak community institutions and their elites used these issues to pressure the Canadian government to defend democratic values before Soviet and Czechoslovak officials. In opposing the communist regime in Czechoslovakia in the two decades after the Soviet-led invasion of their homeland, politically active Czech refugees in Canada raised awareness among their fellow citizens about the totalitarian regime in their old homeland, further entrenching their position within the conservative Cold War consensus in Canada.

Ultimately, the CAC and MMI were ethnic organizations that supported Canada's democratic culture during the Cold War. However, with the same sociocultural groups displaying an aging membership, financial insecurity, and lack of interest among a younger group of Canadian-born community members, many Cold War refugees from Czechoslovakia began to turn their attention toward cultivating their ancestral language, history, and culture for future generations.

CHAPTER
7

Creating Ethnocultural Heritage

When Zdeněk and Dagmar Zimmer arrived in Canada in 1951, they were struck by the country's natural beauty and urban architecture. They made their way to Hamilton, where a Czech friend had settled and married a Canadian woman. They found the city to be an adequate size and employment opportunities to be plentiful. They eventually joined the local CNA branch, where they met fellow compatriots from Czechoslovakia. As Catholics, they sought a local national parish, but Czechs in Hamilton did not have their own church, so the couple attended mass at the local Slovak parish of Saints Cyril and Methodius. Zdeněk found employment in industry and founded the Hamilton Sparta Soccer Club. Dagmar first found work as a sales clerk and volunteered for the Canadian Red Cross, which led to employment at the Ontario Hospital (later renamed the Hamilton Psychiatric Hospital), where in January 1956 she became a certified psychiatric aide and a registered nursing assistant.

In their home, the Czech Canadian couple cultivated many aspects of their ethnocultural heritage. Dagmar established a traditional Czech kitchen but "reinvented" the cuisine to include fish and salad since these items were rarely available in Czechoslovakia. Canadian foods also helped to balance the traditional Czech diet, calorie rich and vitamin deficient. Although the Zimmers accepted a Canadian way of life, they were committed to adapting their Czech world to their new land. Food and sport were two ways in which the Czech couple transplanted their culture to Canada. Zdeněk asserted that, with ethnocultural identity, "we can transfer it to almost any other activity of human life. In other words, we did accept much of [the] Canadian way of living, yet somewhere deep in ourselves there's still the Czech in us, the way we were brought up, our customs. . . . This we will maintain. We always will be Czechs. Even living in Canada and being proud of being Canadian, our origin is Czechoslovakia."[1] Many Czech refugees like the Zimmers looked for ways to re-establish their ethnicity and culture while embracing a new Canadian identity.

When Zdeněk and Dagmar arrived in Canada at the height of the Cold War, the relationship between the Canadian Czechoslovak community and the Communist Party government in Prague was strained. Community members increasingly discussed the need to cultivate their ethnic heritage and democratic identity for successive generations. An important aspect of the community's identity was its struggle against communism. Many individuals within the community had been removed from their homeland for decades and continued to support the liberation of Czechoslovakia. However, after the Warsaw Pact invasion, many 1948ers and 1968ers feared that they would never see the return of a parliamentary democracy in their old homeland. Coupled with the fact that some of their compatriots assimilated into Canadian society through intermarriage with Canadian-born partners, Czech refugees soon believed that the durability of their community's ethnocultural heritage was in question. This observation only heightened their desire to cultivate Czechoslovak ethnocultural heritage in Canada.

The arrival of Prague Spring refugees between 1968 and 1969 and the third wave of Cold War refugees during the 1970s and 1980s galvanized the Canadian Czechoslovak community and breathed new life into community groups across the country. Nonetheless, in the immediate years after the events of 1968, organizations (including the CNAC and MMI) continued to struggle with a lack of financial security as they became increasingly concerned about the promotion of ethnocultural heritage for future generations. Following the introduction in 1971 of the federal multiculturalism policy, Canadian Czechoslovak community groups and associations successfully applied for grants and subsidies that provided much-needed funding for ethnocultural initiatives, including language schools, libraries, radio and television programs, and conferences. Interactions between Czech refugees and federal officials allowed the Czechoslovak community to promote its ethnocultural heritage, especially among its youth members, and to contribute to Canada's multicultural identity. As representatives of various Czechoslovak institutions, Czech refugees were able to increase public recognition of their activities, which included endorsing democratic values, promoting cultural pluralism, and supporting a unified country against an emerging separatist movement in Quebec. During the 1970s and 1980s, the Czechoslovak community moved to a position of greater public visibility and, indeed, a fuller measure of social and cultural citizenship in Canada.

The Advent of Canadian Multiculturalism

Across Canada, ethnocultural institutions increasingly examined how to promote their particular heritage for future generations. For smaller ethnocultural communities, less visible in mainstream society, becoming recognized ethnic communities became an existential matter. Following recommendations of the Royal Commission on Bilingualism and Biculturalism, and universal liberalization of immigration policy with introduction of the points system, in October 1971 Prime Minister Trudeau declared before the House of Commons that multiculturalism was official government policy. It confirmed that the country had no official culture and that English and French remained its two official languages. Canadian citizens of all ethnic, religious, and linguistic backgrounds were considered equal.[2] With the introduction of this policy, ethnocultural groups became able to support their activities and institutions with grants and subsidies under the aegis of multiculturalism. With federal and provincial support, Canadian Czechoslovak organizations successfully funded projects, including Czech- and Slovak-language supplementary schools and community radio and television broadcasts that not only articulated Czechoslovak heritage and democratic identity but also promoted Canadian citizenship and multiculturalism. These ethnocultural activities assisted in combatting public apathy among community members and improved good citizenship. The Department of the Secretary of State, responsible for citizenship and multiculturalism programs, believed that its funding would allow the Canadian Czechoslovak community to achieve greater public visibility, whereby its contribution to Canadian multiculturalism could be better appreciated. Many community members also placed greater emphasis on how the Cold War refugees from Czechoslovakia were integrating into Canadian society.

As a small Canadian Czechoslovak community organization, the Masaryk Memorial Institute was often faced with financial difficulties while promoting ethnocultural heritage among its members. In November 1970, representatives of the MMI inquired at the Department of the Secretary of State's Citizenship Branch if any federal funding was available to support its sociocultural programs. As president of MMI, Bedřich Čecha informed Citizenship Branch officials that his organization wanted to expand its activities even as operating costs continued to increase significantly.[3] The officials replied that previous funding of cultural organizations had been conducted on an experimental basis as a pilot project and that future funding of ethnocultural groups and their projects would depend on cabinet's response to the recommendations of the Royal Commission on Bilingualism and Biculturalism. Financial assistance remained limited to individually assessed projects and their respective merits.[4] Although the institute was initially unsuccessful in securing federal funding to support and expand its services, the organization's sponsorship of the Czechoslovak Studies program at the University of Toronto no longer required a subsidy; the program had become self-sufficient. But this success was short-lived: the Chair for Czechoslovak Studies was later discontinued due to a lack of financial support and mounting opposition from the Canadian Slovak community.[5]

As MMI continued to secure funding for its programs and services—including issuing short-term loans and scholarships, maintaining Masaryktown, and finding accommodations and employment for newly arrived refugees—many smaller Czechoslovak organizations perceived the institute to be withholding funds from the community's other groups. This perception hampered MMI's ability to secure its own financial future. Groups that sought to use the organization's facilities believed that MMI was stealing from them by asking for rental fees. However, these fees were used to pay the organization's taxes and for renovations. In his executive member's report to the MMI community for 1970, W. Bartánus declared that it was "time to realize that we all have to work together, forget our political disputes and rather cultivate the great supply of Czech and Slovak talents, respect one another and most of all work together as a unit to elevate Czech and Slovak culture."[6] Bartánus argued controversially that Masaryktown should be sold in order to establish a financially self-sustaining Czechoslovak centre. Since many community members in Toronto and southern Ontario attended only the annual Czechoslovak Day, Bartánus believed that Masaryktown cost the community in excess of $12,000 annually for one occasion. He claimed that Masaryktown remained a symbol of a "rather expensive sentimentalism" and that selling the property and the old Masaryk Hall would permit the organization to establish a new community centre that better reflected the current needs of the community.[7]

Bartánus's report generated considerable interest from MMI's membership as the organization continued to struggle to meet its financial needs and effectively support recently arrived refugees. To assist ethnocultural communities in their resettlement efforts, in early 1971 the Department of the Provincial Secretary and Citizenship in Ontario published a monthly newspaper, *Newcomer News,* with the goal of assisting adult immigrants in English-language classes to acquire the necessary reading skills. The monthly government newspaper also informed newcomers of upcoming events that could assist them in their resettlement in the province. Provincial Secretary and Minister of Citizenship John Yaremko informed MMI that English-language teachers and newcomers to the province found the publication useful, and the demand for copies steadily increased. Yaremko requested that the institute include copies of the monthly newspaper in its own weekly, *Nový domov.* With the popular bonus supplement delivered to thousands of new Canadians across the province on a regular basis, Yaremko informed *Nový domov* editor Henry Zoder that Ontario's ethnic press provided "a bridge of understanding between the cultures of their readers and that of our way of life, and could be a very effective means for this wider distribution of *Newcomer News.*"[8] Zoder accepted Yaremko's proposal and included 1,000 copies of *Newcomer News* in his weekly.[9]

While the Ontario government sought the cooperation of its ethnocultural communities in the hope that they would assist immigrants and recent arrivals with their integration, the CNAC focused its attention on the size of its membership. In the spring of 1971, the organization requested that its local branches determine the ages of their members and how many of them were active. The CNAC branch in Ottawa consisted of only fifty-seven members, of whom only one person had come to Canada prior to 1939. Another ten individuals had arrived during the Second World War and before the Communist Party takeover in 1948; thirty-one had resettled during the early communist period; and fifteen had arrived following the Soviet-led invasion of Czechoslovakia in 1968. A majority of the branch's members was between thirty and fifty-five years of age.[10] Although many 1968ers had joined Canadian Czechoslovak organizations, including the CNAC and MMI, a significant portion of them remained outside community life. Older branches in rural areas and recently established units in urban centres often suffered from a lack of newcomer involvement. In Batawa, where a significant portion of community members had arrived prior to the Second World War, many no longer frequented scheduled CNAC meetings, and newcomers largely ignored CNAC activities. Similarly, a newly established branch in Halifax suffered from a lack of members and financial support. Although the branch held events, it suffered from the frequent relocation of its members to other parts of Canada. Exemplifying its dire position, the branch held approximately twenty-five dollars in its bank account and could not afford to send a representative to the annual CNAC congress.[11]

The arrival of Czech refugees after the Warsaw Pact invasion bolstered the CNAC, yet many of its branches across Canada remained small and in need of government support for their community programs. During the formative period of multiculturalism in Canada, CNAC members actively lobbied their municipal and provincial governments for grants and subsidies. In the summer of 1972, the branch in Calgary participated in the Alberta Cultural Heritage Conference at the University of Alberta in Edmonton. The conference dealt with the acculturation of cultural groups in the province. In its brief to the conference, the branch argued that no cultural group "should have any privileges which could not be given to all groups, regardless of their numerical strength or length of their establishment in Canada or Alberta."[12] The branch sought to promote tolerance, understanding, and cooperation among ethnic groups and pressured the provincial government to enact legislation that embodied these ideals. The brief suggested that two proposals be implemented. First, the branch argued for the establishment of a multicultural centre in Calgary as a keystone of efforts to support ethnic groups in the region. The branch believed that such a centre could lease space to diverse ethnic organizations for a library, dining room, theatre, and physical activity space. In return, ethnic groups would be able to hold regular meetings and schedule cultural events promoting diversity in Calgary and throughout Alberta. The CNAC branch hoped that provincial and municipal authorities would work with the Canadian government to build the proposed centre. Second, the branch maintained that evening classes for every language spoken in Alberta be equally funded in order to promote fairness and equality among large and financially stable ethnic groups and those such as the CNAC branch, which could not cover the costs of language classes. During the conference, the branch representatives concluded that "the basic right to be taught one's parental language should be extended to all Albertans, regardless of [the] numerical strength of their cultural group. This move would strengthen the feeling of equality among all Albertans."[13]

As CNAC members in Calgary raised awareness of their financial difficulty in cultivating ethnocultural heritage among their small group, MMI suffered from a lack of involvement by its much larger membership. In his annual report to the MMI community, treasurer Jaroslav Forest argued that, though the institute might not have been able to provide the facilities that members desired, the amenities that did exist, including Masaryktown, were underused. It was his contention that, in order for the organization to survive, members had to alter their thinking, establish new goals, and implement them while remaining cognizant of the organization's financial realities.[14] Forest's assertion proved to be correct: in November 1972, the institute's board of directors established the Masaryk Old Age Fund. It was financed through community donations and fundraising activities, including bingo evenings.[15] That month the Women's Council of the CNAC in Toronto continued its fundraising efforts by holding its annual charity bazaar and Christmas Fair at Masaryk Hall. The bazaar was open to the public and consisted of pastries from Czechoslovakia and refreshments, including goulash and soup, delicatessen hors d'oeuvres, jams, jellies, handicrafts, and cookbooks. A new edition of the council's *Czechoslovak Recipes,* originally published in 1963, was also available for purchase.[16]

Along with lobbying efforts, community fairs, and exhibitions, politically active Czech refugees within the Czechoslovak community engaged in public presentations to promote sociocultural citizenship in Canada. On the occasion of Citizenship Day in Winnipeg, CNAC president Jiří Corn delivered a speech before guests at the Manitoba legislature in May 1974. During his remarks, Corn, a 1948er, requested Czech immigrants in attendance to cast their votes in the upcoming federal election and to remain proud of their newly received Canadian citizenship. The CNAC executive noted that new citizens had a duty to cherish their mother tongues and the culture of their old homeland. Corn argued that Canada's ethnocultural mosaic "encourages you to maintain the best from your culture and habits while being a good and honest Canadian citizen. You should integrate into the Canadian society and way of life by maintaining the best from your past and adopting the best from your present Canadian society."[17] The CNAC president concluded his remarks by suggesting that the new Canadian citizens in attendance should participate in all aspects of society and value the freedom and democratic culture available to all in Canada.[18]

While good citizenship remained an important part of the CNAC's agenda, the organization was forced continually to address a more existential concern: an aging membership. The same month the CNAC held its twenty-sixth annual congress in Hamilton. Delegates in attendance at McMaster University were informed that their organization's membership had an average age of sixty years. Batawa's eighty-eight members had an average age of sixty-three years. Conversely, the smallest branch, in Kingston, consisted of thirteen members with an average age of forty years. The CNAC's fourteen branches included 1,485 individuals with an average age of fifty years. The issue was of greatest concern to the smallest branches, which included Calgary, Halifax, Kingston, and Windsor—each with less than fifty members and an average age in the late forties. In the larger centres of Toronto, Montreal, and Hamilton, the average age of CNAC members remained in the mid-fifties. These statistics illustrated that a majority of the association's members were aging. As a result, the association was confronted with the necessity of finding new and young members who would assist in renewing it.[19]

The Dictionary Project

As CNAC branch leaders and the executive in Toronto began to address the organization's need for younger members, they continued to promote ethnic heritage and cultivate Czechoslovak identity in Canada. In attempting to meet public demand for Czech- and Slovak-language materials, the CNAC corresponded with Zdena Salivarová—who along with her husband, Josef Škvorecký, had established the Czech dissident publishing house Sixty-Eight Publishers—to determine the financial viability of producing a Czech-language text. Salivarová informed the CNAC that the dissident publishing house's readership would be interested in the publication of a Czech-English dictionary. In her view, 2,000 copies could be printed, and Sixty-Eight Publishers would act as a distributor to all interested compatriot communities in the West.[20] The project was later titled *Dictionary of Stereotyped, Metaphorical, and Idiomatic Expressions.* Under the authorship of *Nový domov* editor Břetislav Kroulík, the dictionary listed commonly used English-language expressions and conveyed their Czech equivalents. The CNAC argued that the dictionary was necessary because many newcomers from Czechoslovakia struggled to understand English idioms widely used in the Canadian workforce. In seeking support for the project from the federal Citizenship Branch, CNAC member and Brock University professor Victor Fic argued that understanding these idioms would prepare immigrants to secure employment in their chosen fields and "greatly reduce" the "anxiety and emotional trauma of the people who are technically competent but whose competitiveness on the job market is badly handicapped by [a] lack of idiomatic English."[21]

The CNAC applied to the federal government for funding since the dictionary project fell under the Third Language Teaching Aid classification within the Multicultural Grants Program. Grants from the program were available for projects that promoted diversity in Canada through the dissemination of cultural heritage. Similarly, activities that assisted in an ethnocultural group's development were also considered. Prospective projects were required to secure financial support from the local community and to assist immigrants in fully participating in Canadian society.[22] In its grant application, the CNAC indicated that it was comprised of over 8,000 members between eighteen and seventy years of age. As a small and financially sound organization that required further funding to meet its commitments to the Czechoslovak community, the CNAC indicated to the Citizenship Branch that its proposed dictionary would consist of approximately 300 pages of idioms, phrases, and metaphorical expressions in Czech and English. The objective of the dictionary was to improve each Canadian Czech's knowledge of English and benefit professionals, including translators and writers who required a consistent source of terminology. The total cost for the publication of the Czech-English dictionary was $18,100. The CNAC allocated $9,500 to the project and requested that the Citizenship Branch approve $8,600 in federal funding.[23] In April 1975, the branch informed the CNAC that it could financially support the publication and distribution of books only if they were of interest to a significant portion of Canadians. Citizenship Branch officials believed that the dictionary project was limited in terms of how many Canadians would benefit from its publication and withheld funds. Yet officials in Ottawa informed the CNAC that funding for a publication pertaining to an ethnocultural group's history in Canada was readily accepted.[24] Without federal funding, the CNAC project would lie dormant for almost a decade; the Czech-English dictionary was finally published with private support in 1991 by the Toronto-based Moravia Publishing Company. The dictionary became an important resource for Czech refugees who wanted to understand the English language better as they navigated new employment opportunities and social circles or simply desired to increase their level of linguistic competence. In the early 1970s, the CNAC also explored the use of other forms of media to promote the Czechoslovak community and disseminate ethnocultural heritage in Canada.

Radio and Television

Czechoslovak groups and CNAC branches across Canada continued to receive grants from the Canadian government under its strategy of promoting multiculturalism through the cultivation of ethnic culture and identity. In October 1974, the Montreal branch—with a $1,000 federal grant from the Department of the Secretary of State—began a regular weekly radio program in the Czech and Slovak languages. The purpose of the program was to provide a public service to former Czechoslovak nationals in Montreal. The program offered important news to newcomers from Czechoslovakia who lived in Quebec, including information on new laws and regulations in an effort to fight public apathy and to improve good citizenship. Broadcasts also contained interviews with prominent compatriots, including Czech American film director Miloš Forman. The weekly radio broadcast over CFMB 1410's airwaves became popular with members of the community and led some individuals in Montreal to organize public events, including lectures, exhibits, and shows for the Czechoslovak community. Eventually, the broadcast introduced its listeners to twenty-four one-minute announcements on multiculturalism in Canada.

To understand its audience better, the Montreal branch conducted a survey in the spring of 1979 involving a random sample of 350 Czech and Slovak families. Approximately 176 households indicated that the radio broadcasts were beneficial to them. A smaller number indicated that the program's 11:30 p.m. broadcasts were too late, and many listeners advocated for an earlier time slot. About 75 percent of respondents indicated that they tuned in to the program regularly. Younger listeners favoured modern Czech or Slovak music, whereas older members of the community preferred classical or folk music. When it came to preferences in news content, many 1968ers confirmed that they listened attentively to the news from Czechoslovakia rather than domestic events, whereas members of the 1948er generation preferred Canadian news information. The Montreal branch concluded that approximately 2,000–2,500 individuals listened regularly to its radio broadcasts. Since a majority of its members consisted of intellectuals and skilled workers, the community lacked small-business owners who could sponsor the thirty-minute radio program. Unable to find sponsors, the CNAC turned to the Department of the Secretary of State for funding by arguing that

> as ardent Federalists we see that our new home—Canada—is in grave danger. We are shocked with the political orientation of our provincial government and with articles appearing in some French newspapers advocating [for the] elimination of Multiculturalism. Thus, as it is our fervent desire to keep Canada together, we must intensify our efforts to convince every member of our community to work as [an] ambassador of good will, informing his French friends and acquaintances about the immense pitfalls that will be the inevitable consequence of separation of Quebec from the rest of Canada.[25]

The CNAC branch hoped that its broadcasts demonstrated the Czechoslovak community's good citizenship in Canada. In its assessment of the broadcasts, Canadian officials concluded that the Montreal branch was active and responded to the needs of the local Czechoslovak community. The program comprised twenty-five broadcasts per year and discussed the cultural heritage of Czechoslovaks in Quebec in the areas of literature, music, and theatre. Officials believed that funding the Ethnic Broadcast in Czech and Slovak Languages project would promote further understanding of Czechoslovakia and its compatriots in Canada, national unity, and multiculturalism in Quebec at a time when the separatist Parti Québécois was firmly in power.[26]

Two years after the nationalist Slovak community in Ottawa established a local television program in 1978 known as *Slovak Spectrum,* still in existence today, the local CNAC branch sponsored a television show titled *Czechoslovak Television Kaleidoscope: Life of Ethnic Czechs and Slovaks in Their New Homeland.* The program was broadcast once per month and focused on Czechoslovak culture, community news, and Canadian adaptation and multiculturalism. The community television show collected material on the immigration and settlement experiences of Czechoslovaks in Canada to raise awareness of their past historical and political circumstances for future generations, and it showcased how these individuals had integrated into Canadian society. Included in the interviews were representatives of the Multiculturalism section of the Department of the Secretary of State, who also assisted in funding the program with an annual grant of $1,200 for necessary supplies. Similar to other broadcast installments, the recorded interviews were preserved for future generations. For children in the local Czech- and Slovak-language supplementary school in Ottawa, the television show included information on Czechoslovakia's geography and history. Community members also televised discussions with individuals from other ethnic communities to illustrate their shared experiences in Canada. In their evaluation of the television program, Canadian officials concluded that *Czechoslovak Television Kaleidoscope* was a well-produced program and served as an example for other ethnocultural groups in Canada.[27]

Language and Culture

Similar to the CNAC, other Czechoslovak organizations in Canada had mixed results after applying for federal funding for their ethnocultural projects. Initially, MMI was denied a multicultural grant for its sociocultural programs by the Canadian government. This early failure was later reversed with support from the Department of the Secretary of State for the institution's application for funding to promote Czechoslovak culture and the Czech and Slovak languages. In January 1975, Stanley Haidasz, MP for Toronto-Parkdale, announced funding for the institute under the auspices of the federal government's multiculturalism policy. With a grant from the Canadian government, MMI established a community library on the grounds of Masaryktown that became a popular destination for individuals and families searching for Czech- and Slovak-language history books and traditional literature. The federal grant of $800 assisted the institute in repairing old books and purchasing newer Czech- and Slovak-language manuscripts.[28] In 1974, the institute applied for federal funding from the Immigrant Settlement and Adaptation Program under the auspices of the Department of Manpower and Immigration to establish an information office for the Czechoslovak community in Canada. The institute later joined other Czechoslovak community groups in Toronto and created a cultural pavilion for the Metro Toronto Caravan festival. Established in 1968 as a festival celebrating different cultures throughout the city, the international caravan brought the world to Toronto's Canadian-born Anglo-Saxon community. Located at different sites in various ethnic neighbourhoods and presided over by "mayors," pavilions were often located in church basements and community halls and featured ethnic foods, crafts, clothing, and music. As the chosen site of the Czechoslovak community's cultural pavilion, Masaryktown opened its Golden Prague restaurant for the event. The *Toronto Star* later reported that the pavilion was well received by Torontonians.[29] Aside from cultural events, publications, and television and radio programs, the cultivation of the Czech and Slovak languages among younger members was vital within the Czechoslovak community.

Supplementary Schools

Upon obtaining federal funding to support the establishment of a community library and the acquisition of Czech- and Slovak-language literature, MMI turned its attention toward obtaining a grant for its language school. In the late 1970s, MMI received $1,000 per year in federal funding from the Department of the Secretary of State's Supplementary School Assistance Program. Canadian officials used the program to enhance the learning of diverse languages and to promote multiculturalism.[30] The institute informed federal officials that any acquired funds were to subsidize its Czech- and Slovak-language school in an effort to cultivate Czechoslovak cultural and linguistic heritage among younger generations. During the 1979–80 school year, the Czech- and Slovak-language supplementary school organized instruction for four classes of students with a total enrolment of forty-five. Students received weekly instruction for a period of thirty-two weeks per year.

Several subjects were taught, including gymnastics or calisthenics, since the school was part of the patriotic Sokol movement, Czech- and Slovak-language instruction, dance, music and choir, literature and drama, and Czechoslovakia's geography and history.[31] By the beginning of the 1980–81 academic year, the supplementary school had grown to seventy students from Kindergarten to Grade 4. Given an annual federal grant and a donation from MMI, the school did not collect tuition fees and received no other funding. As a result, it ran a small deficit. Similarly, in Ottawa, the supplementary school held classes at a Lutheran church in the Meadowlands area of the city.[32]

The Supplementary School Assistance Program also assisted smaller and less urban Czechoslovak groups. In January 1980, officials from the Department of the Secretary of State informed the Czechoslovak Canadian Cultural Society of Southern Alberta that its new Czech- (and Slovak-) language school in Lethbridge had received $260 for the year. Libby Jonas, an instructor of Russian at the University of Lethbridge and a graduate of Slavic languages from the University of Alberta, served as the school's Czech and Slovak teacher. The school held weekly evening classes, with two hours allocated to language and grammar instruction and one hour to music. The school offered separate Czech- and Slovak-language classes, with Czech students outnumbering their Slovak counterparts three to one. Canadian officials noted that the recently established language school was well organized and offered an excellent opportunity for the retention of ethnic heritage.[33] A month later the department granted the CNAC's Kitchener-Waterloo branch $348 for its language school because of the group's status as a "very small struggling community which greatly appreciates the support."[34] Funds were allocated for supplies and to supplement the teacher's income received from the local school board. Students enrolled in weekly classes and spent one hour on language instruction, thirty minutes on literature and drama, fifteen minutes on geography and history, fifteen minutes on music, and thirty minutes on language-orientation games.[35]

Promoting Heritage

The CNAC and MMI were not the only organizations influential in promoting awareness of Czechoslovakia. Seeking to raise knowledge of Czechoslovak culture and history, the Ottawa chapter of the Czechoslovak Society of Arts and Sciences proposed a project entitled Cultural Integration of Czechoslovak Immigrants to Canadian Cultural Atmosphere and Role of Ethnic Organization to officials in the Department of the Secretary of

State.[36] Founded in Washington in 1958 as an international cultural organization with chapters throughout the Western world, the society promoted the dissemination of knowledge pertaining to Czechoslovakia and its peoples. In Ottawa, the local chapter was made up of intellectuals and professionals, many of them 1948ers and 1968ers. The Ottawa chapter received a grant of $935 from the Department of the Secretary of State and established a resource library for Czechoslovak studies. It also created an informative public program of guest lectures, films, and panel discussions on various topics pertaining to Czechoslovakia and Czechoslovak studies. In assessing the validity of sponsoring the society's project, Canadian officials noted that the society was well respected and included an established group of Czechoslovak scholars whose public lectures, literary evenings, and panel discussions were well attended. The department hoped that its grant would permit the society to move "from a less parochial and isolated stance into a more public and accessible position" whereby its contribution to multiculturalism and Canadian society could be better appreciated.[37]

In a similar fashion, the CNAC branch in Winnipeg applied for federal funding for its project, Presentation of Czechoslovak Literary Heritage to (the) Canadian Public.[38] In November 1980, the Department of the Secretary of State approved a grant of $2,250, which permitted the branch to organize a lecture and panel discussions at the Winnipeg Public Library. The discussions examined current literary trends in Eastern Europe, the role of exiled writers, and the status of Czech and Slovak Canadian literature, in the hope of raising Canadian awareness of Czechoslovak literary life. The lecture coincided with a display of Czech- and Slovak-language books and their English translations published in Canada by Czech and Slovak Canadian authors.[39]

As Canadian Czechoslovak community organizations engaged in promoting multiculturalism and their ethnocultural heritage, many Canadian-born members were increasingly concerned by how refugees from Czechoslovakia were integrating into Canadian society. In May 1983, the CNAC hosted a conference on the "cultural and social integration of immigrants from Czechoslovakia" in Toronto.[40] The conference brought together community leaders, private citizens, and Canadian Czechoslovak professionals and scholars.

Among the many participants, sociologist Jarmila Horná presented her findings from a survey of immigrants from Czechoslovakia in Alberta. She concluded that a majority of the respondents to her survey indicated that they considered themselves as having a distinct dual Canadian and Czech or Slovak ethnicity. More specifically, Horná revealed that postwar refugees from Czechoslovakia in Canada—including 1948ers and 1968ers—preferred the urban and middle-class background of English Canada. A majority of the newcomers in Alberta preferred to compartmentalize their identities. In the private sphere, refugees from Czechoslovakia cultivated an ethnic identity with an emphasis on the culture and language of their former country. Outside the home, these individuals espoused a Canadian identity in which they participated in Canadian arts and purchased Canadian literature and music. They also considered themselves to be Canadians when in the public sphere, including at work, church, and social gatherings. As refugees from Czechoslovakia demonstrated a strong preference for the upper-middle-class culture of English Canada, they also showed diminishing interest in providing an education in the Czech and Slovak languages to successive generations. Horná's study demonstrated that, once in Canada, immigrant adults were preoccupied with English-language courses and college or university studies in order to improve their socioeconomic positions. As a result, a majority of respondents spent less time in the home and rarely participated in ethnic association events or civic organizations because they had not been formally invited.[41] Their emphasis was on improving their language skills and levels of employment through further studies and interactions with a multicultural Canadian population, much to the detriment of community organizations that depended on their support to continue cultivating Czechoslovak heritage in Canada.

▸ ▸ ◂ ◂

In the years immediately after the Warsaw Pact invasion of Czechoslovakia, the CNAC and MMI continued to struggle with a lack of financial security as their memberships fluctuated. Both institutions increasingly recognized that the promotion of Czechoslovak heritage for future generations was vital. As a result, many members of the CNAC and MMI continued to turn to domestic issues. With the Canadian government's introduction of an official multiculturalism policy in 1971, Canadian Czechoslovak institutions were able to support their activities with federal grants and subsidies that promoted the country's diverse ethnic cultures and identities. Canadian Czechoslovak groups were now able to fund projects to establish Czechoslovak heritage and identity in the diaspora, including Czech and Slovak supplementary schools and community radio and television broadcasts, and to promote Canadian multiculturalism within their organizations and the broader community.

These government-supported ethnocultural activities assisted in combatting public apathy among Czech refugees and the broader Canadian Czechoslovak community and strengthened their sense of Canadian citizenship. Similarly, government funding allowed for the Canadian Czechoslovak community to gain greater public visibility, whereby its contribution to Canadian multiculturalism could be better appreciated.

CONCLUSION

Three successive waves of Czech refugees migrated to Canada during the Cold War. These individuals and families were part of a larger wave of migration to the West. From the Communist Party takeover of Czechoslovakia in February 1948 to the fall of the communist regime in December 1989, approximately 550,000 individuals, or 3.5 percent of the total population, emigrated from Czechoslovakia.[1] During this period, 36,531 people claimed Czechoslovakia as their country of citizenship upon entering Canada, meaning that they arrived via another country.

The emigration of Czech refugees was a direct consequence of Cold War politics. Throughout the Cold War, the communist regime cited emigration as an act of betrayal against the state and the Czechoslovak nation. Those who fled from communism were often resented by their fellow compatriots in Czechoslovakia for leaving their homeland; as one refugee put it, they perpetuated an "old myth which dictates that it is a sin to leave your country of birth."[2] Czech refugees who settled in Canada during the Cold War often recalled that compatriots distrusted them simply because they believed that the refugees lived better lives in the West. Individuals who sacrificed much in leaving Czechoslovakia behind did so at high costs to their relatives and friends. Those who fled communism for the West were considered traitors, and their relatives and friends back in Czechoslovakia were often denied access to university study, career advancement, and travel abroad. Then, too, many of the refugees, seemingly too individualistic to join pro-"Czechoslovak" organizations in Canada, often refused to do so out of a genuine fear of reprisal by the Czechoslovak government in Prague. Only a small minority within the Canadian Czechoslovak community had regularized their status as "illegal émigrés" when they left Czechoslovakia "without permission." A majority of individuals did not resolve this issue with Prague. They were *personae non gratae* in their old homeland.

Despite this tension, though, and unlike the 1948ers, both the 1968ers and those who arrived in the 1970s and 1980s were more than likely to be "apolitical." In some instances, Czech refugees refused to seek their relatives and friends because they feared for their safety in Czechoslovakia as government officials scrutinized correspondence between "illegal émigrés" in the West and their contacts at home.[3] For these and other reasons, Canadian Czechoslovak institutions found it difficult to attract recently arrived Czech refugees even though many of them consistently read Canadian Czech- and Slovak-language newspapers and magazines for news about their community.[4]

Yet the Communist Party takeover of February 1948, the Warsaw Pact invasion of 1968, and even the following period of normalization saw thousands of individuals leave their homeland because they had encountered a totalitarian regime that suppressed human rights and civic freedoms on a daily basis. In three successive waves of immigration, ethnic Czechs who supported a pro-"Czechoslovak" identity transplanted their political views and democratic values to Canada.

This study has shown that, beginning in the interwar period, Czech immigrants were preoccupied with forging identities and obtaining acceptance as "desirable" immigrants. For example, the resettlement of Bata Shoe Company workers and their families, and the movement of social democratic Sudeten Germans, many of whom joined Canadian Czechoslovak organizations, also at a time of rising international and domestic political tensions on the eve of the Second World War, had to demonstrate that they were not political subversives, supported democratic values, and were gainfully employed. After the German invasion of the Czech Lands, some Czechs hid their ethnocultural backgrounds in order not to be mistaken as Germans. Nevertheless, during the Second World War, Czechs had to fight against their official status as "enemy aliens" to prove their loyalty to Canada. Postwar Czech refugees only had to look within their own ethnocultural community for an example of how earlier immigrants dealt with pre-existing societal norms as they adapted to their new country.

During the early postwar period, Canada endured a "Red Scare," real and imagined, that manifested itself in what scholars have called "moral panic" about an "influx" of refugees deemed "freedom fighters" but possibly concealing links to Soviet espionage or at least harbouring communist sympathies. These fears among the Canadian population could also be found in a particular form of xenophobia prevalent at the time: suspicion of immigration from Eastern Europe. Although Canadian officials were concerned about the resettlement of "undesirable" individuals and "security risks," they largely viewed the admission of Czech refugees as a positive for a number of reasons, including Cold War politics, an attempt to embarrass the Soviet Union by resettling refugees from behind the Iron Curtain, economic self-interest, and support for international efforts to alleviate the growing postwar European refugee crisis.

Canada's Cold War agenda was bolstered by the selection and admission of these newcomers, many of whom viewed themselves as ardent Cold War warriors whose adherence to anti-communism and pro-democratic values would further legitimize the conservative Cold War consensus in Canadian society. Because public and private gatekeepers believed that it was their patriotic duty to shield their fellow citizens from communist infiltration, they asked questions of and shared concerns with Czechoslovak community "oldtimers" and recently arrived refugees about daily life under the totalitarian regime in Czechoslovakia, their suspected involvement in the communist movement, or their links to espionage. Early Cold War xenophobia was centred on the prospect of Eastern European immigrants concealing their socialist leanings. Although the gatekeepers were intent on instilling a certain Cold War identity on Czech newcomers, the choice to engage with Canadian society rested with the refugees themselves. At every turn, politically engaged Czech refugees worked to convince their fellow Canadians that they were dedicated pro-democrats and anti-communists.

Despite public attitudes that viewed these newcomers either as heroic freedom fighters or as suspicious immigrants because of their ethnocultural and geographic origins, Czech refugees remained intent on demonstrating loyalty to their new homeland, and they opposed leftist politics in Canada and worked against the spread of global communism. Moral panic extended to Czech newcomers, who capitalized on this political climate and used their anti-communist identity to meet existing social and cultural norms in their new country. In the process, they found a strategy to achieve social and cultural citizenship and helped to shape the image of a "good" refugee in Cold War Canada.

Throughout the Cold War, Czech refugees coalesced around their predominantly middle-class and anti-communist identities. As part of this process, they exposed the daily totalitarian repression in Czechoslovakia and thus further legitimized their experiences as refugees and entrenched their standing as "desirable" immigrants in Canada. As such, the Czech newcomers found a comfortable social and cultural citizenship; indeed, they were able to diminish fears about being communist sympathizers or Soviet spies and put under surveillance by the Canadian security establishment. Even those who viewed themselves as émigrés, believing that they would one day return to a democratic Czechoslovakia, fought the moral panic of the spread of global communism by supporting anti-communist efforts and the conservative Cold War consensus. It became clear to many Czech émigrés, especially after the Soviet-led invasions of Hungary in 1956 and Czechoslovakia in 1968, that their wait to return home would last many years if not decades. After 1968, this stark realization compelled even these migrants to turn their attention toward social and cultural citizenship in Canada. Although the idea of "home" for many émigrés was tied to political events in the old homeland, for other Czech migrants the ability to join efforts in combatting the spread of global communism provided them with a path toward full acceptance in Canada.

In order to use their agency and to find a sense of home, politically minded Czech refugees soon joined existing Czechoslovak ethnocultural associations. They found in them a constituency willing to support their pro-democracy values, virulent anti-communism, and anti-Soviet sentiment. As ethnocultural institutions that supported the conservative Cold War consensus, while promoting good citizenship among its members, the Czechoslovak National Association of Canada and the Masaryk Memorial Institute, both headquartered in Toronto, opened their doors to Czech refugees. Many of those who joined were articulate and politically driven. They entrenched their ideological beliefs in these groups and began to portray themselves as the true representatives of the Czechoslovak community. They lobbied their fellow Canadians for political support in returning parliamentary democracy to Czechoslovakia while strengthening democratic values in Canada. It was a strategy that served well their desire for social and cultural citizenship in Canada; politically active Czech refugees were able to integrate fully into their new country.

Several conclusions can be drawn from this study of Czech migration to Canada during the Cold War. After 1945, Canada was in the midst of profound social and economic changes as a large number of displaced persons and political refugees were resettled in the country. Federal authorities were well aware of the need to assist European states in alleviating postwar displacement. At the same time, the Canadian government was concerned about the immigration of Eastern Europeans who might hold leftist sympathies, suffered from psychological or physical trauma, or were members of dysfunctional and immoral family units. Across Canada, public officials and non-governmental professionals pursued policies that heightened the Canadian public's anxiety about the Cold War. As representatives of a predominantly white, Christian, and conservative society during the Cold War, both private and public gatekeepers claimed that newcomers from the Eastern Bloc could compromise the moral and social character of Canadian society. As a result, Canadian citizens became increasingly alarmed by potentially immoral, socially dysfunctional, sexually deviant, and politically divergent European newcomers arriving in Canada.[5]

Nevertheless, Canadian authorities were instrumental in the admission, settlement, and integration of Czech refugees during the Cold War. Federal officials engaged these newcomers who adhered to anti-communist, anti-Soviet, and pro-democratic values. They did so in an attempt to solicit political support to further a general Cold War agenda of protecting the country from communist influence from abroad and, more specifically, to limit the influence of interwar Czech "leftists" in Canada. Federal and provincial cabinet members and government bureaucrats, for example, promoted Canadian citizenship and democratic values when attending newcomer events, such as MMI's annual Czechoslovak Day celebrations at Masaryktown. The interactions between Canadian officials and Czechoslovak community events further helped to legitimize the Czech newcomers' anti-communist agenda.

Politically driven refugees from Czechoslovakia thus joined community organizations such as the CNAC and MMI in an effort to establish themselves as intermediaries between the Czechoslovak community that they hoped to represent and mainstream Canadian society. Within the CNAC and MMI, many 1948ers were joined by 1968ers to cultivate transnational identities, using old political affiliations from Czechoslovakia to promote anti-communist and pro-democratic values in the hope of one day witnessing democratic government return to their old homeland. In helping to minimize communist infiltration within Canadian Czechoslovak organizations, these Cold War refugees attempted to illustrate to Canadian officials that they were also loyal to their new country and its Cold War agenda. The use of their position as Cold War refugees from Czechoslovakia and their anti-communist background ultimately bolstered many newcomers' positions within their ethnocultural community and the broader Canadian society.

The Czech refugees' activities were also shaped by the ethnic organizations that they joined. Those organizations invariably espoused a Czechoslovak identity, and the refugees sought assistance from community institutions for accommodations, employment opportunities, loans, language translation, and social activities. The organizations provided a sense of community and a common ethnocultural understanding.

At the same time, many individuals within the existing Canadian Czechoslovak community were influenced by the anti-communism of the newcomers and supported the return of a democratic system of government to Czechoslovakia. Beginning with the 1948ers, Czech refugees who transplanted their pro-democratic politics and anti-communist sentiments to Canada used persuasive language such as "struggle," "liberation," "movement," "combat," and "fight" to illustrate their opposition to the Soviets and the Czechoslovak government. This use of rhetoric often exceeded reality since the newcomers had little or no real influence over developments in Czechoslovakia or Canadian foreign policy on Czechoslovakia. This study has demonstrated that, during the Cold War, Czech refugees who became members of the Czechoslovak elite used rhetoric to establish an identity that fit into existing anti-communist social, cultural, and political norms in Canada. Through their participation with federal, provincial, and local officials, and members of other Eastern European ethnic communities, these elites denounced leftist political dissent and regarded their activities as outside the liberal democracy in which they lived. In their self-appointed role as citizen allies, these individuals used anti-communist rhetoric to promote "liberty," "freedom," "human rights," and "democracy" in an effort to petition other Canadians not to fall victim to communist propaganda.[6]

Over four decades of the Cold War, the writings, public demonstrations, and protests exemplified forms of self-justification by many 1948ers, 1968ers, and those who arrived in Canada during the 1970s and 1980s. Within these three successive waves of immigration from Czechoslovakia, Czech refugees sought to dispel rumours and allegations of leftist sympathies or communist involvement in their old homeland or in their new homeland. At the same time, as evidence of StB infiltration of Czechoslovak organizations in Canada reveals, some Czech refugees did attempt to shield their pasts or true allegiances from the Czechoslovak community, Canadian officials, and the broader Canadian society. Perhaps their motive was to gain income or influence in the old homeland, and some so-called professional Czechoslovaks did benefit financially and politically from their roles as prominent members of an Eastern European community in Cold War Canada. Other groups, such as the prewar immigrants and their Canadian-born relatives, opposed attempts to use community institutions to help liberate their old homeland from communism, but they were sympathetic to individuals who had escaped from the communist regime in Czechoslovakia. These oldtimers reminded the 1948ers that the Soviet invasion of Hungary in 1956 illustrated that a pro-democracy movement in the Eastern Bloc could be suppressed easily. As a result, both the oldtimers and the 1948ers increasingly turned toward promoting Canadian citizenship and advancing a Czechoslovak ethnocultural heritage for successive generations.

The subsequent resettlement of close to 12,000 refugees from Czechoslovakia during the special program for Prague Spring refugees reinvigorated community institutions, including the CNAC and MMI. The 1968ers lived through two decades of communist rule, and many of them eagerly joined the 1948ers and their agenda of returning a democratic system of government to Czechoslovakia. At the same time, the 1968ers feared for their families and in some cases sought to "normalize relations" with the Prague government. Joining Canadian Czechoslovak organizations gave them a sense of purpose in which they could attempt to influence developments in their homeland and Canadian foreign policy on Czechoslovakia.

As normalization was implemented in Czechoslovakia after the events of 1968, Czech refugees continued to arrive in the 1970s and 1980s and were well received by Canadian authorities, government agencies, and local Czechoslovak groups. With federal, provincial, and privately administered programs for newcomers, more recent Czech refugees were often able to find temporary accommodations, clothing, funds, and employment from mainstream Canadian organizations. These programs helped the newcomers to obtain a high level of assimilation into Canadian society.[7] But Czechoslovak Canadian organizations also served a function on the path toward assimilation. Following the introduction of official multiculturalism by the Canadian government in 1971, Czechoslovak organizations successfully applied for federal funding to support their community libraries, radio and television programs, supplementary language schools, publications, conferences, and community exhibitions.

As a result, newcomers were less involved in the 1948ers' and 1968ers' anti-communist agenda and preferred to support the creation of Czechoslovak heritage in Canada for successive generations, even as they worked at becoming Canadians themselves. Ultimately, adherence to democratic values, opposition to communism in Czechoslovakia, cultivation of Czechoslovak ethnocultural heritage, and facility with the English and French languages accelerated Czech refugees' socioeconomic and political assimilation into Canadian society during the Cold War.

In Czechoslovakia, Communist Party authorities were successfully thwarted from manipulating refugees in Canada into becoming agents for their old homeland. As Cold War newcomers in Canada, Czech refugees played an important role in raising awareness of human rights abuses, censorship, lack of socioeconomic advancement, and daily life under the totalitarian regime in their old homeland. However, Canadian Czechoslovak institutions had little influence over developments in Eastern Europe or Canadian foreign policy on the Eastern Bloc. Cold War Czech refugees continued to believe in the chimera of Czechoslovakia and Czechoslovak civic nationalism, only to be disappointed ultimately by the state's dissolution in 1992 and the formation of the Czech Republic and Slovak Republic in 1993. However, through their efforts to secure human rights and civic freedoms in the old homeland, and simultaneously to pursue Canadian citizenship, Czech refugees presented themselves as newcomers who adhered to middle-class values and supported Canada's conservative Cold War consensus in an effort to attain social and cultural citizenship. Alongside other Cold War newcomers, Czech refugees presented themselves before public and private gatekeepers as citizen allies who could help to shape a multicultural and democratic society in Cold War Canada.

What can we learn about present-day Canadian society and refugee resettlement from this study? The success that Czech refugees found in becoming "good Canadians" during the Cold War was dependent on two factors: first, their ability to use their agency to seek acceptance in a new country; second, evolving notions of Cold War desirability and admissibility regarding immigration from Eastern Europe. This is particularly instructive for scholars of refugee history and culture in a post-9/11 world in which Muslim refugees in the United States and Western Europe, no matter their desire to acquire social and cultural citizenship, are often denied this path because of (mis)perceptions about their political allegiances and ability to integrate.

Although Czech refugees and present-day Muslim refugees maintain their own agency, their experiences have differed based upon bureaucratic and public notions of admissibility and desirability. During the height of the Cold War, the 1952 Immigration Act expanded the classes of individuals deemed "undesirable" to include communist sympathizers, homosexuals, drug traffickers, and persons declared medically unfit, and it prohibited their entry into Canada. Even though they immigrated from a communist satellite state, Czech refugees were perceived by federal officials to have come from a refugee-producing country, hence helping to establish their Cold War desirability within

Canadian society. Muslim refugees, who have sought integration into Western democracies in the post-9/11 period, have continued to encounter varying levels of bureaucratic and public resistance. Implementation of the 2001 Immigration and Refugee Protection Act in response to the 11 September 2001 terrorist attacks on the United States tightened existing immigration regulations to prevent radicals, terrorists, and serious criminals from entering the country. As a result, it has become harder for skilled workers and labourers to immigrate to Canada under the points system. At the time, requirements for refugee admission were further constrained, and individuals wishing to immigrate to Canada as refugees no longer had the right to appeal their cases if they were unsuccessful during their refugee hearings. Who is considered "desirable" for immigration to Canada remains based upon the economic needs of the country, the physical and mental health of the prospective immigrant, and his or her financial security, personal ideology, risk to national security, and past criminality.

Notwithstanding this reality, in autumn 2015 the Canadian government announced the resettlement of approximately 25,000 Syrian refugees, most of them Muslim, prioritizing married couples, families, and children for resettlement. Their admission into Canada is no longer contingent on Cold War views of desirability and admissibility. However, missing from this group of desirable newcomers are single adult males because of a fear among Canadian officials that such men might hold extremist beliefs and have ties to terrorist organizations.[8] Their omission speaks loudly to evolving bureaucratic notions of refugee desirability, sociocultural acceptance, and inclusion within Canadian immigration policy in the early twenty-first century.

ACKNOWLEDGEMENTS

Over the years, many individuals offered their advice and support for my research interests. This book would never have been completed without the generous support of countless individuals. I wish to thank Professor M. Mark Stolárik of the University of Ottawa for first encouraging me to study immigration history. I am indebted to Professor Marlene Epp of the University of Waterloo for graciously accepting to steer me toward the completion of a dissertation that forms the foundation for this book. Professors James W. St.G. Walker and Gary Bruce served as members of my PhD dissertation committee and provided helpful comments and suggestions on earlier versions of the manuscript.

Many friends were present as I shared in the difficulties and successes of researching and writing. As fine scholars in their own right, Christopher Adam and Hristo Kostov provided me with a cluster of like-minded historians who also explored Eastern European immigration to Canada. I am also thankful to have worked alongside a talented group of scholars at the University of Waterloo. Their love of history was infectious, and I am grateful for their friendship. They have made me a better scholar for having studied with them. I must also thank my fellow staff members at the Canadian Museum of Immigration at Pier 21 for their support.

When it came time to conduct archival and oral history research, many individuals generously provided their time and assistance. In particular, I wish to thank Pasang Thackchhoe of the Multicultural History Society of Ontario; Luba Fraštacký of the Thomas Fisher Rare Book Library, University of Toronto; Ron Ward and Oksana Budjko of the Archives of Ontario; and the reference staff at Library and Archives Canada for answering all of my queries and assisting me in accessing their collections. Financial support in the form of an Ontario Graduate Studies Scholarship from the Government of Ontario, and a President's Graduate Scholarship from the University of Waterloo, are gratefully acknowledged. I must also thank the University of

Manitoba Press, in particular Professor Royden Loewen and Jill McConkey, for showing early interest in my work and guiding me through the process of turning my manuscript into a monograph. Any errors or inconsistencies are my responsibility.

My family was a source of support during the research and writing of this book. They have often led me to consider what it means to be a Canadian of Czech ancestry. Their appreciation of the rigours involved in and their enormous support of my work will never be forgotten. Perhaps no one has lived with this project more than my partner, Katharine. Her steadfast patience, advice, encouragement, empathy, and most of all love helped to bring this project to fruition. This book is dedicated to her.

ABBREVIATIONS

AO	Archives of Ontario
CAC	Czechoslovak Association of Canada
CCBA	Canadian Czechoslovak Benevolent Association
CFC	Council of Free Czechoslovakia
CFCR	Canadian Fund for Czechoslovak Refugees
CMIP	Canadian Museum of Immigration at Pier 21
CNA	Czechoslovak National Alliance
CNAC	Czechoslovak National Association of Canada
CSL	Canadian Slovak League
CUARF	Canadian United Allied Relief Fund
CWCF	Czechoslovak War Charities Fund
DEA	Department of External Affairs
DFAIT	Department of Foreign Affairs and International Trade
DND	Department of National Defence
DP	Displaced Person
DPSC	Department of the Provincial Secretary and Citizenship
DSS	Department of the Secretary of State
FLQ	Front de libération du Québec
IB	Immigration Branch
IRO	International Refugee Organization
KGB	Komitet gosudarstvennoy bezopasnosti (Committee for State Security)
KOS	Kanadská Obec Sokolská (Canadian Sokol Organization)

LAC	Library and Archives Canada
MH	Masaryk Hall
MHSO	Multicultural History Society of Ontario
MMI	Masaryk Memorial Institute
MP	Member of Parliament
PCO	Privy Council Office
RCMP	Royal Canadian Mounted Police
SGAC	Sokol Gymnastic Association of Canada
StB	Státní bezpečnost (State Security)
UN	United Nations
UNHCR	United Nations High Commissioner for Refugees
WAFCPP	Welfare Association of Former Czechoslovak Political Prisoners

NOTES

Preface

1 Canada, Department of Manpower and Immigration, *1973 Immigration Statistics,* 13; *1974 Immigration Statistics,* 22; *1975 Immigration Statistics,* 22; *1976 Immigration Statistics,* 26; *1977 Immigration Statistics,* 26; *1978 Immigration Statistics,* 26; *1979 Immigration Statistics,* 26; *1980 Immigration Statistics,* 68; *1981 Immigration Statistics,* 68; *1982 Immigration Statistics,* 36; *1983 Immigration Statistics,* 36; *1985 Immigration Statistics,* 45; *1986 Immigration Statistics,* 45; *1987 Immigration Statistics,* 47; *1988 Immigration Statistics,* 47; *1989 Immigration Statistics,* 47. "Country of Citizenship" figures for 1984 were not available in the Department of Employment and Immigration's annual *Immigration Statistics.*

2 Statistics Canada, *2016 Census of Population, Statistics Canada Catalogue No. 94-580-XCB2006001,* http://www.statcan.gc.ca/cgi-bin/IPS/display?cat_num=98-400-x2016187.

Introduction

1 See Gerald E. Dirks, *Canada's Refugee Policy: Indifference or Opportunism?* (Montreal: McGill-Queen's University Press, 1977); Reginald Whitaker, *Double Standard: The Secret History of Canadian Immigration* (Toronto: Lester and Orpen Dennys, 1987); Gary Marcuse and Reginald Whitaker, *Cold War Canada: The Making of a National Insecurity State, 1945–1957* (Toronto: University of Toronto Press, 1994); Reginald Whitaker and Steve Hewitt, *Canada and the Cold War* (Toronto: James Lorimer, 2003).

2 Reginald Whitaker, "'We Know They're There': Canada and Its Others, with or without the Cold War," in *Love, Hate, and Fear in Canada's Cold War,* ed. Richard Cavell (Toronto: University of Toronto Press, 2004), 45–46.

3 Milda Danys, *DP: Lithuanian Immigration to Canada after the Second World War* (Toronto: Multicultural History Society of Ontario, 1986), 299; Lubomyr Y. Luciuk, *Searching for Place: Ukrainian Displaced Persons, Ottawa, and the Migration of Memory* (Toronto: University of Toronto Press, 2000), xxiii; Franca Iacovetta, *Gatekeepers: Reshaping Immigrant Lives in Cold War Canada* (Toronto: Between the Lines, 2006), 9–19; Francis Peddie, *Young, Well-Educated, and Adaptable: Chilean Exiles in Ontario and Quebec, 1973–2010* (Winnipeg: University of Manitoba Press, 2015), 2.

4 For context, see Iacovetta, *Gatekeepers,* 103–34.

5 Jérôme Elie, "Histories of Refugee and Forced Migration Studies," in *The Oxford Handbook of Refugee and Forced Migration Studies,* ed. Elena Fiddian-Qasmiyeh, Gil Loescher, Katy Long, and Nando Sigona (Oxford: Oxford University Press, 2014), 26–28.

6 Jan Raska, "Who Is Admissible?," *Canadian Museum of Immigration at Pier 21 Blog,* 11 January 2015, http://www.pier21.ca/blog/jan-raska/who-is-admissible.

7 Harold Troper, "In Search of Haven," in *Safe Haven: The Refugee Experience of Five Families,* ed. Elizabeth McLuhan (Toronto: Multicultural Historical Society of Ontario, 1995), 4–7; Marlene Epp, *Refugees in Canada: A Brief History* (Ottawa: Canadian Historical Association, 2017), 10.

8 Elena Jakešová and M. Mark Stolárik, "Slovaks," in *Encyclopedia of Canada's Peoples,* ed. Paul Robert Magocsi (Toronto: University of Toronto Press, 1999), 1178.

9 Madelaine Hron, "The Czech Émigré Experience of Return after 1989," *Slavonic and East European Review* 85, 1 (2007): 54; Dinah A. Spritzer, "Children of '68: Émigrés' Kids Sound Off about Sexism, Their Countrymen's Self-Esteem, and the Liabilities of a Czech Passport," *Prague Post,* 19 May 2005, http://www.praguepost.cz/archivescontent/41029-children-of-68.html. Until the early 1970s, approximately 225,000 individuals fled Czechoslovakia and permanently resettled in the West.

10 Peter Whelan, "203 from Czechoslovakia Combine Joy and Sorrow," *Globe and Mail,* 16 September 1968, 1–2.

11 See Laura Madokoro, "Good Material: Canada and the Prague Spring Refugees," *Refuge: Canada's Periodical on Refugees* 26, 1 (2009): 162.

12 Jaroslav Krejčí and Pavel Machonin, *Czechoslovakia, 1918–92: A Laboratory for Social Change* (New York: St. Martin's Press, 1996), 8–18; Carol Skalník Leff, *National Conflict in Czechoslovakia: The Making and Remaking of a State, 1918–1987* (Princeton, NJ: Princeton University Press, 1988), 48–64.

13 Stanislav J. Kirschbaum, "Whither Slovak Historiography after 1993?," *Canadian Slavonic Papers* 53, 1 (2011): 45–46; Dušan Kováč, "Czechs and Slovaks in Modern History," in *Bohemia in History,* ed. Mikuláš Teich (Cambridge, UK: Cambridge University Press, 1998), 371–76; Elizabeth Bakke, "Czechoslovakism in Slovak History," in *Slovakia in History,* ed. Mikuláš Teich, Dušan Kováč, and Martin D. Brown (Cambridge, UK: Cambridge University Press, 2011), 252–62.

14 For further context, see Jan Raska, "Recreating a Homeland: Czechoslovak Diplomats in Canada during the Second World War," *Canadian Slavonic Papers* 58, 1 (2016): 68–92.

15 Jakešová and Stolárik, "Slovaks," 1172–75.

16 Marek J. Jovanovic, "Czechs," in *Encyclopedia of Canada's Peoples,* ed. Paul Robert Magocsi (Toronto: University of Toronto Press, 1999), 401–05.

17 United Nations High Commissioner for Refugees (hereafter UNHCR), "Convention and Protocol Relating to the Status of Refugees," http://www.unhcr.org/3b66c2aa10.html. The quotation can be found on page 14 of the document.

18 Jacek Z. Adolf, "Adaptation of East European Refugees and Political Émigrés in Toronto, with Special Reference to Immigrants from Poland and Czechoslovakia" (PhD diss., York University, 1977), vii.

19 Ibid.

20 Odd A. Westad, "The Cold War and the International History of the Twentieth Century," in *Cambridge History of the Cold War, Volume I: Origins,* ed. Melvyn P. Leffler and Odd A. Westad (Cambridge, UK: Cambridge University Press, 2010), 3. See also George Orwell, "You and the Atomic Bomb," *Tribune,* 19 October 1945, https://ia800409.us.archive.org/35/items/YouAndTheAtomicBomb-English-GeorgeOrwell/orwellomb.pdf.

21 Mary Louise Adams, *The Trouble with Normal: Postwar Youth and the Making of Heterosexuality* (Toronto: University of Toronto Press, 1997), 22–23.

22 Marcuse and Whitaker, *Cold War Canada*, 5.

23 Adams, *The Trouble with Normal*, 27.

24 Ibid., 18, 27–38.

25 Franca Iacovetta, "Making Model Citizens: Gender, Corrupted Democracy, and Immigrant and Refugee Reception Work in Cold War Canada," in *Whose National Security? Canadian State Security and the Creation of Enemies*, ed. Gary Kinsman, Dieter K. Buse, and Mercedes Steedman (Toronto: Between the Lines, 2000), 158; Iacovetta, *Gatekeepers*, 18–19, 105, 134; Whitaker and Hewitt, *Canada and the Cold War*, 241.

26 Jovanovic, "Czechs," 400; Whitaker, *Double Standard*, 78; Iacovetta, *Gatekeepers*, 105–07; Dirks, *Canada's Refugee Policy*, 234; Ninette Kelley and Michael Trebilcock, *The Making of the Mosaic: A History of Canadian Immigration Policy* (Toronto: University of Toronto Press, 1998), 382.

Chapter 1: Interwar Farm Labourers, Wartime Enemy Aliens, and Allied Citizens

1 Interview with Frank Všetula, © Multicultural History Society of Ontario (hereafter MHSO), Czech Collection, 27 August 1980, CZE-7940-VSE. Martin Bursík was interviewed as part of Všetula's oral history.

2 Jovanovic, "Czechs," 399; Jakešová and Stolárik, "Slovaks," 1170.

3 Canadian Czech-Slovak Benevolent Association, "History of CCBA," http://www.czechslovakbenevolentassoc.ca/html/history-of-ccba.html. For further context, see Edna M. Bosley and Canadian Czechoslovak Benevolent Association (hereafter CCBA), *Pamatník Kanadsko-Československé jednoty, Winnipeg, Manitoba, 1913-1963* (Winnipeg: National Publishers, 1963).

4 Elena Jakešová, "Slovak Emigrants in Canada as Reflected in Diplomatic Documents (1920-1938)," *Slovakia* 35, 64-65 (1991-92): 25. For further context, see Royden Loewen and Gerald Friesen, *Immigrants in Prairie Cities: Ethnic Diversity in Twentieth Century Canada* (Toronto: University of Toronto Press, 2009), 38.

5 Jovanovic, "Czechs," 399–400; Jakešová and Stolárik, "Slovaks," 1170–71.

6 John M. Gibbon, *Canadian Mosaic: The Making of a Northern Nation* (Toronto: McClelland and Stewart, 1938), 314.

7 Interview with Martin Yankovic, © MHSO, Ukrainian Collection, 11 November 1977, UKR-6278-YAN; Interview with Joe Choroš, © MHSO, Czech Collection, 12 July 1977, CZE-1514-CHO.

8 Gregory S. Kealey and Reginald Whitaker, eds., *RCMP Security Bulletins: The War Series (Vol. 2), 1942–1945* (St. John's: Committee on Canadian Labour History, 1989), 380–83.

9 Jakešová, "Slovak Emigrants in Canada, 9; Jakešová and Stolárik, "Slovaks," 1170.

10 Canada, Department of Trade and Commerce, Dominion Bureau of Statistics, *The Canada Year Book, 1938* (Ottawa: King's Printer, 1938), 197–98; *The Canada Year Book, 1942* (Ottawa: King's Printer, 1942), 156; *The Canada Year Book, 1943–44* (Ottawa: King's Printer, 1944), 180; *The Canada Year Book, 1945* (Ottawa: King's Printer, 1945), 171; *The Canada Year Book, 1946* (Ottawa: King's Printer, 1946), 185. Immigrants who self-identified their racial origins as Bohemian and Moravian were included in this study as Czechs. During this period, 973 immigrants claimed their racial origin as Bohemian, whereas 175 immigrants claimed their racial origin as Moravian. The

bureau also identified 23,718 immigrants as having a Slovak racial origin. From 1931 to 1945, 9,577 immigrants gave their nationality as Czechoslovakian.

11 Josef Čermák, *Fragmenty ze života Čechů a Slovaků v Kanadě* (Zlín: Atelier IM, 2000), 22. The organization later established a branch in Toronto in 1927.

12 Canada, Department of the Secretary of State, *The Canadian Family Tree: Canada's Peoples* (Don Mills, ON: Corpus Information Services, 1979), 55.

13 The Czech Lands consist of three historical provinces: Bohemia, Moravia, and Silesia. Together with Slovakia and Subcarpathian Ruthenia, these provinces formed Czechoslovakia.

14 Interview with Všetula.

15 Library and Archives Canada (hereafter LAC), Privy Council Office (hereafter PCO) Fonds, RG2, vol. 1479, file "Orders in Council — Décrets du Conseil," Order-in-Council P.C. 1931-695, 21 March 1931. Dominion Bureau of Statistics, *The Canada Year Book, 1934–35* (Ottawa: King's Printer, 1935), 138. Figures for the years immediately prior to 1931 combine ethnic Czechs and Slovaks into a single group. In 1931, Canadian-born Czechs and Slovaks totalled 8,437 individuals. Approximately 84.7 percent (7,148) of them had parents who were foreign born.

16 LAC, PCO Fonds, RG2, vol. 1479, file "Orders in Council — Décrets du Conseil," Order-in-Council P.C. 1931-695, 21 March 1931.

17 Ibid.

18 Interview with Marie Gabriel, © MHSO, Czech Collection, 19 July 1978, CZE-5166-GAB.

19 Jakešová, "Slovak Emigrants in Canada," 33–35; John Gellner and John Smerek, *The Czechs and Slovaks in Canada* (Toronto: University of Toronto Press, 1968), 80. In 1936, the pro-"Czechoslovak" communists split into two groups: the Slovak communists who supported autonomy for Slovakia, and the Czechs who supported a national Czechoslovak identity.

20 Ibid.

21 Jakešová, "Slovak Emigrants in Canada," 22, 33.

22 Elena Jakešová, *Vystahovalectvo Slovakov do Kanady* (Bratislava: Vydavateľstvo Slovenskej Akademie vied, 1981), 117.

23 Thomas Fisher Rare Book Library, University of Toronto, Ms. Coll. 6, John Reeves Papers, Box 8, Item 3 (Buzek, Karel—official consul of Czech government in exile in 1940s Canada. Interview. Tape.); Archives of Ontario (hereafter AO), MHSO Fonds, Czech Canadian Records, Joseph Čermák Textual Records, F 1405-67-2, barcode B444769, file "Joseph Čermák Papers—Nase Hlasy," publication, *Naše hlasy: Independent Czechoslovak Weekly*, centennial issue, 1967, 27.

24 "Československo pripravené k obrane," *Nová vlasť*, 29 September 1938, 1; Igor Lukeš, *Czechoslovakia between Stalin and Hitler: The Diplomacy of Edvard Beneš in the 1930s* (New York: Oxford University Press, 1996), 237.

25 Edvard Beneš and Milan Hauner, *Fall and Rise of a Nation: Czechoslovakia, 1938–1941* (Boulder, CO: East European Monographs, 2004), 12; Lukeš, *Czechoslovakia between Stalin and Hitler*, 34.

26 Canada, Department of External Affairs (hereafter DEA), *Documents Relating to the German-Czechoslovak Crisis September, 1938* (Ottawa: J.O. Patenaude, 1938), 10–11; Ronald M. Smelser, *The Sudeten Problem, 1933–1938: Volkstumspolitik and the Formulation of Nazi Foreign Policy* (Middletown, CT: Wesleyan University Press, 1975), 3–13.

27 Marek J. Jovanovic, "Creating a New Bohemia: The Czechs in Canada, 1880–1990" (MA thesis, University of Ottawa, 1999), 3; Gus Garber, "Joining Up, 1938," in *The Land Newly Found: Eyewitness Accounts of the Canadian Immigrant Experience*, ed. Norman Hillmer and Jack L. Granatstein (Toronto: Thomas Allen Publishers, 2006), 208.

28 Valerie Knowles, *Strangers at Our Gates: Canadian Immigration and Immigration Policy, 1540–2006* (Toronto: Dundurn Press, 2007), 147–48. Approximately 80,000 anti-Nazi Sudeten Germans fled Germany's annexation of the Sudetenland.

29 Dirks, *Canada's Refugee Policy*, 75–76.

30 Jan Raska, "Mistrusted Strangers at Home: Czechs, Slovaks, and the 'Enemy Aliens' Registration Issue, 1938-1942," *International Journal of Canadian Studies* 38 (2009): 98.

31 Dirks, *Canada's Refugee Policy*, 83–85; Hanns F. Skoutajan, *Uprooted and Transplanted: A Sudeten Odyssey from Tragedy to Freedom, 1938–1958* (Owen Sound, ON: Ginger Press, 2000), 121–23.

32 Interview with Hanns Skoutajan, © MHSO, Czech Collection, 24 November 1978, CZE-0017-SKO; Oral history with Hanns Skoutajan, 22 October 2003, Canadian Museum of Immigration at Pier 21 (hereafter CMIP) Collection [03.10.22HS]; Jonathan F. Wagner, "British Columbia's Anti-Nazi Germans: The Tupper Creek Refugees," *BC Studies* 39 (1978): 6–7; Jonathan F. Wagner, *A History of Migration from Germany to Canada, 1850–1939* (Vancouver: UBC Press, 2006), 172; Helen Raptis, "Teaching Czech German Refugees at Tate Creek, British Columbia, during World War II," *Historical Studies in Education* 24, 2 (2012): 31, 34.

33 Immigration story of Hanns Skoutajan (Czechoslovak immigrant), CMIP Collection [S2012.242.1].

34 "Mayor Says Reds Exploited Parade: Bans Czech Demonstration on Street—Two Arrested," *Montreal Daily Star*, 3 October 1938, 1, 11; "Two Arrested as Nazi-Haters Assemble Here: 2,000 Rally on Fletcher's Field after Mayor Bans Parade," *Montreal Gazette*, 3 October 1938, 1, 4.

35 Věra Olivová, *The Doomed Democracy: Czechoslovakia in a Disrupted Europe, 1914–1938* (London: Sidgwick and Jackson, 1972), 263–64.

36 Stanislav J. Kirschbaum, *A History of Slovakia: The Struggle for Survival* (New York: St. Martin's Press, 1995), 180–81; Yeshayahu Jelínek, *The Parish Republic: Hlinka's Slovak People's Party, 1939–1945* (Boulder, CO: East European Quarterly, 1976), 17–31; Mary Heimann, *Czechoslovakia: The State that Failed* (New Haven, CT: Yale University Press, 2009), 87–89.

37 Hugh L. Agnew, *Czechs and the Lands of the Bohemian Crown* (Stanford: Hoover Institution Press, 2004), 206–08; Edvard Beneš, *Paměti: Od Mnichova k nové válce a k novému vítězství* (Praha: Orbis, 1947), 82.

38 Joseph M. Kirschbaum, *The Truth and Legends about the Origin of the Slovak Republic* (Cleveland: First Catholic Slovak Union, 1974), 6; Agnew, *Czechs and the Lands of the Bohemian Crown*, 208.

39 George F. Kennan, *From Prague after Munich: Diplomatic Papers, 1938–1940* (Princeton, NJ: Princeton University Press, 1968), 82–83; Joseph M. Kirschbaum, *The Slovaks in Canada* (Toronto: Canadian Ethnic Press Association of Ontario, 1967), 154–55.

40 Chad Bryant, *Prague in Black: Nazi Rule and Czech Nationalism* (Cambridge, MA: Harvard University Press, 2007), 28–29.

41 Kirschbaum, *Truth and Legends about the Origin of the Slovak Republic*, 1–8.

42 Beneš and Hauner, *Fall and Rise of a Nation*, 27.

43 Raska, "Mistrusted Strangers at Home," 98; Donald H. Avery, *Reluctant Host: Canada's Response to Immigrant Workers* (Toronto: McClelland and Stewart, 1995), 137.

44 Gerhard P. Bassler, *Sanctuary Denied: Refugees from the Third Reich and Newfoundland Immigration Policy, 1906–1949* (St. John's: Institute of Social and Economic Research, 1992), 28.

45 Interview with Tomáš J. Baťa, © MHSO, Czech Collection, 8 April 1978, CZE-543-BAT; Antonín Čekota, *The Battle of Home: Some Problems of Industrial Community* (Toronto: Macmillan, 1944), 49–50, 129.

46 Interview with Baťa; Thomas J. Baťa and Sonja Sinclair, *Bata: Shoemaker to the World* (Toronto: Stoddart Publishing, 1990), 50–51, 58, 63; Knowles, *Strangers at Our Gates*, 148.

47 Ibid.

48 Interview with Milada Čechová, © MHSO, Czech Collection, 20 June 1978, CZE-5288-CEC.

49 Irving Abella and Harold Troper, *None Is Too Many: Canada and the Jews of Europe, 1933–1948* (Toronto: Lester and Orpen Dennys, 1982), x, 4–5, 73–74, 93–94. Blair was director of the Immigration Branch from 1936 to 1944.

50 Hanna Spencer, *Hanna's Diary, 1938–1941: Czechoslovakia to Canada* (Montreal: McGill-Queen's University Press, 2001), 79, 109–11, 113.

51 McKenzie Porter, "Leon Koerner's One-Man Giveaway Program," *Maclean's*, 4 August 1956, 9, 34–37. After February 1948, Koerner used his business success to send thousands of food parcels to acquaintances behind the Iron Curtain in Czechoslovakia.

52 Dominion Bureau of Statistics, *The Canada Year Book, 1943–44*, 180. In comparison, 291 Slovaks entered Canada as immigrants in 1939. Between 1940 and 1943, eighty-two Slovaks arrived in Canada as immigrants.

53 "Czechs Will Be Free Again," *Montreal Daily Star*, 17 April 1939, 5; Čermák, *Fragmenty ze života Čechů a Slovaků v Kanadě*, 31.

54 Gellner and Smerek, *Czechs and Slovaks in Canada*, 105; Josef Čermák, *It All Started with Prince Rupert: The Story of Czechs and Slovaks in Canada* (Prague: Atelier IM, 2003), 163.

55 "Sjednotenie našej odbojovej práce v Kanade," *Nová vlasť*, 11 April 1940, 2.

56 Interview with Antonín Ronza, © MHSO, Czech Collection, 18 July 1978, CZE-8360-RON.

57 Reginald Whitaker and Gregory S. Kealey, "A War on Ethnicity? The RCMP and Internment," in *Enemies Within: Italian and Other Internees in Canada and Abroad*, ed. Franca Iacovetta, Roberto Perin, and Angelo Principe (Toronto: University of Toronto Press, 2000), 129.

58 "Kanadská vláda oznamuje registrovanie Čechoslovákov," *Nová vlasť*, 2 November 1939, 1; "Registrácia Čechoslovákov ako priateľský národ," *Nová vlasť*, 9 November 1939, 1.

59 "Registrácia," *Nová vlasť*, 12 December 1940, 4.

60 "Ďalšie veľké víťazstvo Československej veci v Kanade," *Nová vlasť*, 3 April 1941, 1.

61 Kirschbaum, *Slovaks in Canada,* 410–11. See document no. 4: "Registration of Slovaks as Enemy Aliens," and document No. 5: "Reply of the Department of Justice on the Registration of Slovaks."

62 Gellner and Smerek, *Czechs and Slovaks in Canada,* 106.

63 Josef Korbel, *The Communist Subversion of Czechoslovakia, 1938–1948: The Failure of Coexistence* (Princeton, NJ: Princeton University Press, 1959), 85.

64 LAC, Masaryk Memorial Institute (hereafter MMI) Fonds, MG28-V110, vol. 5, file "Masaryk School—Reports, 1942–1949; Students' Lists, 1942–1951; Misc., n.d.–1949," memo from Prokop V. Havlík, "Zpráva o československé škole za školní rok 1943–1944—sestavená k valně hromadě Sdružení ČSL," 16 January 1944.

65 Interview with Karol (Karel) Stark, © MHSO, Czech Collection, 28 August 1980, CZE-8359-STA.

66 Rudolf Nekola, *A Gem for the Canadian Mosaic* (Toronto: MMI, 1957), xiv; MMI, "About Us," http://masaryktown.ca/?page_id=225.

67 LAC, MMI Fonds, MG28-V110, vol. 5, file "Masaryk School—Reports, 1942–1949; Students' Lists, 1942–1951; Misc., n.d.–1949," letter from Prokop V. Havlík to unknown, 1–3.

68 LAC, MMI Fonds, MG28-V110, vol. 5, file "Youth Club—Minutes, 1946, 1948, 1949; Membership Lists, n.d.," minutes of Masarykův club mládeže, 17 March 1946.

69 LAC, MMI Fonds, MG28-V110, vol. 5, file "Youth Club—Minutes, 1946, 1948, 1949; Membership Lists, n.d.," minutes of Masarykův club mládeže, 24 March 1946.

70 LAC, MMI Fonds, MG28-V110, vol. 5, file "Youth Club—Minutes, 1946, 1948, 1949; Membership Lists, n.d.," minutes of Masarykův club mládeže, 4 May 1946.

71 LAC, MMI Fonds, MG28-V110, vol. 5, file "Youth Club—Minutes, 1946, 1948, 1949; Membership Lists, n.d.," minutes of Masarykův club mládeže, 7 April 1946.

72 LAC, MMI Fonds, MG28-V110, vol. 2, file "Annual Reports, 1948, 1949, 1953, 1954," Výroční zpráva—Masarykova domu—rok 1948, 3; "Masarykov dom," *Nová vlasť,* 20 February 1947, 4.

73 LAC, Czechoslovak National Association of Canada (hereafter CNAC) Fonds, MG28-V111, vol. 1, file 4, "Minutes—Executive Committee, 1945," Zápis, č. 3/45, 15 February 1945, 1–2. Ottawa allowed the CWCF to use $3,345—or less than two-thirds of 1 percent—to support its administrative costs.

74 Eugen Steiner, *The Slovak Dilemma* (Cambridge, UK: Cambridge University Press, 1973), 77–83; Yeshayahu Jelínek, *Lust for Power: Nationalism, Slovakia, and the Communists, 1918–1948* (Boulder, CO: East European Monographs, 1983), 79–85; Peter A. Toma and Dušan Kováč, *Slovakia: From Samo to Dzurinda* (Stanford: Hoover Institution Press, 2001), 158–59; Agnew, *Czechs and the Lands of the Bohemian Crown,* 223–24; John F.N. Bradley, *Czechoslovakia: A Short History* (Edinburgh: Edinburgh University Press, 1971), 168–69.

75 LAC, CNAC Fonds, MG28-V111, vol. 1, file 9, "Minutes—Executive Committee—Drafts, 1944–1945," Zápisnica, 12 April 1945, 1. Originally founded in 1936 as *Hlas ľudu* (Voice of the People), the pro-communist Slovak-language paper was later renamed *Ľudové zvesti* (People's News) in 1941. The paper was funded by the communist regime in Czechoslovakia after February 1948.

76 Kealey and Whitaker, *RCMP Security Bulletins,* 319.

77 LAC, CNAC Fonds, MG28-V111, vol. 1, file 4, "Minutes—Executive Committee, 1945," Zápis, č. 5/45, 5 April 1945, 2.

78 LAC, CNAC Fonds, MG28-V111, vol. 1, file 4, "Minutes—Executive Committee, 1945," Zápis, č. 6/45, 21 May 1945, 1.

79 LAC, CNAC Fonds, MG28-V111, vol. 1, file 4, "Minutes—Executive Committee, 1945," Zápis, č. 9/45, 15 February 1945, 3.

80 LAC, CNAC Fonds, MG28-V111, vol. 18, file 6, "C.N.A. Czechoslovak War Charities Fund, 1945," letter from A.H. to Rudolf Kočí, č.j. 2105/45, 4 May 1945.

81 LAC, CNAC Fonds, MG28-V111, vol. 21, file 66, "Czechoslovak Military Mission in Montreal, 1945," letter from Karel Buzek to Lieutenant-Colonel Ján Ambruš, Czechoslovak Military Attaché, č.j. 85a/45, 28 February 1945.

82 LAC, CNAC Fonds, MG28-V111, vol. 18, file 6, "C.N.A. Czechoslovak War Charities Fund, 1945," letter from A.H. to Rudolf Kočí, č.j. 1733/45, 12 April 1945.

83 LAC, CNAC Fonds, MG28-V111, vol. 1, file 4, "Minutes—Executive Committee, 1945," Zápis, č. 8/45, 23 August 1945, 1.

84 LAC, CNAC Fonds, MG28-V111, vol. 1, file 4, "Minutes—Executive Committee, 1945," Zápis, č. 9/45, 20 September 1945, 1; LAC, CNAC Fonds, MG28-V111, vol. 2, file 8, "VI Congress, 1945," letter from Karel Buzek to Professor J.J. Zmrhal, 12 November 1945, and letter from Karel Buzek to Professor H. Gordon Skilling, 13 November 1945.

85 Paul McKay, *The Roman Empire: The Unauthorized Life and Times of Stephen Roman* (Toronto: Key Porter Books, 1990), 13; Kirschbaum, *Slovaks in Canada,* 412–13.

86 Kealey and Whitaker, *RCMP Security Bulletins,* 380–83.

87 Ibid.

88 Jovanovic, "Czechs," 402. Finding Aid MSS1179 located at LAC. See http://www.collectionscanada.gc.ca/digital-initiatives/012018-10007-e.html, which indicates that the CNA reached a pinnacle with ninety-two branches.

89 Čermák, *It All Started with Prince Rupert,* 163.

90 Kealey and Whitaker, *RCMP Security Bulletins,* 71.

91 LAC, Immigration Branch (hereafter IB) Fonds, RG76, vol. 617, file 916207, part 10, "Immigration from Czechoslovakia, 1947–1953," memo "Political Adherents to Tiso Regime in Slovakia—Admission to Canada," 27 June 1946, microfilm reel C-10436.

92 LAC, IB Fonds, RG76, vol. 617, file 916207, part 10, "Immigration from Czechoslovakia, 1947–1953," memo from Western District Superintendent, "Look Out No. 10: Immigration Inspectors—Western District," 2 November 1945, microfilm reel C-10436.

93 LAC, IB Fonds, RG76, vol. 617, file 916207, part 10, "Immigration from Czechoslovakia, 1947–1953," memo from Commissioner of Immigration to District Superintendents, 29 October 1945, microfilm reel C-10436.

94 LAC, IB Fonds, RG76, vol. 617, file 916207, part 10, "Immigration from Czechoslovakia, 1947–1953," memo from Pacific District Superintendent to Commissioner of Immigration, 7 November 1945, microfilm reel C-10436.

95 Ibid.

96 LAC, IB Fonds, RG76, vol. 617, file 916207, part 10, "Immigration from Czechoslovakia, 1947–1953," letter from Norman Alexander Robertson to Honourable James Allison Glen, 8 December 1945, microfilm reel C-10436.

97 LAC, CNAC Fonds, MG28-V111, vol. 2, file 6, "VI Congress, 1945," Resoluce VI. Sjezdu—Vítězného Kongresu Československého národního sdružení v Kanadě, 24.-25. XI. 1945.

98 LAC, CNAC Fonds, MG28-V111, vol. 2, file 6, "VI Congress, 1945," Zpráva ústřední tajemníka, br. K. Buzka, na vítězném kongrese Čs. N.S. 24.-25. Listopadu 1945.

99 LAC, CNAC Fonds, MG28-V111, vol. 2, file 6, "VI Congress, 1945," Celkový finančný výkaz administračného fondu od založenia ČSNS v Kanade od juna 1939 do 31 oktobra 1945. The CNA's various war funds included the Cigarette Fund ($20,671.18), Parcel Fund ($1,081.77), Dispatches to USSR Fund ($9,230.09), and raised $30,983.04 for the war effort. Similarly, the CWCF garnered $209,212.42, the United Fund for Czechoslovak Soldiers brought in $19,735.50, the Canadian Aid to Russia Fund gathered $11,859.29, and membership in the Czechoslovak Red Cross garnered $1,806.50. The CNA Radio Fund for broadcasting to the homeland accumulated $1,897.71 and donations to the CNA Administrative Fund totalled $55,427.54. Donations to the latter fund were used to purchase stamps and telegrams and to support publications such as the pro-"Czechoslovak" *Nová vlasť* newspaper in Canada.

100 LAC, CNAC Fonds, MG28-V111, vol. 2, file 6, "VI Congress, 1945," Celkový finančný prehlad odbočiek od založenia ČSNS do 31 oktobra 1945, 1–2.

101 LAC, CNAC Fonds, MG28-V111, vol. 2, file 6, "VI Congress, 1945," Zpráva ústřední tajemníka, br. K. Buzka, na vítězném kongrese Čs. N.S. 24.-25. Listopadu 1945, 2. The Canadian United Allied Relief Fund's members included the Belgian War Relief Fund, Chinese War Relief Fund, Czechoslovak War Charities Fund, Danish Relief Fund, Canada-France Relations Committee, Greek War Relief Fund, Canadian Friends of Luxembourg Fund, Netherlands Relief Fund, Norwegian Relief Fund, United Polish Relief Fund, Yugoslav Relief Fund, and Canadian Aid to Russia Fund.

102 LAC, CNAC Fonds, MG28-V111, vol. 16, file 8, "Head Office—General Correspondence—English Letters, 1946," letter from Karel Buzek to Colonel P.L. Browne, 2 April 1946.

103 LAC, CNAC Fonds, MG28-V111, vol. 18, file 6, "C.N.A. Czechoslovak War Charities Fund, 1945," letter from Colonel P.L. Browne to Karel Buzek, 22 December 1945.

104 LAC, CNAC Fonds, MG28-V111, vol. 2, file 8, "VI Congress, 1945," Zápisnica z Vítazného Kongresu = VI. Výročného sjazdu Československého národného sdruženia v Kanade, 24–25 novembra 1945, 3.

105 LAC, CNAC Fonds, MG28-V111, vol. 11, file 229, "Head Office Correspondence—Chatham, Ont., Branch No. 7, n.d., 1945," letter from John Botek to Karel Buzek, 3 December 1945, and letter from Karel Buzek to John Botek, 29 December 1945.

106 LAC, CNAC Fonds, MG28-V111, vol. 21, file 70, "Czechoslovak Government Ministries, 1946," letter from Czechoslovak Minister of Labour and Social Welfare to Karel Buzek, I 2679/126, 3 December 1945.

107 LAC, CNAC Fonds, MG28-V111, vol. 21, file 66, "Czechoslovak Military Mission in Montreal, 1945," letter from Colonel Karel Lukáš, Czechoslovak Legation Military and Air Attaché in Ottawa, to CNA, Toronto, Čj. 447/45, 4 December 1945, 1. Although 782 men initially applied, 106 were deemed unfit to join.

108 LAC, CNAC Fonds, MG28-V111, vol. 21, file 67, "Czechoslovak Military Mission in Montreal, 1946," letter from J.H. Hogan, Director, Re-Establishment Credit Division, Department of Veterans Affairs, Ottawa, to Allied Force Section.

109 Dominion Bureau of Statistics, *The Canada Year Book, 1938*, 199; *The Canada Year Book, 1939* (Ottawa: King's Printer, 1939), 162; *The Canada Year Book, 1940* (Ottawa:

King's Printer, 1940), 154; *The Canada Year Book, 1942,* 156, 158; *The Canada Year Book, 1943–44,* 180; *The Canada Year Book, 1945,* 171–72; *The Canada Year Book, 1946,* 185; *The Canada Year Book, 1948–49* (Ottawa: King's Printer, 1949), 180. Immigrants who self-identified their racial origins as Bohemian and Moravian were included in this study as Czechs. In all, 401 individuals claimed their racial origin as Bohemian, 54 as Moravian, and 420 as Slovak.

Chapter 2: Postwar Relief, Canadian Citizenship, and Ethnic Heritage

1 LAC, Jan Dočkálek Fonds, MG30-C148, vol. 1, file "Bobřík, 1946, 1947," *Bobřík: Časopis Masarykovy Mládeže v Kanadě* 1 (1946): 1.

2 Ibid.

3 LAC, CNAC Fonds, MG28-V111, vol. 1, file 5, "Minutes—Executive Committee, 1946," Zápisnica, Číslo 1/1946, 10 January 1946, 3.

4 LAC, CNAC Fonds, MG28-V111, vol. 18, file 15, "Parcels to Czechoslovakia, 1946," letter from F.E. Jolliffe, Acting Director of Administrative Services, Post Office Department, to Karel Buzek, 4 January 1946.

5 LAC, CNAC Fonds, MG28-V111, vol. 1, file 5, "Minutes—Executive Committee, 1946," Zápisnica, Číslo 1/1946, 10 January 1946, 1–2.

6 LAC, CNAC Fonds, MG28-V111, vol. 1, file 5, "Minutes—Executive Committee, 1946," Zápisnica, Číslo 2/1946, 28 January 1946, 2 and Zápisnica, Číslo 4/1946, 14 March 1946, 1–2.

7 LAC, CNAC Fonds, MG28-V111, vol. 16, file 8, "Head Office—General Correspondence—English Letters, 1946," Karel Buzek, "Need Still Great," *Toronto Daily Star,* 20 April 1946, 6.

8 LAC, CNAC Fonds, MG28-V111, vol. 1, file 5, "Minutes—Executive Committee, 1946," Zápisnica, Číslo 7/1946, 18 June 1946, 1.

9 LAC, CNAC Fonds, MG28-V111, vol. 16, file 8, "Head Office—General Correspondence—English Letters, 1946," letter from the Office of the Minister, Department of National War Services, to Karel Buzek, 16 April 1946.

10 LAC, CNAC Fonds, MG28-V111, vol. 16, file 8, "Head Office—General Correspondence—English Letters, 1946," letter from Honourable James Joseph McCann, Minister of National War Services, to Karel Buzek, 16 April 1946.

11 LAC, CNAC Fonds, MG28-V111, vol. 1, file 6, "Minutes—Executive Committee, 1947," Zápisnica, Číslo 1/47, 7 January 1947, 1.

12 "Darkové zasielanie do ČSR," *Nová vlasť,* 2 January 1947, 3. An individual package could contain one of the following items: one pound of tobacco (for $2.25), 600 cigarettes (for $4.00), 300 cigarettes (for $2.25), or 120 cigars.

13 "Intervencia delegácie ČSNS vo veci dárkových balíčkov," *Nová vlasť,* 9 January 1947, 3.

14 "K akcii Čs.N.S.," *Ľudové zvesti,* 4 October 1947, 4.

15 "Ústredný výkonný výbor Československého národného sdruzenia, 'Voľa ľudu Rozhoduje,'" *Nová vlasť,* 16 October 1947, 3.

16 Josef Kotrlý, "Csl. Gen. konsulat o sbirce Kanadské dary na Kanadské potreby," *Nová vlasť,* 13 November 1947, 2, 4.

17 LAC, CNAC Fonds, MG28-V111, vol. 30, file 11, "Miscellaneous—General, n.d., 1941–1945," letter from Matuš Pavlík to CNA head office, Toronto, December 1947.

18 LAC, CNAC Fonds, MG28-V111, vol. 16, file 8, "Head Office—General Correspondence—English Letters, 1946," letter from J.D. McFarlane, District Superintendent, to Karel Buzek, 1 February 1946.

19 Ibid.

20 LAC, CNAC Fonds, MG28-V111, vol. 16, file 8, "Head Office—General Correspondence—English Letters, 1946," letter from A.D. Adamson, A/ Immigration Inspector-in-Charge, to Karel Buzek, 27 February 1946.

21 Ibid.

22 LAC, CNAC Fonds, MG28-V111, vol. 23, file 93, "Immigration and Travel—Cunard Line, 1945–1946," DEA, Memorandum to Persons Travelling to Continental Europe, n.d., 1–2.

23 Ibid.

24 LAC, CNAC Fonds, MG28-V111, vol. 23, file 93, "Immigration and Travel—Cunard Line, 1945–1946," Jozef Šimkovič, Application for Eastbound Atlantic Passage, 21 March 1946, and John Somr, Application for Eastbound Atlantic Passage, 30 March 1946, and Antonín Heindl, Application for Eastbound Atlantic Passage, 1 June 1946, and Steve Kulkoský, Application for Eastbound Atlantic Passage, 19 October, 194?.

25 Joseph Rothschild and Nancy M. Wingfield, *Return to Diversity: A Political History of East Central Europe since World War II*, 3rd ed. (New York: Oxford University Press, 2000), 91; Karel Kaplan, *The Short March: The Communist Takeover of Czechoslovakia, 1945–1948* (New York: St. Martin's Press, 1987), 58; Josef Korbel, *Twentieth-Century Czechoslovakia: The Meaning of Its History* (New York: Columbia University Press, 1977), 234–37; Martin Myant, *Socialism and Democracy in Czechoslovakia, 1945–1948* (New York: Cambridge University Press, 1981), 126–29.

26 Mark Kramer, "Stalin, Soviet Policy, and the Consolidation of a Communist Bloc in Eastern Europe, 1944–53," in *Stalinism Revisited: The Establishment of Communist Regimes in East-Central Europe*, ed. Vladimir Tismaneanu (Budapest: CEU Press, 2010), 69.

27 Norman Hillmer and Donald Page, eds., *Documents on Canadian External Relations, Volume 13: 1947* (Ottawa: Communication Group Publishing, 1993), 924. See file DEA/6993-B-40, memo Extension of Czechoslovak Loan, 15 November 1947; Toma and Kováč, *Slovakia*, 170–71; Kaplan, *The Short March*, 61; and Tad Szulc, *Czechoslovakia since World War II* (New York: Viking Press, 1971), 32.

28 LAC, DEA Fonds, RG25, vol. 5874, file 50165-40, part 1.1, "Czechoslovakia—Political Situation—General File," R.M. Macdonnell, Chargé d'Affaires, Canadian Legation, Prague, to Secretary of State for External Affairs, 9 January 1948, 1. See also LAC, W.L. Mackenzie King Papers, Memoranda and Notes, 1940–50, MG26-J4, vol. 248, despatch 3 from Canadian Legation, Prague, 8 January 1948, microfilm reel H-1478, C-166701-166704.

29 Ibid. R.M. Macdonnell was appointed chargé d'affaires to the Canadian Legation in Prague in March 1947.

30 Canada, Department of Foreign Affairs and International Trade (hereafter DFAIT), *Documents on Canadian External Relations*, vol. 14, chap. 12, Europe, the Soviet Union, and the Middle East, part 1, Czechoslovakia, 1047, file DEA/7121-40, R.M. Macdonnell, Chargé d'Affaires, Canadian Legation, Prague, to Secretary of State for External Affairs, 23 February 1948, despatch 37, http://www.international.gc.ca/department/history-histoire/dcer/details-en.asp?intRefid=10735.

31 Ibid.

32 LAC, DEA Fonds, RG25, vol. 5874, file 50165-40, part 1.1 and part 1.2, "Czechoslovakia—Political Situation—General File," R.M. Macdonnell, Chargé d'Affaires, Canadian Legation, Prague, to Secretary of State for External Affairs, 24 February 1948, 1.

33 Ibid.

34 Korbel, *Communist Subversion of Czechoslovakia, 1938–1948,* 214–15; Jon Bloomfield, *Passive Revolution: Politics and the Czechoslovak Working Class, 1945–1948* (New York: St. Martin's Press, 1979), 207–08; Zbyněk Zeman and Antonín Klimek, *The Life of Edvard Beneš, 1884–1948: Czechoslovakia in Peace and War* (Oxford: Clarendon Press, 1996), 268–70; Bradley, *Czechoslovakia,* 176–78; Myant, *Socialism and Democracy in Czechoslovakia, 1945–1948,* 207; John Crane and Sylvia Crane, *Czechoslovakia: Anvil of the Cold War* (New York: Praeger, 1991), 315.

35 F. Gregory Campbell, "Empty Pedestals?," *Slavic Review* 44, 1 (1985): 1; Hubert Ripka, *Czechoslovakia Enslaved: The Story of the Communist Coup d'État* (London: Victor Gollancz, 1950), 290–95; Edward Táborský, *President Edvard Beneš: Between East and West, 1938–1948* (Stanford: Hoover Institution Press, 1981), 228–29; Edward Táborský, *Communism in Czechoslovakia: 1948–1960* (Princeton, NJ: Princeton University Press, 1961), 22.

36 DFAIT, *Documents on Canadian External Relations,* vol. 14, chap. 12, Europe, the Soviet Union, and the Middle East, part 1, Czechoslovakia, 1048, file DEA/7121-40, despatch 41 from Chargé d'Affaires in Czechoslovakia to Secretary of State for External Affairs, 26 February 1948, http://www.international.gc.ca/department/history-histoire/dcer/details -en.asp?intRefid=10736.

37 Associated Press, "Czech Reds Seize Power, Control Police," *Globe and Mail,* 25 February 1948, 1.

38 Associated Press, "Czech Communists Rule; Subdue Student Protest," *Globe and Mail,* 26 February 1948, 2.

39 "1948 Secret Revealed: Czech Papers in Coldwell Bedroom," *Globe and Mail,* 30 March 1955, 1.

40 Canadian Press, "'Not In' or 'Not Available,' Czech Minister Won't Talk," *Globe and Mail,* 27 February 1948, 3; "Dr. Nemec Still Out," *Ottawa Evening Citizen,* 27 February 1948, 1.

41 "Strangling Czech Liberty," *Ottawa Evening Citizen,* 25 February 1948, 30. The *Ottawa Citizen* was known as the *Ottawa Evening Citizen* at the time of this editorial.

42 Ibid.

43 Joseph Kotrlý, "Former Czech Consul Tells of Red 'Web,'" *Halifax Chronicle Herald,* 26 March 1948, 8; LAC, DEA Fonds, RG25, vol. 8560, file 12467-D-40, part 1.1, "RCMP Reports re Re-Admission of Canadians from Czechoslovakia—Individual Cases," letter from N.O. Jones, Inspector, RCMP, to Registrar, Canadian Citizenship Registration Branch, Department of Citizenship and Immigration, 19 September 1957.

44 Joseph Kotrlý, "Communists Move in Canada in a Secret Manner," *Halifax Chronicle Herald,* 29 March 1948, 5. Exacerbating the frustrations felt by Prague's diplomats in Canada and the CNA was Canada's delay in establishing a permanent legation in Prague. Ottawa's diplomatic presence in Czechoslovakia had been terminated in September 1944 when Chargé d'Affaires Pierre Dupuy concluded his mission.

The Canadian government delayed opening an office in Czechoslovakia because it required additional personnel in its diplomatic corps. A Canadian presence in the country resumed on 24 March 1947 when R.M. Macdonnell was appointed chargé d'affaires in Prague. See John Hilliker and Donald Barry, *Canada's Department of External Affairs, Volume II: Coming of Age, 1946–1968* (Montreal: McGill-Queen's University Press, 1995), 12. See DFAIT, *Heads of Post List*, http://www.international.gc.ca/department/ history-histoire/heads_of_posts_search-en.asp.

45 LAC, CNAC Fonds, MG28-V111, vol. 29, file 10, "Senate Standing Committee on Immigration and Labour, C.N.A. Memorandum, Committee Reports, etc., n.d. 1944, 1946"; Canada, Parliament, Senate, *Speech of the Hon. Arthur W. Roebuck, Senator, on Immigration in the Senate of Canada, Ottawa, on Thursday, April 4, 1946* (Ottawa: Edmond Cloutier, Printer to the King's Most Excellent Majesty, 1946), 1.

46 Ibid.

47 Alvin Finkel, "Canadian Immigration Policy and the Cold War, 1945–1980," *Journal of Canadian Studies* 21, 3 (1986): 54–55.

48 Ibid.

49 Whitaker, *Double Standard*, 18–19. The Security Panel, consisting of senior civil servants, military intelligence officers, and RCMP officials, maintained a permanent secretariat in the Privy Council Office.

50 Adams, *The Trouble with Normal*, 22–24; Howard Margolian, *Unauthorized Entry: The Truth about Nazi War Criminals in Canada, 1946–1956* (Toronto: University of Toronto Press, 2000), 35–36.

51 Ibid. The panel's agenda was soon broadened to include immigrant vetting, since Canada had closed its immigration offices in Europe in the 1930s. With British authorities indicating that they would no longer examine prospective immigrants for entry into Canada, the Security Panel proposed that the RCMP become responsible for the security screening of immigrants seeking to enter the country from overseas.

52 Mark Wyman, *DP: Europe's Displaced Persons, 1945–1951* (Philadelphia: Balch Institute Press, 1990), 190.

53 Milda Danys, *DP*, 213–14.

54 LAC, CNAC Fonds, MG28-V111, vol. 16, file 8, "Head Office—General Correspondence—English Letters, 1946," letter from Senator Arthur W. Roebuck to Karel Buzek, 12 June 1946.

55 LAC, CNAC Fonds, MG28-V111, vol. 16, file 8, "Head Office—General Correspondence—English Letters, 1946," letter from Karel Buzek to Senator Arthur W. Roebuck, 17 June 1946.

56 Canada, Parliament, Senate, *Proceedings of the Standing Committee on Labour and Immigration: Session of Wednesday, July 24, 1946* (Ottawa: Minister of Supply and Services, 1946), 216–20.

57 "Oznameni o repatriaci a pasech," *Nová vlasť*, 16 January 1947, 1.

58 Jaroslav Vaculík, "Reemigrace zahraničních Čechů a Slováků v letech 1945–1948," *Slezský sborník* 93, 1–2 (1995): 54.

59 LAC, CNAC Fonds, MG28-V111, vol. 1, file 5, "Minutes—Executive Committee, 1946," Zápisnica, Číslo 10/1946, 22 November 1946, 1.

60 "Uvaha k starému a novému roku," *Nová vlasť*, 2 January 1947, 1.

61 "Novi Kanadskí občania," *Nová vlasť*, 2 January 1947, 2.

62 "Vitame noveho csl. vyslanca v Kanade," *Nová vlasť,* 13 February 1947, 1–2. After the resignation of Czechoslovak Ambassador to Canada František Pavlásek in 1946, Prague's legation in Ottawa was led by Chargé d'Affaires Karel Sakh. Newly appointed Czechoslovak Ambassador to Canada František Němec had previously fought for the Republican cause during the Spanish Civil War. In 1940, Němec was named minister of social welfare in the Czechoslovak government-in-exile in London.

63 Josef Kotrlý, "Jen manželky a děti připustene do Kanady," *Nová vlasť,* 20 February 1947, 1.

64 Canada, Parliament, House of Commons, *House of Commons Debates: Official Report, Third Session – Twentieth Parliament, Volume 3* (Ottawa: King's Printer and Controller of Stationery, 1947), 2644-2646; Reginald Whitaker, *Canadian Immigration Policy since Confederation* (Ottawa: Canadian Historical Association, 1991), 14.

65 LAC, CNAC Fonds, MG28-V111, vol. 1, file 6, "Minutes—Executive Committee, 1947," Zápisnica, Číslo 4/47, 27 May 1947, 3.

66 LAC, CNAC Fonds, MG28-V111, vol. 29, file 2, "Questionnaires, 1947," Dotazník (Winnipeg), n.d., 1947.

67 LAC, CNAC Fonds, MG28-V111, vol. 29, file 2, "Questionnaires, 1947," Dotazník (Kingston), n.d., 1947.

68 LAC, CNAC Fonds, MG28-V111, vol. 29, file 2, "Questionnaires, 1947," Dotazník (Oshawa), n.d., 1947.

69 LAC, CNAC Fonds, MG28-V111, vol. 31, file 11, "Montreal Branch—Slovak School—Student Lists, Agendas of Meetings, etc., n.d., 1947," Návrh stanov organizácie, n.d., 1. Montreal was also home to approximately 3,000 Canadians of Slovak origin.

70 LAC, CNAC Fonds, MG28-V111, vol. 29, file 2, "Questionnaires, 1947," Dotazník (Montreal), n.d., 1947.

71 Martin Dudák, "Na Prahu Nového roku," *Nová vlasť,* 25 December 1947, 1.

72 Miroslav Vitula, "Z historie českých a slovenských krajanu v Kanadě do roku 1939," *Časopis Matice Moravské* 118, 1 (1999): 108.

73 "*Nova Vlast'* po 14 rokoch končí svoje poslanie medzi našim ľudom v Kanade: Posledne číslo, ktore sa dostava do ruk čitateľov," *Nová vlasť,* 5 February 1948, 1, 4.

74 LAC, MMI Fonds, MG28-V110, vol. 2, file "Annual Reports, 1948, 1949, 1953, 1954," Výroční zpráva, Masarykova domu, rok 1948, 2, 4; LAC, MMI Fonds, MG28-V110, vol. 7, file "Miscellaneous—Bingo," "Masaryk Memorial Institute Incorporated and the Bingo Games," 3 April 1965, 1.

75 Ibid.

76 LAC, MMI Fonds, MG28-V110, vol. 1, file "Rules and Regulations, n.d.," "Rules and Regulations Applicable to All Members and Non Members while on Property of Masaryktown."

77 LAC, MMI Fonds, MG28-V110, vol. 2, file "Annual Reports, 1948, 1949, 1953, 1954," Výroční zpráva, Masarykova domu, rok 1948, 4.

78 LAC, MMI Fonds, MG28-V110, vol. 7, file "Czechoslovak Day, 1948," poster of Československý den, 11 July 1948; Interview with Stark.

79 LAC, MMI Fonds, MG28-V110, vol. 2, file "Correspondence 1948," letter from Výbor Masarykového Domu to F. Smajkal, 10 June 1948.

80 LAC, MMI Fonds, MG28-V110, vol. 2, file "Correspondence 1948," letter from unknown to *Enterprise,* 20 June 1948.

81 Ibid.

82 Aloysius Balawyder, "Canadian-Slavic Cultural Nationalism and the Canadian Government's Reaction," *Canadian Review of Studies in Nationalism* 16, 1–2 (1989): 200.

83 LAC, MMI Fonds, MG28-V110, vol. 5, file "Masaryk School—Reports, 1942–1949; Students' Lists, 1942–1951; Misc., n.d.–1949," Oběžník, 12 October 1949, 1; Nekola, *A Gem for the Canadian Mosaic,* xiv.

84 Dominion Bureau of Statistics, *The Canada Year Book, 1947* (Ottawa: King's Printer, 1947), 133; *Canada Year Book, 1948–49,* 179. In all, fifty-eight individuals claimed their racial origin as Bohemian, and another twelve immigrants claimed their racial origin as Moravian. These immigrants used historical ethnic identifiers for the Czech Lands (Bohemia and Moravia). They were included in this study as Czechs. Similarly, 111 individuals indicated that they were Slovaks.

Chapter 3: Aftermath of the Communist Takeover

1 Interview with Marie Flosman, © MHSO, Czech Collection, 29 May 1978, CZE-5533-FLO; AO, MHSO, Czech Canadian Records, Marie Flosman Textual Records, F 1405-67-21, barcode B444769, file "Marie Flosman Papers—Flosman, Frantisek—Personal Id. Papers, 1950–1951," Marie Flosman, Certificate of Identity for the Purposes of Immigration to Canada, International Refugee Organization, Serial No. 2G-11408.

2 Justine Faure, "Les exilés tchécoslovaques de 1948: Un exile politique au service de la politique étrangère américaine," *Materiaux pour l'histoire de notre temps* 60, 1 (2000): 61; Hron, "Czech Émigré Experience of Return after 1989," 54; Bořivoj Čelovský, *Emigranti: Dopisy politických uprchlíků z prvních let po "Vítězném únoru" 1948* (Ostrava: Tilia, 1998), 142; Jan Filípek, *Reflections and Perspectives: Czechoslovaks after Forty Years in Exile* (Palm Springs, CA: Palm Springs Publishing, 1988), 1–2; Mario Hikl, *A Short History of the Czechoslovak People in Canada* (Toronto: Across-Canada Press, 1955), 19.

3 In the early 1950s, Masaryk Hall changed its name to Masaryk Memorial Hall. In 1960, it was incorporated and became Masaryk Memorial Institute.

4 LAC, Department of the Secretary of State (hereafter DSS) Fonds, RG6, accession 1986–87/319, box 87, file 9-334-1, memo from Jean Boucher, Director, Citizenship Branch, Department of Citizenship and Immigration, to Deputy Minister, Department of Citizenship and Immigration, 23 March 1961.

5 Interview with Stark; Aloysius Balawyder, "Canadian-Slavic Cultural Nationalism and the Canadian Government's Reaction," *Canadian Review of Studies in Nationalism* 16, 1–2 (1989): 202–03; Gellner and Smerek, *Czechs and Slovaks in Canada,* 109; Bosley and CCBA, *Pamatník Kanadsko-Československé podporující jednoty,* 27.

6 Interview with Stark.

7 For an example, see Franca Iacovetta, "Freedom Lovers, Sex Deviates, and Damaged Women: Iron Curtain Refugee Discourses in Cold War Canada," in *Love, Hate, and Fear in Canada's Cold War,* ed. Richard Cavell (Toronto: University of Toronto Press, 2004), 84–86.

8 "Couple sudète sorti de l'enfer tchècoslovaque: M. et Mme. Kuttig ont quitté Prague mercredi dernier—Les élections: Un affreux truquage," *Le Devoir,* 1 March 1948, 10; untitled, *Globe and Mail,* 2 March 1948, 13.

9 Warren Baldwin, "Czech Ottawa Minister Quits to Protest Action of Reds in Homeland," *Globe and Mail,* 4 March 1948, 17.

10 Canadian Press, "À Prague," *Le Devoir,* 3 March 1948, 1; "Two Czechoslovakian Envoys Quit: Protest Coup in Homeland," *Winnipeg Free Press,* 3 March 1948, 1.

11 "Czech Minister Asks to Stay Here," *Montreal Daily Star,* 4 March 1948, 4; "More Czechs Quit," *Winnipeg Free Press,* 4 March 1948, 1; "Czech Consul Will Quit if Benes Out," *Winnipeg Free Press,* 4 March 1948, 1.

12 DFAIT, *Documents on Canadian External Relations,* vol. 14, chap. 9, Immigration, part 3, Refugees from Eastern Europe, 800, file DEA/233-A (S), memo from Assistant Undersecretary of State for External Affairs to Secretary of State for External Affairs, 22 March 1948, http://www.international.gc.ca/department/history-histoire/dcer/details-en.asp?int Refid=10540; Avery, *Reluctant Host,* 158–59. On 16 March 1948, Order-in-Council P.C. 1108 formally permitted former Czechoslovak minister in Canada František Němec, commercial attaché Karel Bala, and First Secretary Karel Moudrý, including their families and some members of the embassy's clerical and domestic staff, to remain in Canada. See DFAIT, *Documents on Canadian External Relations,* vol. 14, chap. 9, Immigration, part 3, Refugees from Eastern Europe, 801, file PCO/volume 66, memo from Secretary of State for External Affairs to Cabinet, 7 May 1948, http://www.international.gc.ca/department/history-histoire/dcer/details-en.asp?intRefid=10541.

13 "Démission du consul général de Tchécoslovaquie," *Le Devoir,* 6 March 1948, 3–4.

14 Baldwin, "Czech Ottawa Minister Quits to Protest Action of Reds in Homeland," 17. St. Laurent noted before the House of Commons that approximately $1.4 million in trade credits could be removed in light of the Communist Party takeover.

15 "Canada Still to Send Envoy to Prague; Dominion Won't Sever Relations or Cut Off Loan to Czechs," *Vancouver Sun,* 4 March 1948, 3; Canadian Press, "Attitude canadienne," *Le Devoir,* 27 February 1948, 1.

16 Josef Škvorecký, "Bohemia of the Soul," *Daedalus* 119, 1 (1990): 111–12; Filípek, *Reflections and Perspectives,* 60–61.

17 Ibid.

18 Oral history with Milan Gregor, 3 August 2002, CMIP Collection [02.08.03MG].

19 LAC, W.L. Mackenzie King Papers, Memoranda and Notes, 1940–50, MG26-J4, vol. 248, memo, Possible Movement of Czech Democratic Refugees to Canada, n.d., microfilm reel H-1478, C166715; LAC, IB Fonds, RG76, vol. 662, file B83052, part 1, "Czechoslovak Displaced Persons (Lists)," telegram from Canadian Delegation, Preparatory Commission of the International Refugee Organization, Geneva, to Secretary of State for External Affairs, Ottawa, 14 May 1948, 1–3, microfilm reel C-10597.

20 Ibid.

21 Čelovský, *Emigranti,* 142. In 1953, hundreds of Czech political refugees returned to Communist Czechoslovakia as the five-year agreement on refugee status concluded. For more on Czech refugees and IRO eligibility, see Gerard D. Cohen, *In War's Wake: Europe's Displaced Persons in the Postwar Order* (Oxford: Oxford University Press, 2012), 51–57.

22 LAC, IB Fonds, RG76, vol. 662, file B83052, part 1, "Czechoslovak Displaced Persons (Lists)," letter from R.J. McPherson for Robert J. Corkery, Chief, Department of Repatriation and Resettlement, Preparatory Commission of the International Refugee Organization, Geneva, to Canadian Immigration Mission, Karlsruhe, 7 June 1948, and memo for file, O. Cormier, Consul General, Canadian Immigration Mission, Karlsruhe, 8 June 1948, microfilm reel C-10597.

23 LAC, IB Fonds, RG76, vol. 662, file B83052, part 1, "Czechoslovak Displaced Persons (Lists)," memo from Commissioner of Immigration, Overseas Service, to Department of Mines and Resources, Ottawa, 18 June 1948, microfilm reel C-10597.

24 LAC, IB Fonds, RG76, vol. 662, file B83052, part 1, "Czechoslovak Displaced Persons (Lists)," letter from Louis St. Laurent, Secretary of State for External Affairs, to Humphrey Mitchell, Minister of Labour, 29 June 1948, 2, microfilm reel C-10598. Ten days later the Canadian Immigration Mission in Karlsruhe sent a telegram to the Immigration Branch in Ottawa informing officials that refugees from Czechoslovakia were being processed at the Regensburg and Schwabach reception centres and then screened by the United States Army Counter Intelligence Corps before being sent to one of the permanent refugee camps in the American Zone of Occupation.

25 Ibid.

26 Ibid.

27 LAC, IB Fonds, RG76, vol. 662, file B83052, part 1, "Czechoslovak Displaced Persons (Lists)," telegram from Canadian Immigration Mission, Karlsruhe, to IB, Ottawa, 22 June 1948, microfilm reel C-10597; LAC, W.L. Mackenzie King Papers, Memoranda and Notes, 1940–50, MG26-J4, vol. 248, memo, "Possible Movement of Czech Democratic Refugees to Canada," n.d., microfilm reel H-1478, C166715.

28 Faure, "Les exilés tchécoslovaques de 1948," 61; Hikl, *Short History of the Czechoslovak People in Canada,* 13.

29 Bořivoj Čelovský, *Politici bez moci: První léta exilové rady svobodného Československa* (Šenov u Ostravy: Tilia, 2000), 14.

30 Faure, "Les exilés tchécoslovaques de 1948," 61.

31 Dushan Břesky, "Czech Poet in Canada: Pavel Javor's Life and Work," *Canadian Ethnic Studies* 10, 1 (1978): 78.

32 Dominion Bureau of Statistics, *The Canada Year Book, 1948–1949,* 174.

33 Igor Lukeš, "Czechoslovak Political Exile in the Cold War: The Early Years," *Polish Review* 47, 3 (2002): 333.

34 Dominion Bureau of Statistics, *The Canada Year Book, 1951* (Ottawa: King's Printer, 1951), 143, 145–47.

35 Škvorecký, "Bohemia of the Soul," 121.

36 Interview with Ana Lanc, © MHSO, Czech Collection, 1 August 1978, CZE-5164-LAN.

37 Interview with Stark; Interview with Louis Urban, © MHSO, Czech Collection, 10 August 1978, CZE-5171-URB.

38 Interview with František Braun, © MHSO, Czech Collection, 5 September 1978, CZE-5163-BRA.

39 Ibid.

40 LAC, IB Fonds, RG76, vol. 617, file 916207, part 11, "Immigration from Czechoslovakia, 1947–1953," R.M. Macdonnell, Despatch No. 99, 5 May 1948, microfilm reel C-10436.

41 Ibid.

42 LAC, IB Fonds, RG76, vol. 617, file 916207, part 11, "Immigration from Czechoslovakia, 1947–1953," R.M. Macdonnell, Despatch No. 186, 5 August 1948, microfilm reel C-10436.

43 DFAIT, *Documents on Canadian External Relations,* vol. 14, chap. 9, Immigration, part 3, Refugees from Eastern Europe, 800, file DEA/233-A (S), memo from Assistant Undersecretary of State for External Affairs to Secretary of State for External Affairs, 22 March 1948, http://www.international.gc.ca/department/history-histoire/dcer/details-en.asp?int Refid=10540.

44 LAC, DEA Fonds, RG25, vol. 4042, file 10515-40, part 1, "Canadian Fund for Czechoslovak Refugees—Establishment and Activities of," letter from W.P.J. O'Meara, Assistant Undersecretary of State, to Undersecretary of State for External Affairs, 22 April 1949.

45 Ibid.

46 Pamphlet, CMIP Collection [DI2013.793.20a]; Interview with Josef Čermák, © MHSO, Czech Collection, 29 March 1977, CZE-0014-CER; Čermák, *It All Started with Prince Rupert,* 190.

47 Pamphlet, CMIP Collection [DI2013.793.22b].

48 LAC, DEA Fonds, RG25, vol. 4042, file 10515-40, part 1, "Canadian Fund for Czechoslovak Refugees—Establishment and Activities of," memo from G.G. Crean, Defence Liaison Division, to United Nations Division, 3 May 1949.

49 LAC, CNAC Fonds, MG28-V111, vol. 13, file 302, "Head Office Correspondence—St. Ann's, Ont., Branch No. 68, n.d., 1949," letter from Mike Nikodem and Jan Krejčík to IB, Department of Mines and Resources, Ottawa, 31 March 1949.

50 LAC, CNAC Fonds, MG28-V111, vol. 13, file 302, "Head Office Correspondence—St. Ann's, Ont., Branch No. 68, n.d., 1949," letter from Karel Buzek to Jan Krejčík, 26 March 1949.

51 LAC, CNAC Fonds, MG28-V111, vol. 13, file 302, "Head Office Correspondence—St. Ann's, Ont., Branch No. 68, n.d., 1949," letter from A.H. Creighton, District Superintendent of Colonization, to Karel Buzek, 25 March 1949.

52 Dominion Bureau of Statistics, *The Canada Year Book, 1950* (Ottawa: King's Printer, 1950), 183.

53 LAC, CNAC Fonds, MG28-V111, vol. 13, file 282, "Head Office Correspondence—Kitchener, Ont., Branch No. 25, n.d., 1949," letter from M.F. Kousal to Karel Buzek, 20 January 1949, and letter from Karel (Karol) Stark to Karel Buzek, 14 March 1949.

54 Jan Dočkálek, "Na Cestu," *Čas,* 1 June 1949, 2.

55 Ken J. Couch, "A Letter from the Mayor of Trenton," *Čas,* 1 June 1949, 8.

56 LAC, DEA Fonds, RG25, vol. 4018, file 10254-40, part 1, "Council of Free Czechoslovakia—Activities and Reports," letter from Karel Stark, President, and P.V. Havlík, Secretary, CNAC, to unknown, n.d.

57 Prokop V. Havlík, "Z Čs. N.S. v Kanadě Do Montrealu Que.!," *Čas,* 27 July 1949, 1.

58 "To Our Readers," *Čas,* 8 August 1949, 8.

59 Beth Paterson, "24 D.P.s, Bound for Universities, Voice Joy at Arriving in Canada," *Montreal Gazette,* 9 September 1949, 3.

60 DFAIT, *Documents on Canadian External Relations,* vol. 15, chap. 1, Conduct of External Relations, part 4, Diplomatic and Consular Representation, section E, Czechoslovakia, Hungary, Poland, and Yugoslavia, 14, file DEA/10926-40, memo from European Division to Acting Undersecretary of State for External Affairs, "Arguments for and against Maintaining Canadian Diplomatic Missions in Satellite Countries," 18 November 1949, http://www.international.gc. ca/department/history-histoire/dcer/details-en.asp?intRefid=8626.

61 LAC, DEA Fonds, RG25, accession 1977–78/84, vol. 2493, file 10463-W-40, "Annual Review of Events in Czechoslovakia by the Canadian Minister at Prague," Circular Document No. C27/51, Annual Review of Events in Czechoslovakia—1950, from Secretary of State for External Affairs to Minister of External Affairs, 30 March 1951, 6; Warren Baldwin, "Ottawa Reprisal Seen as Czechs Oust Pair," *Globe and Mail,* 23 January 1950, 1; Canadian Press, "Ottawa Delays Retaliation Move against Czechs," *Globe and Mail,* 24 January 1950, 3; Frank Flaherty, "Two Czech Employees Have to Leave Canada as Expulsion Reprisal," *Globe and Mail,* 3 February 1950, 3; Canadian Press, "Ousted Czech Sorry to Leave," *Globe and Mail,* 7 February 1950, 2.

62 DFAIT, *Documents on Canadian External Relations,* vol. 16, chap. 1, Conduct of External Relations, part 1, Diplomatic and Consular Representation, section C, Czechoslovakia, 5, file L.S.L./volume 8, memo from Undersecretary of State for External Affairs to Prime Minister, 24 January 1950, http://www.international.gc.ca/department/history-histoire/dcer/details-en.asp?intRefid=7026; Baldwin, "Ottawa Reprisal Seen as Czechs Oust Pair," 1; Canadian Press, "Ottawa Delays Retaliation Move against Czechs," 3; Flaherty, "Two Czech Employees Have to Leave Canada as Expulsion Reprisal," 3; Canadian Press, "Ousted Czech Sorry to Leave," 2.

63 DFAIT, *Documents on Canadian External Relations,* vol. 16, chap. 1, Conduct of External Relations, part 1, Diplomatic and Consular Representation, section D, Iron Curtain Missions: Assessment, 7, file DEA/10926-40, memo from Acting Undersecretary of State for External Affairs to Secretary of State for External Affairs, 2 March 1950, http://www.international.gc.ca/department/history-histoire/dcer/details-en.asp?intRefid=7028. See Enclosure 1—Notes on Functions of Canadian Posts in Poland and Czechoslovakia, 28 February 1950; also see Enclosure 2—Memorandum: Usefulness of Iron Curtain Missions, 28 February 1950.

64 Ibid.

65 Ibid.

66 Interview with Josef Kubánek, © MHSO, Czech Collection, 14 July 1978, CZE-5291-KUB.

67 Táborský, *Communism in Czechoslovakia,* 474.

68 LAC, IB Fonds, RG76, vol. 617, file 916207, part 11, "Immigration from Czechoslovakia, 1947–1953," memo from J.A. Irwin to Secretary of State for External Affairs, 4 May 1950, microfilm reel C-10436.

69 LAC, IB Fonds, RG76, vol. 617, file 916207, part 11, "Immigration from Czechoslovakia, 1947–1953," memo from Benjamin Rogers to Secretary of State for External Affairs, 4 June 1952, microfilm reel C-10436.

70 Immigration Story of the Valentin Family (Czechoslovak immigrants), CMIP Collection [S2012.651.1].

71 LAC, IB Fonds, RG76, vol. 617, file 916207, part 11, "Immigration from Czechoslovakia, 1947–1953," memo from J.A. Irwin to Secretary of State for External Affairs, 4 May 1950, microfilm reel C-10436.

72 LAC, IB Fonds, RG76, vol. 617, file 916207, part 11, "Immigration from Czechoslovakia, 1947–1953," memo on Czechoslovak Immigration, 22 December 1950, microfilm reel C-10436.

73 Ibid. Dastich had been promoted to the rank of brigadier general on 1 May 1945 and later worked as a Czechoslovak military diplomat in Budapest and Berlin. On 31 December 1948, he resigned to protest the Communist Party takeover of his homeland, later settling in the United States, where he was active in the Council of Free Czechoslovakia.

74 Finkel, "Canadian Immigration Policy and the Cold War," 54, 58.

75 Canada, Department of National Defence (hereafter DND), Directorate of History and Heritage, Kardex, 112.3M2 (D329), "Fort Churchill, Jul. 48 / Oct. 51," Appendix A: Extracts from Current Intelligence Appreciation of Forms and Scales of Attack Covering Period 1949/50.

76 LAC, DND Fonds, RG24, file 762-215, "Canadian Joint Intelligence Bureau Information on—Czechoslovakia," memo from Joint Intelligence Bureau—Ottawa JIB (Can) 19/48—Czechoslovakia: Realignment within the Soviet Sphere of Influence, 1 May 1948, microfilm reel C-11642, 1.

77 Ibid.

78 LAC, DND Fonds, RG24, file 762-215, "Canadian Joint Intelligence Bureau Information on—Czechoslovakia," Annex I—World War II Developments, 17 May 1948, microfilm reel C-11642, 3.

79 LAC, DND Fonds, RG24, file 9490-34-82, "War Office Reports on Czechoslovakia," memo of conversation with Arnošt Heidrich (former secretary general of the Czechoslovak Foreign Office), n.d., microfilm reel C-11653, 2.

80 UNHCR, "Convention and Protocol Relating to the Status of Refugees," http://www.unhcr.org/3b66c2aa10.html. The quotation can be found on page 14 of the document. The convention came into force on 22 April 1954.

81 Ibid.

82 LAC, MMI Fonds, MG28-V110, vol. 3, file "Correspondence, 1951," letter from Gustav Přístupa to Mr. Dowson [sic], Department of Labour, 23 May 1951.

83 LAC, MMI Fonds, MG28-V110, vol. 3, file "Correspondence, 1951," letter from W.W. Dawson, Department of Labour, to Gustav Přístupa, 28 May 1951.

84 LAC, MMI Fonds, MG28-V110, vol. 7, file "Miscellaneous—Parkdale Baptist Church, Toronto—Anniversary Booklet, Invitations, n.d., 1960, 1967," 25. Výročí československěho baptistickěho sboru v Torontě, n.d.

85 Associated Press, "Czech Engineer Races Train to Freedom from Iron Curtain: Brake Lines Cut in Dash to Germany," *Globe and Mail,* 12 September 1951, 1. See also "Engineered Freedom Train," *Globe and Mail,* 17 September 1951, 9; *New York Times* Service, "32 Who Race Train to Freedom Coming to Canada," *Globe and Mail,* 25 September 1951, 1.

86 Associated Press, "Czech Engineer Races Train to Freedom from Iron Curtain: Brake Lines Cut in Dash to Germany."

87 "Czech Who Fled Reds with Train Offered Job Here," *Globe and Mail,* 15 September 1951, 1.

88 *New York Times* Service, "32 Who Race Train to Freedom Coming to Canada."

89 Kingsley Brown, "Knew Lives in Danger, So Stole Train, Fled," *Globe and Mail,* 25 October 1951, 13.

90 Karel Ruml, *Z deníku Vlaku Svobody* (Brno: Barrister and Principal, 2001), 123, 126–27.

91 Immigration Record issued to Bohumír Říbek by the International Refugee Organization, 19 April 1949, CMIP Collection [DI2013.839.28].

92 Letter typed for Bohumír Říbek appealing the International Refugee Organization's decision declaring him ineligible for assistance, 18 May 1949, CMIP Collection [DI2013.839.25]; Immigration Record issued to Bohumír Říbek by the International Refugee Organization, 3 October 1949, CMIP Collection [DI2013.839.27]; Memorandum of Undertaking issued to Bohumír Říbek by the Canadian Department of Labour, 20 October 1950, CMIP Collection [DI2013. 839.10]; Identification Card issued to Bohumír Říbek, 30 October 1950, CMIP Collection [DI2013.839.23].

93 LAC, MMI Fonds, MG28-V110, vol. 3, file "Correspondence, 1951," letter from Zdeněk Štřelec to Gustav Přístupa, 31 October 1951.

94 LAC, MMI Fonds, MG28-V110, vol. 3, file "Correspondence, 1951," letter from A.D. Adamson, Immigration Inspector-in-Charge, to Gustav Přístupa, 24 April 1951; Antonín Sevelka Jr., email message to the author, 22 March 2016.

95 LAC, MMI Fonds, MG28-V110, vol. 3, file "Correspondence, 1951," letter from Zdeněk Němeček to Gustav Přístupa, 15 December 1951.

96 LAC, MMI Fonds, MG28-V110, vol. 3, file "Correspondence, 1951," letter from Masaryk Memorial Hall to OPAL Manufacturing Company, 1 June 1952.

97 LAC, CNAC Fonds, MG28-V111, vol. 1, file 8, "Minutes—Executive Committee, 1948–1953," Zápisnica zo širšieho výkonného výboru ČSNS v Kanade, 14 October 1951.

98 LAC, IB Fonds, RG76, vol. 617, file 916207, part 11, "Immigration from Czechoslovakia, 1947–1953," memo from Benjamin Rogers to Secretary of State for External Affairs, 4 June 1952, microfilm reel C-10436.

99 Ibid.

100 Harold Troper, "Canadian Immigration Policy since 1945," *International Journal* 48, 2 (1993): 262.

101 LAC, CNAC Fonds, MG28-V111, vol. 33, file 5, "Toronto Branch No. 24—Miscellaneous, n.d., 1944–1945, 1955," letter from Karel Stark, Antonín Daičar, Gustav Přístupa, and Prokop V. Havlík to the Publisher, *Toronto Telegram,* 1 April 1952. The Communist Party of Canada was banned in 1940. In 1943, the Labour-Progressive Party was founded as its successor. The letter also pointed to the 1950 visit of approximately 500 CNA members to Parliament Hill, where they were met by Prime Minister Louis St. Laurent.

102 "Democratic Slovaks Honor Former Leaders," *Toronto Daily Star,* 4 May 1953, 14.

103 "Czechs Say Wreath Tribute to Traitor," *Toronto Daily Star,* 16 May 1953, 2.

104 LAC, Canadian Slovak League (hereafter CSL) Fonds, MG28-V47, vol. 2, file "Correspondence," Resolution to His Worship, Allan A. Lamport, Mayor of the City of Toronto, and to the Controllers of the City of Toronto, n.d., 1–3. After declaring Slovak independence in March 1939, Tiso served as Slovakia's head of state for twenty months before Slovakia officially joined the Axis coalition in November 1940.

105 Ibid.

106 Interview with Vít Wágner, © MHSO, Czech Collection, 26 August 1980, CZE-7955-WAG.

Chapter 4: Community Tensions and Ideological Divisions

1 Marika Robert, "How an Immigrant Girl Fell in Love with Canada," *Maclean's*, 23 April 1960, 24–27, 40, 45–46.

2 Ibid. For another example, see Lucie Pelikánová, "Oskar Sýkora ml., DDS, PhD—Zubní lékař a doktor filosofie v jednom dni," in *Neviditelné oběti komunismu*, ed. Jakub Hodbod', Jan Goll, and Václav Ulvr (Liberec: Gymnázium F.X. Šaldy v Liberci, 2006), 61–62; also see Bořivoj Čelovský, *Šel jsem svou cestou* (Opava: Vademecum, 1996), 89–95.

3 Iacovetta, *Gatekeepers*, 5; Kelley and Trebilcock, *The Making of the Mosaic*, 313.

4 Bruce MacDonald, "Can't Protest Czech Ad Giving Amnesty—Ottawa," *Toronto Daily Star*, 14 June 1955, 2; Canadian Press, "Pearson Sure Czechs Here Won't Be Led Astray by Ad," *Globe and Mail*, 16 June 1955, 11; V.G. Stafl, "Scorn Red Amnesty," *Toronto Daily Star*, 25 June 1955, 6.

5 Ibid.

6 Prokop Tomek, "The Highs and Lows of Czech and Slovak Émigré Activism," in *Anti-Communist Minorities in the U.S.: Political Activism of Ethnic Refugees*, ed. Ieva Zake (New York: Palgrave Macmillan, 2009), 123. For more information on the StB and its intelligence activities, see Ladislav Bittman, *The Deception Game: Czechoslovak Intelligence in Soviet Political Warfare* (Syracuse: Syracuse University Research Corporation, 1972).

7 Eric Geiger, "Red Espionage Ring Is Bared in Ottawa by Toronto Czech: Gets Orders to Spy on 20 New Canadians from Ottawa Czech Legation," *Toronto Daily Star*, 28 October 1955, 5.

8 See LAC, DEA Fonds, vol. 8560, file 12467-D-40, part 1.1, "RCMP Reports re Re-Admission of Canadians from Czechoslovakia—Individual Cases."

9 Geiger, "Red Espionage Ring Is Bared in Ottawa by Toronto Czech," 1, 5.

10 Eric Geiger, "Spy Recruiting Said 'Warning' of Reds' Intent," *Toronto Daily Star*, 31 October 1955, 25.

11 Interview with George Corn, © MHSO, Czech Collection, 29 March 1977, CZE-0401-COR; Miroslav Ivanov, *Čech v Kanadě* (Prague: Faun, 1994), 91, 151.

12 Geiger, "Spy Recruiting Said 'Warning' of Reds' Intent," 27.

13 Geiger, "Red Espionage Ring Is Bared in Ottawa by Toronto Czech," 1, 5; Geiger, "Spy Recruiting Said 'Warning' of Reds' Intent," 25, 27; Eric Geiger, "Barred, Soundproof Ottawa Cellar Used to Discuss Czech Spy Plot," *Toronto Daily Star*, 29 October 1955, 1, 4.

14 George Štembera, "Czech Asked to Get Data for Blackmail of AVRO Employees," *Toronto Daily Star*, 31 October 1955, 1, 4.

15 LAC, MMI Fonds, MG28-V110, vol. 3, file "Correspondence, 1955," letter from Gustav Přístupa to Honourable M. Pearson, DFAIT, 14 November 1955; LAC, DEA Fonds, RG25, vol. 4018, file 10254-40, part 1, "Council of Free Czechoslovakia—Activities and Reports," memo from Václav Peřina, L. Vánra [sic], J. Jonák, and V. Trnka to Lester Bowles Pearson, Secretary of State for External Affairs, 31 October 1955; Eric Geiger, "Czechs Fight Reds, Ignore Threat, Blackmail, Blacklist," *Toronto Daily Star*, 31 October 1955, 25.

16 Prokop V. Havlík, "Vyzvědačství," *Nový domov*, 5 November 1955, 3.

17 Ibid.

18 LAC, MMI Fonds, MG28-V110, vol. 3, file "Correspondence, 1955," letter from Gustav Přístupa to Honourable M. Pearson, DFAIT, 14 November 1955.

19 LAC, DEA Fonds, RG25, accession 1977–78/84, vol. 2493, file 10463-W-40, "Annual Review of Events in Czechoslovakia by the Canadian Minister at Prague," Despatch No. 154, Annual Review for Czechoslovakia for the Year 1955, from Chargé d'Affaires, Prague, to Secretary of State for External Affairs, 12 March 1956, 10–11. The number of successful exist visa applicants rose insignificantly from four in 1954 to seventeen in 1955. Canadian Chargé d'Affaires in Prague John McLaurin Teakles indicated that the majority of successful applicants were older relatives of individuals living in Canada.

20 Canadian Press, "Easier to Seal Lips: Reds Sending Appeals for Refugees' Return," *Globe and Mail,* 22 June 1956, 15.

21 Robert Taylor, "Soviet Envoy Expelled as Spy Tries to Buy Super Jet Data," *Toronto Daily Star,* 24 September 1956, 1–2.

22 LAC, DEA Fonds, RG25, vol. 4150, file 232-AX-40, vol. 1, "Immigration from Czechoslovakia," memo, Masaryk Memorial Hall, n.d.

23 LAC, DEA Fonds, RG25, vol. 4150, file 232-AX-40, vol. 1, "Immigration from Czechoslovakia," memo from Lester Bowles Pearson, Secretary of State for External Affairs, to Honourable J.W. Pickersgill, Minister of Citizenship and Immigration, 30 July 1956.

24 Ibid.

25 Eric Geiger, "'Anti-Red' Goes Back Secretly to Prague," *Toronto Daily Star,* 13 October 1956, 29.

26 Eric Geiger, "Claims Czech in Toronto Was Spy for Five Years," *Toronto Daily Star,* 22 October 1956, 2.

27 Ibid.

28 LAC, CNAC Fonds, MG28-V111, vol. 14, file 6, "Head Office—General Correspondence, 1950–1954," letter from Josef Ludvík to Československé národní sdruženi v Kanadé, odbočka c. 24 Toronto, 21 October 1956; LAC, CNAC Fonds, MG28-V111, vol. 14, file 7, "Head Office—General Correspondence, 1955–1957," letter from Jan Polanský and Jan Kalla to Karel Buzek, 1 November 1956, and letter from Karel Buzek to Jan Polanský, 7 November 1956.

29 LAC, CNAC Fonds, MG28-V111, vol. 32, file 2, "Ottawa Branch—Minutes, 1970—1977," Pozvánka na valnou hromadu ottawské odbočky Československé národního sdružení v Kanadě, CNA, Ottawa Branch, 14 January 1957, 1–2.

30 Karel Buzek, "Czech People Still Seek Freedom," *Globe and Mail,* 7 November 1956, 6.

31 Vladimír V. Kusin, *The Intellectual Origins of the Prague Spring: The Development of Reformist Ideas in Czechoslovakia, 1956–1967* (Cambridge, UK: Cambridge University Press, 1971), 26–27.

32 Bosley and CCBA, *Pamatník Kanadsko-Československé podporující jednoty,* 37.

33 LAC, DEA Fonds, RG25, accession 1977–78/84, vol. 2493, file 10463-W-40, "Annual Review of Events in Czechoslovakia by the Canadian Minister at Prague," Circular Document No. A. 35/57, Annual Review for Czechoslovakia, 1956, from Secretary of State for External Affairs to Heads of External Affairs Posts Abroad, 21 March 1957, 5.

34 Claire E. Nolte, *The Sokol in the Czech Lands until 1914: Training for the Nation* (Basingstoke, UK: Palgrave Macmillan, 2002), 1, 3, 181–82; Sokol Canada, "Sokol Canada 1911, " http://www.sokolcanada.ca/uploads/3/4/6/8/34680982/Sokol_canada_history_august_29_zas.docx; Josef Čermák, "63. Czechoslovak (Czech and Slovak) day at Masaryktown," http://czechfolks.com/2011/07/23/163-czechoslovak-czech-and-slovak-day-at-masaryktown/.

35 LAC, MMI Fonds, MG28-V110, vol. 6, file "Sokol—Slets, 1950, 1955, 1964, 1965," pamphlet, *Canadian Sokol Festival, Montreal, 1955*, and pamphlet, *You'll Be Spending Wisely When You Advertise in the . . . Canadian Sokol Slet (Festival) Publication*; file "Sokol—Statutes, n.d.," memo, Navrh: Stanovy Ústředí československého Sokolstva v zahraničí, n.d.; Gellner and Smerek, *Czechs and Slovaks in Canada*, 112.

36 LAC, MMI Fonds, MG28-V110, vol. 6, file "Sokol—Correspondence, 1947–1967, 1975," letter from A. Alex. Cattanach, Department of the Secretary of State to Messrs. Robertson, Lane, Perrett, Frankish and Estey, Barristers, 10 June 1957.

37 Ibid.

38 LAC, Sokol Gymnastic Association of Canada (hereafter SGAC) Fonds, MG28-V136, accession 1982/0550, vol. 1, file "Windsor Branch," letter from Prokop V. Havlík to J. Kostka and J. Kostková, 13 September 1958.

39 Ivanov, *Čech v Kanadě*, 154–55; LAC, MMI Fonds, MG28-V110, vol. 7, file "Sokol Bulletin, 1958, 1964, 1965," SGAC—Bulletin, 14 April 1958. From 13 August 1957 to 31 January 1958, SGAC fundraised $9,138.69 from members and $1,021 from non-members. For a period of five years, the association borrowed $3,500 from its members and a further $900 from non-members. Additionally, $4,400 was given to the SGAC by members. With fundraising, the SGAC purchased land for $7,500 and redeveloped its building to host activities at 1621 Dupont Street for $33,224.22.

40 LAC, MMI Fonds, MG28-V110, vol. 7, file "Sokol Bulletin, 1958, 1964, 1965," *SGAC—Bulletin*, 6 May 1958.

41 Christian P. Champion, "Courting 'Our Ethnic Friends': Canadianism, Britishness, and New Canadians, 1950–1970," *Canadian Ethnic Studies* 38, 1 (2006): 24, 30.

42 Ibid.

43 J.W. Pickersgill, "Twenty-Fifth Anniversary of Sokol Toronto," *Nový domov*, 24 November 1956, 1.

44 E.W. Harris, "Minister of Finance, Ottawa, Hon. E.W. Harris," *Nový domov*, 1 December 1956, 1.

45 Paul Martin, "Twenty-Fifth Anniversary of Sokol Toronto," *Nový domov*, 24 November 1956, 1–2.

46 LAC, DEA Fonds, RG25, accession 1977–78/84, vol. 2493, file 10463-W-40, "Annual Review of Events in Czechoslovakia by the Canadian Minister at Prague," Circular Document No. A. 19/58, Annual Review for Czechoslovakia, 1958, from Secretary of State for External Affairs to Heads of External Affairs Posts Abroad, 24 February 1957 [sic], 6.

47 LAC, DEA Fonds, RG25, vol. 4150, file 232-AX-40, vol. 1, "Immigration from Czechoslovakia," memo from Defence Liaison (2) Division to DEA, Consular Division, 22 September 1958; Interview with Dagmar Zimmer, © MHSO, Czech Collection, 25 July 1978, CZE-5165-ZIM.

48 LAC, DEA Fonds, RG25, accession 1977–78/84, vol. 2493, file 10463-W-40, "Annual Review of Events in Czechoslovakia by the Canadian Minister at Prague," Circular Document No. A. 23/59, Annual Review for Czechoslovakia, 1958, from Secretary of State for External Affairs to Heads of Posts Abroad, 13 February 1959, 5.

49 John Sawatsky, *Men in the Shadows: The RCMP Security Service* (Toronto: Doubleday Canada, 1980), 174–76.

50 Bořivoj Čelovský, *Moje střetnutí s rozvědkou StB* (Ostrava: Tilia, 2003), 34–35, 48–49, 90–94.

51 LAC, DEA Fonds, RG25, vol. 8560, file 12467-D-40, part 1.2, "RCMP Reports re Re-Admission of Canadians from Czechoslovakia—Individual Cases," memo, Attention: Defence Liaison Division (2), from Superintendent W.H. Kelly, Assistant Director of Security and Intelligence, to Undersecretary of State for External Affairs, 9 June 1961.

52 LAC, CNAC Fonds, MG28-V111, vol. 32, file 7, "Ottawa Branch—Correspondence, 1950–1960," letter from Jaroslav A. Brouček to J. Diefenbaker, Prime Minister of Canada, 23 August 1960.

53 CNAC, *Charta, stanovy, jednací šrád* (Hamilton: CNAC, 1961), 6; Bosley and CCBA, *Pamatník Kanadsko-Československé podporující jednoty,* 28.

54 CNAC, *Charta, stanovy, jednací šrád,* 4–5, 10–11; LAC, CNAC Fonds, MG28-V111, vol. 32, file 7, "Ottawa Branch—Correspondence, 1950–1960," memo, Československému národnímu sdružení v Kanadé bylo chartou vydanou federální vládou v Ottawé zákonné povoleno používat všech práv a výsad pro tyto účely, n.d.

55 LAC, DSS Fonds, RG6, accession 1986–87/319, box 87, file 9-334-1, memo from Jean Boucher, Director, Citizenship Branch, Department of Citizenship and Immigration, to Deputy Minister, Department of Citizenship and Immigration, 23 March 1961.

56 LAC, DEA Fonds, RG25, vol. 8437, file 10254-40, part 2, "Activities of Czechoslovakians in Canada and Abroad: General," letter from Paul A. Demers for Acting Director, Companies Division, Department of the Secretary of State, to Undersecretary of State for External Affairs, Ottawa, 6 April 1960.

57 LAC, DEA Fonds, RG25, vol. 8437, file 10254-40, part 2, "Activities of Czechoslovakians in Canada and Abroad: General," letter from John Lucas, President, and Frank Kvetan, Secretary, CSL, to Companies Division, Department of the Secretary of State, Ottawa, 7 March 1960.

58 LAC, DSS Fonds, RG6, accession 1986–87/319, box 87, file 9-334-1, memo from Jean Boucher, Director, Citizenship Branch, Department of Citizenship and Immigration, to Deputy Minister, Department of Citizenship and Immigration, 23 March 1961; "Steel City Campaign Promises to Be Hot One: Ellen Keeps Home Fires Burning," *Ottawa Citizen,* 19 March 1963, 7.

59 LAC, SGAC Fonds, MG28-V136, accession 1982/0550, vol. 2, file "Windsor Branch," Zápis o schuzce zastupcu KOS a Kanadského sokola, okrsku Čsl. sokola v zahraničí, konane dne 31 května 1961 v sokolovne na Dupont Street, 1 June 1961.

60 LAC, MMI Fonds, MG28-V110, vol. 7, file "Sokol Bulletin, 1958, 1964, 1965," *Canadian Sokol: Official Publication of the SGAC* 1 (15 January 1962).

61 LAC, MMI Fonds, MG28-V110, vol. 7, file "Sokol Bulletin, 1958, 1964, 1965," *Sokol—Toronto News Letter,* December 1964, 1–2, and *Sokol—Toronto News Letter,* January 1965, 1, 5.

62 LAC, MMI Fonds, MG28-V110, vol. 3, file "Correspondence, January–June 1963," letter from Ruth Petříčková to Prokop V. Havlík, 1 March 1963; Jovanovic, "Czechs," 402.

63 LAC, MMI Fonds, MG28-V110, vol. 3, file "Correspondence, August–December 1963," letter from Ruth Petříčková to J. Kubík, 19 September 1963.

64 Čermák, *It All Started with Prince Rupert*, 200–01.

65 "Santa Claus Won't Miss Young Czech Stowaway," *Toronto Daily Star*, 24 December 1962, 1; "A New Home for a Stowaway," *Globe and Mail*, 14 February 1963, 3; "Freezing, Fearful Flight Described by Czech Boy," *Toronto Daily Star*, 14 February 1963, 25.

66 LAC, DEA Fonds, RG25, vol. 8437, file 10254-40, part 2, "Activities of Czechoslovakians in Canada and Abroad: General," message from Canadian Permanent Mission, Geneva, to DEA, 2 January 1963.

67 LAC, MMI Fonds, MG28-V110, vol. 3, file "Correspondence, June–December 1962," letter from Prokop V. Havlík to Mr. Casselman, Acting Superintendent of Immigration, Department of Citizenship and Immigration, Pier 21, 28 December 1962.

68 "Freezing, Fearful Flight Described by Czech Boy," *Toronto Daily Star*, 14 February 1963, 25.

69 LAC, MMI Fonds, MG28-V110, vol. 3, file "Correspondence, June–December 1961," letter from Prokop V. Havlík to Frank Clifton, President, Reorganized Church of Jesus Christ of Latter Day Saints, 5 October 1961.

70 LAC, MMI Fonds, MG28-V110, vol. 3, file "Correspondence, September–December 1959," letter from Yaroslav Hueber, counsel for the appellant, to unknown, n.d.

71 Ibid.

72 LAC, MMI Fonds, MG28-V110, vol. 3, file "Correspondence, January–March 1964," Questionnairre [sic] for Charity, 11 March 1964, and letter from unknown to Mrs. A. Fisher, Postmaster, Renabie, Ontario, 10 March 1964, and letter from W.A. Moore, Manager, Renabie Mines Limited, to MMI, 16 March 1964.

73 LAC, MMI Fonds, MG28-V110, vol. 2, file "Annual Reports, 1963, 1965, 1967, 1970," Výroční zpráva za rok 1964, 2.

74 Ibid.

75 LAC, MMI Fonds, MG28-V110, vol. 3, file "Correspondence, August–December 1963," Memorandum to Institutions, from Neil M. Morrison and Paul Lacoste, Co-Secretaries, Royal Commission on Biculturalism and Bilingualism, to Prokop V. Havlík, 10 October 1963.

76 LAC, MMI Fonds, MG28-V110, vol. 3, file "Correspondence, August–December 1963," letter from Stanley Haidasz, Parliamentary Secretary to Minister of National Health and Welfare, to Prokop V. Havlík, 22 October 1963.

77 Richard Heyman, "Making a Scene about Language Rights," *Canadian Journal of Education* 4, 1 (1979): 58–59.

78 CNAC, *Brief to the Royal Commission on Bilingualism and Biculturalism by the Czechoslovak National Association of Canada* (Toronto: CNAC, 1963), 1–2.

79 Ibid.

80 Ibid.

81 Ibid.

82 LAC, MMI Fonds, MG28-V110, vol. 3, file "Correspondence, September–December 1959," letter from Yaroslav Hueber, counsel for the appellant, to unknown, n.d.; LAC, MMI Fonds, MG28-V110, vol. 7, file "Miscellaneous—Bingo," "Masaryk Memorial Institute Incorporated and the Bingo Games," 3 April 1965, 1, 6–14.

83 LAC, MMI Fonds, MG28-V110, vol. 5, file "Scholarships, 1962–64," see newspaper clipping "University Scholarship Masaryk Memorial Institute Inc.," *Nový domov,* 16 May 1964.

84 Ibid.

85 LAC, DEA Fonds, RG25, vol. 5009, file 232-AX-40, vol. 2, "Immigration from Czechoslovakia," letter 317, from John Alexander McCordick, Canadian Ambassador to Czechoslovakia, to Undersecretary of State for External Affairs, 8 May 1963; LAC, DEA Fonds, RG25, vol. 4150, file 232-AX-40, vol. 1, "Immigration from Czechoslovakia," memo for the minister, from Norman Alexander Robertson to Honourable Howard Charles Green, Minister of External Affairs, 19 July 1962; LAC, DEA Fonds, RG25, vol. 8948, part 1, file 20-Czech-1-4, "Political Affairs—Policy and Background—Internal Policy," memo, Czechoslovak Socialist Republic, 11 April 1964, 3; Hilliker and Barry, *Canada's Department of External Affairs, Volume II,* 173.

86 LAC, DEA Fonds, RG25, vol. 5009, file 232-AX-40, vol. 2, "Immigration from Czechoslovakia," letter C-58, from Undersecretary of State for External Affairs to John Alexander McCordick, Canadian Ambassador to Czechoslovakia, 29 May 1963.

87 LAC, DEA Fonds, RG25, vol. 5009, file 232-AX-40, vol. 2, "Immigration from Czechoslovakia," letter C-513, from John Alexander McCordick, Canadian Ambassador to Czechoslovakia, to Undersecretary of State for External Affairs, 18 September 1963.

88 LAC, DEA Fonds, RG25, vol. 8948, part 1, file 20-Czech-1-4, "Political Affairs—Policy and Background—Internal Policy," memo, Confidential: Czechoslovakia, August 1966, 3.

89 Canada, Parliament, House of Commons, *House of Commons Debates: Official Report, First Session—Twenty Seventh Parliament, Volume 8* (Ottawa: Queen's Printer and Controller of Stationery, 1967), 8651–54; Dirks, *Canada's Refugee Policy,* 228–29.

90 John Sawatsky, *For Services Rendered: Leslie James Bennett and the RCMP Security Service* (Toronto: Doubleday Canada, 1982), 220–23; LAC, DEA Fonds, RG25, vol. 8560, file 12467-D-40, part 1.1, "RCMP Reports re Re-Admission of Canadians from Czechoslovakia—Individual Cases," letter from N.O. Jones, Inspector, RCMP, to Registrar, Canadian Citizenship Registration Branch, Department of Citizenship and Immigration, 19 September 1957.

91 Ibid.

92 LAC, CNAC Fonds, MG28-V111, vol. 3, file 15, "XVIII Congress, 1966," letter from Antonín Daičar and Jiří Corn to Paul Martin, Secretary of State for External Affairs, 5 December 1966, 2–3.

93 Ibid.

94 LAC, CNAC Fonds, MG28-V111, vol. 3, file 15, "XVIII Congress, 1966," Československé národní sdružení v Kanadé centennial kongres, Ottawa, Ontario—1. Dubna 1967, 12.

95 LAC, CNAC Fonds, MG28-V111, vol. 14, file 8, "Head Office—General Correspondence, 1967–1968," letter, "Why Canadian Czechs and Slovaks Will Not Demonstrate against Mr. Novotný, President of Czechoslovakia and Canada's Guest at Expo 67," from Antonín Daičar and Jiří Corn to unknown, Secretary of State for External Affairs, n.d., 3.

96 Canadian Press, "Michener, Pearson Welcome Novotny," *Globe and Mail,* 15 May 1967, 11; Canadian Press, "Czech President to Talk Trade during Visit," *Toronto Daily Star,* 15 May 1967, 3; United Press International, "Czech Chief Calls Newsman a Spy," *Toronto Daily Star,* 15 May 1967, 2; Lewis Seale, "Seek New Wheat Pact in Czech-Ottawa Talks," *Globe and Mail,* 16 May 1967, 10.

97 LAC, Lubor J. Zink Fonds, R11600-0-6-E, vol. 2, file 1, "Correspondence. June 1967," letter from Dr. Petr Zenkl, Chairman, and Dr. Matej Josko, Vice-Chairman, CFC, to Lubor J. Zink, 24 May 1967, and letter from J. Josten, Managing Editor, *Lady of Lambeth,* to Colin Welch, Deputy Editor, *Daily Telegraph,* 22 May 1967, and letter from Joška Pejskar, Editor, *České slovo,* to Lubor Zink, 4 June 1967, and letter from Alois Stana to Lubor Zink, 7 June 1967.

98 Martin O'Malley, "Concentration Camp Crony Greets Czech President at Expo," *Globe and Mail,* 17 May 1967, 9; Richard Snell, "Smiles, Tears, as Czech Chief Meets Pal from Prison Camp," *Toronto Daily Star,* 16 May 1967, 2; "War Camp Crony Greets Czech Chief," *Toronto Daily Star,* 17 May 1967, 3; "Czechoslovakian President," photo, *Toronto Daily Star,* 17 May 1967, 3.

99 Josef V. Polišenský, *Canada and Czechoslovakia* (Prague: Orbis, 1967), 10, 46.

100 LAC, CNAC Fonds, MG28-V111, vol. 33, file 2, "Hamilton Branch No. 34—Correspondence, 1967–1968," DEA, Notice Concerning Claims of Canadian Citizens against Czechoslovakia, May 1967. In this notice, the department could not guarantee that individual and business claims would be submitted to Prague and requested that the attached questionnaire be submitted to Ottawa with supporting evidence before 1 September 1967.

101 LAC, CNAC Fonds, MG28-V111, vol. 14, file 8, "Head Office—General Correspondence, 1967–1968," letter from Antonín Daičar and Jiří Corn to Paul Martin, Secretary of State for External Affairs, 10 May 1967, 2–3.

102 Sawatsky, *For Services Rendered,* 220–23, 273–74.

103 Canada, Parliament, *Proceedings of the Special Joint Committee of the Senate and the House of Commons on Immigration* (Ottawa: Supply and Services, 1968), 806–07.

104 Interview with Lida Havrlant, © MHSO, Czech Collection, 16 March 1978, CZE-0544-HAV.

105 Korbel, *Twentieth-Century Czechoslovakia,* 276.

106 LAC, MMI Fonds, MG28-V110, vol. 4, file "Correspondence, July–December 1967," letter from Ervin Sypták, MMI President, and H. Kubík, MMI Office Manager, to unknown, 24 August 1967.

107 LAC, MMI Fonds, MG28-V110, vol. 2, file "Annual Reports, 1963, 1965, 1967, 1970," Výroční zpráva za rok 1967—Zpráva referenta pro občanství a styk s úřady.

108 LAC, CNAC Fonds, MG28-V111, vol. 14, file 8, "Head Office—General Correspondence, 1967–1968," letter from Antonín Daičar and Jiří Corn to Walter Koerner, 3 June 1968.

109 Ibid.

110 LAC, MMI Fonds, MG28-V110, vol. 2, file "Annual Financial Statements, 1970–1973," "Combined Financial Statements: Masaryk Memorial Institute Incorporated, Toronto," 30 November 1973, 16; Ian Willoughby, "Professor Lubomír Doležel—Now Retired Doyen of Czech Studies in Toronto," *Radio Prague,* 3 May 2010, http://www.radio.cz/en/section/one-on-one/professor-lubomir-dolezel-now-retired-doyen-of-czech-studies-in-toronto.

111 Iacovetta, *Gatekeepers,* 291–92.

Chapter 5: Warsaw Pact Invasion

1 Immigration Story of Libor and Jiřina Roštík (Czechoslovak immigrants), CMIP Collection [S2012.2110.1]; Canadian Press, "Czechoslovaks Given Status as Immigrants," *Globe and Mail,* 14 December 1968, 4.

2 See Whitaker and Hewitt, *Canada and the Cold War,* 165–69.

3 For an overview of each constituency's role in the reform movement in Czechoslovakia, see Vladimír Kusin, *Political Groupings in the Czechoslovak Reform Movement* (New York: Columbia University Press, 1972), and Jaroslav Krejčí, *Social Change and Stratification in Postwar Czechoslovakia* (New York: Columbia University Press, 1972).

4 Jeremi Suri, "The Promise and Failure of 'Developed Socialism': The Soviet 'Thaw' and the Crucible of the Prague Spring, 1964–1972," *Contemporary European History* 15, 2 (2006): 133–58; Galia Golan, "Youth and Politics in Czechoslovakia," *Journal of Contemporary History* 5, 1 (1970): 4; Otto Ulč, *Politics in Czechoslovakia* (San Francisco: W.H. Freeman, 1974), 28–29.

5 H. Gordon Skilling, *Czechoslovakia's Interrupted Revolution* (Princeton, NJ: Princeton University Press, 1976), 217–21; Hans Renner, *A History of Czechoslovakia since 1945* (London: Routledge, 1989), 55–59; Benjamin B. Page, *The Czechoslovak Reform Movement, 1963–1968: A Study in the Theory of Socialism* (Amsterdam: Gruner, 1973), 64.

6 Ibid.

7 Cynthia Paces, *Prague Panoramas: National Memory and Sacred Space in the Twentieth Century* (Pittsburgh: University of Pittsburgh Press, 2009), 211; Korbel, *Twentieth-Century Czechoslovakia,* 285–86; Martin Myant, *The Czechoslovak Economy, 1948–1988: The Battle for Economic Reform* (Cambridge, UK: Cambridge University Press, 1989), 157; Zdeněk Suda, *The Czechoslovak Socialist Republic* (Baltimore: Johns Hopkins University Press, 1969), 115–17; Zdeněk Suda, *Zealots and Rebels: A History of the Ruling Communist Party of Czechoslovakia* (Stanford: Hoover Institution Press, 1980), 322–23.

8 Zbyněk Zeman, *Prague Spring: A Report on Czechoslovakia, 1968* (Harmondsworth, UK: Penguin Books, 1969), 152–53; Szulc, *Czechoslovakia since World War II,* 341–46; Zdeněk Kříšťufek, *The Soviet Regime in Czechoslovakia* (Boulder, CO: East European Monographs, 1981), 143; David W. Paul, *Czechoslovakia: Profile of a Socialist Republic at the Crossroads of Europe* (Boulder, CO: Westview Press, 1981), 83; *Zdeněk Mlynář, Nightfrost in Prague: The End of Humane Socialism* (New York: Karz, 1980), 139–40.

9 For a chronology of the Prague Spring movement, see Zdeněk Hejzlar and Vladimír V. Kusin, *Czechoslovakia, 1968–1969: Chronology, Bibliography, Annotation* (New York: Garland Publishing, 1975).

10 LAC, DEA Fonds, vol. 8948, file 20-Czech-1-4, part 3, "Political Affairs—Policy and Background—Internal Policy Trends—Czechoslovakia," telegram from Alan Renouf, Ambassador, Australian Embassy, Belgrade, to Australian DEA, Canberra, 23 January 1968, 1, 3.

11 LAC, DEA Fonds, vol. 8948, file 20-Czech-1-4, part 3, "Political Affairs—Policy and Background—Internal Policy Trends—Czechoslovakia," confidential memo from DEA to Peter Walker, Government House, Ottawa, 21 June 1968, 2–3. Ottawa did not release this figure to the Communist Party authorities.

12 LAC, DEA Fonds, vol. 8948, file 20-Czech-1-4, part 3, "Political Affairs—Policy and Background—Internal Policy Trends—Czechoslovakia," telegram no. 126, from Malcolm Norman Bow, Ambassador, Canadian Embassy, Prague, to Marcel Cadieux, Undersecretary of State for External Affairs, Ottawa, 14 February 1968, and memo from Arthur Redpath Menzies, High Commissioner, Canadian High Commission, Canberra, to Marcel Cadieux, Undersecretary of State for External Affairs, DEA, Ottawa, 18 April 1968, 1, and confidential memo from DEA to Peter Walker, Government House, Ottawa, 21 June 1968, 1–2.

13 Geraint Hughes, "British Policy towards Eastern Europe, and the Impact of the 'Prague Spring,' 1964–1968," *Cold War History* 4, 2 (2004): 124–25; Kieran Williams, *The Prague Spring and Its Aftermath: Czechoslovak Politics, 1968–1970* (Cambridge, UK: Cambridge University Press, 1997), 97–100.

14 Galia Golan, *The Czechoslovak Reform Movement: Communism in Crisis, 1962–1968* (London: Cambridge University Press, 1971), 323–24; Galia Golan, *Reform Rule in Czechoslovakia: The Dubček Era, 1968–1969* (Cambridge, UK: Cambridge University Press, 1973), 230–32; Jiři Valenta, *Soviet Intervention in Czechoslovakia, 1968: Anatomy of a Decision* (Baltimore: Johns Hopkins University Press, 1979), 71–85.

15 Pavel Tigrid, *Why Dubcek Fell* (London: Macdonald, 1971), 93; Williams, *Prague Spring and Its Aftermath*, 100–03; Zvi Y. Gitelman, "Public Opinion in Czechoslovakia," in *Public Opinion in European Socialist Systems*, ed. Walter D. Connor and Zvi Y. Gitelman (New York: Praeger, 1977), 96; Barbara W. Jancar, *Czechoslovakia and the Absolute Monopoly of Power: A Study of Political Power in a Communist System* (New York: Praeger Publishers, 1971), 203–04; Vladimír V. Kusin, "A Note on K 231," *Soviet Studies* 24, 1 (1972): 77–85.

16 Jeffrey Simon, *Warsaw Pact Forces: Problems of Command and Control* (Boulder, CO: Westview Press, 1985), 50.

17 Valenta, *Soviet Intervention in Czechoslovakia*, 85–92.

18 Suri, "Promise and Failure of 'Developed Socialism,'" 153; Hughes, "British Policy towards Eastern Europe," 126.

19 Korbel, *Twentieth-Century Czechoslovakia*, 301–08; Williams, *Prague Spring and Its Aftermath*, 112; Mark Kramer, "The Prague Spring and the Soviet Invasion in Historical Perspective," in *The Prague Spring and the Warsaw Pact Invasion of Czechoslovakia in 1968*, ed. Gunter Bischof, Stefan Karner, and Peter Ruggenthaler (Plymouth, MA: Lexington Books, 2010), 48–51; Karen Dawisha, *The Kremlin and the Prague Spring* (Berkeley: University of California Press, 1984), 319–20; Paulina Břeň, *The Greengrocer and His TV: The Culture of Communism after the 1968 Prague Spring* (Ithaca, NY: Cornell University Press, 2010), 27–28; Jiří Pelikán, ed., *The Secret Vysočany Congress: Proceedings and Documents of the Extraordinary Fourteenth Congress of the Communist Party of Czechoslovakia, 22 August 1968* (London: Allen Lane, 1971). Williams noted that initially 165,000 Warsaw Pact soldiers invaded Czechoslovakia on 20–21 August 1968. Meanwhile, Kramer indicated that the figure was 170,000.

20 Ivan Stražnický and Marta Stražnický, "After the Prague Spring," in *The Land Newly Found: Eyewitness Accounts of the Canadian Immigrant Experience*, ed. Norman Hillmer and Jack L. Granatstein (Toronto: Thomas Allen Publishers, 2006), 282.

21 Interview with Hana Semerád, © MHSO, Czech Collection, August 1978, CZE-8352-SEM.

22 Hron, "Czech Émigré Experience of Return after 1989," 54; Spritzer, "Children of '68." Up to the early 1970s, approximately 225,000 individuals had fled Czechoslovakia and permanently resettled in the West.

23 Troper, "In Search of Haven," 9; Troper, "Canadian Immigration Policy since 1945," 271–72; Whitaker, *Double Standard*, 6–9; Dirks, *Canada's Refugee Policy*, 233–34, 255; Victor Malarek, *Heaven's Gate: Canada's Immigration Fiasco* (Toronto: Macmillan, 1985), 102; Freda Hawkins, *Canada and Immigration: Public Policy and Public Concern* (Montreal: McGill-Queen's University Press, 1988), 38, 384.

24 Troper, "Canadian Immigration Policy since 1945," 271–72.

25 Madokoro, "Good Material," 168.

26 LAC, CNAC Fonds, MG28-V111, vol. 14, file 8, "Head Office—General Correspondence, 1967–68," letter from Antonín Daičar, CNAC President, and Jiří Corn, CNAC Secretary General, to Mitchell Sharp, Secretary of State for External Affairs, 26 July 1968.

27 LAC, CNAC Fonds, MG28-V111, vol. 14, file 8, "Head Office—General Correspondence, 1967–68," message from Marcel Cadieux, Undersecretary of State for External Affairs, to Czechoslovak Democratic Organizations in Canada, Toronto, 7 August 1968.

28 "Invasion Disappointing to Sharp, 'No Immediate Threat to Peace,'" *Globe and Mail*, 21 August 1968, 1–2. At the time, Canada remained without an ambassador in Prague. Malcolm Bow had concluded his service in Czechoslovakia and returned home to Canada. On 6 December, Minister of External Affairs Mitchell Sharp announced the appointment of Thomas Blake Burrill Wainman-Wood as the new Canadian ambassador to Prague. Bow was appointed to lead the department's disarmament division. See Canadian Press, "Wainman-Wood Gets Czech Post," *Globe and Mail*, 7 December 1968, 12.

29 Victor Mackie, "Ottawa Blasts Russian Move: Czech Crisis Forces Trudeau to Cut Short Holiday Trip," *Winnipeg Free Press*, 21 August 1968, 1, 4.

30 LAC, CNAC Fonds, MG28-V111, vol. 4, file "(Proposals and Resolutions, n.d., 1968–1975)," untitled resolution, CNAC, MMI, Permanent Conference of Slovak Democratic Exiles, and Czechoslovak Society for Arts and Sciences, n.d.

31 Marcel Desjardins, "Retour subit de M. Trudeau," *Le Droit*, 21 August 1968, 1; Greg Connolley, "Intervention Is Denounced," *Ottawa Citizen*, 21 August 1968, 1.

32 Marcel Desjardins, "Le Canada en faveur d'un vote de blame contre l'URSS—Trudeau," *Le Droit*, 22 August 1968, 1–2; Frank Jones, "'A Whole Generation Will Die' Czech Says," *Toronto Star*, 22 August 1968, 4.

33 LAC, CNAC Fonds, MG28-V111, vol. 4, file "(Proposals and Resolutions, n.d., 1968–1975)," untitled resolution, CNAC, MMI, Permanent Conference of Slovak Democratic Exiles, and Czechoslovak Society for Arts and Sciences, n.d.; W.A. Wilson, "Canada Urges UN Censure," *Montreal Daily Star*, 21 August 1968, 2; Connolley, "Intervention Is Denounced," 1.

34 Andrew Geller, "Slovaks Seek Canada's Aid," *Montreal Gazette*, 22 August 1968, 3.

35 LAC, Josef Hlávka Fonds, MG31-H101, vol. 1, letter from Don MacKenzie, Secretary, Office of the Prime Minister, to Joseph Hlávka, 27 August 1968; LAC, CCBA Fonds, MG28-V125, accession 1984/0377, vol. 2, file "Canadian Czechoslovak Benefit Association," letter from Mitchell Sharp, Secretary of State for External Affairs, to J. Hamata, President, CCBA, Winnipeg, 30 August 1968; Mackie, "Ottawa Blasts Russian Move," 4.

36 LAC, CNAC Fonds, MG28-V111, vol. 4, file "(Proposals and Resolutions, n.d., 1968–1975)," statement by the Secretary of State for External Affairs, 21 August 1968.

37 Fernand Beauregard, "Le Canada va-t-il passer aux actes?," *La Presse,* 22 August 1968, 1; Wilson, "Canada Urges UN Censure," 1.

38 Robert Bothwell, *Alliance and Illusion: Canada and the World, 1945–1984* (Vancouver: UBC Press, 2007), 284.

39 Paul Kidd, "Immediate Withdrawal Demanded," *Ottawa Citizen,* 22 August 1968, 1; Mackie, "Ottawa Blasts Russian Move," 1; "Soviet Troops Seize Reform Leaders, Fire on Czechs in Prague Streets: Didn't Ask Reds Prague Tells UN," *Globe and Mail,* 22 August 1968, 1–2; United Nations Security Council, "Situation in Czechoslovakia: Initial Proceedings," *Repertoire of the Practice of the Security Council,* http://www.un.org/en/sc/repertoire/66-68/Chapter%208/66-68_08-14Situation%20in%20Czechoslovakia.pdf, see 171–73. Council members voted ten votes for, two votes against, with three abstentions. One of the two votes against came from the Soviet Union.

40 LAC, CNAC Fonds, MG28-V111, vol. 14, file 8, "Head Office—General Correspondence, 1967–68," message from Henry Weisbach, President, and Karl Heeb, Secretary, to Jiří Corn, CNAC Secretary General, Toronto, 22 August 1968. In 1952, the Trans-Canada Alliance of German-Canadians was founded. In 1984, its successor organization, the German-Canadian Congress, was established.

41 Ibid.

42 LAC, CNAC Fonds, MG28-V111, vol. 14, file 8, "Head Office—General Correspondence, 1967–68," message from Henry Weisbach, President, and L. Lowit, Secretary, to Jiří Corn, CNAC Secretary General, Toronto, 22 August 1968.

43 LAC, CNAC Fonds, MG28-V111, vol. 33, file 3, "Hamilton Branch No. 34—Correspondence, 1968," Oběžník, J.G. Corn, Secretary General, CNAC, Toronto, 10 September 1968, 3; "Metro's Czechoslovak Community Plans Convoy to Take Plea to PM," *Globe and Mail,* 22 August 1968, 8; "150 Metro Czechs Will Ask PM for Tough Line on Crisis," *Toronto Star,* 22 August 1968, 1.

44 "150 Metro Czechs Will Ask PM for Tough Line on Crisis," *Toronto Star,* 22 August 1968, 1.

45 "Demonstrace," *Nový domov,* 24 August 1968, 2; Burt Heward, "Czechs Ask More than Talk," *Ottawa Citizen,* 23 August 1968, 17; Rick Mackie, "Uneasy Truce between Protestors, Police Marks Night Demonstration," *Ottawa Citizen,* 23 August 1968, 17; David Smithers, "Invasion Beginning of the End for Russia, Says Ex-Czech MP," *Ottawa Citizen,* 23 August 1968, 17.

46 LAC, CNAC Fonds, MG28-V111, vol. 2, file 16, "Minutes—Head Office and Branches, 1969–1974," letter, Sestry a bratři, from CNAC Winnipeg Branch to unknown, n.d.; "Vigil Set at Cenotaph for Czechs," *Winnipeg Free Press,* 22 August 1968, 4.

47 Heather Chisvin, "Czech Freedom Wreath Placed on Cenotaph," *Winnipeg Free Press,* 23 August 1968, 3.

48 "Les tchèques protestant durement et ne ménagent pas leur mots," *Le Droit,* 23 August 1968, 2–3; "Hands Tied: Trudeau," *Winnipeg Free Press,* 23 August 1968, 1; "Demonstrace," *Nový domov,* 24 August 1968, 8; Kirk Smith, "Silent Sincere Pickets Protest at Soviet Embassy," *Ottawa Citizen,* 22 August 1968, 54; Canadian Press, "'You Murderers,'" photo, *Ottawa Citizen,* 23 August 1968, 3; Canadian Press, "Thoughts of Homeland Bring Tears," photo, *Ottawa Citizen,* 23 August 1968, 21.

49 Canadian Press, "Czech Ottawa Envoys Back Dubček Reforms," *Montreal Daily Star,* 23 August 1968, 1; "Hands Tied: Trudeau," *Winnipeg Free Press,* 23 August 1968, 1.

50 Canadian Press, "Montreal Czechs Protest," *Winnipeg Free Press,* 24 August 1968, 8; "Slovaks to March Tonight," *Montreal Star,* 23 August 1968, 3; Canadian Press, "200 Montreal Students Picket," *Ottawa Citizen,* 22 August 1968, 54.

51 LAC, CSL Fonds, MG28-V47, vol. 2, file "Clippings," Mark Starowicz, "A Proud Czech Communist Who Isn't So Proud Any More," *Toronto Daily Star,* 23 August 1968, 4; Joseph M. Kirschbaum, *The Ideological Orientation of the Canadian Slavic Press* (Toronto: Inter-University Committee on Canadian Slavs, 1971), 301–02.

52 Anthony X. Sutherland, *The Canadian Slovak League* (Toronto: CSL, 1984), 82.

53 LAC, CNAC Fonds, MG28-V111, vol. 14, file 8, "Head Office—General Correspondence, 1967–68," message from Mitchell Sharp, Secretary of State for External Affairs, to Antonín Daičar, CNAC President, and Jiří Corn, CNAC Secretary General, Toronto, 28 August 1968.

54 LAC, SGAC Fonds, MG28-V136, accession 1982/0550, vol. 1, "Our Answer to the Soviets: No More Talks! Get Out! Save Dubček, Save Czechoslovakia," editorial, *Naše hlasy,* n.d.

55 LAC, MMI Fonds, MG28-V110, vol. 4, file "Correspondence, 1968," letter from George Ben and Jiří Corn, Committee Organizing Protest against Soviet Aggression in Czechoslovakia, to MMI, Toronto, 3 September 1968.

56 LAC, MMI Fonds, MG28-V110, vol. 4, file "Correspondence, 1968," untitled declaration, Toronto, 29 August 1968. The twenty-five organizations that signed the declaration were CNAC, MMI, CSL, Slovak Canadian Professional and Businessmen's Association, Canadian Polish Congress, Canadian Veterans 601 (Czechoslovak Branch), Hungarian Canadian Federation, Byelorussian Canadian Alliance, Latvian National Federation in Canada, Estonian Central Council in Canada, Sokol Canada, Association of Czechoslovak Sportsmen of Western World, Serbian Cultural Club "St. Sava," United Steel Workers of America Toronto Area Council, Czechoslovak Society of Arts and Sciences, Canadian Loyalist Movement, Armenian Community Centre ARF, Bratstvo Ukrainci Katoliku, Serbian National Committee, Serbian Cultural Club "Bishop Dr. Nikolan," Ukrainian Canadian Committee Toronto Branch, Ukrainian National Federation of Canada, Slovenian National Federation of Canada, Romanian National Front, and Permanent Conference of Slovak Democratic Exiles.

57 LAC, MMI Fonds, MG28-V110, vol. 4, file "Correspondence, 1968," letter from George Ben and Jiří Corn, Committee Organizing Protest against Soviet Aggression in Czechoslovakia, to MMI, Toronto, 3 September 1968.

58 Louise Holborn, *Refugees: A Problem of Our Time: The Work of the United Nations High Commissioner for Refugees, 1951–1972, vol. 1* (Metuchen, NJ: Scarecrow Press, 1975), 516–17.

59 Gil Loescher, *The UNHCR and World Politics: A Perilous Path* (Oxford: Oxford University Press, 2001), 178.

60 Madokoro, "Good Material," 165–66.

61 Troper, "In Search of Haven," 9.

62 Canada, Department of Manpower and Immigration, *The Immigration Program* (Ottawa: Minister of Supply and Services, 1974), 108–09; Dirks, *Canada's Refugee Policy*, 233; Kelley and Trebilcock, *Making of the Mosaic*, 363.

63 Department of Manpower and Immigration, *The Immigration Program*, 109. For a brief account of a Manpower counsellor's experience in resettling 1968ers in Trail, British Columbia, see Bernard Brodie, "Czechoslovakia 1968: The Canada Manpower Perspective," *CIHS Bulletin: The Newsletter of the Canadian Immigration Historical Society* 35 (1999): 2–6.

64 Greg Connolley, "Govt. Denies Any Delays in Speeding Czechs Here," *Ottawa Citizen*, 6 September 1968, 1.

65 Tim Creery, "Red Tape Holding Up Immigration," *Ottawa Citizen*, 6 September 1968, 25.

66 John Zawisza, "The Czechoslovakian Refugee Movement, 1968," *CIHS Bulletin: The Newsletter of the Canadian Immigration Historical Society* 46 (2005): 5.

67 Dirks, *Canada's Refugee Policy*, 234.

68 LAC, CNAC Fonds, MG28-V111, vol. 33, file 3, "Hamilton Branch No. 34—Correspondence, 1968," Oběžník, J.G. Corn, Secretary General, CNAC, Toronto, 10 September 1968, 1–2.

69 Ibid.

70 LAC, IB Fonds, RG76, vol. 691, file 568-3-23, part 4, "28th Parliament, First Session, House of Commons, Unnumbered Questions—Czech Refugees, Polish Seamen, Black Writers' Congress, Military Deserters, etc.," Question Period response from Allan MacEachen, Minister, Department of Manpower and Immigration, n.d., microfilm reel C-10688.

71 Clair Balfour, "Going to Like Canada, Czech Refugee Says," *Globe and Mail*, 13 September 1968, 4.

72 Whelan, "203 from Czechoslovakia Combine Joy and Sorrow," 1–2.

73 Eva Marha, "Czechs/Slovaks," in *Safe Haven: The Refugee Experience of Five Families*, ed. Elizabeth McLuhan (Toronto: MHSO, 1995), 61–62.

74 Reuters, "Rush of Czech Refugees Handled in Crash Program," *Globe and Mail*, 16 September 1968, 17.

75 "After 20 Hard Years, Former Czech Judge Seeks Fourth Career," *Globe and Mail*, 17 September 1968, 5.

76 Whelan, "203 from Czechoslovakia Combine Joy and Sorrow," 1–2; "Přiletěli: Vítame Československé uprchlíky do Toronta a celé Kanady," *Nový domov*, 21 September 1968, 1; Joe Bissett, "The Czechoslovakian Refugee Movement, 1968," *CIHS Bulletin: The Newsletter of the Canadian Immigration Historical Society* 46 (2005): 1–4.

77 "Přiletěli: Vítame Československé uprchlíky do Toronta a celé Kanady," *Nový domov*, 21 September 1968, 1.

78 Jarmila L.A. Horná, "The Entrance Status of Czech and Slovak Immigrant Women," in *Two Nations, Many Cultures: Ethnic Groups in Canada*, ed. Jean Leonard Elliott (Scarborough, ON: Prentice-Hall, 1979), 272, 277–78.

79 Škvorecký, "Bohemia of the Soul," 122–23; Josef Škvorecký, "A Country after My Own Heart," *Maclean's* 87, 3 (1974): 24–25, 74–76; Mark Sarner, "Portrait of a Political Exile: Why Josef Škvorecký, Czechoslovakia's Preeminent Novelist, Is Very Much at Home in Cabbagetown," *Toronto Life* 11 (1977): 38; Josef Škvorecký, "At Home in Exile: Czech Writers in the West," *Books Abroad* 50, 2 (1976): 308–13. For information on Sixty-Eight Publishers and Czech dissident publishing houses in the West, see Jana Prokop, "Bibliography of Czech Dissidents," *Nationalities Papers* 11, 1 (1983): 93–99. Among the many dissident publishing houses, CCC (Czechoslovak Cultural Club) in Munich, Index in Cologne, Konfrontation in Zurich, and Sixty-Eight Publishers in Toronto were the most prominent.

80 Canada, Parliament, House of Commons, *House of Commons Debates: Official Report, First Session—Twenty Eighth Parliament, Volume 1* (Ottawa: Queen's Printer and Controller of Stationery, 1969), 18–19, 60, 67–68.

81 John Kraglund, "New Conductor Becomes a Refugee: Ancerl in Toronto a Year Early," *Globe and Mail*, 13 September 1968, 1; Jo Carson, "Blacky Had to Stay in Prague," *Globe and Mail*, 24 September 1968, 10.

82 Canadian Press, "Special Team Sent to Help Czech Refugees," *Globe and Mail*, 18 September 1968, 8; Dirks, *Canada's Refugee Policy*, 234; Charles Murrow, "Sacrifice and Bravery as the Prague Spring Ends," *CIHS Bulletin: The Newsletter of the Canadian Immigration Historical Society* 46 (2005): 15.

83 Marha, "Czechs/Slovaks," 34; Stražnický and Stražnický, "After the Prague Spring," 284.

84 House of Commons, *House of Commons Debates: Official Report, First Session—Twenty Eighth Parliament*, 60.

85 Canadian Press, "Czech 'Cream' Allegation Is Denied," *Globe and Mail*, 20 September 1968, 4.

86 LAC, CNAC Fonds, MG28-V111, vol. 14, file 9, "Head Office—General Correspondence, September–December, 1968," letter from Alex Havrlant, CNAC Vice-President, to Board of Education, City of Toronto, 7 October 1968, and letter from Alex Havrlant, CNAC Vice-President, to Jiří Corn, CNAC Secretary General, Toronto, 17 October 1968.

87 LAC, MMI Fonds, MG28-V110, vol. 7, file "Miscellaneous—Information for Newcomers, n.d.," brochure, *První směrnice pro nové příchozí*, MMI, Toronto, n.d. For example, a minimum of three years of experience was needed for hairdressers and five years for mechanics and electricians. Refugees were informed that the minimum wage for workers was set at $4.25 per hour, whereas carpenters made $4.15, electricians $4.70, construction workers $2.75, house painters $3.45, and installation workers $4.67. Masaryk Memorial Institute also advised newcomers that registration with a union could cost more than $150.

88 Loren Lind, "A Penniless Czech Finds a Place to Live and a Job in Toronto," *Globe and Mail*, 25 September 1968, 37.

89 Interview with Jarmila Lenk, © MHSO, Czech Collection, 15 August 1978, CZE-5170-LEN.

90 Interview with Marie Vejvalková, © MHSO, Czech Collection, 5 June 1978, CZE-5531-VEJ.

91 Interview with Ludmila Kotáčková, © MHSO, Czech Collection, 28 May 1978, CZE-5529-KOT.

92 Lind, "A Penniless Czech Finds a Place to Live and a Job in Toronto," 37.

93 LAC, CNAC Fonds, MG28-V111, vol. 33, file 3, "Hamilton Branch No. 34—Correspondence, 1968," Oběžník, J.G. Corn, Secretary General, CNAC, 28 August 1968, 1.

94 LAC, CNAC Fonds, MG28-V111, vol. 2, file 16, "Minutes—Head Office and Branches, 1969–1974," letter, Sestry a bratři, from CNAC Winnipeg Branch to unknown, n.d.

95 LAC, CNAC Fonds, MG28-V111, vol. 2, file 16, "Minutes—Head Office and Branches, 1969–1974," letter, Zpráva o činnosti odbočky Edmonton, from Eric Z. Schoengut, President, CNAC Edmonton Branch, to unknown, n.d.

96 LAC, CNAC Fonds, MG28-V111, vol. 4, file 2, "Reports, n.d., 1968–1973," report, Canadian Fund for Czechoslovak Refugees in Canada, n.d.

97 LAC, MMI Fonds, MG28-V110, vol. 4, file "Correspondence, 1968," telegram from Senator Andy Thompson to MMI, 26 October 1968.

98 LAC, MMI Fonds, MG28-V110, vol. 4, file "Correspondence, 1968," letter from Ervin Sypták, MMI President, and Jan Stríček, MMI Secretary, to Mr. and Mrs. Nathan Phillips, 29 October 1968, and letter from Ervin Sypták, MMI President, and Jan Stríček, MMI Secretary, to Charles White, Supervisor of Immigrant Settlement Services, Canada Manpower Centre, Toronto, 29 October 1968, and letter from Ervin Sypták, MMI President, and Jan Stríček, MMI Secretary, to L.E. Fox, Clerk of the Court, Court of Canadian Citizenship, Toronto, 29 October 1968, and letter from Ervin Sypták, MMI President, and Jan Stríček, MMI Secretary, to Controller Margaret Campbell, City Hall, Toronto, 29 October 1968, and letter from Ervin Sypták, MMI President, and Jan Stríček, MMI Secretary, to Mr. and Mrs. Z. Jarmicki, President, Canadian Polish Congress, Toronto, 29 October 1968.

99 LAC, CNAC Fonds, MG28-V111, vol. 33, file 4, "Hamilton Branch No. 34—Correspondence, 1969," Zpráva odbočky Hamilton za rok 1968–69, František Braun, President, and Eva Kraus, Secretary, CNAC, Hamilton Branch, 28 April 1969.

100 LAC, DEA Fonds, vol. 8948, file 20-Czech-1-4, part 3, "Political Affairs—Policy and Background—Internal Policy Trends—Czechoslovakia," memo from R.B. Curry, Assistant Deputy Minister (for Deputy Minister), to Allan MacEachen, Minister of Manpower and Immigration, Ottawa, 15 October 1968, 1–2.

101 AO, Department of the Provincial Secretary and Citizenship (hereafter DPSC) Fonds, RG 8-5, barcode B229098, file "Citizenship—Czech and Slovak Refugees," article, Canadian Press, "Door Closing on Czech Refugees," 4 January 1969.

102 "Haven Granted to 10,000, Czech Program to End," *Globe and Mail,* 4 January 1969, 1.

103 LAC, CNAC Fonds, MG28-V111, vol. 14, file 11, "Head Office—General Correspondence, April–July 1969," letter from R. Talbot, Director, Technical Services, Ontario Region, Department of Manpower and Immigration, to Jiří (George) Corn, Secretary General, CNAC, Toronto, 2 May 1969.

104 Margaret Mironowicz, "It's Been a Long, Hard Road to Their New Home," *Toronto Star,* 26 September 1973, B3; LAC, CNAC Fonds, MG28-V111, vol. 3, file 19, "XXII Congress, Winnipeg, 1970," Zpráva sociální referentky—Ústředí Československého národního sdružení v Kanadě, Ruth Petříčková, social officer, CNAC Head Office, 1969.

105 LAC, CNAC Fonds, MG28-V111, vol. 2, file 16, "Minutes—Head Office and Branches, 1969–1974," news release, z Ústředí ČSNS, CNAC press service, Toronto, n.d., 1; LAC, Josef Hlávka Fonds, MG31-H101, vol. 1, Československého národního sdružení v Kanadě—XXI. Kongres J.A. Komenský, 1592–1670, Chateau Laurier, 3.–4. května 1969—Ottawa, 16.

106 LAC, Josef Hlávka Fonds, MG31-H101, vol. 1, Československého národního sdružení v Kanadě—XXI. Kongres J.A. Komenský, 1592–1670, Chateau Laurier, 3–4. května 1969—Ottawa, 7–8, 16, 18–22; LAC, CNAC Fonds, MG28-V111, vol. 3, file 17, "XX Congress, Batawa, 1968," letter, Oběžník č.5, from J.G. Corn and E. Talacko, CNAC Head Office, Toronto, to CNAC Branches, Members of CNAC Central Council, Affiliated Groups in Canada, and Compatriot Press, 28 March 1969.

107 Marha, "Czechs/Slovaks," 61.

108 Michael Lanphier, "Canada's Response to Refugees," *International Migration Review* 15, 1–2 (1981): 113–14.

109 Paul Martin, "Canadian Senators Visit Czechoslovakia," *External Affairs* 21, 8 (1969): 311–13.

110 LAC, CNAC Fonds, MG28-V111, vol. 4, file "(Proposals and Resolutions, n.d., 1968–1975)," press release, Czechoslovak Day in Toronto, CNAC, Toronto, 6 July 1969.

111 Ibid.

112 AO, DPSC Fonds, RG 8-5, barcode B229098, file "Citizenship—Czech and Slovak Refugees," memo from J.S. Yoerger, Deputy Minister, DPSC, to D.R. Colombo, Director, Citizenship Branch, 28 October 1969.

113 Canada, Parliament, House of Commons, *House of Commons Debates: Official Report, Second Session—Twenty Eighth Parliament, Volume 1* (Ottawa: Queen's Printer for Canada, 1970), 524–25.

114 "Czechoslovakian Refugees Adapt to Canada," Edmond Ziegler, 1972–78, CMIP Collection [D2014.103.1].

115 Ron Heatley, *Czechoslovakian Refugee Study: A Report on the Three-Year Study of the Economic and Social Adaptation of Czechoslovakian Refugees to Life in Canada, 1968–1969 to 1971–1972* (Ottawa: Manpower and Immigration Canada, 1975), 1, 5–6.

116 Ibid., 3; Lanphier, "Canada's Response to Refugees," 114; Bernard Brodie, "The Czechoslovaks of 1968/69," *CIHS Bulletin: The Newsletter of the Canadian Immigration Historical Society* 26 (1997): 6; Ed Ziegler, "The Adaptation of Czechoslovak Refugees in Canada, 1969–1972," *CIHS Bulletin: The Newsletter of the Canadian Immigration Historical Society* 54 (2008): 5–7.

117 Heatley, *Czechoslovakian Refugee Study,* 2; Department of Manpower and Immigration, *The Immigration Program,* 109; Department of the Secretary of State, *The Canadian Family Tree,* 56; Lanphier, "Canada's Response to Refugees," 114.

118 "Czechoslovakian Refugees Adapt to Canada," Edmond Ziegler, 1972–78, CMIP Collection [D2014.103.1].

119 Canada, Department of Manpower and Immigration, *Immigration Statistics 1968* (Ottawa: Queen's Printer for Canada, 1969), 10–11; Canada, Department of Manpower and Immigration, *Immigration Statistics 1969* (Ottawa: Queen's Printer for Canada, 1970), 10–11, 22.

Chapter 6: Opposing the Communist Regime

1 Interview with Ladislav Šolc, © MHSO, Czech Collection, July 1980, CZE-8360-SOL; Interview with Iva Rousová, © MHSO, Czech Collection, c. 1978, CZE-8353-ROU.

2 Hron, "Czech Émigré Experience of Return after 1989," 54.

3 LAC, CNAC Fonds, MG28-V111, vol. 34, file "Welfare Association of Former Czechoslovak Political Prisoners—Minutes, 1970–1973," letter from Milo Komínek, Secretary, WAFCPP, to CNAC, Toronto, 27 January 1970.

4 LAC, CNAC Fonds, MG28-V111, vol. 34, file "Welfare Association of Former Czechoslovak Political Prisoners—Minutes, 1970–1973," letter from Milo Komínek, Secretary, WAFCPP, to Members, Toronto, 26 January 1970.

5 LAC, CNAC Fonds, MG28-V111, vol. 3, file 19, "XXII Congress, Winnipeg, 1970," "Resolution of the Czechoslovak National Association of Canada," n.d., 2. For information on the Brezhnev Doctrine, see Robert L. Hutchings, *Soviet East European Relations: Consolidation and Conflict, 1968–1980* (Madison: University of Wisconsin Press, 1983), 42–44.

6 Whitaker and Hewitt, *Canada and the Cold War*, 170–74.

7 LAC, CNAC Fonds, MG28-V111, vol. 3, file 19, "XXII Congress, Winnipeg, 1970," "Resolution of the Czechoslovak National Association of Canada," n.d., 3.

8 University of British Columbia, Department of Botany, "Vladimir Krajina," http://botany.ubc.ca/people/vladimir-krajina.

9 Ibid.

10 LAC, CNAC Fonds, MG28-V111, vol. 3, file 19, "XXII Congress, Winnipeg, 1970," letter from Vladimír Krajina to Pierre Elliott Trudeau, Prime Minister of Canada, Ottawa, 11 May 1970, 1–2.

11 Ibid.

12 LAC, MMI Fonds, MG28-V110, vol. 4, file "Correspondence, 1970," letter from Milo Komínek, Secretary, WAFCPP, to MMI, Toronto, 27 May 1970, and letter from Manager, MMI, to WAFCPP, Toronto, 9 June 1970.

13 LAC, CNAC Fonds, MG28-V111, vol. 4, file "(Proposals and Resolutions, n.d., 1968–1975)," Proclamation from A. Daičar, CNAC President, and J.G. Corn, CNAC Secretary General, Toronto, 21 August 1970.

14 Whitaker and Hewitt, *Cold War Canada*, 178–79.

15 LAC, CNAC Fonds, MG28-V111, vol. 15, file 14, "Head Office—General Correspondence, July–December 1970," letter from Antonín Daičar, President, and Jiří G. Corn, Secretary General, CNAC, to Pierre Elliott Trudeau, Prime Minister, Ottawa, 27 October 1970.

16 Ibid.

17 AO, DPSC Fonds, RG 8-5, barcode B229098, file "Citizenship—Czech and Slovak Refugees," article "Prague Starts Blackmailing 70,000 Exiles: Trials for Unauthorized Departure to Be Paid in Foreign Currencies by Refugees or Relatives—Solicitors Letters Despatched All over the World—KGB Advisers behind Foreign Currency Drive," *F.C.I.—Free Central European News Agency*, 18 November 1970.

18 AO, DPSC Fonds, RG 8-5, barcode B229098, file "Citizenship—Czech and Slovak Refugees," letter from JUDr. Nittel, Prague, to Otakar Šindelář, Niagara Falls, ON, 20 October 1970.

19 AO, DPSC Fonds, RG 8-5, barcode B229098, file "Citizenship—Czech and Slovak Refugees," flyer from Toronto Area Co-Ordinating Committee of Czech and Slovak Democratic Organizations to unknown, 1 December 1970, and flyer entitled "Ethnic Scene from Ethnic Liaison Council" to unknown, December 1970. The twelve groups consisted of the Club of Newcomers of Czech and Slovak Origin in Canada, Czechoslovak Baptist Church, Canadian Fund for Czechoslovak Refugees and Information Service, Permanent Conference of Slovak Democratic Exiles in Canada, Royal Canadian Legion, Branch 601 (Czechoslovak), St. Paul's Evangelical Lutheran Church, St. Wenceslaus Roman Catholic Church, Soccer Club "Sparta," Sokol Gymnastic Association of Toronto, Union of Czechoslovak Protestants in Canada, Union of Czechoslovak Sportsmen Abroad—Toronto Branch, and Welfare Association of Former Czechoslovak Political Prisoners (Canada).

20 Ibid.

21 AO, DPSC Fonds, RG 8-5, barcode B229098, file "Citizenship—Czech and Slovak Refugees," article, "Prague Starts Blackmailing 70,000 Exiles: Trials for Unauthorized Departure to Be Paid in Foreign Currencies by Refugees or Relatives—Solicitors Letters Despatched All over the World—KGB Advisers behind Foreign Currency Drive," *F.C.I.—Free Central European News Agency*, 18 November 1970.

22 AO, DPSC Fonds, RG 8-5, barcode B229098, file "Citizenship—Czech and Slovak Refugees," flyer from Toronto Area Co-Ordinating Committee of Czech and Slovak Democratic Organizations to unknown, 1 December 1970, and flyer entitled "Ethnic Scene from Ethnic Liaison Council" to unknown, December 1970.

23 LAC, CNAC Fonds, MG28-V111, vol. 2, file 16, "Minutes—Head Office and Branches, 1969–1974," letter, Zpráva o činnosti za odobi 1970–71, from M. Schiller, Officer, CNAC Vancouver Branch, to unknown, 7 March 1971.

24 LAC, CNAC Fonds, MG28-V111, vol. 3, file 20, "XXIII Congress, Niagara Falls, 1971," Resolution of XXIII Congress of CNAC—1971, J.G. Corn, President, and Alex Havrlant, Secretary General, CNAC, n.d., 1–2.

25 Ota Hora, "Attitudes towards Canadian Foreign Policy—'It Is Time to Unite All Forces against Soviet Imperialism and Its Tyranny, *Nový domov*, Toronto, June 19, 1971," in *Immigration and the Rise of Multiculturalism*, ed. Howard Palmer (Vancouver: Copp Clark, 1975), 204.

26 LAC, CNAC Fonds, MG28-V111, vol. 3, file 21, "XXIV Congress, Kitchener, 1972," Československé národní sdružení v Kanadě—24. Kongres—Inn of the Black Walnut, King and Benton, Kitchener, ON, 13. V. 1972, 4–5; LAC, CNAC Fonds, MG28-V111, vol. 4, file "(Proposals and Resolutions, n.d., 1968–1975)," proposal, Vydání pohlednic k 21. srpnu 1968, CNAC, n.d.

27 Ibid.

28 LAC, CNAC Fonds, MG28-V111, vol. 4, file "(Proposals and Resolutions, n.d., 1968–1975)," "Proclamation of the Czechoslovak National Association of Canada, Toronto, 21 August 1971."

29 LAC, CNAC Fonds, MG28-V111, vol. 3, file 25, "Congress of Western Canada Chapters, Edmonton, 1972," Československé národní sdružení v Kanadě—I. Kongres západnich provincií—Edmonton, AB, 8–9 duben 1972, 2–3.

30 LAC, CNAC Fonds, MG28-V111, vol. 15, file 17, "Head Office—Correspondence, January–June 1972," letter from Mitchell Sharp, Secretary of State for External Affairs, to Alex Havrlant, Secretary General, CNAC, Toronto, 13 January 1972, 1–3.

31 Ibid.

32 LAC, CNAC Fonds, MG28-V111, vol. 4, file "(Proposals and Resolutions, n.d., 1968–1975)," Resolution, Association nationale tchécoslovaque du Canada, Toronto, 14 May 1972.

33 LAC, CNAC Fonds, MG28-V111, vol. 4, file "(Proposals and Resolutions, n.d., 1968–1975)," letter to the editor from J.G. Corn, CNAC President, Toronto, 14 May 1972.

34 LAC, CNAC Fonds, MG28-V111, vol. 4, file "(Proposals and Resolutions, n.d., 1968–1975)," *Mémoire de la communauté éthnique de la province de Québec* from Polish Congress of Quebec, Ukrainian Canadian Committee (Quebec Section), Alliance of Hungarian Associations, United Croats of Canada, Hellenic Canadian Community of Montreal, Romanian Association of Canada, Baltic Federation in Canada (Quebec Branch), Grand Committee of Churches and Hungarian Associations, Social Culture Club Giovanni Caboto, Order of Italo-Canadians, CSL (Montreal Branch), and CNAC (Montreal Branch) to Robert Bourassa, Premier, and Government of Quebec, 14 May 1972, 1–3.

35 LAC, CNAC Fonds, MG28-V111, vol. 33, file 14, "Ottawa Branch No. 89—Miscellaneous, 1970–1976," letter from J.G. Corn, President, CNAC, to Commonwealth Heads of Government Conference, Ottawa, 7 August 1973.

36 Ibid.

37 LAC, CNAC Fonds, MG28-V111, vol. 29, file 3, "Pamphlets, Programs, and Brochures, n.d., 1969–1974," postal seals "21 August, Day of Soviet Shame," CNAC, Toronto, 1973.

38 LAC, MMI Fonds, MG28-V110, vol. 4, file "Correspondence, 1973," see newspaper clipping, "Moment of Prayer for Captive People," photo, *St. Catharines Standard,* 21 August 1973.

39 LAC, CNAC Fonds, MG28-V111, vol. 33, file 14, "Ottawa Branch No. 89—Miscellaneous, 1970–1976," letter from O. Hora and J. Kouba, CNAC Ottawa Branch, to Press Gallery, Parliament Hill: Assignment Editors, 13 August 1973, and letter from K. Hrubý, Chairman, CNAC Ottawa Branch, to unknown, 20 August 1970, 2, and letter from O. Hora and J. Kouba, CNAC Ottawa Branch, to Press Gallery, Parliament Hill: Assignment Editors, n.d., 2.

40 LAC, CNAC Fonds, MG28-V111, vol. 29, file 7, "Grant Applications—Secretary of State, 1974–1975," article, Victor Žícha, "Proč ještě nejste členem ČSNS," *Věstník: Československých spolků v Montreale* 10, 4 (1973): 1.

41 "Kursy státního občanství," *Věstník: Československých spolků v Montreale* 10, 3 (1973): 3.

42 LAC, CNAC Fonds, MG28-V111, vol. 33, file 14, "Ottawa Branch No. 89—Miscellaneous, 1970–1976," letter from Louis Urban, President, and Zdeněk Otruba, Secretary General, CNAC, to CNAC Membership, 9 October 1975, and memo "Případ Morcinek," from CNAC, Toronto, n.d.

43 LAC, CNAC Fonds, MG28-V111, vol. 33, file 14, "Ottawa Branch No. 89—Miscellaneous, 1970–1976," article, Peter Worthington, "Deportation to Certain Jail," *Toronto Sun,* 11 December 1975, 11.

44 Ibid.

45 "Such Ship-Jumpers Need a Break," *Toronto Star,* 7 April 1976, B4.

46 Worthington, "Deportation to Certain Jail," 11; Canada, Parliament, House of Commons, *House of Commons Debates: Official Report, First Session—Thirtieth Parliament, Volume 12* (Ottawa: Queen's Printer for Canada, 1976), 12399, 12406.

47 LAC, CNAC Fonds, MG28-V111, vol. 4, file "(Proposals and Resolutions, n.d., 1968–1975)," XXVII Congress of the Czechoslovak National Association of Canada, "Resolution of the Czechoslovak National Association of Canada, Toronto, 25 May 1975," 1–2.

48 Ibid.

49 LAC, CNAC Fonds, MG28-V111, vol. 4, file "(Proposals and Resolutions, n.d., 1968–1975)," J.G. Corn, CNAC President, "Proclamation of the Czechoslovak National Association of Canada on Détente, Toronto, May 1975," 2–3.

50 LAC, CNAC Fonds, MG28-V111, vol. 3, file 24, "Congress XXVII, Toronto, 1975," Československé národní sdružení v Kanadě—27.Kongres T.G. Masaryka, 24–25 května 1975, 6. The Foreign Claims Commission agreed to hold an initial amount of $1 million in compensation. Prague would subsequently forward yearly payments of $500,000 until the aforementioned amount of $3.25 million was reached. Once all claims had been received and processed from former Czechoslovak nationals residing in Canada, repayments would first be made to individuals with claims below $1 million.

51 Vladimír V. Kusin, "Challenge to Normalcy: Political Opposition in Czechoslovakia, 1968–1977," in *Opposition in Eastern Europe,* ed. Rudolf L. Tokes (Baltimore: Johns Hopkins University Press, 1979), 51.

52 Janusz Bugajski, *Czechoslovakia: Charter 77's Decade of Dissent* (New York: Praeger, 1987), 10.

53 Jiří Pelikán, *Socialist Opposition in Eastern Europe: The Czechoslovak Example* (London: Allison and Busby, 1976), 105.

54 Interview with Břetislav Marek, © MHSO, Czech Collection, 19 June 1978, CZE-5287-MAR.

55 Kirschbaum, *History of Slovakia,* 242. On 27 April 1978, VONS (Výbor na obranu nespravedlivě stíhaných—Committee for the Defence of the Unjustly Persecuted) was established by a group of Charter 77 signatories. The committee supported persons harassed by the police and prosecuted by the communist legal system. The committee assisted defendants in finding financial aid and legal representation.

56 Kusin, "Challenge to Normalcy," 52; Bugajski, *Czechoslovakia,* 11; Carol Skalník Leff, *The Czech and Slovak Republics: Nation versus State* (Boulder, CO: Westview Press 1997), 61.

57 David W. Paul, *The Cultural Limits of Revolutionary Politics: Change and Continuity in Socialist Czechoslovakia* (Boulder, CO: East European Quarterly, 1979), 34–35; Ladislav Holy, *The Little Czech and the Great Czech Nation* (Cambridge, UK: Cambridge University Press, 1996), 29; Vladimír V. Kusin, *From Dubcek to Charter 77: A Study of "Normalization" in Czechoslovakia, 1968–1978* (New York: St. Martin's Press, 1978), 308.

58 Canadian Press, "Ottawa Cautions Czechs," *Zpravodaj,* January 1978, 2.

59 Škvorecký, "Bohemia of the Soul," 127; Interview with Semerád.

60 České slovo "Emigrantské cesty do staré vlasti," *Kanadské listy,* 15 April 1984, 1; Anthony Bailey, "Letter from Prague," *New Yorker,* 23 July 1979, 77.

61 České slovo "Emigrantské cesty do staré vlasti," *Kanadské listy,* 15 April 1984, 1.

62 Kelley and Trebilcock, *Making of the Mosaic,* 406.

63 Ota Hora, "Úvahy Při podepsání dohody mezi kanadskou vladou a Československým národním sdružením v Kanadě o sponsorovaní politických uprchlíku z Československa," *Naše hlasy,* 2 August 1980, 2.

64 Canada, Department of Manpower and Immigration, *1970 Immigration Statistics* (Ottawa: Information Canada, 1971), 5; *1971 Immigration Statistics* (Ottawa: Information Canada, 1972), 5; *1972 Immigration Statistics* (Ottawa: Information Canada, 1974), 5; *1973 Immigration Statistics* (Ottawa: Information Canada, 1975), 5; *1974 Immigration Statistics* (Ottawa: Information Canada, 1975), 5; *1975 Immigration Statistics* (Ottawa: Minister of Supply and Services Canada, 1976), 5; *1976 Immigration Statistics* (Ottawa: Minister of Supply and Services Canada, 1977), 5; Canada, Department of Employment and Immigration, *1977 Immigration Statistics* (Ottawa: Minister of Supply and Services Canada, 1978), 5; *1978 Immigration Statistics* (Ottawa: Minister of Supply and Services Canada, 1980), 5; *1979 Immigration Statistics* (Ottawa: Minister of Supply and Services Canada, 1981), 5.

65 "Noví uprchlíci stále přicházejí," *Kanadské listy*, 15 October 1982, 6.

66 David R. Francis, "Flying to Freedom via a Canadian Fuel Stop: Czechoslovak 'Vacationers' Heading to Cuba Defect in Montreal," *Christian Science Monitor*, 2 December 1986, http://www.csmonitor.com/1986/1202/ofect.html.

67 William Barrett, "Czechs Defect to Canada on Planes that 'Never Land at Mirabel,'" *Montreal Gazette*, 29 October 1985, A1.

68 Rick Davey, "Czechs Fly to Freedom through Montreal Airport," *Toronto Star*, 20 January 1986, A11.

69 Lidia Ribeiro, *Profils des communautés culturelles du Québec* (Québec: Gouvernement de Québec, Ministère des communautés culturelles et de l'immigration, 1991), 1–2, 4; John Kralt, *Atlas of Residential Concentration for the Census Metropolitan Area of Montreal* (Ottawa: Multiculturalism Directorate, 1986), 26. By the mid-1980s, Quebec was home to approximately 6,605 individuals from Czechoslovakia. Czech Quebecers accounted for 1,525 persons, Slovak Quebecers numbered 1,395 individuals, with 1,160 identifying themselves as "Czechoslovaks." The remaining 2,520 people were counted as having multiple origins. A majority of these individuals (88.7 percent) resided in Montreal. Approximately 68.8 percent of the population was foreign born. According to the 1986 Canadian Census, 4,920 Czechs and Slovaks lived in Montreal.

70 Miloš Šuchma, "Imigrační situace a možnosti naší pomoci," *Věstník* 1, 1 (1986): 1.

71 Filípek, *Reflections and Perspectives*, 62.

72 "Problemy exulantu," *Kanadské listy*, 15 April 1984, 6.

73 Marta Procházka, "An Absurd Way of Life: A Very Unusual Feeling," *Canadian Ethnic Studies* 25, 2 (1993): 127–30.

74 Ivo Moravec, *Tightrope Passage: Along the Refugee Route to Canada* (Toronto: McClelland and Stewart, 1997), 52–54, 191–93.

75 Francis, "Flying to Freedom via a Canadian Fuel Stop."

76 "Pomožte nám sponzorovat tyto rodiny a jednotlivce," *Věstník* 3, 2 (1987): 7.

77 "Statistika sponsorovani odbočkami v roce 1988," *Věstník* 4, 2 (1989): 6. The CNAC's Toronto Branch sponsored ninety-six refugees, followed by thirty in Vancouver, fifteen each in Edmonton and Kitchener-Waterloo-Guelph, twelve in Ottawa, seven in Hamilton, five in Montreal, and two in Winnipeg.

78 Douglas Martin, "A Canada Airport Lures Would-Be Defectors," *New York Times*, 13 February 1985, http://www.nytimes.com/1985/02/13/world/a-canada-airport-lures-would-be-defectors.html?pagewanted=all; Peggy Curran, "Immigration Moves to Stop Czechs Landing at Mirabel," *Montreal Gazette*, 27 July 1989, B1.

79 Canada, Department of Employment and Immigration, *1980 Immigration Statistics* (Ottawa: Minister of Supply and Services, 1982), 10; *1981 Immigration Statistics* (Ottawa: Minister of Supply and Services, 1983), 10; *1982 Immigration Statistics* (Ottawa: Minister of Supply and Services, 1984), 18; *1983 Immigration Statistics* (Ottawa: Minister of Supply and Services, 1985), 18, 62; *1984 Immigration Statistics* (Ottawa: Minister of Supply and Services, 1986), 50; *1985 Immigration Statistics* (Ottawa: Minister of Supply and Services, 1987), 49; *1986 Immigration Statistics* (Ottawa: Minister of Supply and Services, 1988), 49; *1987 Immigration Statistics* (Ottawa: Minister of Supply and Services, 1989), 51; *1988 Immigration Statistics* (Ottawa: Minister of Supply and Services, 1990), 51; *1989 Immigration Statistics* (Ottawa: Minister of Supply and Services, 1991), 51.

80 Hašek, "Dedication of K-231 Monument," 1; MMI, "Monument"; Čermák, *It All Started with Prince Rupert,* 273.

81 Mark Bastien, "Czech-Canadian Rewarded in Returning Home to Help," *Edmonton Journal,* 13 December 1989, A17.

82 As an English-language translator for the dissident movement, Rita Klímová coined the term "Velvet Revolution." A trained economist, Klímová became Czechoslovakia's last ambassador to the United States prior to dissolution of the country in 1992.

83 Robert G. McRae, *Resistance and Revolution: Vaclav Havel's Czechoslovakia* (Ottawa: Carleton University Press, 1997), 199–201.

84 Nomi Morris, "'Hero of Hope' Draws Tears, Cheers, in Metro," *Toronto Star,* 20 February 1990, A2; "Czechoslovakia, Quebec Sign Co-Operation Deal," *Toronto Star,* 20 February 1990, A2; Peter Adler, "Czech President Asks for Business, Not Charity," *Toronto Star,* 19 February 1990, A14; Čermák, *It All Started with Prince Rupert,* 199–200.

85 Ibid.

86 Paul Koring, "Echo of Ethnic Bitterness Greets Havel at Ottawa Meeting of Czechoslovaks," *Globe and Mail,* 19 February 1990, A1, A2; McRae, *Resistance and Revolution,* 201; H. Gordon Skilling, *The Education of a Canadian: My Life as a Scholar and Activist* (Montreal: McGill-Queen's University Press, 2000), 372–73. The Slovak World Congress was founded in New York in 1970 by Canadian Slovak businessman Stephen Roman. The congress serves as an international body representing various Slovak organizations and societies around the world.

87 Canada, Department of Employment and Immigration, *1990 Immigration Statistics* (Ottawa: Minister of Supply and Services, 1991), 9, 51; *1991 Immigration Statistics* (Ottawa: Minister of Supply and Services, 1992), 51; *1992 Immigration Statistics* (Ottawa: Public Works and Government Services Canada, 1994), 55. These figures were derived from the table "Country of Last Permanent Residence by Class."

88 Czech and Slovak Association of Canada, "Brief History and Archives, " https://www.cssk.ca/brief-history-and-activities/.

89 Ribeiro, *Profils des communautés culturelles du Québec,* 1–4.

Chapter 7: Creating Ethnocultural Heritage

1 Interview with Zimmer. František Zimmer was interviewed as part of Dagmar Zimmer's oral history.

2 Michael Dewing, "Parliament of Canada, Background Paper: PRB09-20E, Canadian Multiculturalism," http://www.parl.gc.ca/Content/LOP/

ResearchPublications/prb0920-e.htm#2-The%20Formative; Miriam V. Richter, *Creating the National Mosaic: Multiculturalism in Canadian Children's Literature from 1950 to 1994* (Amsterdam: Editions Rodopi, 2001), 37.

3 LAC, DSS Fonds, RG6, accession 1986–87/319, box 87, file 9-334, part 1, "Masaryk Memorial Institute Inc.," letter from Bedřich Čecha, MMI President, and J. Václav Šauer to the Secretary of State, Ottawa, 13 November 1970.

4 LAC, DSS Fonds, RG6, accession 1986–87/319, box 87, file 9-334, part 1, "Masaryk Memorial Institute Inc.," letter from Stan Zybala, Assistant Chief, Ethnic Participation Division, Citizenship Branch, Department of the Secretary of State, to Jindra Zoder, Toronto, 29 March 1971.

5 LAC, MMI Fonds, MG28-V110, vol. 2, file "Annual Reports, 1972–1974," Jerry (Jaroslav) Forest, Treasurer's Report 1972, Výroční zpráva za rok 1972, n.d.

6 LAC, MMI Fonds, MG28-V110, vol. 2, file "Annual Reports, 1963, 1965, 1967, 1970," W. Bartánus, Executive Member's Report, Výroční zpráva za rok 1970, n.d.

7 Ibid.

8 LAC, MMI Fonds, MG28-V110, vol. 4, file "Correspondence, 1971," letter from John Yaremko, Provincial Secretary and Minister of Citizenship, to H. Zoder, *Nový domov* Editor, Toronto, 20 October 1971.

9 LAC, MMI Fonds, MG28-V110, vol. 4, file "Correspondence, 1971," letter from Henry Zoder, *Nový domov* Editor, to John Yaremko, Provincial Secretary and Minister of Citizenship, Toronto, 8 November 1971.

10 LAC, CNAC Fonds, MG28-V111, vol. 15, file 17, "Head Office—Correspondence, January–June 1972," Dotazník from CNAC to CNAC Ottawa Branch, 26 May 1971.

11 LAC, CNAC Fonds, MG28-V111, vol. 2, file 16, "Minutes—Head Office and Branches, 1969–1974," letter from K. Jatel, CNAC Batawa Branch, to Emil Talacko, 7 March 1971, and letter, Československé národní sdružení v Kanadě pobočka v Halifaxu, N.S.—Zpráva o činnosti za rok 1970, from M.J. Mácalík, CNAC Halifax Branch, to unknown, 3 April 1971.

12 LAC, CNAC Fonds, MG28-V111, vol. 4, file 2, "Reports, n.d., 1968–1973," report, "Brief to Be Presented to the Alberta Cultural Heritage Conference, June 16–18, 1972 University of Alberta in Edmonton by Czechoslovak National Association of Canada—Calgary Branch," n.d.

13 Ibid.

14 LAC, MMI Fonds, MG28-V110, vol. 2, file "Annual Reports, 1972–1974," Jerry (Jaroslav) Forest, Treasurer's Report 1972, Výroční zpráva za rok 1972, n.d.

15 LAC, MMI Fonds, MG28-V110, vol. 2, file "Annual Financial Statements, 1970–1973," "Combined Financial Statements: Masaryk Memorial Institute Incorporated," Toronto, 30 November 1973, 16.

16 LAC, CNAC Fonds, MG28-V111, vol. 29, file 3, "Pamphlets, Programs, and Brochures, n.d., 1969–1974," pamphlet, "Charity Bazaar of the Women's Council of the CNAC," Toronto, 4 November 1972. See Edith Feldman, ed., *Czechoslovak Recipes—Women's Council of the Czechoslovak National Association* (Toronto: CNAC, 1963).

17 LAC, CNAC Fonds, MG28-V111, vol. 33, file 14, "Ottawa Branch No. 89—Miscellaneous, 1970–1976," "Remarks Delivered by J.G. Corn on the Occasion of Citizenship Day in Winnipeg, Manitoba on 29 May 1974 in Parliament Buildings, Winnipeg."

18 Ibid.

19 LAC, CNAC Fonds, MG28-V111, vol. 3, file 23, "XXVI Congress, Hamilton, 1974," Československé národní sdružení v Kanadě—26.Kongres "Bedřicha Smetany"—McMaster University, Hamilton, ON, 11 května 1974, 25.

20 LAC, CNAC Fonds, MG28-V111, vol. 29, file 7, "Grant Applications—Secretary of State, 1974–1975," draft letter from Zdena Škvorecký to CNAC, Toronto, n.d. The draft is attached to a letter from J.G. Corn, President, CNAC, to Sixty-Eight Publishers, Toronto, 29 May 1974.

21 LAC, CNAC Fonds, MG28-V111, vol. 29, file 7, "Grant Applications—Secretary of State, 1974–1975," draft letter from Victor M. Fic, Professor, Department of Politics, Brock University, St. Catharines, ON, to J. Jaworski, Canadian Citizenship Branch, Department of the Secretary of State, Ottawa, 18 October 1973.

22 LAC, CNAC Fonds, MG28-V111, vol. 29, file 7, "Grant Applications—Secretary of State, 1974–1975," Guidelines for Submissions for Grants under the Multicultural Program, Citizenship Branch, Department of the Secretary of State, Bernard Ostry, Assistant Undersecretary of State, Ottawa, n.d., 1.

23 LAC, CNAC Fonds, MG28-V111, vol. 29, file 7, "Grant Applications—Secretary of State, 1974–1975," "Secretary of State, Citizenship Branch Grant Application Form" prepared by Jiri G. Corn, President, CNAC, Toronto, 12 June 1974, 2, 4–5. In its funding application, the association noted that it had received approximately $2,702 in membership dues, $5,206 in private donations, $4,880 from federal departments and agencies, and $31,386 from other activities, for a total of $44,174. Conversely, the CNAC claimed $37,825 in expenditures, which included $1,200 for part-time salaries, $534 for travel, $4,591 for office rent, and $31,500 for cultural gifts and support for other initiatives. From the estimated total cost for publication of the dictionary, $10,200 was to go to materials, $5,600 to honoraria, $1,500 to publicity, $600 to typing, and $200 to travel.

24 LAC, CNAC Fonds, MG28-V111, vol. 16, file 23, "Head Office—Correspondence, January–May 1975," letter from Stan Zybala, Multicultural Program, Canadian Citizenship Branch, Department of the Secretary of State, to Anthony Daičar, CNAC, Batawa, 17 April 1975.

25 LAC, DSS Fonds, RG6, accession 1989–90/157 GAD, box 13, file 9264-B, "Czechoslovak National Association of Canada: Ethnic Broadcast in Czech and Slovak Language," Czechoslovak Broadcast CFMB Radio 1410 Report 1978, Prepared for the Department of the Secretary of State, Multiculturalism and Citizenship Branch, Victor G. Žícha, 6 June 1979, 1–4.

26 LAC, DSS Fonds, RG6, accession 1989–90/157 GAD, box 13, file 9264-B, "Czechoslovak National Association of Canada: Ethnic Broadcast in Czech and Slovak Language," letter from Steve E. Paprocki, Minister of State for Multiculturalism, to Dr. Victor Žícha, CNAC, Montreal, 14 August 1979. See attached "Grant Assessment Form" in French.

27 LAC, DSS Fonds, RG6, accession 1989–90/157 GAD, box 52, file "Czechoslovak Television Kaleidoscope—Life of Ethnic Czechs and Slovaks in Their New Homeland," letter from Jim Fleming, Minister of State for Multiculturalism, to Arnošt Wagner, Producer, Czechoslovak Television Kaleidoscope, Ottawa, 17 June 1980. See attached "Grant Application Form" and "Grant Assessment Form." The *Slovak Spectrum* television program is still in existence today.

28 LAC, CNAC Fonds, MG28-V111, vol. 16, file 23, "Head Office—Correspondence, January–May 1975," press release from Stanley Haidasz, Member of Parliament for Parkdale, ON, Ottawa, 27 January 1975.

29 LAC, MMI Fonds, MG28-V110, vol. 2, file "Annual Reports, 1972–1974," S.P. Viezner, Secretary's Report, 1974, Výroční zpráva za rok 1974, 29 May 1975; Peter Small, "Caravan Founder Changed the City," *Toronto Star,* 8 August 2001, B1, B4.

30 LAC, DSS Fonds, RG6, accession 1989–90/157 GAD, box 47, file 0760-C, "Citizenship Sector—Masaryk Memorial Institute Inc.—Teaching Czech," letter from Jim Fleming, Minister of State for Multiculturalism, to Karel Jeřábek, MMI President, 13 February 1981.

31 LAC, DSS Fonds, RG6, accession 1989–90/157 GAD, box 6, file 9887-C, "Masaryk Memorial Institute Inc. Czechoslovak Supplementary School," "Grant Assessment Form," 24 December 1979, and letter from Steve E. Paproski, Minister of State for Multiculturalism, to Jaroslav Forest, MMI, Czechoslovak Supplementary School, Toronto, 6 February 1980.

32 LAC, DSS Fonds, RG6, accession 1989–90/157 GAD, box 47, file 0760-C, "Citizenship Sector—Masaryk Memorial Institute Inc.—Teaching Czech," "Grant Application Form—Multicultural Program—Secretary of State," 22 October 1980; LAC, CNAC Fonds, MG28-V111, vol. 32, file 2, "Ottawa Branch—Minutes, 1970–1977," Pozvánka na valnou hromadu ottawské odbočky Československé národního sdružení v Kanadě, 1977, 6.

33 LAC, DSS Fonds, RG6, accession 1989–90/157 GAD, box 4, file 9750-D, "Czechoslovak Canadian Cultural Society of Southern Alberta—Czech Language School," letter from Steve E. Paprocki, Minister of State for Multiculturalism, to Libby Jonas, Czechoslovak Canadian Cultural Society of Southern Alberta, Lethbridge, 9 January 1980. See attached "Grant Assessment Form." The society was incorporated on 11 October 1978.

34 LAC, DSS Fonds, RG6, accession 1989–90/157 GAD, box 4, file 9882-C, "Czechoslovak Canadian Cultural Society of Southern Alberta—Czech Language School," letter from Steve E. Paprocki, Minister of State for Multiculturalism, to Martin Jelinowicz, CNAC, Kitchener-Waterloo, 6 February 1980. See attached "Grant Assessment Form."

35 Ibid.

36 Ibid.

37 LAC, DSS Fonds, RG6, accession 1989–90/157 GAD, box 52, file 0305-C, "Czechoslovak Society of Arts and Sciences—Cultural Integration of Czechoslovak Immigrants to Canadian Cultural Atmosphere and Role of Ethnic Organization," letter from Jim Fleming, Minister of State for Multiculturalism, to Jaromír Smrčka, Ottawa, 10 October 1980. See attached "Recommendation for Approval Form."

38 LAC, DSS Fonds, RG6, accession 1989–90/157 GAD, box 52, file 0081-D, "Czechoslovak National Association of Canada—Winnipeg Branch—Presentation of Czechoslovak Literary Heritage to Canadian Public," letter from Jim Fleming, Minister of State for Multiculturalism, to J.M. Dobrovolný, CNAC, Winnipeg, 5 November 1980. See attached "Grant Application Form."

39 Ibid.

40 Jarmila L.A. Horná, "Social Problems in Integration of Immigrants from Czechoslovakia," in *Czechoslovak National Association of Canada Conference on*

Cultural and Social Integration of Immigrants from Czechoslovakia, ed. Victor Fic (Toronto: CNA of Canada, 1983), 35–42.

41 Ibid.

Conclusion

1 Hron, "Czech Émigré Experience of Return after 1989," 47.

2 Procházka, "An Absurd Way of Life," 133; Hron, "Czech Émigré Experience of Return after 1989," 51.

3 Adolf, "Adaptation of East European Refugees and Political Émigrés in Toronto," 205, 281.

4 Ibid.

5 For further context, see Iacovetta, *Gatekeepers,* 18–19.

6 Ibid.

7 Jovanovic, "Czechs," 404.

8 For example, see Rosemary Barton, "Canada's Syrian Refugee Plan Limited to Women, Children, and Families," *CBC News,* 22 November 2015, http://www.cbc.ca/news/politics/canada-refugee-plan-women-children-families-1.3330185.

BIBLIOGRAPHY

Archival Collections

Archives of Ontario

Department of the Provincial Secretary and Citizenship Fonds (RG 8-5)

Joseph Čermák Textual Records (F 1405-67-02)

Marie Flosman Textual Records (F 1405-67-21)

Canadian Museum of Immigration at Pier 21

Archival Collection

Digital Image Collection

Department of External Affairs and International Trade

Documents on Canadian External Relations (vols. 14, 15, 16)

Directorate of History and Heritage, Department of National Defence

Fort Churchill, July 48/October 51 (Kardex, 112.3M2 [D329])

Library and Archives Canada

Canadian Czechoslovak Benevolent Association Fonds (MG28-V125)

Canadian Slovak League Fonds (MG28-V47)

Czechoslovak National Association of Canada Fonds (MG28-V111)

Department of External Affairs Fonds (RG25)

Department of the Secretary of State Fonds (RG6)

Department of National Defence Fonds (RG24)

Immigration Branch Fonds (RG76)

Jan Dočkálek Fonds (MG30-C148)

Josef Hlávka Fonds (MG31-H101)

Lubor J. Zink Fonds (R11600-0-6-E)

Masaryk Memorial Institute Fonds (MG28-V110)

Privy Council Office Fonds (RG2)

Sokol Gymnastic Association of Canada Fonds (MG28-V136)

William Lyon Mackenzie King Papers, Memoranda and Notes, 1940–50 (MG26-J4)

Thomas Fisher Rare Book Library, University of Toronto

John Reeves Papers (Ms. Coll. 6)

Oral History Collections

Canadian Museum of Immigration at Pier 21
Oral History Collection
Story Collection

Multicultural History Society of Ontario
Czech Collection
Slovak Collection
Ukrainian Collection

Newspapers and Magazines

Čas
Christian Science Monitor
Le Devoir
Le Droit
Edmonton Journal
Globe and Mail
Halifax Chronicle Herald
Kanadské listy
L'udové zvesti
Maclean's
Montreal Gazette
Montreal Herald
Montreal Star
Naše hlasy
New Yorker
New York Times
Nová vlasť
Nový domov
Ottawa Citizen
Prague Post
La Presse
Radio Prague
Toronto Life
Toronto Star
Tribune
Vancouver Sun
Věstník
Věstník: Československých spolků v Montreale
Winnipeg Free Press
Zpravodaj

Government Publications

Canada. Department of Citizenship and Immigration. *1992 Immigration Statistics.* Ottawa: Public Works and Government Services Canada, 1994.

———. Department of Employment and Immigration. *1977 Immigration Statistics.* Ottawa: Minister of Supply and Services Canada, 1978.

———. *1978 Immigration Statistics.* Ottawa: Minister of Supply and Services Canada, 1980.

———. *1979 Immigration Statistics.* Ottawa: Minister of Supply and Services Canada, 1981.

———. *1980 Immigration Statistics.* Ottawa: Minister of Supply and Services, 1982.

———. *1981 Immigration Statistics.* Ottawa: Minister of Supply and Services, 1983.

———. *1982 Immigration Statistics.* Ottawa: Minister of Supply and Services, 1984.

———. *1983 Immigration Statistics.* Ottawa: Minister of Supply and Services, 1985.

———. *1984 Immigration Statistics.* Ottawa: Minister of Supply and Services, 1986.

———. *1985 Immigration Statistics.* Ottawa: Minister of Supply and Services, 1987.

———. *1986 Immigration Statistics.* Ottawa: Minister of Supply and Services, 1988.

———. *1987 Immigration Statistics.* Ottawa: Minister of Supply and Services, 1989.

———. *1988 Immigration Statistics.* Ottawa: Minister of Supply and Services, 1990.

———. *1989 Immigration Statistics.* Ottawa: Minister of Supply and Services, 1991.

———. *1990 Immigration Statistics.* Ottawa: Minister of Supply and Services, 1991.

———. *1991 Immigration Statistics.* Ottawa: Minister of Supply and Services, 1992.

———. Department of External Affairs. *Documents Relating to the German–Czechoslovak Crisis September, 1938.* Ottawa: J.O. Patenaude, 1938.

———. Department of Industry, Trade, and Commerce. Dominion Bureau of Statistics. *The Canada Year Book, 1969.* Ottawa: Queen's Printer, 1969.

———. Department of Manpower and Immigration. *1967 Immigration Statistics.* Ottawa: Queen's Printer and Controller for Stationery, 1968.

———. *1968 Immigration Statistics.* Ottawa: Queen's Printer, 1969.

———. *1969 Immigration Statistics.* Ottawa: Queen's Printer for Canada, 1970.

———. *1970 Immigration Statistics.* Ottawa: Information Canada, 1971.

———. *1971 Immigration Statistics.* Ottawa: Information Canada, 1972.

———. *1972 Immigration Statistics.* Ottawa: Information Canada, 1974.

———. *1973 Immigration Statistics.* Ottawa: Information Canada, 1975.

———. *1974 Immigration Statistics.* Ottawa: Information Canada, 1975.

———. *1975 Immigration Statistics.* Ottawa: Minister of Supply and Services Canada, 1976.

———. *1976 Immigration Statistics.* Ottawa: Minister of Supply and Services Canada, 1977.

———. *The Immigration Program.* Ottawa: Minister of Supply and Services, 1974.

———. Department of the Secretary of State. *The Canadian Family Tree: Canada's Peoples.* Don Mills, ON: Corpus Information Services, 1979.

———. Department of Trade and Commerce. Dominion Bureau of Statistics. *The Canada Year Book, 1934–35.* Ottawa: King's Printer, 1935.

———. *The Canada Year Book, 1938.* Ottawa: King's Printer, 1938.

———. *The Canada Year Book, 1939.* Ottawa: King's Printer, 1939.

———. *The Canada Year Book, 1940.* Ottawa: King's Printer, 1940.

———. *The Canada Year Book, 1942.* Ottawa: King's Printer, 1942.

———. *The Canada Year Book, 1943–44.* Ottawa: King's Printer, 1944.

———. *The Canada Year Book, 1945.* Ottawa: King's Printer, 1945.

———. *The Canada Year Book, 1946.* Ottawa: King's Printer, 1946.

———. *The Canada Year Book, 1947.* Ottawa: King's Printer, 1947.

———. *The Canada Year Book, 1948–1949.* Ottawa: King's Printer, 1949.

———. *The Canada Year Book, 1950.* Ottawa: King's Printer, 1950.

———. *The Canada Year Book, 1951.* Ottawa: King's Printer, 1951.

———. Parliament. *Proceedings of the Special Joint Committee of the Senate and the House of Commons on Immigration.* Ottawa: Supply and Services, 1968.

———. Parliament. House of Commons. *House of Commons Debates: Official Report, First Session—Thirtieth Parliament, Volume 12.* Ottawa: Queen's Printer for Canada, 1976.

———. *House of Commons Debates: Official Report, First Session—Twenty Eighth Parliament, Volume 1.* Ottawa: Queen's Printer and Controller of Stationery, 1969.

———. *House of Commons Debates: Official Report, First Session—Twenty Seventh Parliament, Volume 8.* Ottawa: Queen's Printer and Controller of Stationery, 1967.

———. *House of Commons Debates: Official Report, Second Session—Twenty Eighth Parliament, Volume 1.* Ottawa: Queen's Printer for Canada, 1970.

———. *House of Commons Debates: Official Report, Third Session—Twentieth Parliament, Volume 3.* Ottawa: King's Printer and Controller of Stationery, 1947.

———. Parliament. Senate. *Proceedings of the Standing Committee on Labour and Immigration: Session of Wednesday, July 24, 1946.* Ottawa: Minister of Supply and Services, 1946.

———. Parliament. Senate. *Speech of the Hon. Arthur W. Roebuck, Senator, on Immigration in the Senate of Canada, Ottawa, Thursday, on April 4, 1946.* Ottawa: Edmond Cloutier, Printer to the King's Most Excellent Majesty, 1946.

———. Statistics Canada. *2016 Census of Population. Statistics Canada Catalogue No. 98-400-X2016187.* http://www.statcan.ca/cgi-bin/IPS/display?cat_num=98-400-X2016187.

Dewing, Michael. "Parliament of Canada, Background Paper: PRB09-20E, Canadian Multiculturalism." http://www.parl.gc.ca/Content/LOP/ResearchPublications/prb0920-e.htm#2-The%20Formative.

Heatley, Ron. *Czechoslovakian Refugee Study: A Report on the Three-Year Study of the Economic and Social Adaptation of Czechoslovakian Refugees to Life in Canada, 1968–1969 to 1971–1972.* Ottawa: Manpower and Immigration Canada, 1975.

Kralt, John. *Atlas of Residential Concentration for the Census Metropolitan Area of Montreal.* Ottawa: Multiculturalism Directorate, 1986.

Ribeiro, Lidia. *Profils des communautés culturelles du Québec.* Québec: Gouvernement de Québec, Ministère des communautés culturelles et de l'immigration, 1991.

United Nations High Commissioner for Refugees. "Convention and Protocol Relating to the Status of Refugees." http://www.unhcr.org/3b66c2aa10.html.

United Nations Security Council. "Situation in Czechoslovakia: Initial Proceedings." *Repertoire of the Practice of the Security Council.* http://www.un.org/en/sc/repertoire/66-68/Chapter%208/66-68_08-14-Situation%20in%20Czechoslovakia.pdf.

Secondary Sources

Abella, Irving, and Harold Troper. *None Is Too Many: Canada and the Jews of Europe, 1933–1948.* Toronto: Lester and Orpen Dennys, 1982.

Adams, Mary L. *The Trouble with Normal: Postwar Youth and the Construction of Heterosexuality.* Toronto: University of Toronto Press, 1997.

Adolf, Jacek Z. "Adaptation of East European Refugees and Political Émigrés in Toronto, with Special Reference to Immigrants from Poland and Czechoslovakia." PhD diss., York University, 1977.

Agnew, Hugh L. *The Czechs and the Lands of the Bohemian Crown.* Stanford: Hoover Institution Press, 2004.

Avery, Donald H. *Reluctant Host: Canada's Response to Immigrant Workers.* Toronto: McClelland and Stewart, 1995.

Bakke, Elisabeth. "Czechoslovakism in Slovak History." In *Slovakia in History*, edited by Mikuláš Teich, Dušan Kováč, and Martin D. Brown, 247–68. Cambridge, UK: Cambridge University Press, 2011.

Balawyder, Aloysius. "Canadian-Slavic Cultural Nationalism and the Canadian Government's Reaction." *Canadian Review of Studies in Nationalism* 16, 1–2 (1989): 197–205.

Barton, Rosemary. "Canada's Syrian Refugee Plan Limited to Women, Children, and Families." *CBC News*, 22 November 2015. http://www.cbc.ca/news/politics/canada-refugee-plan-women-children-families-1.3330185.

Bassler, Gerhard P. *Sanctuary Denied: Refugees from the Third Reich and Newfoundland Immigration Policy, 1906–1949.* St. John's: Institute of Social and Economic Research, 1992.

Baťa, Thomas J., and Sonja Sinclair. *Bata: Shoemaker to the World.* Toronto: Stoddart Publishing, 1990.

Beneš, Edvard. *Paměti: Od Mnichova k nové válce a k novému vítězství.* Praha: Orbis, 1947.

Beneš, Edvard, and Milan Hauner. *Fall and Rise of a Nation: Czechoslovakia, 1938–1941.* Boulder, CO: East European Monographs, 2004.

Bissett, Joe. "The Czechoslovakian Refugee Movement, 1968." *CIHS Bulletin: The Newsletter of the Canadian Immigration Historical Society* 46 (2005): 1–4.

Bittman, Ladislav. *The Deception Game: Czechoslovak Intelligence in Soviet Political Warfare.* Syracuse, NY: Syracuse University Research Corporation, 1972.

Bloomfield, Jon. *Passive Revolution: Politics and the Czechoslovak Working Class, 1945–1948.* New York: St. Martin's Press, 1979.

Bosley, Edna M., and Canadian Czechoslovak Benevolent Association. *Pamatník Kanadsko-Československé podporující jednoty, Winnipeg, Manitoba, 1913–1963.* Winnipeg: National Publishers, 1963.

Bothwell, Robert. *Alliance and Illusion: Canada and the World, 1945–1984.* Vancouver: UBC Press, 2007.

Bradley, John F.N. *Czechoslovakia: A Short History.* Edinburgh: Edinburgh University Press, 1971.

Břeň, Paulina. *The Greengrocer and His TV: The Culture of Communism after the 1968 Prague Spring.* Ithaca: Cornell University Press, 2010.

Břesky, Dushan. "Czech Poet in Canada: Pavel Javor's Life and Work." *Canadian Ethnic Studies* 10, 1 (1978): 75–84.

Brodie, Bernard. "Czechoslovakia 1968: The Canada Manpower Perspective." *CIHS Bulletin: The Newsletter of the Canadian Immigration Historical Society* 35 (1999): 2–6.

———. "The Czechoslovaks of 1968/69." *CIHS Bulletin: The Newsletter of the Canadian Immigration Historical Society* 26 (1997): 5–6.

Bryant, Chad. *Prague in Black: Nazi Rule and Czech Nationalism.* Cambridge, MA: Harvard University Press, 2007.

Bugajski, Janusz. Czechoslovakia: *Charter 77's Decade of Dissent.* New York: Praeger, 1987.

Campbell, F. Gregory. "Empty Pedestals?" *Slavic Review* 44, 1 (1985): 1–15.

Canadian Czech-Slovak Benevolent Association. "History of CCBA." http://www.czechslovakbenevolentassoc.ca/html/history-of-ccba.html.

Čekota, Antonín. *The Battle of Home: Some Problems of Industrial Community.* Toronto: Macmillan, 1944.

Čelovský, Bořivoj. *Emigranti: Dopisy politických uprchlíků z prvních let po "Vítězném únoru" 1948.* Ostrava: Tilia, 1998.

———. *Moje střetnutí s rozvědkou StB.* Ostrava: Tilia, 2003.

———. *Politici bez moci: První léta exilové rady svobodného Československa.* Šenov u Ostravy: Tilia, 2000.

———. *Šel jsem svou cestou.* Opava: Vademecum, 1996.

Čermák, Josef. *Fragmenty ze života Čechů a Slovaků v Kanadě.* Zlín: Atelier IM, 2000.

———. *It All Started with Prince Rupert: The Story of Czechs and Slovaks in Canada.* Prague: Atelier IM, 2003.

———. "63. Czechoslovak (Czech and Slovak) day at Masaryktown." http://czechfolks.com/2011/07/23/163-chechoslovakczech-and-slovak-day-at-masaryktown/.

Champion, Christian P. "Courting 'Our Ethnic Friends': Canadianism, Britishness, and New Canadians, 1950–1970." *Canadian Ethnic Studies* 38, 1 (2006): 23–46.

Cohen, Gerard D. *In War's Wake: Europe's Displaced Persons in the Postwar Order.* Oxford: Oxford University Press, 2012.

Crane, John, and Sylvia Crane. *Czechoslovakia: Anvil of the Cold War.* New York: Praeger, 1991.

Czech and Slovak Association of Canada. "Brief History and Activities." https://www.cssk.ca/brief-history-and-activities/.

Czechoslovak National Association of Canada. *Brief to the Royal Commission on Bilingualism and Biculturalism by the Czechoslovak National Association of Canada.* Toronto: Czechoslovak National Association, 1963.

———. *Charta, stanovy, jednací šrád.* Hamilton: Czechoslovak National Association of Canada, 1961.

Danys, Milda. *DP: Lithuanian Immigration to Canada after the Second World War.* Toronto: Multicultural History Society of Ontario, 1986.

Dawisha, Karen. *The Kremlin and the Prague Spring.* Berkeley: University of California Press, 1984.

Dirks, Gerald E. *Canada's Refugee Policy: Indifference or Opportunism?* Montreal: McGill-Queen's University Press, 1977.

Elie, Jérôme. "Histories of Refugee and Forced Migration Studies." In *The Oxford Handbook of Refugee and Forced Migration Studies,* edited by Elena Fiddian-Qasmiyeh, Gil Loescher, Katy Long, and Nando Sigona, 23–35. Oxford: Oxford University Press, 2014.

Epp, Marlene. *Refugees in Canada: A Brief History.* Ottawa: Canadian Historical Association, 2017.

Faure, Justine. "Les exilés tchécoslovaques de 1948: Un exile politique au service de la politique étrangère américaine." *Materiaux pour l'histoire de notre temps* 60, 1 (2000): 61–66.

Feldman, Edith, ed. *Czechoslovak Recipes—Women's Council of the Czechoslovak National Association.* Toronto: Czechoslovak National Association of Canada, 1963.

Filípek, Jan. *Reflections and Perspectives: Czechoslovaks after Forty Years in Exile.* Palm Springs, CA: Palm Springs Publishing, 1988.

Finkel, Alvin. "Canadian Immigration Policy and the Cold War, 1945–1980." *Journal of Canadian Studies* 21, 3 (1986): 53–70.

Garber, Gus. "Joining Up, 1938." In *The Land Newly Found: Eyewitness Accounts of the Canadian Immigrant Experience,* edited by Norman Hillmer and Jack L. Granatstein, 208. Toronto: Thomas Allen Publishers, 2006.

Gellner, John, and John Smerek. *The Czechs and Slovaks in Canada.* Toronto: University of Toronto Press, 1968.

Gibbon, John M. *Canadian Mosaic: The Making of a Northern Nation.* Toronto: McClelland and Stewart, 1938.

Gitelman, Zvi Y. "Public Opinion in Czechoslovakia." In *Public Opinion in European Socialist Systems,* edited by Walter D. Connor and Zvi Y. Gitelman, 83–103. New York Praeger, 1977.

Golan, Galia. *The Czechoslovak Reform Movement: Communism in Crisis, 1962–1968.* London: Cambridge University Press, 1971.

———. *Reform Rule in Czechoslovakia: The Dubček Era, 1968–1969.* Cambridge, UK: Cambridge University Press, 1973.

———. "Youth and Politics in Czechoslovakia." *Journal of Contemporary History* 5, 1 (1970): 3–22.

Hawkins, Freda. *Canada and Immigration: Public Policy and Public Concern.* Montreal: McGill-Queen's University Press, 1988.

Heimann, Mary. *Czechoslovakia: The State that Failed.* New Haven, CT: Yale University Press, 2009.

Hejzlar, Zdeněk, and Vladimír V. Kusin. *Czechoslovakia, 1968–1969: Chronology, Bibliography, Annotation.* New York: Garland Publishing, 1975.

Heyman, Richard. "Making a Scene about Language Rights." *Canadian Journal of Education* 4, 1 (1979): 54–66.

Hikl, Mario. *A Short History of the Czechoslovak People in Canada.* Toronto: Across-Canada Press, 1955.

Hilliker, John, and Donald Barry. *Canada's Department of External Affairs, Volume II: Coming of Age, 1946–1968.* Montreal: McGill-Queen's University Press, 1995.

Hillmer, Norman, and Donald Page, eds. Department of External Affairs. *Documents on Canadian External Relations, Volume 13: 1947.* Ottawa: Communication Group Publishing, 1993.

Holborn, Louise. *Refugees: A Problem of Our Time: The Work of the United Nations High Commissioner for Refugees, 1951–1972, Volume 1.* Metuchen, NJ: Scarecrow Press, 1975.

Holý, Ladislav. *The Little Czech and the Great Czech Nation.* Cambridge, UK: Cambridge University Press, 1996.

Hora, Ota. "Attitudes towards Canadian Foreign Policy—'It Is Time to Unite All Forces against Soviet Imperialism and Its Tyranny, *Nový Domov*, Toronto, June 19, 1971.'" In *Immigration and the Rise of Multiculturalism,* edited by Howard Palmer, 204–5. Vancouver: Copp Clark, 1975.

Horná, Jarmila L.A. "The Entrance Status of Czech and Slovak Immigrant Women." In *Two Nations, Many Cultures: Ethnic Groups in Canada,* edited by Jean Leonard Elliott, 270–79. Scarborough, ON: Prentice-Hall, 1979.

———. "Social Problems in Integration of Immigrants from Czechoslovakia." In *Czechoslovak National Association of Canada Conference on Cultural and Social Integration of Immigrants from Czechoslovakia,* edited by Victor Fic, 31–48. Toronto: Czechoslovak National Association of Canada, 1983.

Hron, Madelaine. "The Czech Émigré Experience of Return after 1989." *Slavonic and East European Review* 85, 1 (2007): 47–78.

Hughes, Geraint. "British Policy towards Eastern Europe, and the Impact of the 'Prague Spring,' 1964–1968." *Cold War History* 4, 2 (2004): 115–39.

Hutchings, Robert L. *Soviet East European Relations: Consolidation and Conflict, 1968–1980.* Madison: University of Wisconsin Press, 1983.

Iacovetta, Franca. "Freedom Lovers, Sex Deviates, and Damaged Women: Iron Curtain Refugee Discourses in Cold War Canada." In *Love, Hate, and Fear in Canada's Cold War,* edited by Richard Cavell, 77–107. Toronto: University of Toronto Press, 2004.

———. *Gatekeepers: Reshaping Immigrant Lives in Cold War Canada.* Toronto: Between the Lines, 2006.

———. "Making Model Citizens: Gender, Corrupted Democracy, and Immigrant and Refugee Reception Work in Cold War Canada." In *Whose National Security? Canadian State Security and the Creation of Enemies,* edited by Gary Kinsman, Dieter K. Buse, and Mercedes Steedman, 154–70. Toronto: Between the Lines, 2000.

Ivanov, Miroslav. *Čech v Kanadě.* Prague: Faun, 1994.

Jancar, Barbara W. *Czechoslovakia and the Absolute Monopoly of Power: A Study of Political Power in a Communist System.* New York: Praeger Publishers, 1971.

Jakešová, Elena. "Slovak Emigrants in Canada as Reflected in Diplomatic Documents (1920–1938)." *Slovakia* 35, 64–65 (1991–92): 7–35.

———. *Vystahovalectvo Slovakov do Kanady.* Bratislava: Vydavatel'stvo Slovenskej Akademie Vied, 1981.

Jakešová, Elena, and M. Mark Stolárik. "Slovaks." In *Encyclopedia of Canada's Peoples,* edited by Paul Robert Magocsi, 1168–79. Toronto: University of Toronto Press, 1999.

Jelínek, Yeshayahu A. *Lust for Power: Nationalism, Slovakia, and the Communists, 1918–1948.* Boulder, CO: East European Monographs, 1983.

———. *The Parish Republic: Hlinka's Slovak People's Party, 1939–1945.* Boulder, CO: East European Quarterly, 1976.

Jovanovic, Marek J. "Creating a New Bohemia: The Czechs in Canada, 1880–1990." MA thesis, University of Ottawa, 1999.

———. "Czechs." In *Encyclopedia of Canada's Peoples,* edited by Paul Robert Magocsi, 397–405. Toronto: University of Toronto Press, 1999.

Kaplan, Karel. *The Short March: The Communist Takeover of Czechoslovakia, 1945–1948.* New York: St. Martin's Press, 1987.

Kealey, Gregory S., and Reginald Whitaker, eds. *RCMP Security Bulletins: The War Series (Vol. 2), 1942–1945.* St. John's: Committee on Canadian Labour History, 1989.

Kelley, Ninette, and Michael Trebilcock. *The Making of the Mosaic: A History of Canadian Immigration Policy.* Toronto: University of Toronto Press, 1998.

Kennan, George F. *From Prague after Munich: Diplomatic Papers, 1938–1940.* Princeton, NJ: Princeton University Press, 1968.

Kirschbaum, Joseph M. *The Ideological Orientation of the Canadian Slavic Press.* Toronto: Inter-University Committee on Canadian Slavs, 1971.

———. *The Slovaks in Canada.* Toronto: Canadian Ethnic Press Association of Ontario, 1967.

———. *The Truth and Legends about the Origin of the Slovak Republic.* Cleveland: First Catholic Slovak Union, 1974.

Kirschbaum, Stanislav J. *A History of Slovakia: The Struggle for Survival.* New York: St. Martin's Press, 1995.

———. "Whither Slovak Historiography after 1993?" *Canadian Slavonic Papers* 53, 1 (2011): 45–63.

Knowles, Valerie. *Strangers at Our Gates: Canadian Immigration and Immigration Policy, 1540–2006.* Toronto: Dundurn Press, 2007.

Korbel, Josef. *The Communist Subversion of Czechoslovakia, 1938–1948: The Failure of Coexistence.* Princeton, NJ: Princeton University Press, 1959.

———. *Twentieth-Century Czechoslovakia: The Meaning of Its History.* New York: Columbia University Press, 1977.

Kováč, Dušan. "Czechs and Slovaks in Modern History." In *Bohemia in History,* edited by Mikuláš Teich, 364–79. Cambridge, UK: Cambridge University Press, 1998.

Kramer, Mark. "The Prague Spring and the Soviet Invasion in Historical Perspective." In *The Prague Spring and the Warsaw Pact Invasion of Czechoslovakia in 1968,* edited by Gunter Bischof, Stefan Karner, and Peter Ruggenthaler, 35–60. Plymouth, MA: Lexington Books, 2010.

———. "Stalin, Soviet Policy, and the Consolidation of a Communist Bloc in Eastern Europe, 1944–53." In *Stalinism Revisited: The Establishment of Communist Regimes in East-Central Europe,* edited by Vladimir Tismaneanu, 51–102. Budapest: CEU Press, 2010.

Krejčí, Jaroslav. *Social Change and Stratification in Postwar Czechoslovakia.* New York: Columbia University Press, 1972.

Krejčí, Jaroslav, and Pavel Machonin. *Czechoslovakia, 1918–92: A Laboratory for Social Change.* New York: St. Martin's Press, 1996.

Křýštufek, Zdeněk. *The Soviet Regime in Czechoslovakia.* Boulder, CO: East European Monographs, 1981.

Kusin, Vladimír V. "Challenge to Normalcy: Political Opposition in Czechoslovakia, 1968–1977." In *Opposition in Eastern Europe,* edited by Rudolf L. Tokes, 26–59. Baltimore: Johns Hopkins University Press, 1979.

———. *From Dubček to Charter 77: A Study of "Normalization" in Czechoslovakia, 1968–1978.* New York: St. Martin's Press, 1978.

———. *The Intellectual Origins of the Prague Spring: The Development of Reformist Ideas in Czechoslovakia, 1956–1967.* Cambridge, UK: Cambridge University Press, 1971.

———. "A Note on K 231." *Soviet Studies* 24, 1 (1972): 77–85.

———. *Political Groupings in the Czechoslovak Reform Movement.* New York: Columbia University Press, 1972.

Lanphier, Michael. "Canada's Response to Refugees." *International Migration Review* 15, 1–2 (1981): 113–30.

Loescher, Gil. *The UNHCR and World Politics: A Perilous Path.* Oxford: Oxford University Press, 2001.

Loewen, Royden, and Gerald Friesen. *Immigrants in Prairie Cities: Ethnic Diversity in Twentieth-Century Canada.* Toronto: University of Toronto Press, 2009.

Luciuk, Lubomyr Y. *Searching for Place: Ukrainian Displaced Persons, Ottawa, and the Migration of Memory.* Toronto: University of Toronto Press, 2000.

Lukeš, Igor. "Czechoslovak Political Exile in the Cold War: The Early Years." *Polish Review* 47, (2002): 332–43.

———. *Czechoslovakia between Stalin and Hitler: The Diplomacy of Edvard Beneš in the 1930s.* New York: Oxford University Press, 1996.

Madokoro, Laura. "Good Material: Canada and the Prague Spring Refugees." *Refuge: Canada's Periodical on Refugees* 26, 1 (2009): 161–71.

Malarek, Victor. *Heaven's Gate: Canada's Immigration Fiasco.* Toronto: Macmillan, 1985.

Marcuse, Gary, and Reginald Whitaker. *Cold War Canada: The Making of a National Insecurity State, 1945–1957.* Toronto: University of Toronto Press, 1994.

Marha, Eva. "Czechs/Slovaks." In *Safe Haven: The Refugee Experience of Five Families,* edited by Elizabeth McLuhan, 19–64. Toronto: Multicultural Society of Ontario, 1995.

Martin, Paul. "Canadian Senators Visit Czechoslovakia." *External Affairs* 21, 8 (1969): 310–14.

Masaryk Memorial Institute. "About Us." http://masaryktown.ca/?page_id=225.

———. "Monument." http://masaryktown.ca/?page_id= 437.

McRae, Robert G. *Resistance and Revolution: Vaclav Havel's Czechoslovakia.* Ottawa: Carleton University Press, 1997.

Mlynář, Zdeněk. *Nightfrost in Prague: The End of Humane Socialism.* New York: Karz, 1980.

Moravec, Ivo. *Tightrope Passage: Along the Refugee Route to Canada.* Toronto: McClelland and Stewart, 1997.

Murrow, Charles. "Sacrifice and Bravery as the Prague Spring Ends." *CIHS Bulletin: The Newsletter of the Canadian Immigration Historical Society* 46 (2005): 15–16.

Myant, Martin. *The Czechoslovak Economy, 1948–1988: The Battle for Economic Reform.* Cambridge, UK: Cambridge University Press, 1989.

———. *Socialism and Democracy in Czechoslovakia, 1945–1948.* New York: Cambridge University Press, 1981.

Nekola, Rudolf. *A Gem for the Canadian Mosaic.* Toronto: Masaryk Memorial Institute, 1957.

Nolte, Claire E. *The Sokol in the Czech Lands until 1914: Training for the Nation.* Basingstoke, UK: Palgrave Macmillan, 2002.

Olivová, Věra. *The Doomed Democracy: Czechoslovakia in a Disrupted Europe, 1914–1938.* London: Sidgwick and Jackson, 1972.

Pačes, Cynthia. *Prague Panoramas: National Memory and Sacred Space in the Twentieth Century.* Pittsburgh: University of Pittsburgh Press, 2009.

Page, Benjamin B. *The Czechoslovak Reform Movement, 1963–1968: A Study in the Theory of Socialism.* Amsterdam: Gruner, 1973.

Paul, David W. *The Cultural Limits of Revolutionary Politics: Change and Continuity in Socialist Czechoslovakia.* Boulder, CO: East European Quarterly, 1979.

———. *Czechoslovakia: Profile of a Socialist Republic at the Crossroads of Europe.* Boulder, CO: Westview Press, 1981.

Peddie, Francis. *Young, Well-Educated, and Adaptable: Chilean Exiles in Ontario and Quebec, 1973–2010.* Winnipeg: University of Manitoba Press, 2015.

Pelikán, Jiří. *Socialist Opposition in Eastern Europe: The Czechoslovak Example.* London: Allison and Busby, 1976.

———, ed. *The Secret Vysočany Congress: Proceedings and Documents of the Extraordinary Fourteenth Congress of the Communist Party of Czechoslovakia, 22 August 1968.* London: Allen Lane, 1971.

Polišenský, Josef V. *Canada and Czechoslovakia.* Prague: Orbis, 1967.

Procházka, Marta. "An Absurd Way of Life: A Very Unusual Feeling." *Canadian Ethnic Studies* 25, 2 (1993): 119–35.

Prokop, Jana. "Bibliography of Czech Dissidents." *Nationalities Papers* 11, 1 (1983): 93–99.

Raptis, Helen. "Teaching Czech German Refugees at Tate Creek, British Columbia, during World War II." *Historical Studies in Education* 24, 2 (2012): 31–46.

Raska, Jan. "Mistrusted Strangers at Home: Czechs, Slovaks, and the 'Enemy Aliens' Registration Issue, 1938–1942." *International Journal of Canadian Studies* 38 (2009): 91–117.

———. "Recreating a Homeland: Czechoslovak Diplomats in Canada during the Second World War." *Canadian Slavonic Papers* 58, 1 (2016): 68–92.

———. "Who Is Admissible?" Canadian Museum of Immigration at Pier 21 Blog, 11 January 2015. http://www.pier21.ca/blog/jan-raska/who-is-admissible.

Renner, Hans. *A History of Czechoslovakia since 1945.* London: Routledge, 1989.

Richter, Miriam V. *Creating the National Mosaic: Multiculturalism in Canadian Children's Literature from 1950 to 1994.* Amsterdam: Editions Rodopi, 2001.

Ripka, Hubert. *Czechoslovakia Enslaved: The Story of the Communist Coup d'État.* London: Victor Gollancz, 1950.

Rothschild, Joseph, and Nancy M. Wingfield. *Return to Diversity: A Political History of East Central Europe since World War II.* 3rd ed. New York: Oxford University Press, 2000.

Ruml, Karel. *Z deníku Vlaku Svobody.* Brno: Barrister and Principal, 2001.

Sawatsky, John. *For Services Rendered: Leslie James Bennett and the RCMP Security Service.* Toronto: Doubleday Canada, 1982.

———. *Men in the Shadows: The RCMP Security Service.* Toronto: Doubleday Canada, 1980.

Simon, Jeffrey. *Warsaw Pact Forces: Problems of Command and Control.* Boulder, CO: Westview Press, 1985.

Skalník Leff, Carol. *The Czech and Slovak Republics: Nation versus State.* Boulder, CO: Westview Press, 1997.

———. *National Conflict in Czechoslovakia: The Making and Remaking of a State, 1918–1987.* Princeton, NJ: Princeton University Press, 1988.

Skilling, H. Gordon. *Czechoslovakia's Interrupted Revolution.* Princeton, NJ: Princeton University Press, 1976.

———. *The Education of a Canadian: My Life as a Scholar and Activist.* Montreal: McGill-Queen's University Press, 2000.

Skoutajan, Hanns F. *Uprooted and Transplanted: A Sudeten Odyssey from Tragedy to Freedom, 1938–1958.* Owen Sound, ON: Ginger Press, 2000.

Škvorecký, Josef. "At Home in Exile: Czech Writers in the West." *Books Abroad* 50, 2 (1976): 308–13.

———. "Bohemia of the Soul." *Daedalus* 119, 1 (1990): 111–39.

Smelser, Ronald M. *The Sudeten Problem, 1933–1938:* Volkstumspolitik *and the Formulation of Nazi Foreign Policy.* Middletown, CT: Wesleyan University Press, 1975.

Spencer, Hanna. *Hanna's Diary, 1938–1941: Czechoslovakia to Canada.* Montreal: McGill-Queen's University Press, 2001.

Sokol Canada. "Sokol Canada 1911." http://www.sokolcanada.ca/uploads/3/4/6/8/34680982/Sokol_canada_history_august_29_zas.docx.

Steiner, Eugen. *The Slovak Dilemma.* Cambridge, UK: Cambridge University Press, 1973.

Stražnický, Ivan, and Marta Stražnický. "After the Prague Spring." In *The Land Newly Found: Eyewitness Accounts of the Canadian Immigrant Experience,* edited by Norman Hillmer and Jack L. Granatstein, 281–84. Toronto: Thomas Allen Publishers, 2006.

Suda, Zdeněk. *The Czechoslovak Socialist Republic.* Baltimore: Johns Hopkins University Press, 1969.

———. *Zealots and Rebels: A History of the Ruling Communist Party of Czechoslovakia.* Stanford: Hoover Institution Press, 1980.

Suri, Jeremi. "The Promise and Failure of 'Developed Socialism': The Soviet 'Thaw' and the Crucible of the Prague Spring, 1964–1972." *Contemporary European History* 15, 2 (2006): 133–58.

Sutherland, Anthony X. *The Canadian Slovak League.* Toronto: Canadian Slovak League, 1984.

Szulc, Tad. *Czechoslovakia since World War II.* New York: Viking Press, 1971.

Táborský, Edward. *Communism in Czechoslovakia, 1948–1960.* Princeton, NJ: Princeton University Press, 1961.

———. *President Edvard Beneš: Between East and West, 1938–1948.* Stanford: Hoover Institution Press, 1981.

Tigrid, Pavel. *Why Dubcek Fell.* London: Macdonald, 1971.

Toma, Peter A., and Dušan Kováč. *Slovakia: From Samo to Dzurinda.* Stanford: Hoover Institution Press, 2001.

Tomek, Prokop. "The Highs and Lows of Czech and Slovak Émigré Activism." In *Anti-Communist Minorities in the U.S.: Political Activism of Ethnic Refugees,* edited by Ieva Zake, 109–26. New York: Palgrave Macmillan, 2009.

Troper, Harold. "Canadian Immigration Policy since 1945." *International Journal* 48, 2 (1993): 255–81.

———. "In Search of Haven." In *Safe Haven: The Refugee Experience of Five Families,* edited by Elizabeth McLuhan, 1–18. Toronto: Multicultural Historical Society of Ontario, 1995.

Ulč, Otto. *Politics in Czechoslovakia.* San Francisco: W.H. Freeman, 1974.

University of British Columbia. Department of Botany. "Vladimir Krajina." http://botany.ubc.ca/people/vladimir-krajina.

Vaculík, Jaroslav. "Reemigrace zahraničních Čechů a Slováků v letech 1945–1948." *Slezský sborník* 93, 1–2 (1995): 53–58.

Valenta, Jiři. *Soviet Intervention in Czechoslovakia, 1968: Anatomy of a Decision.* Baltimore: Johns Hopkins University Press, 1979.

Vitula, Miroslav. "Z historie českých a slovenských krajanu v Kanadě do roku 1939." *Časopis Matice Moravské* 118, 1 (1999): 97–110.

Wagner, Jonathan. "British Columbia's Anti-Nazi Germans: The Tupper Creek Refugees." *BC Studies* 39 (1978): 3–19.

———. *A History of Migration from Germany to Canada, 1850–1939.* Vancouver: UBC Press, 2006.

Westad, Odd A. "The Cold War and the International History of the Twentieth Century." In *Cambridge History of the Cold War, Volume I: Origins,* edited by Melvyn P. Leffler and Odd A. Westad, 1–19. Cambridge, UK: Cambridge University Press, 2010.

Whitaker, Reginald. *Canadian Immigration Policy since Confederation.* Ottawa: Canadian Historical Association, 1991.

———. *Double Standard: The Secret History of Canadian Immigration.* Toronto: Lester and Orpen Dennys, 1987.

———. "'We Know They're There': Canada and Its Others, with or without the Cold War." In *Love, Hate, and Fear in Canada's Cold War,* edited by Richard Cavell, 35–56. Toronto: University of Toronto Press, 2004.

Whitaker, Reginald, and Steve Hewitt. *Canada and the Cold War.* Toronto: James Lorimer, 2003.

Whitaker, Reginald, and Gregory S. Kealey. "A War on Ethnicity? The RCMP and Internment." In *Enemies Within: Italian and Other Internees in Canada and Abroad,* edited by Franca Iacovetta, Roberto Perin, and Angelo Principe, 128–47. Toronto: University of Toronto Press, 2000.

Williams, Kieran. *The Prague Spring and Its Aftermath: Czechoslovak Politics, 1968–1970.* Cambridge, UK: Cambridge University Press, 1997.

Wyman, Mark. *DP: Europe's Displaced Persons, 1945–1951.* Philadelphia: Balch Institute Press, 1990.

Zawisza, John. "Processing of the Czechoslovakian Refugee Movement, Vienna, Austria (Sep.–Nov. 1968)." *CIHS Bulletin: The Newsletter of the Canadian Immigration Historical Society* 46 (2005): 4–8.

Zeman, Zbyněk. *Prague Spring: A Report on Czechoslovakia, 1968.* Harmondsworth, UK: Penguin Books, 1969.

Zeman, Zbyněk, and Antonín Klimek. *The Life of Edvard Beneš, 1884–1948: Czechoslovakia in Peace and War.* Oxford: Clarendon Press, 1996.

Ziegler, Ed. "The Adaptation of Czechoslovak Refugees in Canada, 1969–1972." *CIHS Bulletin: The Newsletter of the Canadian Immigration Historical Society* 54 (2008): 5–7.

INDEX

D

E

F

W

Y

Z